THE GREAT AIR RACE

JOHN LANCASTER

THE GREAT AIR RACE

Glory, Tragedy, and the Dawn of American Aviation

Liveright Publishing Corporation

A Division of W. W. Norton & Company
Celebrating a Century of Independent Publishing

frontispiece: Library of Congress

Copyright © 2023 by John Lancaster

For information about permission to reproduce selections from this book,
write to Permissions, Liveright Publishing Corporation, a division of
W. W. Norton & Company, Inc., 500 Fifth Avenue, New York, NY 10110

For information about special discounts for bulk purchases, please
contact W. W. Norton Special Sales at specialsales@wwnorton.com or
800-233-4830

Manufacturing by Lake Book Manufacturing
Book design by Patrice Sheridan
Production manager: Julia Druskin

ISBN 978-1-63149-637-0

Liveright Publishing Corporation
500 Fifth Avenue, New York, N.Y. 10110
www.wwnorton.com

W. W. Norton & Company Ltd.
15 Carlisle Street, London W1D 3BS

1 2 3 4 5 6 7 8 9 0

In memory of my parents,
Paul and Susan Lancaster

CONTENTS

PART III TRIUMPH

PART IV FOUNDATION

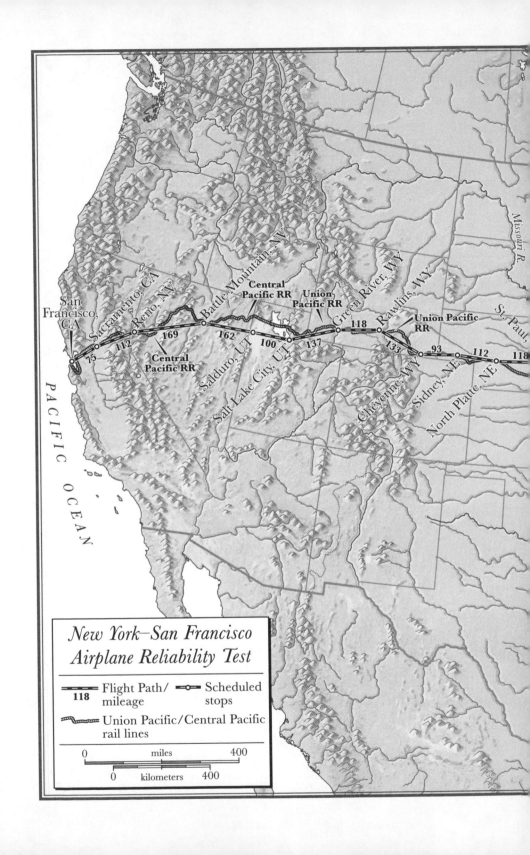

San Francisco, CA

Sacramento, CA

Reno, NV

Battle Mountain, NV

Central Pacific RR

Union Pacific RR

Green River, WY

Rawlins, WY

Union Pacific RR

St. Paul,

Missouri R.

Central Pacific RR

Salduro, UT

Salt Lake City, UT

Cheyenne, WY

Sidney, NE

North Platte, NE

75   112   169   162   100   137   118   133   93   112   118

PACIFIC OCEAN

New York–San Francisco Airplane Reliability Test

———— Flight Path/
118   mileage

⚬═⚬ Scheduled
stops

〜〜 Union Pacific/Central Pacific
rail lines

0   miles   400

0   kilometers   400

PROLOGUE

The snow came on suddenly, as it often does in the Wyoming high country, all but blinding the two aviators in their wood-and-fabric biplane. Hunched in the open front cockpit, Lt. Edward V. Wales reduced power and descended to within a few hundred feet of the ground, where the visibility was slightly better. But there was little room to spare beneath the clouds. Soon after the aircraft leveled off, the terrain started to rise. Wales advanced the throttle and began a slow climb.

Before leaving Rawlins some twenty minutes earlier, Wales and the man who rode in the cockpit behind him, Lt. William Goldsborough, had decided to fly the direct compass line to the temporary airfield at Fort D. A. Russell in Cheyenne, on the far side of the Medicine Bow Mountains. They briefly had considered a safer route along the Union Pacific Railroad tracks, which ran north of the highest peaks before veering south toward Laramie and Cheyenne. But the detour would have cost them valuable time—another forty minutes or so at least—and the two were in a hurry.

Now Wales was having second thoughts. The blizzard showed no sign of abating, and he knew that the tallest mountains were still ahead. Better to follow the railroad after all. He banked the DH-4 into a left turn, then flattened the wings on a new compass heading to the north.

Neither man was particularly worried. They could still see the ground and were making good progress. It wouldn't be long before they picked up the railroad and with it an unobstructed path across the prairie to Cheyenne, where fuel and food awaited. They could make up the lost time on the next couple of legs. With a tailwind and a bit of luck they might even reach Omaha by sunset. In the meantime, Wales was careful to maintain an even distance between the biplane and the moderate uphill slope. At more than 8,000 feet above sea level, the air was bitingly cold, but the aviators were used to it by now.

An isolated ranch house passed beneath their wings. Glimpsing a group of cattlemen in the snow, Goldsborough stuck an arm out of the cockpit and gave them a friendly wave. The cowboys would have heard the thunder of the big V-12 and if they were close enough would have recognized the tricolor roundels of the U.S. Army Air Service.

It was early in the afternoon of October 9, 1919.

———

A little more than twenty-four hours earlier, the two flyers had departed San Francisco on the first leg of a grand adventure—a coast-to-coast airplane race, the likes of which the world had never seen. As conceived by William "Billy" Mitchell, the brash, sharp-elbowed brigadier general and war hero who would one day be celebrated as the father of the U.S. Air Force, the "Reliability and Endurance Test," as the race was officially known, would be unprecedented not only in length and duration but also in number of participants. More than sixty airplanes divided into two groups—one on Long Island, the other in San Francisco—would take off for the opposite coast some 2,700 miles distant, crossing in the middle and competing for the fastest flying and elapsed times.

It was a bold and risky undertaking. Though the race was open only to qualified military aviators, none of the men who signed up had attempted a journey of such improbable length—and for good reason. Like all aircraft of the day, the surplus warplanes they would fly were almost comically ill-suited for long-distance travel or arguably for any travel at all. Open cockpits offered scant protection against wind and cold. Engine noise was, quite literally, deafening. Engines were unreliable and sometimes caught fire in flight. Crude flight instruments were of marginal value to pilots trying to keep their bearings in clouds and fog.

But that was only part of the challenge. The route across the country was almost entirely lacking in permanent airfields—or any form of aviation infrastructure. There was no radar, air traffic control system, or radio network. Weather forecasts were rudimentary and often wrong.

In the absence of electronic beacons or formal aviation charts, pilots followed railroad tracks or compass headings that wandered drunkenly with every turn. Every hour or two—they hoped—they would land at one of twenty "control stops" between the coasts. Most were makeshift grass or dirt airfields that had been hastily demarcated and stocked with fuel, spare parts, and other supplies, sometimes just hours before the start of the race. Despite these slapdash preparations, Mitchell and his colleagues in the Air Service decided at the last minute to double the length of the race—instead of a one-way flight between the coasts, it would be a round-trip journey of 5,400 miles. It was as if, in the absence of anything resembling a national air transportation system, Mitchell had decided simply to will one into being.

———

His motives were nakedly political. Though it had given birth to the airplane, the United States had been a latecomer to World War I and had fallen behind Europe in aviation, as clashing armies competed for dominance of the air over the Western Front. Now, as the United States rushed to demobilize, Mitchell feared that its long-term security was at risk. The country needed a robust aviation industry to fulfill both military and commercial needs. Part of the solution, he believed, was a cabinet-level department of aeronautics to include an independent air force, as called for by several bills pending in Congress. He also sought to protect the Air Service from the worst of postwar budget cuts. A gifted showman, Mitchell conceived the race as a stunt to demonstrate the transformative potential of aviation and rally the public behind his goals in Washington. To that end, he had a powerful ally in Otto Praeger, the driven, sometimes-ruthless Texan who ran the fledgling U.S. Air Mail Service and embraced the contest as a prelude to a transcontinental airmail route.

In one sense, at least, Mitchell's timing was good. Despite the victory in Europe eleven months earlier, the country was fearful, anxious, and in need of a little distraction. The influenza pandemic, which ultimately would kill about 675,000 Americans, only recently had begun to recede. Many cities were in turmoil, as nativist mobs fueled by racism and anti-communist paranoia visited their fury on immigrants, unions, and especially African Americans, several hundred of whom were lynched during the so-called Red Summer of 1919. And Washington was rife with rumor and speculation over the health of President Woodrow B. Wilson, who recently had suffered a stroke. Against that backdrop, the contest came as a welcome respite—an irresistible pageant of grit, daring, and skill that would play out over many days and thousands of miles.

The press certainly covered it that way. In reporters' telling, "the world's greatest air race"—or sometimes simply "the air derby"—was a sporting event as compelling as the World Series, which was still under way as the race began. Daily box scores ranked pilots by their flying times on each leg. Photos of grinning airmen next to their machines appeared in newspapers across the country. The *New York Times* ran more than thirty stories on the contest, eight of them on the front page. As news of the competition spread, crowds at some control stops along the route grew so large that police were called in to keep them from interfering with takeoffs and landings. Library shelves were stripped of books on aeronautics.

The country's fascination with the race owed as much to the contestants as it did to the novelty of the airplane. Reporters made much of the rivalries between these mythic, seemingly fearless "birdmen." Among them were an ordained Baptist minister whose German police dog shared the rear cockpit with his mechanic; a swaggering, cigar-smoking former track star who flew with crutches in the cockpit and metal braces on the legs he had shattered in a crash in France; and several bona fide combat "aces," one of them a general's son who had twice managed to escape from German imprisonment after he was shot down behind enemy lines. For the duration of the race and sometimes beyond, these and other contestants would attain a celebrity to rival that of sports heroes and silent-film stars.

None could doubt their courage. Before it finally ended at sunset on October 31, nine men would be dead, victims of unseasonably bad weather or lapses in judgment or skill, sometimes in combination. It was a shocking toll even apart from the dozens more who dropped out of the race because of accidents, mechanical problems, or sheer exhaustion. In the end, a spectacle designed in part to promote the safety and reliability of air travel arguably did the opposite. Some editorialists all but accused Mitchell of murder.

Yet there is no denying the aviators' role as pioneers in the same tradition as Charles A. Lindbergh or the first astronauts. As they hop-scotched from one improvised airfield to the next, they blazed the trail for the first crude version of a transcontinental air route. Just eleven months later, the U.S. Post Office inaugurated its coast-to-coast airmail service along essentially the same path, fulfilling Praeger's dream and opening the door to commercial air travel. Henry H. "Hap" Arnold—a Mitchell contemporary who helped organize the race and later commanded U.S. air forces in World War II—would one day describe the contest as "the foundation of commercial aviation in the United States."

The contest came at a critical time in American aviation. Though the airplane had shown its potential in war, it had yet to prove its utility in peacetime. Airmail was still in its infancy, and—except for a few short-lived experiments before World War I—commercial passenger service had not yet been realized. At least in civilian life, the airplane was little more than a curiosity, flown mostly by the "gypsy flyers"—later known as barnstormers—who eked out a living at fairgrounds or borrowed pastures, where they put on air shows or carried passengers on $15 joyrides. But the race between the coasts cast aviation in an entirely new light. The chain of designated airfields that spanned the continent, the communication and logistics networks that tied them together, the great distances covered by the flyers, the regular arrivals and departures—all foreshadowed the rapidly approaching age of modern air travel. Nearly eight years before Lindbergh's electrifying flight from New York to Paris in the *Spirit of St. Louis*, the transcontinental contest vividly demonstrated the airplane's potential as an instrument of everyday commerce. It was the opening of the latest and most thrilling chapter in the long quest to shrink the world.

———

More than a century later, the transcontinental race is all but forgotten. I hadn't even heard of it until a few years ago, when the germ of a book idea—on airplane racing between the world wars—led me to a used copy of *The Speed Seekers*, an exhaustive look at the subject by Thomas G. Foxworth that was published in 1976. Most of the book focused on short races over closed courses—aerial equivalents of the Indianapolis 500—that drew huge crowds in the 1920s and 1930s. But it also included a short section on the transcontinental race. Intrigued, I walked over to the Library of Congress, near my home in Washington, D.C., and searched the electronic catalog for a book on the contest. I was a little surprised that I couldn't find one. Widening my net, I consulted other aviation histories, but with one or two exceptions, most ignored the subject or mentioned it only in passing. One of the best and most comprehensive accounts that I could find was a master's thesis submitted by a young Air Force officer, Ray L. Bowers, at the University of Wisconsin in 1960.

I learned more from old newspapers preserved on microfilm or in digital databases. As I read their stories on the contest, soaking up details of ice-covered wings, balky engines, and tricky crosswind landings on dangerous fields, I became convinced that the race was worth more scrutiny than it had received. It not only signified a threshold moment in aviation history but also was a great adventure story, one that captured the actual *experience* of flying open-cockpit biplanes in that era.

The subject played to an abiding passion. Although I spent most of my career as a newspaper reporter, including eight years as a foreign correspondent, I've had a lifelong interest in airplanes and flying. As a child I was an avid builder of model planes, and my bookshelves were filled with aviation-themed works by Ernest K. Gann, Antoine de Saint-Exupéry, and other writers. The summer after graduating from college I fulfilled my boyhood fantasy by earning a private pilot's license. I loved the challenge of flying and the unparalleled sense of freedom it offered, the exhilaration of takeoff and the gratifying squeak of my wheels on asphalt when I made a smooth landing. I even toyed with the idea of flying as a career. That was a passing fancy. After taking my first newspaper job in Des Moines, I decided there were better uses of my time and money than buzzing cornfields in a rented Cessna. But my fascination with airplanes and the people who flew them never waned.

The transcontinental race gave me a reason (my wife would call it an excuse) to start flying again. I wanted to retrace the flyers' original route as part of my research, landing at the same towns and cities, flying low and slow so I could see the country as they had. I signed up for flying lessons at a small airport outside Washington, D.C., where I slowly relearned the skills I'd lost over nearly four decades. After countless laps around the traffic pattern and a lot of bounced landings, my instructor signed me off as competent to fly the small two-seater I had bought secondhand a few months earlier.

My flight across the country and back in the early summer of 2019 went far more smoothly than it did for the aviators who covered the same distance a century earlier. This came as no surprise. Unlike its rickety, cloth-covered forebears, my airplane had a carbon-fiber fuselage, a reliable fuel-injected engine, an autopilot, and a digital instrument panel that took the guesswork out of navigating or avoiding bad weather. Air traffic controllers guided me through crowded airspace and made sure I arrived safely at my destination. And if all else failed, I could have yanked a handle beside my seat and deployed a parachute from a canister behind the cockpit; attached to the airframe, the parachute was designed to lower the whole plane gently to earth, like a space capsule returning from orbit. This modern innovation, an increasingly common feature of light aircraft, is a big source of comfort when flying over water or rough terrain.

But judgment and skill still matter, and there were times when I was deficient in both. This led to several memorable scares, one caused by my failure to fully advance the throttle on takeoff—a cardinal sin that in other circumstances might have been my last. Every pilot has similar stories. The important thing is to learn from them. They help keep us humble. They remind us that sometimes it all comes down to luck.

———

Wales and Goldsborough were somewhere in the vicinity of Oberg Pass when Wales decided to deviate from the compass line and turn north in the direction of the railroad. The pass was a broad saddle between two moderate peaks—Pennock Mountain to the south and Coad Mountain to the north—that in clear weather would have posed no threat. But now, with snow whipping past his cockpit, Wales could barely make out the rocks and sagebrush just a few hundred feet below. The path ahead was invisible. With only his compass and a crude map to guide him, he had no way of knowing that the biplane was heading straight for Coad Mountain.

Wales realized his mistake too late. As the DH-4 neared the top of the 9,300-foot peak, dark trees and scrub emerged through the veil of snow. The plane was less than 200 feet above a rocky gulch. With only a second or two to react, Wales attempted to turn away, stepping on the rudder bar and shoving the stick to one side. But the plane was flying too slowly for its wings to maintain lift in a turn. With the telltale shudder of an aerodynamic stall, the DH-4 dropped its nose and entered the first revolution of a spin. Wales was out of options. He did not have the time or altitude to recover. The men could only watch as the mountain rushed to meet them.

PART I

———◆———

The Air Service

1

The Honeymoon Special

At 2:00 p.m. on the first day of March 1919, New Yorkers out for a Saturday stroll looked up to see biplanes performing stunts over Madison Square Garden. The aircraft had been dispatched by the U.S. Army Air Service to promote the New York Aeronautical Exposition, the first large-scale display of airplanes and aviation technology in the United States since the end of the Great War less than four months earlier. The exposition was due to open in just a few hours. Thirty minutes later, as the Army aviators flew home to their nearby base at Hazelhurst Field on Long Island, the show's general manager ascended to the roof of the Garden's handsome Beaux-Arts structure at Twenty-Fifth Street and Madison Avenue, where he released 250 hydrogen-filled balloons. Each carried a ticket to the event. By the time darkness fell, an estimated 10,000 people had converged on the Garden, forming an eight-column line that stretched around the block. The opening of the doors triggered a stampede. Police, overwhelmed, called in reinforcements from a nearby station on East Twenty-Second Street.

Once they had elbowed their way inside, the visitors gaped. Weeks of feverish preparations had transformed the cavernous main hall into a fanciful tableau of an airfield in the French countryside, with a painted backdrop of forests, pastures, and airplane silhouettes. Suspended from the ceiling was a huge, elongated kite balloon—or "sausage," as troops called it—designed to loft artillery spotters over the battlefields of the

Western Front, and a smaller barrage balloon, used to deter enemy air attacks by means of dangling cables or nets.

But it was the airplanes below that truly set the crowd aflutter. Crammed in at angles on the exhibition floor and in the adjacent Sixty-Ninth Regiment Armory—the Garden being too small to accommodate all of the manufacturers who wished to show off their wares—were more than thirty of the latest and most sophisticated models made by domestic and foreign manufacturers. Many had been developed for use in battle. Among them were several multi-engine bombers, including a towering Italian-made Caproni triplane with three stacked wings and a wingspan of nearly 100 feet. There was a Navy flying boat with its fabric skin removed so that viewers could marvel at its intricate wooden frame. There was a DH-4 biplane, a powerful two-seat bomber and reconnaissance aircraft that was based on a British design and built in Ohio by the Dayton-Wright Airplane Company. And for sheer sex appeal, none could rival the nimble single-seat fighters, known as "pursuit" planes, that were scattered among the larger machines. They and the men who flew them had captured the public's imagination with their spiraling duels over France and Belgium—an intensely personal form of combat that evoked knights in the age of chivalry, at least to those unfamiliar with its horrors. One of the warplanes on display—a French-made Nieuport—was the same type flown by American combat aces such as Eddie Rickenbacker and Douglas Campbell, the latter being one of a number of prominent aviators on hand for opening night. Nearby was a Spad,* the sturdy little fighter that also was made in France and flown to glory by that country's top-scoring ace, René Fonck.

One combat plane in particular stood out, distinguished by its sleek construction and the black iron crosses on its camouflaged wings and fuselage. It was a Fokker D.VII seized from Germany as a trophy of war.

———

For American aviation, the exposition was a kind of coming-out party. It was sponsored by the Manufacturers Aircraft Association, the fledgling

———

* "Spad" was an acronym for its manufacturer, Societé Pour L'Aviation et ses Dérivés.

U.S. industry's trade group, in close coordination with the Air Service, then part of the Army and the forerunner of today's Air Force. Both wanted to show off their wartime achievements while building public enthusiasm for aviation in all its forms. In January 1918, President Wilson had barred aircraft manufacturers from displaying their products at exhibitions, lest they draw scrutiny from German spies. Now the veil of secrecy had been lifted.

To promote its cause, the Air Service had granted permission for officers who wished to attend the exposition to do so without taking leave, reserving a Pullman railcar for those traveling from Washington, D.C. On opening night, aviators in bobtailed Army tunics circulated among the aircraft, gesturing to control sticks and rudder bars as they explained the finer points of loops, spins, and coordinated turns to admiring young "adorables," as one reporter wrote. There were booths displaying reconnaissance cameras, aerial photographs, and a revolutionary new device called a radio telephone; every afternoon during the exposition, an Air Service operator would hold scratchy conversations with aviators in wireless-equipped DH-4s circling overhead. Images of gunnery practice and exploding bombs flickered on a movie screen.

Despite the patriotic atmosphere, visitors could not help but notice that many of the military aircraft on display had been manufactured abroad. The United States had fielded only one model—the DH-4—in combat over the Western Front. Other domestic offerings had come too late for the fighting but not for the exposition.

But an industry that had lagged its foreign competition during the war was determined to dominate the peace. "A most important and valuable application not yet encouraged in this country is the carrying of passengers," wrote Glenn L. Martin, one of the country's leading aircraft designers, in the 25-cent souvenir catalog for the exposition. "Important centers such as Philadelphia and New York should have a ten or twelve-passenger machine leaving a well-equipped airdrome in both cities every half hour."

This was a thinly veiled sales pitch. The Glenn L. Martin Company's huge, twin-engine bomber—one of the featured attractions at the

Garden—also came in a transport version, with glass windows, extra headroom, and seats for ten passengers. During the second week of the show, the Air Service arranged for reporters to take a ride in one of the planes, which circled the sixty-story Woolworth Building in Manhattan, buffeted by forty-mile-an-hour winds, before returning to Hazelhurst Field. "Throughout the trip, despite the wind, the absence of a chill in the air seemed remarkable," one reporter wrote.

Martin's rivals also were looking ahead. The Dayton-Wright Airplane Company, builder of the DH-4, displayed a civilian prototype of that aircraft called the Honeymoon Special, which had a "luxuriously upholstered" rear cockpit outfitted for newlyweds. "The car is equipped with a buffet arrangement, with a sandwich box and thermos bottles," the *New York Times* reported. "For the young bride there has been installed a vanity case, locker, and mirror set, for the groom a smoking outfit and luggage compartment, and for the comfort of both a wind shield to ward off wind and rain." The "sky chauffeur" sat in front.

Smaller models displayed at the Garden were aimed at sportsmen. Among them was the endearingly named Chummy Flyabout, a two-seat monoplane made by the Gallaudet Aircraft Corporation of East Greenwich, Rhode Island. It was powered by two twenty-horsepower motorcycle engines, each of which drove a pusher propeller behind the wings. The Loening Kitten—a tiny seaplane having a wingspan of just nineteen feet and designed to be carried on ships or submarines—was thought to have similar appeal. Manufacturers of aircraft engines, parts, laminated wooden propellers, and flight instruments took up their own exhibition space.

———

Soon after the doors of the exposition opened, the keynote speaker arrived. Brig. Gen. William "Billy" Mitchell had recently turned thirty-nine. Undeniably handsome, he had a strong, well-formed nose, a dimpled chin, and deep creases bracketing his mouth. A prominent lower lip hinted at a pugnacious streak. At five feet nine-and-one-half inches, Mitchell was slightly taller than the average American man in 1919, with a lean 150-pound frame that reflected a lifetime of outdoor activity, much of it on horseback, and an austere diet that eschewed red meat (he also shunned tobacco). He carried himself ruler straight, as if his spine were made of steel, which in some respects it was.

No American in uniform believed more fervently in the promise of aviation or advocated more fiercely on its behalf. As the commander of American air operations at the front, Mitchell had demonstrated physical courage, boundless energy, and a prescient understanding of a new medium of battle—the atmosphere—most famously in orchestrating the biggest air assault of the war the previous September during the battle of St. Mihiel. His military prowess was matched only by his flamboyance. A bon vivant with more than a touch of vanity, he established his first field headquarters in an eighteenth century French chateau, amused himself by hunting wild boar, and hurtled around the countryside in a requisitioned Mercedes racing car. He sometimes carried a walking cane, though his legs were perfectly sound, or a leather riding crop, which he liked to rap smartly across his glossy cordovan boots. Completing the image were tan, British-style riding breeches, known as pinks, and a tailored blouse of Mitchell's own design, with enormous patch pockets on the breast.

People who met Mitchell rarely forgot him. There was a quickness about him, in his movements as well as his speech—a brusque, rapid-fire patter that projected both high intelligence and impatience, though the latter sometimes got the better of the former. Mitchell's men loved him for his vivid personality and swagger, his superiors less so, and partly for the same reasons. "He had a charming quality, and also an asinine quality," a contemporary would recall. But there was no denying the medals he had earned or the celebrity that followed him home and which now attended his first public appearance on U.S. soil since he sailed for Europe nearly two years earlier.

As Mitchell entered the Garden, members of an Air Service detail from Hazelhurst Field snapped to attention. Buglers preceded him onto the exhibition floor, where he was formally greeted by an official from the manufacturers' group. As the Army musicians tooted out a call signaling the presence of a general officer, Mitchell climbed the stairs to the speaker's platform that had been erected near the Martin Bomber. His remarks were brief and immodest. "In the air fighting up to the time the Armistice was signed, the American aviation forces brought down four and one-half times as many German airplanes as the enemy brought down American machines," he declared. "When the war ended the Air Service of the United States Army excelled that of any army in all branches of aerial tactics." The first claim was an exaggeration—the actual ratio was less than three-to-one—the second a debatable one. But the crowd was in no mood to quibble and greeted Mitchell's words with hearty applause.

It was a triumphal moment, not only for Mitchell and the Air Service but also, it seemed, for the industry that had organized the exposition. More than eighty American manufacturers of aircraft, engines, components, and accessories had turned out to display their products. How could anyone who wandered among their booths or listened to Mitchell's words doubt the country's ability to dominate this thrilling new field?

In fact, there was every reason to do so. The exposition was a mirage. American aviation was in deep trouble. And no one was more worried about it than Billy Mitchell.

2

Willie

He came from money. His grandfather saw to that. Alexander Mitchell was in his early twenties when in 1839 he left his native Scotland to start a bank in Wisconsin, using seed money from a patron back home. During the next three decades he built a business and financial empire that grew to include the Chicago, Milwaukee and St. Paul Railway, one of the nation's largest with 5,000 miles of track. By then he was the wealthiest man in Wisconsin, having amassed a fortune estimated at $20 million. The very picture of a nineteenth century robber baron, though perhaps more principled than some, he and his second wife, Martha, built a grand home in Milwaukee and another one in Florida, to which they escaped by private railcar during the winter. He once outbid John D. Rockefeller at an art auction in New York. In the 1870s, Alexander served two terms in Congress, and Martha helped lead the effort to preserve George Washington's estate at Mount Vernon.

Alexander's son, John Lendrum Mitchell, was cut from different cloth. Born in 1842 and educated for much of his youth in Europe, he was a dreamy intellectual with eclectic interests and a strong sense of *noblesse oblige*. He fought for the Union in the Civil War, then joined his father's banking business and entered into an unhappy twelve-year marriage that ended scandalously in 1877, amid public charges of infidelity on both sides. He remarried the following year and promptly decamped with his new wife, Harriet, to France, where he indulged his interests in art and history. It was there, in Nice, that Billy Mitchell was born on December 29, 1879.

"Willie," as his family called him, was the first of the couple's seven children. He was three when his parents took him home to Milwaukee, as fluent in French as English. His father rejoined the family banking business and established himself as a civic leader, serving as head of the Milwaukee school system and helping to found an agriculture school at the University of Wisconsin. A gentle, unassuming man with spectacles and a long gray beard, John began to dabble in Democratic politics and eventually served in the U.S. Senate.

Willie was a happy child—bright, curious, and rarely at rest. Soon after returning from France, John Mitchell built a fourteen-bedroom mansion on a sprawling country estate outside Milwaukee called Meadowmere, where he bred horses and experimented with the latest scientific farming methods. Willie thrived in this bucolic setting, which included a fishpond as well as stables and a track. He learned to ride well enough that he would one day compete in international polo matches. Whenever he could slip away from his Scottish nanny, he roamed freely over the 480-acre grounds, climbing the tallest trees and terrorizing small animals with the air rifle his father had given him at age five.

Mitchell was ten when he left home for Racine College, an Episcopal boys' boarding school. He was a good student, if the subject interested him, and a better athlete. At the same time, he often tested the patience of authority figures, as he would throughout his life. One school report chided him for "talking before grace in the dining room, boisterous conduct at the table and disorder in the dormitory."

Mitchell was keenly aware of his place in the aristocracy, with a sense of entitlement to match. As a teenager he wrote a plaintive letter to his mother demanding that she send him more spending money, because "there are lots of fellows here who are a great deal poorer than we are and they get it." In fact, the family's resources were under strain and nearly collapsed during the financial panic of 1893, when John began his first term in the Senate. Alexander Mitchell had died in 1887, and John shared little of his aptitude for business. He barely kept the banking operation afloat and was forced to sell some of the best horses he kept at Meadowmere. But the near-calamity does not appear to have made much of an impression on Billy, whose habit of squeezing his adored "Mummy" for cash would follow him into adulthood.

His relationship with his father was loving but distant. After Billy wrote him a letter boasting of various athletic achievements, John Mitchell replied with mild sarcasm. "Your letter is silent as to your studies," he wrote. "This comes of over-modesty, I suppose."

———

The younger Mitchell would never share his father's zeal for scholarly pursuits and abandoned them at the first opportunity. It came during his freshman year at Columbian College (now George Washington University) in Washington, D.C., as the nation prepared for war. The flashpoint was Cuba, then a Spanish colony in the midst of an insurrection. On February 15, 1898, a mysterious explosion destroyed the battleship USS *Maine* in Havana Harbor. Though the cause of the blast has never been established, Americans were quick to point a finger at Spain; in April of that year, Congress authorized President William McKinley to drive Spanish forces from the island. The teenage Mitchell looked on from the Senate gallery as the measure was debated.

Though his father was among those voting in favor of war, he had done so reluctantly and was wary of the expansionist fever gripping the country. Not so his son. Fired by patriotism and a sense of personal destiny, Mitchell returned to Wisconsin to join the First Wisconsin Volunteer Infantry—the same state militia in which his father once served. Thanks to the elder Mitchell's influence, he spent just seven days as an enlisted man before he was commissioned as a second lieutenant in the Signal Corps, the Army's communications branch. He trained in Florida and sailed for Cuba in December. Much to his disappointment, he arrived too late for any fighting—six months had passed since Teddy Roosevelt and his Rough Riders charged up San Juan Hill—though not too late to witness Spain's formal surrender at the governor-general's palace in Havana. The moment captured for Mitchell his sense that America had a vital role to play on the world stage, and he along with it.

Geopolitics aside, Mitchell loved the adventure and challenges of Army life. During the eight months he spent with occupation forces in Cuba, he supervised the installation of 137 miles of telegraph line, much of it through dense jungle. It was no small achievement for a nineteen-year-old, and his superiors could not help but be impressed.

They were similarly impressed, when, a year later, Mitchell found himself in the Philippines, where Filipino independence fighters were waging guerrilla war against American forces that had recently taken over the colony from Spain. Mitchell commanded a signal company assigned to string telegraph lines among Army units on the island of Luzon. It was a brutal task, and not just because of the swampy terrain or the malaria that periodically wracked him with fever and chills. Mitchell and his men came under regular attack, affording him his first taste of the combat he so desperately craved. He proved to have a cool head under fire, once leading fifteen men on a daring night raid that captured a senior guerrilla commander. He boasted of his exploits in letters home and asked his parents to buy him a Mauser pistol during a trip to Germany.

Mitchell's next assignment was no less daunting for its lack of gunfire. In 1901, he was sent to Alaska, where the Signal Corps was trying to build a telegraph network. The territory was then a trackless wilderness, and the work was going slowly, in part because it largely stopped during the brutal Alaskan winter. By now in the regular Army, Mitchell turned the project into a year-round operation, traveling by dogsled and sleeping in snow caves while his team surveyed the land and distributed line and poles for installation when the ground thawed. Once, in subzero weather, he plunged with his sled into a partially frozen river, drenching himself to the shoulders. His dog team pulled him out, but his clothes instantly froze "hard as boards." He would have died if not for a downed tree, which provided fuel for a fire. By the time he left Alaska in July 1903, the territory had a functioning telegraph system, and Mitchell was considered one of the most capable young officers in the Army.

His personal life also was filled with promise. In December, shortly before his twenty-fourth birthday, Mitchell married Caroline Stoddard, a comely young Vassar graduate and aspiring novelist who was the daughter of wealthy family friends from Rochester, New York. Mitchell's next postings—at Fort Leavenworth, Kansas, and Cuba—were happy ones. In 1907, the couple returned to Leavenworth after Mitchell was awarded a prestigious slot at the School of the Line, the Army's version of graduate school.

It was around this time that he began to make a name for himself as a military thinker. A fluid writer, he had dazzled superiors with lucid and meticulous reports from the field. Now he began to air his views more widely, suggesting in an article written for *Cavalry Journal* in 1906 that airplanes and submarines were the weapons of the future. In 1913, after several short assignments elsewhere, he was posted to Washington, D.C., as the youngest officer on the Army's General Staff.

———

Life in the capital agreed with the Mitchells. Now with two young daughters, they purchased a gracious townhouse near DuPont Circle and joined the city's social elite, mingling with generals and politicians at dinner parties and private clubs. Never one to skimp on luxuries, Mitchell kept three horses, one reserved for polo; Caroline busied herself with golf and shopping expeditions to Woodward & Lothrop, the city's fanciest department store.

Unfortunately, the couple's monthly expenses far exceeded Mitchell's modest Army pay. As bills piled up, he borrowed from banks and earned extra money writing articles on national security for the *Chicago Tribune* and other outlets, using a pseudonym because of Army rules against freelancing. He explored a dubious plan to import animal hides from South America. And just as he had as a youth, he regularly wrote home asking his mother for money, arguing that keeping up appearances was essential to his career.

If so, the money was well spent. A rising star on the General Staff, he frequently was called upon to advise lawmakers on military legislation and, after August 1914, to track developments on the European battle-front for the War Department. One of the most important was the growing use of airplanes as weapons. As it happens, Mitchell had befriended one of the Army's first aviators, who in early 1916 took him up on his first airplane ride. Mitchell was hooked, and the timing was propitious: He had just been placed in temporary command of the Army's tiny Aviation Section, which was then within the Signal Corps.

The new assignment came with a promotion to major, though not with flight training—Mitchell was considered too old at thirty-six. Undeterred, he learned to fly at his own considerable expense, traveling every weekend for several months to the Curtiss Aviation School in Newport News, Virginia. His enthusiasm exceeded his ability. Not long after his first solo flight, he managed to flip a plane on its back while landing. "What did I do wrong?" Mitchell asked after extricating himself from the inverted cockpit.

It was not the first time Mitchell had shown a willingness to go it alone. In 1915, he gave a lecture in which he asserted that the United States was unprepared for war. His remarks found their way into the press, earning him a mild reprimand. Mitchell's outspokenness began to grate on his superiors, who concluded that his talents might be better suited to the field. By early 1917, after Germany broke its pledge to refrain from submarine attacks on ships from the United States and other neutral countries, war seemed inevitable. The Army needed a man on the scene to observe and report back on the Allies' use of aircraft. Sending Mitchell would solve two problems at once. He sailed for France in March.

3

The Western Front

Mitchell had been right that the United States was ill prepared for the fighting that lay ahead. In April 1917 the Army could muster only 128,000 men, a number that would grow to 4 million by the end of World War I. The country's air force was in even worse shape. From the beginning, military leaders had failed to appreciate the transformative potential of the Wright brothers' achievement, and in this they were not alone. The Wrights' first successful flight test at Kitty Hawk, North Carolina, on December 17, 1903, was all but ignored by the press, as was their steady progress over the next few years. This was partly because the brothers were reluctant to publicize their invention, fearing that rivals would steal their ideas. But it also stemmed from a failure of imagination; until they saw it with their own eyes, reporters, like the public, had a hard time believing that the Wrights had accomplished what they said they did.

Attitudes began to shift in the summer of 1908, when Orville Wright began a series of test flights for the Army at Fort Myer, Virginia,* and Wilbur Wright began demonstrating one of their machines in

---

* On September 17, 1908, Lt. Thomas Selfridge, who was flying with Orville as a passenger, was killed in aviation's first fatal crash. Orville was seriously injured but resumed the test flights after he recovered.

Europe. European inventors had made some progress on their own, but Wilbur's exhibition flights, some lasting more than two hours, caused a sensation and were prominently reported in newspapers back home. The brothers from Ohio finally began to get the recognition they deserved. In the summer of 1909, the Army purchased one of their planes—a Wright Military Flyer—for $30,000 after Orville and a passenger completed a speed trial at an average of forty-two-and-a-half miles an hour.

In the meantime, rival manufacturers began to emerge in the United States, and with them a new breed of daredevils who began making exhibition flights around the country. The shows drew large crowds, perhaps because they sometimes ended in spectacular wrecks. But progress was not as swift as it might have been. Patent disputes between the Wright brothers and their main competitor, Glenn H. Curtiss, stifled innovation, and Congress was slow to provide backing for the new technology. Though the federal government had lately begun to expand its role in American life, many lawmakers clung to the laissez-faire economic traditions of the nineteenth century. They saw little need for the government to support what manufacturers would surely accomplish on their own, just as the Wright brothers had.

The outbreak of war in 1914 began to change that calculus, by revealing the airplane's potential as a weapon. In 1915, Congress created a government body—the National Advisory Committee for Aeronautics—charged with directing research into aviation. But Congress provided just $5,000 to fund the organization, whose twelve members—including aeronautical experts from the War Department and the Smithsonian Institution—were expected to volunteer their time.

Such was the state of aviation in those days that even some of the leading names in the field were skeptical about its prospects. The same year the committee was formed, Jerome Hunsaker, who taught the first aeronautical engineering course at the Massachusetts Institute of Technology, was approached by a former student who expressed interest in taking a job with Glenn L. Martin. Hunsaker tried to dissuade him. "This airplane business will never amount to very much," he advised.*

It was a different story on the other side of the Atlantic, where monarchs and parliaments were generally more open to the idea of intervening in the marketplace on behalf of new technologies. Aeronautical laboratories backed by governments and wealthy industrialists sprang up in Britain, France, and Germany, absorbing some of their best scientists and engineers in the years before the war. In the late summer of 1913, Hunsaker and another American academic, Albert F. Zahm, toured the foreign laboratories on behalf of the Smithsonian and were bowled over by what they saw. "The work of this committee is manifold and comprehensive," Zahm wrote of the British Advisory Committee for Aeronautics, which was established by Prime Minister Herbert H. Asquith in 1909 to oversee research at government and private facilities. "Whirling table measurements, wind-tunnel measurements, testing of engines, propellers, woods, metals, fabrics, varnishes, hydromechanics studies, meteorological observations, mathematics investigations in fluid dynamics, the theory of gyroscopes, airplane and dirigible design—whatever studies will promote the art of air craft construction and navigation may be prosecuted by this committee."

Such efforts lent momentum to an industry that already had established an early lead over its American competition. Two French brothers, Gabriel and Charles Voisin, opened the world's first factory for the commercial production of aircraft in 1906. Four more would open in France by the end of 1909, the same year another Frenchman, Louis Blériot, crossed the English Channel in a monoplane of his own design. From 1908 to 1913, the French government invested $22 million in aviation,

---

* The student, Donald Douglas, wisely ignored the advice. He went on to found the Douglas Aircraft Company, maker of the legendary DC-3 and the precursor of the McDonnell Douglas Corporation.

while the United States spent just $435,000. Germany led the pack at $28 million.

The pace of aircraft development in Europe accelerated sharply with the outbreak of war. At first the warring powers used airplanes for reconnaissance and artillery spotting—mobile versions of tethered observation balloons, which armies had deployed since the late eighteenth century and now bobbed in the air currents above the Western Front. The planes lacked armaments, and aviators from opposing sides often greeted each other with a gentlemanly wave. That soon changed, as commanders on both sides saw the wisdom of dominating the skies above the battlefield, especially once they grasped the intelligence threat posed by enemy reconnaissance aircraft. Aviators began plinking at each other with sidearms and rifles, soon replaced by swivel-mounted machine guns. Smaller single-seat scout, or pursuit, aircraft were deployed to attack enemy planes and balloons. Planes became faster, more maneuverable, and more lethal, especially with the advent of synchronizing gears that allowed machine guns to be fired through spinning propellers without shooting them off. Aviators chased each other through the sky at heights of up to 20,000 feet, groggy from lack of oxygen and numb with cold, in dizzying mortal contests that often ended in agony, as their wood-and-fabric planes burned easily, and they flew without parachutes. The era of the dogfight had arrived. So, too, had the first crude attempts at aerial bombardment, and with it the threat to industrial and civilian targets far behind enemy lines, a development with harrowing implications for future wars.

Back in the United States, the Army still had one boot firmly planted in the cavalry age—literally so in the case of its aviators, who were required to wear spurs until 1917. Similar attitudes prevailed at the Navy, whose admirals could scarcely imagine the day when aircraft would pose a threat to their seemingly invincible battleships. After the war, Mitchell would challenge the Navy's hubris, with astonishing results, but for now, skepticism prevailed. In part because the War Department waited three years before dispatching an observer—Mitchell—to report back on the air war in Europe, military leaders in the United States were mostly ignorant of just how far their country had fallen behind. Moreover, in 1916, the Army's first deployment of airplanes to anything resembling a combat zone had not inspired confidence.

In March of that year, Gen. John "Black Jack" Pershing, who soon would command U.S. forces in Europe, led horse-mounted troops across the southern U.S. border in pursuit of the Mexican revolutionary and outlaw Pancho Villa. The expedition came in response to a cross-border raid by Villa and his men that killed or wounded two dozen Americans in Columbus, New Mexico. Pershing's troops were supported by the Army's first air combat unit, the accurately named First Aero Squadron, which was equipped with eight Curtiss JN-3 biplanes. The outdated JN-3, or "Jenny," had a top speed of seventy-five miles an hour and could barely fly two hours on a tank of gas. Though sometimes useful for reconnaissance and delivering messages, the Jennies lacked sufficient power to clear the 10,000-foot mountains of the Mexican desert. Pilots often damaged their planes in forced landings after losing their bearings or suffering engine failures. Propellers cracked and delaminated in the dry heat. The planes were scrapped within a month, and more powerful Curtiss R-2s sent as replacements fared little better.

The First Aero Squadron's sorry record in Mexico confirmed the views of many in the Army's upper ranks that airplanes were dangerous and unreliable. With Congress sharing that jaundiced attitude, aviation remained an afterthought in military budgets. By the time the United States formally entered the war on April 6, 1917, the Army's air component—still within the Signal Corps but soon to become the discrete Army branch known as the Air Service—could muster just thirty-five pilots and fifty-five aircraft, of which "51 were obsolete and 4 were obsolescent," as Pershing later quipped. All had been designed for training rather than combat. The Navy's aviation arm was equally underwhelming.

———

Mitchell arrived in Paris on April 10, just four days after the United States declared war on Germany. Bursting with his usual manic energy, he established a temporary headquarters in space donated by the American Radiator Company—the War Department having neglected to provide him any funds for an office or staff—and immediately began schooling himself in every aspect of military aviation as practiced by those who knew it best. He toured the front as a guest of the French army, crouching in trenches as shells shrieked overhead and catching his first glimpse of French and German airplanes in combat. He traveled to Britain for an audience with that country's leading air strategist, Maj. Gen. Hugh Trenchard. And he repeatedly took to the skies in risky forays across enemy lines, first as a passenger in the rear cockpit of French observation planes, later as the pilot of a two-seat Spad emblazoned with his personal insignia, a silver eagle on a scarlet disc that was inspired by the United States' official seal.*

These experiences shaped his views on air power and informed the detailed reports he sent back to the War Department. By now Mitchell was not alone in recognizing just how far the United States had fallen behind in aviation. A new federal entity, the Aircraft Production Board, shared his sense of alarm, as did some in Congress. The turning point came in late May, when the French government cabled an urgent appeal for airplanes and engines. Military leaders reacted quickly, making plans for the manufacture of 20,474 new airplanes in just twelve months—a wildly ambitious goal for the nation's tiny aircraft industry, which assembled most of its products by hand. Congress supported the plans with the largest single-purpose appropriation—$640 million—in U.S. history to that point. The War Department promised to "darken the skies over Germany with airplanes."

The threat would prove hollow. Though the industry tooled up rapidly—by the end of the war, twelve-cylinder Liberty aircraft engines were rolling off assembly lines at the rate of 150 per day—manufacturers were hamstrung by shortages of designers and engineers as well as essential materials such as spruce, the strong, springy wood used for aircraft frames and ribs. Castor beans, whose oil was used as an engine lubri-

---

* Years later, Mitchell told Paul Garber, the head of the Smithsonian Institution's new aviation museum, that his mechanic had copied the design from a dollar bill.

cant, had to be imported from India until farmers in the United States could start growing enough on their own. Profiteering and corruption caused further delays. To be fair, the country's aircraft industry would end the war in much better shape than it started—production increased roughly 18-fold from 1917 to 1918, driving rapid improvements in airframe design, engines, instruments, and manufacturing techniques. But the gains would come too late to make a significant difference at the front. France, Britain, and Italy would supply most of the planes that Americans flew against the Germans.

The country did a better job with pilots, training about 10,000 by the end of the war. Mitchell would play a central role in preparing them for combat, organizing them into squadrons, and leading them into battle. But it did not happen right away—American aviators would not join the fray until the spring of 1918, just six months before the Armistice—and Mitchell would make plenty of enemies in the meantime.

———

After Pershing and his staff arrived in Paris in June 1917, he named Mitchell as the chief aviation officer of the newly formed American Expeditionary Forces. But Mitchell soon clashed with other senior officers, irritated by their insistence on being heard despite their lack of flying credentials and experience at the front. He was bitterly disappointed when, in September, Pershing named an artilleryman to take over what was now called the Air Service. Pershing softened the blow by promoting Mitchell to colonel and putting him in charge of air operations near the front, where he would oversee combat training and preparations for the coming American offensive. Mitchell was mollified by the vote of confidence, but not for long.

In November, Mitchell was passed over a second time when Pershing named Brig. Gen. Benjamin Foulois to run the Air Service. Foulois, a veteran Army flyer, knew Mitchell from Washington and considered him a self-promoting loudmouth. The antipathy was mutual. When Foulois showed up at Mitchell's office in the French city of Toul, which was supposed to serve as Foulois's new headquarters, Mitchell attempted to remove its furniture—including even the telephone—claiming he needed it for himself. Foulois, citing Mitchell's "extremely childish attitude," tried to get him shipped home. Pershing might well have complied with Foulois's request—he'd had his own run-ins with Mitchell—had he not recognized his talents as a combat leader. Eventually even Foulois came around. When Pershing brought in yet another non-flying general, Mason Patrick, to head the Air Service, Foulois graciously conceded that Mitchell should run its frontline operations while Foulois would focus on logistics and training.

Mitchell would more than vindicate Pershing's faith. In the summer of 1918, he began preparing for a massive air assault in support of the first major American ground offensive of the war. Half a million American doughboys would attack German forces in the St. Mihiel salient, an irregular bulge on the Western Front that encompassed the French town of St. Mihiel. For Mitchell, the battle of St. Mihiel was an opportunity to test his air-power theories on a grand scale. At his headquarters near the front, Mitchell spent weeks huddling with his officers over a huge relief map, drafting orders for his squadrons, and overseeing the assembly of a massive air armada of 1,481 planes and 30,000 officers and enlisted men. The multinational force—American, French, British, and Italian—was secretly distributed among fourteen airfields, where planes were parked in hangars to hide them from German observation aircraft.

Pershing had scheduled the attack for the morning of September 12. Ground troops advanced from their trenches as planned, but heavy rains turned airfields to mud and prevented many planes from taking off—or completing their missions when they did. Moreover, as Mitchell had observed from the cockpit of his Spad just a few days earlier, German forces already had begun withdrawing from the salient, allowing some to escape. Nevertheless, Mitchell and his commanders achieved much of what they had hoped. Over four days, despite poor visibility and low clouds, pursuit planes flew hundreds of sorties across the battle lines, overwhelming their German foes and clearing a path for reconnaissance flights, which brought back valuable intelligence on the disposition of German troops. Allied bombers, some flying at night, hammered ammunition dumps and an important rail line, while smaller planes unleashed their machine guns on retreating German troops and convoys of horse-drawn wagons. More than sixty German aircraft were shot down, in addition to twelve observation balloons. Mitchell himself made repeated flights over the battlefield to assess the progress of his aviators.

In the end, their work was more disruptive than decisive, but it helped clear a path for the First Army's infantry and tanks, which succeeded in retaking the salient in just four days. The air offensive was not without cost—forty Air Service aviators were killed and another sixteen were shot down and taken prisoner. Even so, it was a proud moment for the fledgling Air Service, and especially for Mitchell. Pershing recommended him for promotion to brigadier general and for the Distinguished Service Cross, the second highest award after the Medal of Honor.

————

St. Mihiel marked the high point of Mitchell's wartime career. During the next two months, the Air Service would support an even bigger—and far more costly—American offensive against experienced German troops dug in between the Argonne Forest and the river Meuse. The American flyers did their part, but their mission was plagued by shortages of aircraft and supplies, as well as by infighting between Mitchell and ground commanders irked by his high-handed ways.

Still, Mitchell remained convinced that air power might yet deliver a knockout blow. During the Meuse-Argonne campaign, he and his Allied partners began planning for bombing raids deep inside Germany, and he even proposed training American soldiers in the use of parachutes, so they could be dropped behind enemy lines. These bold ideas were never implemented—the German capitulation in November came too early for that—though both would prove their worth soon enough, in another war against the same foe. In the end, air power played a secondary role in the Allied victory. But its potential could no longer be dismissed, nor could the sacrifices of the aviators who showed what was possible, even with the crude technology of the day.

To soldiers enduring the misery of trench warfare, military flyers often were seen as playboys who enjoyed a pampered life behind the lines, romancing local women and drinking in cafés while ground forces did most of the fighting and dying. The last part was certainly true, at least in terms of absolute numbers. But it's also true that aviators faced daunting odds. Of 740 American planes assigned to squadrons that flew in combat, more than a third—290—were lost to enemy action, and 569 Air Service flyers were killed, wounded, captured, or reported missing. Accidents took the lives of another 319. Among them was Mitchell's younger brother, John, whose skull was crushed when he was thrown from his cockpit during a botched landing attempt in May. For the rest of the war, Mitchell wore the mother-of-pearl cufflinks that he had saved from his brother's belongings before shipping them home.

Yet victory and its aftermath were heady times for Mitchell. Driving through Paris in the evening of the Armistice of November 11, he was mobbed by jubilant French aviators who recognized him from the St. Mihiel campaign. "Vive notre general Américain!" they shouted, clambering onto the running boards and hood of his vehicle. The celebrations would last for months, and Mitchell was in no hurry to get home. He served briefly with occupation forces in Germany, where Marshal Philippe Pétain, known for his leadership of French forces at Verdun in 1916, awarded him the Legion of Honor. He then traveled to Britain for consultations with the Royal Air Force and a "delightful chat" with King George V at Buckingham Palace.

Even on his voyage home in February 1919 aboard the Cunard liner *Aquitania*, he could not bring himself to relinquish the spotlight. The ship carried first-class passengers on its upper decks and troops below. Every morning, Mitchell conducted a top-to-bottom inspection, strutting the decks with a retinue of aides and pausing now and then to touch up his boots with a handkerchief. Civilians aboard were alternately annoyed and bemused by this "plumed fellow with the aura of banner, spear, and shield," recalled a *Chicago Tribune* reporter who happened to be among them. "No one ever had a better time being a general."

When the ship steamed into New York Harbor on February 28, Air Service planes flew out from Long Island to welcome him home as Caroline, "sick with excitement," waited on the pier. Two days later, after Mitchell's appearance at the New York Aeronautical Exposition at Madison Square Garden, the couple boarded an afternoon train for Washington.

"At home at last," Caroline wrote in her diary that night.

4

Aftermath

At the end of a workday in June 1919, after Mitchell had been back in Washington for three months, he invited a fellow officer home for dinner. As Caroline busied herself in the kitchen, Mitchell led his guest to the basement, where he showed him a copper still. "I'm running a little experiment," he offered. "I thought you'd like to watch." Six months earlier, Mitchell had taken it as a personal affront when Congress ratified the Eighteenth Amendment, which banned the manufacture and sale of "intoxicating liquors." In a small act of rebellion, he had prepared sour mash—grain fermented with water and yeast—that he now deemed ready for production. "You know, these people back here passed this Prohibition law while we were fighting for the country," he complained to his guest. "They can't do that to me." Mitchell ignited a burner beneath the still, triggering a process that ended with "white lightning" dripping from a tube. The two men filled their glasses and got pleasantly drunk.

Mitchell had more on his mind than Prohibition. His guest that night was Maj. Reed M. Chambers, an ace who had served with Eddie Rickenbacker in the famed Ninety-Fourth Aero Squadron, known informally as the "Hat in the Ring" squadron for its jaunty emblem of an inverted Uncle Sam top hat inside a red circle. A few months shy of his twenty-fifth birthday, Chambers, like many of his comrades, saw little future in the peacetime Air Service and a few days earlier had turned in his resignation. He had agreed to work for the automobile company that Rickenbacker was planning to start. After dining upstairs with Caroline, the two men resumed their vigil over the bubbling apparatus in the basement, and Mitchell revealed the reason behind his invitation. "I got your resignation," he said. "You can't do it. Too many of the old-timers have left, and we need you in the service. We've got to keep a cadre of experienced men in there, to get this thing reorganized." He dangled before Chambers the command of a squadron at Selfridge Field in Michigan, and Chambers agreed to stay on.

———

It was a small victory in a losing campaign. The boys were coming home, and the country was demobilizing, whether Mitchell liked it or not. As combat squadrons disbanded, flyers, mechanics, and other Air Service personnel boarded ships in St. Nazaire or other French ports bound for Boston, Massachusetts, or Hoboken, New Jersey. Across the United States, most training airfields were abandoned or turned over to other uses. The urgency of war was supplanted by the humdrum of peace. In January 1919, a memo had gone out from headquarters warning against "the shooting of wild fowl with machine guns from airplanes." Curtiss JN-4 trainers were sold to the public for $300. In France, nearly 2,300 surplus Air Service planes were stripped of guns and usable parts, then pushed into heaps and set alight. News of the airplane bonfires caused a minor scandal in Congress, though the Air Service argued that the planes were obsolete and not worth the cost of shipping home. The War Department puzzled over what to do with thousands of Liberty aircraft engines and 30 million feet of aircraft-grade lumber.

Most alarming to Mitchell, the Air Service was hemorrhaging talent. Except for a handful of career Army officers, most of its aviators had been commissioned on an emergency basis in 1917 and 1918, and the War Department was eager to shed them from its payroll. By the end of 1919, the Air Service would retain only about 1,300 officers, down from 20,000 at the signing of the Armistice. One of Mitchell's aides captured the prevailing mood after an inspection tour of Langley Field in Hampton, Virginia, near the mouth of the Chesapeake Bay. "The esprit de corps," he wrote in July 1919, "was very noticeable on account of its total absence."

Mitchell's postwar frustrations had been compounded by his failure, once again, to land the job he thought he was due. At the time of the Armistice, he and many of his fellow aviators believed that he was the natural choice to run the postwar Air Service. But Pershing had instead filled the post with Maj. Gen. Charles T. Menoher, a 56-year-old artillery-man. A trim, stern-looking man with receding gray hair and a cool gaze, Menoher, like Mitchell, was the son of a Civil War veteran and a proven combat commander widely admired by his men, having led the highly successful Forty-Second Division during the Meuse-Argonne offensive. There the resemblance ended, however. In contrast to the outspoken and sometimes-volatile Mitchell, the new Air Service chief was low-key, methodical, and careful in his choice of words. Menoher was raised in Johnstown, Pennsylvania, where his father worked as a carpenter, and briefly taught school before winning an appointment to the U.S. Military Academy at West Point. Known for his "sweet tenor voice," he sang in the choir and in 1886 graduated sixteenth in a class of seventy-seven. He served in Cuba and the Philippines during the Spanish-American War.

Like Pershing, a West Point classmate, Menoher was a traditional-ist who believed that for the foreseeable future, battles would be won or lost by soldiers on the ground, with aircraft in a supporting role. But the new Air Service chief was no Luddite. After returning from the Philip-pines, he had helped to orchestrate the Field Artillery's transition from the black-powder cannons of the nineteenth century to more capable, mobile weapons such as a field howitzer that could be taken apart and packed on a mule. He understood the importance of aviation, if not yet its full potential, and would do his best to protect the Air Service during the rush to demobilize. In a speech at Madison Square Garden at the end of the New York Aeronautical Exposition in March, Menoher even endorsed the idea of a military aviation academy modeled after West Point and the U.S. Naval Academy at Annapolis.

Though denied the prize he had sought, Mitchell would occupy a prominent role in the postwar Air Service as the head of its Training and

Operations Group—in effect, Menoher's second in command. The new Air Service chief valued Mitchell's experience and often deferred to him, at least at first. But the two were destined to clash. Menoher, after all, did not wear aviator's wings on his uniform, nor did he share Mitchell's zeal for shaking up the existing order. Which is exactly what Mitchell intended to do. Almost as soon as he returned to Washington, Mitchell embarked on the quest that would define much of his postwar career.

He believed the time had come for an independent air force. Mitchell got the idea from Britain, whose Royal Air Force had been formed in 1918 by merging the air arms of the British Army and the Royal Navy. He had come to believe in the wisdom of this arrangement even before he shipped home. He was sure the United States would soon face new threats from Japan or perhaps a resurgent Germany—whose army, he noted with uncanny foresight, had "marched back in good order"—and that air power would decide these future conflicts. He was equally confident that air power would be wielded most effectively by an independent U.S. service with the same standing as the Army and the Navy. He began lobbying for a cabinet-level department of aeronautics with responsibility for all aspects of civil and military aviation, including an air force. It was easy to imagine who Mitchell had in mind to run the new branch of the armed forces.

Building on his social and political connections in Washington, Mitchell cultivated powerful allies in Congress, where several bills for the new aeronautics department would be introduced by the end of 1919. Additional support came from aviators who had served with Mitchell in France and now worked with him at Air Service headquarters in the Munitions Building, the hulking, two-block-long edifice on Constitution Avenue that was erected in less than six months during the war.* But institutional resistance ran deep. Mitchell's proposal put him at odds with not only Menoher and the rest of the General Staff of the Army but also Newton D. Baker, the secretary of war, who shared the prevailing view

---

* The Munitions Building, near the present-day Vietnam War Memorial, was demolished in 1970.

of the airplane as a promising but not epoch-making weapon. The Navy, fighting to protect its share of a shrinking military budget, objected on similar grounds. Mitchell did not help his cause by overreaching. Among the blizzard of memos he sent to Menoher during the spring of 1919 was one proposing the construction of two aircraft carriers with 900-foot flight decks—not for the Navy but for the Air Service. Before long, admirals would become apoplectic at the mention of his name.

————

Mitchell's crusade for an independent air force was closely wrapped up with his other main preoccupation: how to promote the development of aviation in the absence of a war. The Armistice had shut down most aircraft production in the United States, as the War Department abruptly canceled orders for 13,000 planes. Within a few months, some manufacturers had closed their doors while others struggled to survive. In Seattle, the Boeing Airplane Co. began making furniture and speedboats. Manufacturers' troubles had serious implications for national defense. A thriving commercial aircraft industry was essential, both to drive innovation and also to maintain production capacity that could be geared up rapidly in times of war.

There was, however, a problem: Except for a few wealthy sportsmen, there were no buyers for new aircraft. Many Americans had yet to even lay eyes on an airplane; if they had, it was probably a war-surplus Jenny with a barnstormer in the cockpit. Practical uses were still mostly theoretical. In Europe, by contrast, several commercial airlines would be established by the end of 1919, including one that flew passengers between London and Paris in converted Farman F-60 Bombers (another was KLM, the Dutch carrier, which is still flying today). The threat of foreign domination became a recurring theme in aviation publications such as *Flying* and *Air Service Journal*, which in January 1919 ran a front-page story under the headline "U.S. Lags Far Behind Europe in Preparations for Air Transport."

Glenn L. Martin, whose modified bomber had carried reporters over Manhattan during the aeronautical exposition in March, was not the only aircraft designer who hoped to close that gap. Soon after the Armistice, Glenn H. Curtiss and his team at the Curtiss Aeroplane & Motor Corporation in upstate New York began work on their own "intercity" biplane, completing the first one in July. Powered by three radial engines, the Curtiss Eagle carried eight passengers in wicker seats and cruised at a respectable ninety miles an hour. "Steadier than any Pullman," pronounced *Flying* magazine editor Evan J. David after riding along on a demonstration flight in late September. Another passenger marveled at its spacious interior. "The ladies in our party were particularly enchanted to discover that they did not have to remove their hats, and that the pressure of the wind did not even disturb their hair."

Perhaps no commercial aircraft sparked as much interest in 1919 as "the Lawson Air Liner," though the attention owed as much to its eccentric namesake and builder as to any innovations in design. Alfred W. Lawson was a onetime professional baseball player with an eclectic prewar career as a writer, spiritualist, and publisher of aviation magazines. He claimed he was called to aviation by God and in 1916 prophesied that its development would ultimately lead to a superhuman being who would "live in the upper stratas of the atmosphere and never come down to earth at all." In the meantime, though, he would focus on building a multi-engine passenger plane.

In the summer of 1919, the first Lawson Air Liner was unveiled at company headquarters in Milwaukee. Propelled by two Liberty engines, it was a blunt-nosed biplane with a roomy, Pullman-style cabin, smoked celluloid windows, and twenty-six wicker seats upholstered in green leather. Pilot and copilot controlled the plane with giant spoked wheels, like something out of Jules Verne. In September, Lawson and his Air Liner began a publicity tour of the Northeast that included a stop in Washington, where senators and other dignitaries accompanied him on a brief flight over the capital. Mitchell was not among them, though he did get a chance to examine the aircraft on the ground, later pronouncing it "a good first attempt." Around the same time, Lawson announced that he had begun building a new version equipped with sleeping berths as well as a lavatory and a smoking compartment. It was part of his plan to offer regularly scheduled passenger service—"the Millionaire's Special"—between New York and San Francisco. He claimed that the journey would take just thirty-six hours, including stops along the way, and that the flights would begin by the summer of 1920. "Book your passage in advance," urged one ad.

Never mind the lack of airfields, aeronautical maps, radio networks, or anything resembling an established route—Lawson's claims were credulously reported in the press, which shared its readers' faith in the boundless if yet unrealized potential of aviation in peacetime. The optimism was in some sense understandable. Almost every week brought news of some record-shattering flight, as aviators competed to fly faster, higher, and farther than ever before. Other stories celebrated "firsts" of a more prosaic nature, such as the San Francisco police department's use of an open-cockpit biplane to retrieve a petty criminal from Alameda across San Francisco Bay—a flight that marked "the inauguration of aerial transport of prisoners," or so the Alameda police chief claimed. A police officer and a pilot occupied the rear cockpit while the prisoner sat in front, wearing a leather flying helmet but no handcuffs. "Elaboration of this statement would be superfluous," the *San Francisco Chronicle* dryly observed.

In early October came news of another milestone—"the longest airplane trip ever undertaken by a woman civilian," according to the *New York Times*. This bold but unverifiable claim centered on Nellie Cox, the glamorous wife of a Texas oil millionaire, Seymour J. Cox, who recently had purchased a Curtiss Oriole biplane and hired an Air Service veteran as its pilot. The couple had a nine-year-old son who was due to start boarding school in New York. In late September, Seymour Jr. and his mother donned matching leather flying gear, squeezed into the open cockpit behind the pilot, and took off from Houston. The flight north took more than a week, in part because Mrs. Cox—petite, blue-eyed, and "golden haired"—insisted on diverting to Cincinnati so she could wave gaily to the crowd at the first game of the World Series. On the last leg of their journey, near Binghamton, New York, the trio narrowly escaped death when the pilot lost sight of the ground in fog. He put the plane into a shallow dive and broke out of the clouds a few feet above the treetops. Ninety minutes later they completed their 2,000-mile journey at Roosevelt Field on Long Island.

The following day, a reporter tracked Mrs. Cox to the Hotel Vanderbilt on Park Avenue. "The wind doesn't hurt my complexion and I'm never cold," she declared. "I think flying is the ideal way of traveling for a woman."

Newspapers could not get enough of such stories, which seemed to confirm the *Times*' declaration back in March, at the close of the New York Aeronautical Exposition, that the world was indeed "on the threshold of a new age." That was true enough, but in the short term, at least, the aircraft industry was gasping. Both Mitchell and Menoher were skeptical that it could survive, let alone catch up with its European competition, without government support. To that end, they embraced new missions aimed at proving the airplane's value in peacetime. In the spring, Army pilots began patrolling for forest fires in California, an effort deemed so successful it soon was expanded to Oregon. Aerial cameras and photography techniques developed for battlefield reconnaissance were promoted for commercial uses, such as mapping cities and advertising real estate. And in June, military pilots began flying border patrols in Texas after several violent incidents linked to Pancho Villa, who was still at large more than three years after Pershing's ill-fated invasion of northern Mexico. Mitchell took a particular interest in the border operation. During a visit to an Army airfield in El Paso over the Fourth of July weekend, he commandeered a plane and browbeat a grizzled old cavalry colonel who had never been aloft into joining him on an illegal flight across the Rio Grande.

———

Such field trips were a balm for the restless airman, who rarely missed an opportunity to get out of Washington. Whenever possible he flew himself, as in early September, when he hopped down to Langley Field on some official pretext and returned with two quarts of fresh oysters. The ever-vigilant Air Service press operation touted the flight as "the first time that oysters have been delivered via airplane." In the capital, by contrast, Mitchell seemed to spend much of his time in congressional hearing rooms, lobbying for his independent air force and budget. "We ask for 1,050 airplanes, at an average cost of $30,000" each, Mitchell said at one such appearance in June. In a statement to the House and Senate on July 30, Menoher, his boss, noted that "the government is practically the only market for the aircraft manufacturers" and pleaded for help to keep them afloat. Otherwise, he warned, "within six months all aircraft manufacturers will be out of the aircraft business and the government will have no source from which to obtain its airplanes and airplane engines."

Menoher was exaggerating, but there was no denying his larger point. The scandalous failures of aircraft procurement during the war had dimmed public and congressional enthusiasm for government spending on new airplanes, especially now that the fighting had ended. In the end, Congress approved only $25 million for the Air Service's 1920 budget, less than a third of what Mitchell and Menoher had requested (and about 5 percent of its wartime peak). The threadbare budget would allow the Air Service to continue tinkering with prototypes at its main engineering facility at McCook Field in Dayton, Ohio. But it also ensured that military orders for new aircraft would slow to a trickle over the next few years—enough to support a few manufacturers, perhaps, but hardly the basis for a thriving industry. For aviation to truly prosper in the United States, its citizens would need to embrace the airplane as a practical means of transportation and commerce, just as they had embraced passenger trains in the nineteenth century and more recently had fallen in love with automobiles. But what would it take to win them over?

5

The Flying Parson

Early on the morning of August 25, 1919, a crowd began to gather at Roosevelt Field, on the flat, airplane-friendly terrain of Long Island's Hempstead Plains, near the town of Mineola. Named for Quentin Roosevelt, a son of the former president who had been killed thirteen months earlier in aerial combat over France, the field was part of a sprawling Air Service training complex that included two adjacent facilities, Hazelhurst Field and Mitchel Field. New York City was just twenty miles to the west. The previous month, thousands had gathered at Roosevelt Field to witness the arrival of a huge British dirigible, the R.34, after a perilous four-day crossing of the Atlantic. The spectators had been delighted when one of its officers parachuted onto the field from 2,000 feet, then coolly stepped out of his harness to direct ground personnel who secured the giant airship.

Now they came to witness another aviation milestone. Some rode the train from Manhattan; others arrived in motorcars from the summer colonies of Long Island's North Shore, where vacation season was in full swing. They parked along a road beneath a billboard advertising Wrigley's chewing gum. By 8:30 a.m., the crowd had swelled to roughly 2,000.

Nearly thirty biplanes were lined up on the patchy grass-and-dirt airfield. Some—DH-4s and foreign-made fighters—were in military garb. Others, such as a Curtiss Oriole painted in vermilion, were of obvious civilian origin. If all went according to plan, they soon would take off in sequence on the first leg of a 1,042-mile sprint to Toronto and back—the longest airplane race ever attempted on any continent. A smaller group would depart simultaneously from Leaside Aerodrome near Toronto, flying the route in the opposite direction. The Air Service had supplied most of the pilots in the contest—civilians and Canadian military aviators made up the rest—and Menoher himself had come up from Washington to officiate.

If only the weather would cooperate. Low clouds hung over the field, threatening rain. As spectators clustered around the airplanes, pilots and mechanics made last-minute adjustments to engines and flying wires, glancing every now and then at the sky.

———

The Air Service had embraced the contest in hopes that it would boost the struggling aircraft industry. A successful showing could help persuade the public that airplanes had evolved into practical traveling machines. Americans had been promised that day was coming but had yet to see much evidence for it. They were starting to get impatient. Even before the United States joined the war in Europe, ticket sales to the air shows known as flying circuses—the main source of income for flyers at the time—had begun to taper off. It wasn't clear when, if ever, the airplane would become a useful feature of everyday life and not just "a provider of sensational amusement," as *Scientific American* put it. Competition over long distances, the magazine argued, would hasten the arrival of that day.

One of the nation's most prominent newspaper publishers agreed. In 1910, William Randolph Hearst offered a $50,000 prize to the first pilot to fly across the country in thirty days or less. The challenge proved irresistible to Calbraith P. Rodgers, a wealthy, 32-year-old blue blood whose great grandfather, Commodore Matthew Calbraith Perry, led the Navy flotilla that forced Japan to open its ports to Western trade in 1854. Rodgers would attempt the journey in a Wright Flyer. On September 17, 1911, he took off from a racetrack at Sheepshead Bay, Brooklyn, followed by a train carrying spare parts. He would need them in abundance. By the time he finally reached California forty-nine days later, his plane had crashed and been rebuilt so many times that its only original parts were its rudder and engine drip pan. He crashed again just nine miles short of his destination in Long Beach, breaking both his legs and his collarbone. After a month-long recovery, he strapped his crutches to a wing and completed his journey to the Pacific, eighty-four days after he had started. Though Rodgers had missed Hearst's deadline by nearly two months, he had demonstrated that crossing the continent by airplane was at least possible. *Scientific American*, taking note of the achievement, predicted that passengers and mail would soon follow.

That they would, though not as quickly as the magazine's editors might have hoped. Despite the rapid aeronautical advances of the war, aviators attempting long-distance flights in 1919 still faced innumerable challenges—as U.S. Navy aviators discovered in May, when they set out to fly from Newfoundland to Lisbon in three Curtiss flying boats. The ocean crossing went awry almost from the start. Even before they reached their first refueling stop in the Azores, two of the planes got lost in poor visibility and landed in heavy seas, suffering damage that prevented them from taking off again. One taxied to the archipelago under its own power, a 52-hour ordeal during which crew members slaked their thirst with rusty radiator water. The second was taken under tow by one of the ships that the Navy wisely had positioned along the route. It sank within hours. Only one of the three flying boats managed to reach the Azores without mishap. After subsequent delays caused by weather and engine trouble, it finally reached Lisbon on May 27, more than ten days after leaving Newfoundland. A steamship could have covered the distance in far less time.

A few weeks later in June, the Navy flyers were upstaged by two Britons, John Alcock and the American-born Arthur Whitten Brown, in a Vickers Vimy biplane. But their sixteen-hour flight from Newfoundland to Ireland—the first nonstop crossing of the Atlantic—was hardly an endorsement of the pleasures and convenience of modern air travel. Navigating by sextant, the men flew through rain, sleet, and icy fog, at one point pulling out of a spiraling dive just sixty feet above the waves. Brown, the copilot, repeatedly climbed onto the wings to clear engine intakes of ice with his bare hands. Their flight ended with a crash-landing in a bog near Galway. Brown quit flying and resumed his career as an engineer. Alcock died in France six months later when his plane hit a tree in fog.

———

The New York–Toronto race, announced in June 1919, was sponsored by the Aero Club of Canada and the American Flying Club, the latter founded by Air Service veterans in 1918 and headquartered at East Thirty-Eighth Street in Manhattan. Word of the contest spread quickly, especially after the Hotel Commodore in Manhattan put up $10,000 in prize money. The race was open to any qualified aviator—a loose category in the days before government licensing—and many among the Air Service's diminishing cadre of pilots were eager to take part, despite Army rules preventing them from accepting cash prizes.

But first they had to get permission. For that they could thank Lt. Col. Harold E. Hartney, a Canadian-born ace and one of the most accomplished aerial tacticians of the war.

Hartney was an unlikely looking warrior. Slight and sparrow-like, with pinched features, prominent ears, and a stubby mustache, he had a punctilious manner that may have reflected his training as an attorney; in the days before the St. Mihiel attack, Billy Mitchell was bemused by his habit of cocking his head and murmuring, "precisely, precisely," as the two discussed battle plans. Born in Ontario in 1888, Hartney worked for a brother's law firm in Saskatchewan after earning his degree, and he married in 1914. Eleven months later he joined the British Royal Flying Corps, which taught him to fly and assigned him to a squadron at the front in 1916.

He proved his combat prowess from the start. In his first dogfight, he shot down two enemy planes, one of them in flames, before he was himself forced down, gliding to a shell-pocked field with fabric torn from his wings and bullets in the water jacket of his engine. Hartney, who estimated that "most green pilots at the front live about five days," continued to defy the odds. After he was shot down a second time—possibly by

Baron Manfred von Richthofen, the German "ace of aces"—he regained consciousness with his face in the mud and a 775-pound Rolls Royce engine resting on his back. He was rescued by Australian soldiers and spent seven months recuperating. He transferred to the Air Service and in early 1918 rejoined the fighting, first as a squadron leader, then as commander of the storied First Pursuit Group, home to the leading American aces of the war.

Hartney now worked for Mitchell in Washington, part of the tight circle of "air-minded" loyalists who shared Mitchell's vision of an independent air arm. Mitchell had great faith in his wartime comrade, allowing him to take his children for an airplane ride at Bolling Field.

———

In late July 1919, Hartney wrote a memo to Mitchell and Menoher, arguing for the Air Service's participation in the New York–Toronto race. "It will certainly encourage the industry in this country," he wrote. The contest, he continued, would promote the "safety, reliability, and permanence" of aviation while highlighting "the great war progress that the science has made, and with which the public is very unfamiliar." He asked that he and other Air Service pilots be permitted to fly "regular government machines" in the race, or, if that were not possible, Fokker pursuit aircraft that had been seized from Germany at the end of the war and shipped to the United States as war booty.

Both were open to the idea, though Menoher initially ruled that Air Service pilots would have to compete in civilian planes. But he soon agreed to the use of military aircraft. Now that the Air Service chief was fully aboard, what started as an independent venture became a quasi-military operation. Mitchell's office issued detailed rules for what was now called "an aerial reliability contest." Pilots were required to make three refueling stops—in Albany, Syracuse, and Buffalo—where they were to remain on the ground for at least thirty minutes. Landings between these "control stops" for repairs and other purposes were permitted but would count against total flying time. Competitors' planes were required to pass a safety inspection and were barred from flying after sunset. A few days before the start, Mitchell dispatched ground crews—an officer and ten enlisted men—to each of the three control stops, along with fuel, spare parts, wind socks, medical kits, and truck-mounted searchlights to serve as beacons in murky weather.

American and Canadian organizers exploited the contest for maximum publicity, touting it as a kind of dress rehearsal for commercial aviation. Among other things, they arranged for flyers starting in New York to carry copies of the *New York Times* for speedy delivery to Toronto, as well as a letter from President Wilson to the Prince of Wales—the future King Edward VII—who was touring Canada at the time. The prince, in turn, drafted a letter to Wilson. A Canadian pilot was tasked with carrying it to New York, where an Air Service plane would be standing by to fly it on to Washington "in the shortest possible time," as Menoher decreed in a telegram to a subordinate. (The plan was scrapped after the prince did not turn up for the start in Toronto.) Menoher told reporters that the contest would "simulate the actual conditions of a commercial airplane passenger and freight route," noting that "regular stops will be made, as on a regular aerial line."

In that sense, it was perhaps fitting that the race began—or more precisely, didn't begin—with a stumble that would be familiar to any present-day air traveler: a weather delay. Shortly before the scheduled start time of 9:00 a.m. at Long Island's Roosevelt Field, a sudden downpour sent spectators scurrying for shelter in nearby wooden hangars and barracks. Around midday, the rain stopped, and "a happy, joyous throng" reassembled on the sodden field. An Air Service pilot was dispatched on a quick reconnaissance flight and returned minutes later to report that the sun was shining over Long Island Sound. At 1:57 p.m., Menoher dropped a handkerchief and the first of twenty-eight aircraft lifted from the field. Bad weather also had delayed the start for the twelve planes leaving from Toronto.

———

The break in the overcast proved fleeting. For the next several days, pilots who had expected clear late-summer skies battled rain, fog, thun-

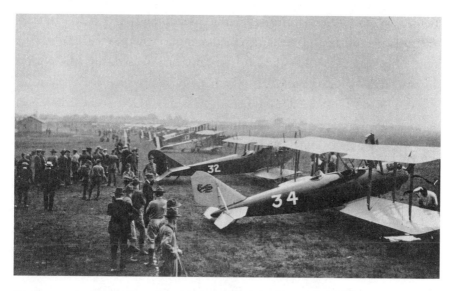

Civilian and military planes lined up at Roosevelt Field for the start of the New York–Toronto race. *National Archives.*

derstorms, and gale-force winds over Lake Ontario. A Canadian military aviator landed in New York with no feeling in his left arm; it had been damaged by German bullets in the war and froze when he was forced to climb above thunderclouds. Weather wasn't the only challenge. At Albany's tiny municipal field, several accidents were caused by overeager spectators who surged into the path of landing aircraft. One was piloted by Capt. Field Kindley, a top-scoring combat ace, who would have shredded them with his propeller had he not whipped his DH-4 into a stall and veered into an embankment, opening a gash above his left eye. Hartney, who witnessed the crash, sent a telegram to Menoher praising Kindley's heroism and recommending him for another medal. Another decorated pilot, Austen Crehore, crashed into trees while taking similar evasive action, suffering injuries that landed him in the hospital for three months. Many other flyers dropped out or made forced landings with mechanical problems of one sort or another.

Despite these difficulties, the New York–Toronto race was widely judged a success. There were no fatalities, and thirty-two of fifty-three pilots—including Hartney in a Royal Aircraft Factory S.E.5, a British-made single-seat fighter—managed to complete the round-trip journey before the race officially ended at midnight on August 30. "The performance I consider was extremely good when the weather conditions are taken into consideration," Col. Gerald Brant, the chief of the Air Service's Eastern Department, wrote in a letter to Mitchell after completing the round-trip flight. "I think we may congratulate ourselves that the Air Service gave such a creditable performance."

Mitchell surely agreed, especially after the American Flying Club completed its tally of flying times and pronounced an Air Service pilot the winner. He was a 27-year-old lieutenant named Belvin Womble Maynard. Dodging storms and buffeted by fierce winds, Maynard had flown his DH-4 from New York to Toronto and back in just seven hours, forty-five minutes, and fifteen seconds, not counting refueling stops, for a blistering average pace of 134 miles an hour over the ground. It was an impressive feat of airmanship, especially for a pilot who was then virtually unknown to the American public.

———

The Air Service's newest hero was a complicated figure who defied familiar stereotypes. To all appearances, he was every inch the dashing aviator, with electric-blue eyes, a well-formed jaw, and floppy brown hair that he combed nearly straight back in the style of the day. Like Lindbergh, to whom he would later be compared, he had an arrogant streak. At the same time, Maynard could come across as shy, even bashful, with a soft southern drawl and a deliberate manner; one of the first things he did after every landing was to carefully remove and polish his rimless spectacles. His background also set him apart. Married with two small children, he was an ordained Baptist minister who did not smoke or drink alcohol and frowned on those who did. Moreover, unlike many of the contestants, he had never flown in combat.

The second of eight children, Maynard came from a prominent family in the hilly Piedmont region of North Carolina. His father was a physician and pharmacist who turned to dairy farming when Belvin was about thirteen. Belvin attended a private, Baptist-affiliated high school, where he was warned against the evils of "selfishness and commercialism" and spent two periods a week in Bible study. He was fifteen when he declared his intention to join the ministry. But he also pursued more secular interests, such as baseball and singing in a quartet. In his spare time, he enjoyed tinkering with farm machinery and automobiles, acquiring an intimate knowledge of engines that would serve him well as an aviator. At sixteen he built a mechanical hay press.

In 1912, Maynard married his high-school sweetheart, Essie Goodson, a bright, sensible young woman with curly brown hair. He was ordained as a minister the following year, around the time he entered Wake Forest College to pursue a divinity degree. Then he and Essie had the first of their three children. Struggling to pay the bills, Maynard dropped out of Wake Forest and moved his family north, where he took a job as a machinist at the Remington Arms Company in Eddystone, Pennsylvania. He was drafted in 1917 and soon transferred to the Air Service.

After two months of ground school in Ohio, Maynard was sent to Issoudun, France, where the Air Service had established a vast training complex. It was there that he got his wings and his first assignment: test-flying newly delivered aircraft, so their engines and rigging could be fine-tuned before they were sent to the front. He soon earned a reputation as one of the best American pilots in France. During eighteen months at Issoudun, he logged more than 700 hours above the French countryside, often in aerobatic maneuvers. Crowds gathered to watch him perform. On a clear Sunday morning in April 1919, five months after the Armistice, he set a new world record for continuous loops, completing 318 in sixty-seven minutes. A witness recalled the precision with which his single-seat Sopwith Pup, trailing a thin stream of oil smoke, inscribed perfect circles that began and ended at the same altitude, as if Maynard were following "a mechanical groove in the heavens." He was said to have never had an accident, an extraordinary achievement in itself.

Maynard shipped home in June, with plans to resume his theological studies in the fall. In the meantime he was assigned to the Air Service complex at Long Island, where he shared a small cottage at Mitchel

Field with his wife, two small children, and Trixie, a German police dog that an Army friend had brought home from France. His victory in the New York–Toronto race launched him from obscurity. Headline writers soon would anoint him with the nickname by which he forever would be known: "The Flying Parson."

6

Praeger

On a cold gray morning in the winter of 1915–16, Otto Praeger entered the office of his boss, the postmaster general of the United States, to find him standing at a window, gazing up Pennsylvania Avenue toward the U.S. Capitol. The two were close friends. Albert Burleson, a former congressman from Texas, had hired Praeger in 1914 as postmaster general of Washington, D.C., then promoted him to a senior headquarters job, with oversight of mail transportation throughout the country. Both shared a love of hunting and fishing. On this particular morning, when Burleson sent word that he wanted to see him, Praeger expected nothing more than an amiable chat, perhaps on whether the bass were biting in the Potomac River channels where they often wet their lines.

But Burleson had something else on his mind as he peered out his office window. It was not a view to lift the spirits. Slush filled the streets, and mist trailed from clouds so low they almost seemed to brush the top of the Capitol dome. He turned to his colleague. "Do you think that airplanes could operate in this kind of weather?"

Praeger was skeptical—the only airplane he'd seen up close was a Wright Military Flyer piloted by Orville Wright at Fort Myer in 1908 or 1909—and he told his boss as much. Burleson pushed back. "We have come a long way since those flights," he said. "If I am convinced that the airplane can operate dependably in any kind of weather—of course, not worse than this—I will put the air mail in the postal service. Don't you see how that would speed up the mails? You and I will both see the day when the mail time between New York and San Francisco is cut in half, maybe more." He ordered Praeger to "make a study" of the matter.

———

Linking the coasts by airmail was but the latest chapter in a story that arguably began in 1803, when President Thomas Jefferson dispatched Meriwether Lewis and William Clark on their famous exploration of the vast wilderness west of the Mississippi that was then virtually unknown to white men. The expedition, which began in St. Louis and ended at the mouth of the Columbia River on the Pacific coast, opened the door to the settlement of the West—first by traders and fur trappers, then by pioneers in wagon trains along the Oregon Trail, which originated in Missouri. In the 1840s and 1850s, more than 400,000 people would follow its ruts across the Great Plains to new lives in the Pacific Northwest and California.

Faster options soon presented themselves, for communication as well as people. By the late 1850s, stagecoaches operated by the Overland Mail Company were carrying both mail and passengers on a southern route from Memphis to San Francisco, completing the 2,800-mile journey in an average of twenty-one-and-a-half days. The much-mythologized relay riders of the Pony Express, who galloped from St. Joseph, Missouri, to Sacramento in about ten days, shrank the continent still further.

Technology sped that process. The Pony Express operated for just eighteen months, rendered almost instantly obsolete by the completion of the transcontinental telegraph in 1861. Even more important was the transcontinental railroad—"a big iron needle stitching the country together," in the words of the writer Jessamyn West—which was completed on May 10, 1869, with the driving of the Golden Spike at Promontory Summit, Utah. Almost in a hammer stroke, people, letters, newspapers, and freight began crossing the country with unprecedented speed—as few as 100 hours from coast to coast.

The mass production of automobiles that began in the early 1900s opened a new era that would transform American culture and development. By 1919, that revolution was well under way, with roughly 6.5 million automobiles in private ownership in the United States. As a means of traveling more than a few miles, however, automobiles left much to be desired, and not just because they were expensive, noisy, and unreliable. Roads between towns and cities were mostly unpaved—bone-jarring in the best of times, quagmires in wet weather. As auto manufacturers realized, this deficit in the nation's infrastructure was a serious deterrent to car sales, to say nothing of tourism and other forms of commerce. Congress showed little interest in fixing the problem.

Carl Fisher would lead the way. A former racing car driver who built the Indianapolis Motor Speedway and started a company that made carbide gas headlights, Fisher launched his crusade after losing his way one night on a country road outside Indianapolis. It was the summer of 1912. He and two friends had taken a wrong turn after driving out of the city in an open-topped car to buy cider. Darkness fell and it started to rain. Thoroughly drenched, Fisher shimmied up a telephone pole to read a small sign at the top, hoping it might provide a clue as to his whereabouts. It was an ad for chewing tobacco. Fisher had had enough. Determined to do something about the dismal state of the nation's road network, he persuaded friends in the industry to join him on a project of spectacular ambition.

They called it the Lincoln Highway. It would span the breadth of the country, running for 3,239 miles from New York's Times Square to Lincoln Park in San Francisco. Henry Joy, the president of the Packard Motor Car Company, took charge of fund-raising and a spirited publicity campaign, under the banner of the Lincoln Highway Association. Besides stoking newspaper coverage and distributing pennants, stationery, and radiator badges, the group published guidebooks for intrepid motorists—something of a leap of faith, as the highway at that point was little more than a line on a map. Nevertheless, the concept won support from state and local governments as well as businesses along the route. Painted signposts soon followed, along with scattered mile-long sections paved with concrete, mostly in the Midwest. These widely spaced segments were called "seedling miles" because they presumably would grow into longer paved stretches once motorists came to appreciate their benefits.

In the meantime, though, driving the Lincoln Highway was not for the faint of heart—as the Army was among the first to discover. On the morning of July 7, 1919, a convoy of eighty-one military vehicles—trucks, kitchen trailers, touring cars, motorcycles, ambulances, and a massive, tractor-like wrecker called a Militor—rumbled out of downtown Washington, D.C., and snaked along country roads through Maryland to Gettysburg, Pennsylvania. There it joined the Lincoln Highway and set out for San Francisco, led by a white Packard Twin Six driven by the highway association's chief publicist. In a brilliant promotional coup, the association had persuaded the War Department to authorize the expedition, the purpose of which, according to an official Army report, was to encourage the highway's development as both a "military and economic asset."

It also would serve as an important test. The Army's transition from horse-drawn to motorized vehicles had begun with Pershing's incursion into Mexico and continued on the Western Front during World War I. But the shift was far from complete. For the Army's Motor Transport Corps, which was barely a year old, the transcontinental journey was a prime opportunity to assess the performance of its latest and most capable vehicles.

It was a test they barely passed. The convoy progressed smoothly enough in the eastern half of the country, where long stretches of the route were graded and graveled, in addition to the concrete seedling miles and other short sections surfaced in brick. Once the convoy passed Omaha, though, its movement slowed to a crawl. In the Great Plains and through the mountains and deserts that lay beyond, much of the "highway" was little more than a wagon trail. Army engineers were frequently called upon to reinforce flimsy bridges or build new ones over dry creek beds, using timber they carried for the purpose. After heavy rains, trucks sank to the axles in mud, straining engines and frying clutches as drivers sought to rock them free. The Militor with its mighty power winch more than proved its worth, repeatedly coming to the aid of mired or disabled vehicles—until it, too, broke down for good near Salt Lake City.

On the morning of September 6, after sixty-two days on the road, the convoy limped into San Francisco, minus the Militor and five other vehicles. Riding along was a personable young lieutenant colonel from Kansas named Dwight D. Eisenhower, who had been drafted for the journey in part because of his familiarity with tanks. The memory stayed with him. As president in 1956, Eisenhower would sign the bill creating the Interstate Highway System, having learned better than most the value of good roads. As for the Lincoln Highway, it was quickly forgotten, subsumed by the network of numbered state highways—some built with federal funds—that followed the first national highway bill passed by Congress in 1921. But the Lincoln Highway had served its purpose. And now the U.S. Post Office was poised to play a similar pioneering role by opening an air route across the country.

———

At the time of his meeting in Burleson's office, Otto Praeger was in his mid-forties, with soft, unremarkable features, a retreating hairline, and a pasty complexion that belied his fondness for the outdoors. He wore rumpled suits and was habitually in a rush; when leaving on a business trip, he would stuff a toothbrush into his shirt pocket because he couldn't be bothered to pack any luggage. But Praeger's disheveled air masked an intensity that sometimes shaded into ruthlessness. Like Burleson, Praeger was a Texan, forged in the dust and heat of the brawling, barely settled West. The son of German immigrants, he was raised in San Antonio, where his father owned a hardware store, at a time when the city was served by stagecoaches, and cowboys with six-guns gambled in saloons.

After dropping out of high school, Praeger took a job as a reporter for the *San Antonio Express*, covering local politics and crossing paths with the likes of Kit Carson and "Buffalo Bill" Cody. In his early twenties, thirsting for adventure, he persuaded his editors to send him on a 1,700-mile bicycle trip through Mexico. He pedaled across deserts and over mountains, once dispatching a rattlesnake with his pistol, and ended his three-month journey in Mexico City, where he interviewed President Porfirio Díaz in his hilltop palace. In 1904, his journalism career took him to

Washington as a correspondent for the *Dallas News*. It was there that he befriended Burleson, who hired him at the Post Office in 1914, at the start of the Wilson administration.

Like the president they served, both Burleson and Praeger were staunch supporters of the Progressive movement, with its emphasis on government action, experts, and technological innovation (if not on racial justice; Burleson, like Wilson, was a segregationist). One of Praeger's first assignments was to replace horse-drawn mail wagons with motorized versions, first in Washington and then—after Burleson promoted him to second assistant postmaster general in 1915—in Chicago and other major cities. The mail wagons were owned by private contractors with powerful allies in Congress. But Praeger outmaneuvered them, canceling the delivery contracts in favor of trucks owned by the Post Office; by 1920, more than 2,600 were in use.

The Post Office had begun experimenting with airmail in 1911, when Burleson's predecessor as postmaster general, Frank H. Hitchcock, authorized a demonstration—really more of a stunt—at an aviation meet on Hempstead Plains on Long Island in late September. A bag of letters and postcards collected from spectators was placed aboard a Blériot monoplane and flown six miles to Mineola, where the pilot heaved it over the side. The bag ruptured on impact, scattering its contents like a piñata. Congress, unimpressed, denied Hitchcock's request for funding to pursue the idea. Burleson fared little better, at least at first. But the politics surrounding airmail turned more favorable with the outbreak of fighting in Europe and the rapid advances in aeronautics that followed. Lawmakers belatedly began to grasp the potential of aviation, and not just for military purposes.

Praeger had a hand in this. In late 1916, in a report written at his urging, the recently formed National Advisory Committee for Aeronautics advised Congress that airplanes were now reliable enough to be trusted with the nation's correspondence. It recommended that the Post Office test the proposition by establishing regular airmail service between Washington and New York or Philadelphia. Congress responded with $100,000 in funds.

Praeger got to work. As the advisory committee had recommended, he would start small, with flights between New York and Washington. The Army offered to supply Curtiss Jenny trainers—modified with mail compartments in place of forward cockpits—as well as pilots for the new service, reasoning that it would provide valuable training for those who would soon be flying along the Western Front. After Praeger sought assurances that the military pilots would not be deterred by bad weather, a senior officer promised that the airmail service would not be "a pink tea flying affair" and "would be flown daily, rain or shine." The Post Office agreed to contribute airfields, hangars, mechanics, and supplies such as gasoline and oil. The route would include a refueling stop at a field near Philadelphia because the Jennies did not have the range to complete the 200-mile flight between Washington and New York in one hop.

———

The new service started with a humiliating pratfall. On May 15, 1918, the first mail plane from the capital took off from the Polo Field, a grassy clearing between the Tidal Basin and the Potomac River, before a large crowd that included President Wilson and his wife. But instead of flying toward Philadelphia, Lt. George L. Boyle headed south—he had followed the wrong rail line—and overturned his plane while attempting to land in Waldorf, Maryland, to ask directions. The mail was removed and taken to New York by train. "Wrong Way Boyle," as he was known ever after, was soon assigned to other duties.

Subsequent efforts fared better. Despite the lack of aeronautical maps or reliable compasses, mail pilots learned to navigate the route by means of roads, rail lines, or other landmarks, often in fog or rain. By June the airmail route had been extended from New York to Boston. Nevertheless, Praeger was unhappy with the Army's performance. No one took more seriously the words chiseled above the entrance of New York City's main Post Office building when it opened in 1914—"Neither snow nor rain nor heat nor gloom of night stays these couriers from the swift completion of their appointed rounds"—which were borrowed from Herodotus and considered the Post Office's unofficial motto. The Army pilots, he believed, lacked that sense of mission and were too quick to cancel flights in the face of bad weather. "Their hearts are set on service in France," Praeger complained to his boss. There was some truth to this. It was one thing to risk your life in aerial combat. It was quite another to do it as a mail carrier.

In August, the Army and the Post Office parted ways. The breakup was in some ways a blessing. Praeger hired Benjamin Lipsner, an Army officer with an engineering background, to run the fledgling U.S. Air Mail Service and replaced the departing military pilots with experienced civilian flyers. Praeger now had sole authority over the mail pilots, which meant he could order them to fly even when prudence counseled otherwise; before giving them jobs, he had insisted that they agree in writing to fly in marginal weather. In November, two of his most capable pilots tested his resolve by refusing to take off from New York in heavy fog. Praeger responded with a telegram to the postal official who ran the airmail field at Belmont Park: "START THE MAIL SHIP WITHOUT A MINUTE'S DELAY." The pilots were unmoved. Praeger fired them.

Pilots got the message. By the end of October, the Post Office could boast in press releases that the Air Mail Service had completed all but two flights on the New York–Washington route during the previous two months (though it failed to mention that many of the flights were hours late). In the meantime, Praeger's ambitions had grown. During the summer he had begun making plans for a transcontinental route to San Francisco, part of a nationwide web that eventually would link such far-flung cities as New Orleans and Minneapolis. He would start by extending the existing route to Chicago.

In late August 1918, Praeger dispatched one of his top aides, John A. Jordan, to Cleveland and Bryan, Ohio, and other intermediate stops along the route. Jordan's mission was to persuade city officials, business leaders, and "enthusiastic women of wealth" to provide both airfields and hangars, which were beyond the means of Praeger's threadbare budget. Then in his early sixties, Jordan was a civil engineer who had helped rebuild San Francisco after the 1906 earthquake and liked to be addressed by the honorific "Colonel" (he had never served in the military). He proved to be a deft salesman—and in any case, communities were thrilled to be included on the new route. Then came the Armistice in November, and with it an offer from the War Department to supply the Air Mail Service with surplus DH-4s that were no longer needed in France. They were faster and could carry more mail over greater distances than the 140-horsepower Jennies they would replace.

———

Praeger was determined to launch the new service by mid-December. It was a tight schedule in the best of circumstances. Planes needed to be tested and prepared, airfields and ground crews organized, and pilots provided with information on landmarks and procedures. Then, in early December, Lipsner decided that he had had his fill of Praeger's bullying and announced his resignation—an embarrassing rupture that made the front page of the *New York Times*. Despite the turmoil, Praeger insisted on forging ahead.

It was a decision he soon would regret. Early on the morning of December 18, the first mail plane dispatched along the new route took off from Belmont Park on Long Island, only to return minutes later with engine trouble. The mail was transferred to a replacement plane, and the same pilot again departed the field. This time he lost his bearings and landed twelve miles short of his destination in Bellefonte, Pennsylvania. The relay pilot who had been standing by took off anyway, without the mail, in order to keep to the schedule. Then he, too, got lost, setting down ten miles short of the airfield that had been prepared on the shore of Lake Erie in Cleveland. The first eastbound flight on the route, scheduled for the same day, had a similar result. After a long delay, a mail pilot took off from Chicago's Grant Park in the late afternoon but soon ran out of daylight. He was forced to land at Ashburn Field on the outskirts of the city, less than twenty miles from where he started.

"All that remains of the New York to Chicago airmail service," the *New York Tribune* reported the next morning, "is a trail of broken or lost aeroplanes across the country from Belmont Park to Defiance, Ohio."

The next few days brought more of the same. A mortified Praeger had no choice but to suspend the flights.

————

It was a bleak period for the Air Mail Service. Even as Praeger reckoned with the fallout from the New York–Chicago debacle, he was fighting a fierce rearguard action to prevent the Army, now scrambling to find new peacetime missions, from taking over the operation. The Army's crusade had many supporters in Congress. In mid-December, a House committee voted to place the Air Mail Service under the control of the Army Air Service. Only desperate lobbying by Praeger and Burleson prevented the measure from becoming law. By January 1919, as he turned his attention once more to the New York–Chicago route, Praeger knew that this time, he could not afford to fail.

That he didn't owes much to the efforts of one man. Soon after Lipsner's departure, Praeger had hired a young Air Service officer, James Edgerton, to run the airmail operation, luring him back to civilian life with a $3,600 yearly salary that was twice his Army pay. Edgerton was an inspired choice. The previous spring, he had demonstrated both skill and courage while detailed to fly the New York–Washington route. Praeger had been particularly impressed when Edgerton, racing to keep the mail on schedule, risked a dangerous night flight from Philadelphia to Washington, guided to a landing on the tiny Polo Field by the headlamps of automobiles parked along the side.

Praeger now had a trusted lieutenant to oversee preparations for the expanded Air Mail Service. In a matter of a few months, Edgerton added to the roster of experienced pilots, hiring several civilians who had served as flight instructors for the Air Service. He managed the complex logistics of readying airfields, distributing spare parts and fuel, and building communication networks. He developed new rules for the training and discipline of pilots, and saw to it they were followed. He pioneered the use of checklists, such as one that listed fourteen steps for starting a Liberty engine, which a century later remain central to aviation safety culture.

The new route opened in phases, starting with the leg from Cleveland to Chicago on May 15, 1919, followed by the New York–Cleveland segment in July. The launch of the extended service was not without setbacks. Worst among them were the Air Mail Service's first fatalities—a pilot who jumped to his death when his plane caught fire after taking off from Cleveland, and another who was killed in the Appalachian Mountains of West Virginia after losing his way in clouds. Pilots continued to balk at Praeger's demand that they fly regardless of weather; after two were fired for resisting his edict, others staged a short-lived walkout, telling the press that their lives were worth more than "a two-cent stamp."

Still, the Air Mail Service had come a long way since the fiasco of the attempted launch in December 1918. For the most part, mail flights started on time and were completed without drama. A letter sent by air from New York could now reach Chicago in just seven hours, less than half the time it took to cover the same distance by train. It was a remarkable achievement that hinted of things to come. As the aviation historian William M. Leary has written, "The 755 miles of the New York–Chicago route, equivalent to the distance from London to Madrid, was a pioneering venture of the first magnitude. Never before had anyone, anywhere, attempted to operate a scheduled airplane service over such distances."

Praeger was not about to stop there. He soon turned his attention to the next stage of his plan—extending the airmail clear across the country, from New York to San Francisco, a distance of 2,700 miles by air. In a speech in Alabama in August 1919, Praeger declared that if Congress provided the funds, the Air Mail Service was prepared to start flying the transcontinental route almost immediately. "Commercial aviation has arrived, and it cannot be stopped," he declared. What he didn't know then was that Billy Mitchell and the Air Service would soon lead the way.

7

"The Greatest Airplane Race
Ever Flown"

The summer of 1919 was winding down. Billy Mitchell was busy, as always, but not so busy that he couldn't find time for frequent trips across the Anacostia River to Bolling Field, where he liked to shoot trap or go for joyrides in government airplanes. Sometimes he got home early enough to take the children for a jaunt in the family Stutz before dinner. On weekends there was horseback riding in the Virginia countryside, fishing on a creek near the Potomac, or tennis at the Chevy Chase Club, where he and Caroline often lingered for dinner with friends. The nation still basked in the afterglow of victory in the Great War. On Wednesday, September 17, Mitchell joined a phalanx of mounted officers who accompanied Gen. John Pershing down Pennsylvania Avenue at the head of the Army's First Division, to the cheers of an estimated 400,000 people. The Air Service had arranged for a wireless-equipped DH-4 to fly overhead, so its pilot could report on the parade's progress through loudspeakers on the reviewing stand.

Such welcome distractions aside, Mitchell continued to agitate relentlessly on behalf of commercial aviation and his proposal for an independent air force. The two were closely related, and both depended heavily on public support. But words alone were not sufficient. To rally the country to his cause, Mitchell needed action, a real-world demonstration that would put to rest any remaining doubts about the practical benefits of aviation.

A day after the victory parade, in a telegram to the Air Service's regional commanders in New York, Chicago, and San Francisco, he revealed his plan for doing just that: a transcontinental air race.

————————

It was not an original idea. Only a month earlier, the Air Service's recently departed publicity chief, Capt. Charles J. Glidden, had announced plans for a "transcontinental aerial derby" sponsored by the Aerial League of America, one of several private groups dedicated to promoting aviation in the country. Glidden was a wealthy adventurer and entrepreneur who had joined the Air Service as a reservist in 1917. Gregarious and energetic, with a bristly mustache and a generous waistline, he personified the boundless technological optimism of the age; in the early 1900s, he arguably had done as much to promote the automobile as Henry Ford or any of the movers and shakers behind the Lincoln Highway. Now, at sixty-two, he was determined to do the same for the airplane.

Glidden built his fortune on another modern marvel. A native of Lowell, Massachusetts, he was working in a telegraph office in New Hampshire when Alexander Graham Bell paid a visit. Though still a teenager, Glidden must have impressed the famous inventor, who asked him to help test a new device for transmitting the human voice over telegraph lines. Inspired by the results, Glidden and several partners then established Lowell's first telephone exchange, laying the groundwork for what would become the New England Telephone and Telegraph Company. The same syndicate eventually built a network of regional telephone companies that extended as far west as Texas. Among other lasting influences, Glidden is credited with the rise of female switchboard "operators," whose voices, he believed, carried better than men's over the telephone.

Around the turn of the century, Glidden cashed out of his communications empire and embraced a new passion. He believed fervently in the promise of the automobile, and not just as a plaything for the rich. Like Ford, he saw it as transportation for the masses. To promote its use and build support for road improvements, he sponsored an annual motorcar rally called the Glidden Tour that was widely covered in the press. But nothing so demonstrated Glidden's cheerful faith in motor vehicles as his decision to circle the globe in one. On two extended journeys between 1904 and 1908, Glidden, his wife, and a mechanic drove more than 46,000 miles in his British-made Napier touring car, venturing as far north as the Arctic Circle in Sweden and as far south as New Zealand and Fiji, where a tribal chief—and reformed cannibal—accepted his offer of a ride ("You would make good eating," the chief said with a grin, or so Glidden later claimed). "A Napier will go anywhere," he liked to boast, and for the most part, it did. In regions more easily traveled by rail than by road, such as the American West, Glidden fitted his Napier with flanged wheels and raced along the tracks at sixty miles an hour.

Inevitably, Glidden found his way into the sky. In the first decade of the new century, he was one of the nation's most prominent "aeronauts," making dozens of ascents above the New England countryside in a hydrogen-filled balloon named *Boston*. He wrote and lectured widely on ballooning, which he believed "should properly take its place along with polo, golf, automobiling, and yachting as an adjunct to country estates." Soon he trained his focus on the more practical possibilities of powered flight. In 1910, after officiating at an aviation meet near Boston organized by the Harvard Aeronautical Society, he offered to sponsor an annual airplane race from Boston to Los Angeles, "much after the style of the automobile tours" conducted in his name. The following year, newspapers reported on his plans to launch a commercial airline service from Boston to Washington, D.C., that would use five-passenger biplanes.

Neither idea bore fruit, but Glidden was not the type to abandon his dreams. His concept of an aerial version of the Glidden Tour stuck with him through the war. In cooperation with the Aerial League of America, he announced in New York on August 18, 1919—just days after his discharge from the Army—a New York–San Francisco aerial derby. Like his prewar automobile rally, the derby was conceived with a practical purpose: "to test the efficiency of different types of aircraft for touring and every day transportation," as the *Boston Globe* reported. It would be open to both civilian and military pilots, including foreigners, who would compete for $100,000 in prize money. They would fly defined legs with compulsory stops, spaced at intervals of up to 250 miles. Retired Adm. Robert Peary, the polar explorer and chairman of the Aerial League of America, would head a committee charged with writing the rules.

A month later, the Air Service announced its own transcontinental race, and Glidden's derby fell by the wayside. Did Mitchell hijack the idea? It's impossible to know. He surely knew of Glidden's plan and could not have relished the idea of the Air Service being upstaged by civilians. Alternatively, even if Glidden had slipped quietly into retirement, Mitchell might well have launched the race on his own initiative, particularly after the successful New York–Toronto race in late August. Either way, it was the right moment. Regional commanders were alerted to the plan in a telegram from Air Service headquarters on September 18:

THE COURSE WILL BE APPROXIMATELY NEW YORK CLEVELAND CHICAGO OMAHA CHEYENNE SALT LAKE SAN FRANCISCO PERIOD   LANDING PLACES WITH GAS COMMA OIL ETCETERA WILL BE REQUIRED APPROXIMATELY EVERY ONE HUNDRED FIFTY TO TWO HUNDRED MILES PERIOD   SUBMIT A PROJECT BY WIRE COVERING THE LANDING PLACES AND WHAT YOU NEED TO HANDLE IT IN THE WAY OF FUNDS PERIOD   MITCHELL PERIOD

The contest would hew to the model established by the New York–Toronto race, with pilots starting simultaneously on both ends of the route—in this case, New York and California. After news of the race became public, Peary graciously wrote Mitchell to offer the Aerial League's support.

———

Original or not, Mitchell's plan was staggeringly ambitious. Over the coming weeks, the depleted Air Service would struggle mightily to carry out his orders, which would test the capabilities of pilots and aircraft in a way they had never been tested in peace or war. As Americans would soon learn, there were many good reasons why an airplane race on such a scale had never been attempted. At the very least, the concept was bold, attention-getting, and borderline reckless—entirely consistent with Mitchell's personality.

Among the biggest challenges was the calendar. Forecasters in the Weather Bureau, a branch of the Department of Agriculture, advised Mitchell to hold the race during the first three weeks of October, before the onset of harsh weather, particularly over the mountains. On that basis, Mitchell set the start date for October 8, which left barely three weeks to prepare. Mitchell and Charles Menoher sought to make the best of the tight schedule by adopting it as part of the rationale for the contest. Not only was it a "reliability test" that would reveal both the limits and capabilities of aviation technology as it existed in 1919; it also would serve as a "maneuver problem" that would challenge the Air Service's ability to shuffle men, supplies, and airplanes over great distances on extremely short notice, as might be required in times of war. In other words, it was a field exercise on a countrywide scale.

That it might have been. But above all it was a competition among men—a test of skill, courage, and endurance that was sure to be greeted as such by the press and public. Mitchell understood this as well as anyone. As he promised his boss on October 3, the contest "will be the greatest airplane race ever flown."

8

Spaatz

Twilight was settling over the eucalyptus groves and handsome Mission-style buildings of the Presidio, the breathtaking military outpost that had guarded the entrance to San Francisco Bay since Spanish colonial times. Ruth Spaatz loved this time of day. As she often did in the late summer of 1919, she strolled down a hill to the small airfield on the waterfront, where she took up a familiar position along the fence. She knew her husband would not fly after sunset, at least not in peacetime, and thus would soon be home. Sure enough, it wasn't long before she heard a faint, familiar buzz. Moments later, she watched as a biplane tilted toward the field, then straightened into the wind before flaring to a gentle landing on the hard-packed dirt. Ruth's husband, Maj. Carl A. "Tooey" Spaatz,* cut the ignition, and the propeller shuddered to a stop.

Spaatz was wiry and "strong as hickory," as an aviation journalist would later write, with red hair and prominent freckles. His narrow mouth turned down slightly at the corners, giving him a cool, sardonic look that did not invite familiarity. Spaatz was famously reserved. "I never learned anything while talking," he once said. But his taciturnity concealed a rebellious streak; as a West Point cadet, Spaatz had been

---

* Born Carl Spatz, he changed his last name to Spaatz, pronounced "spots," in 1938, at the urging of his wife and daughters, who thought the original sounded too much like the cloth ankle covers known as spats.

a habitual rule-breaker who narrowly escaped expulsion for possessing liquor. Even now, at twenty-eight, he was a nonconformist who disdained petty Army rules and liked to unwind by strumming ragtime tunes on his guitar.

Nonconformity was almost a prerequisite for aviators in 1919, and Spaatz, like his friend Billy Mitchell, had thrived in the Army's aviation arm, which was generally more freewheeling than other parts of the service. A high degree of competence, and no small measure of nerve, surely helped.

Of German heritage, Spaatz grew up in a stolid middle-class household in Boyerston, Pennsylvania, where his father ran the local newspaper, juggling his publishing duties with service as a state legislator. The younger Spaatz entered West Point in 1910 and almost instantly regretted it, submitting his resignation within weeks of his arrival. A family friend persuaded him to stay at the military academy, where fellow "plebes" began calling him Tooey because he resembled a red-haired upperclassman of that name.* But Spaatz never took to cadet life. He earned middling grades—except in math, for which he had an aptitude—and piled up so many demerits that he was still marching them off on graduation day. Perhaps the best that can be said of Spaatz's time at West Point is that it exposed him to flying—and that was mostly by happenstance.

The introduction came on May 10, 1910, when Spaatz was still a plebe. Glenn H. Curtiss, the aviation pioneer and the Wright brothers' main business rival, had chosen that day for a flight from Albany to New York, competing for a $10,000 prize offered by the New York *World*. The flight would pass directly in front of West Point's campus overlooking the Hudson River. Spaatz watched from a bluff, spellbound, as Curtiss's pusher-driven biplane wobbled into view, tossed around by winds made stronger by the funneling effect of nearby mountains. Just as Curtiss drew near, a downdraft pushed him toward the water, rocking his aircraft so violently that it nearly dragged a wingtip on the surface.

---

* The upperclassman was Francis Joseph Toohey, though "Tooey" is the common spelling of Spaatz's nickname.

Spaatz never looked back. After graduating from West Point in 1914, he served briefly with an infantry company in Hawaii—it was there that he met Ruth, a colonel's daughter who was then seventeen—before transferring to the Signal Corps' Aviation Section, precursor to the Air Service. At the Army's flight school in San Diego, his instructor flew with him for just fifty minutes before signing him off on his first solo flight (an absurdly compressed schedule by modern standards, which require at least ten hours of dual instruction before students are permitted to fly on their own). In the spring of 1916, Spaatz graduated from flight school. He joined the First Aero Squadron in New Mexico, where he flew Curtiss R-2s in support of Pershing's ill-fated Mexico expedition. He kept in touch with Ruth, who married him in July 1917, choosing Tooey over continuing her undergraduate studies at Berkeley. Two weeks later he shipped out for France.

————

Air Service pilots were still months away from combat. In the meantime, Spaatz would play a central role in preparing them for it, as director of training at the Air Service's Third Instructional Center, near the town of Issoudun about 130 miles south of Paris. The training center was an aerial finishing school, offering advanced instruction to officers who had learned to fly in the United States and were destined for pursuit squadrons at the front (a smaller number, including Belvin Maynard, also received their initial flight training at Issoudun). At least, that was the plan. In the fall of 1917, the base barely existed in anything but name. Flying cadets lived in tar-paper shacks and had to ride trucks into Issoudun, seven miles distant, just to take a bath. Morale was at rock bottom because no airplanes had yet arrived in which the students could train. They filled their time with manual labor, such as building duckboards across the mud.

————

From these humble beginnings, the base rapidly evolved into the largest and busiest aviation training complex the world had ever known, with ten airfields, paved roads, power plants, hospitals, sports leagues, vaudeville shows, a cemetery (morbidly named Field 13), and a rail spur to Issoudun. Spaatz had a hand in this transformation, but his priority was the flight curriculum. Under the critical eye of mostly French instructors, cadets began their training on Field No. 1, where they taxied back and forth at high speed in clipped-wing monoplanes known as "penguins" because they were designed to remain earthbound. After demonstrating sufficient mastery of the twitchy, hard-to-control machines, they graduated to Field No. 2, where they took to the air in Nieuport fighters. These posed their own set of challenges. In certain wind conditions, the high-performance Nieuports had a tendency to ground loop, or spin around, on landing, often breaking their fragile lower wings. (After eighty-two were put out of commission in just two days, the base commander, a cavalry officer with no flight experience, tried to solve the problem by issuing a written order: Henceforth, he decreed, there would be "no more rough landings.") Cadets then moved on to cross-country flights, aerobatics, and specialized classes geared to air combat, such as gunnery and formation flying. At Field No. 8, near the end of their training, they flew against instructors in mock dogfights, using gun cameras to record their "victories."

The exuberance of youth, to say nothing of the inherent dangers of flying in 1918, inevitably took its toll. "Any aviator who stunts close to the ground," Spaatz warned his cadets in April, "clearly demonstrates that his reasoning powers are at fault and therefore, his services as an aviator will not be valuable." But the accident rate proved stubbornly persistent. Roughly one in twenty-five cadets who started the course at Issoudun did not live to complete it.

By the summer of 1918, Spaatz had wearied of the losses as well as the job and its manifold administrative headaches, which included an outbreak of venereal disease. What's more, he worried that the war would end before he ever got a chance to prove himself in combat. When Mitchell ordered him back to the United States to oversee pursuit training there, Spaatz pleaded with him to reconsider. Mitchell agreed to delay the move so that Spaatz could spend a few weeks flying with a squadron at the front.

The concession almost cost him one of his best officers. Spaatz, fly-ing a Spad, got his first taste of combat on September 15, toward the end of the St. Mihiel offensive, when he shot down a single-seat Fokker. But his biggest test came eleven days later. After taking off from an air-field in northwestern France, Spaatz and his squadron mates got into a prolonged dogfight with seven German Fokkers. Spaatz shot down two of them but lost track of time and ran out of fuel over enemy territory. He glided to no-man's land and crash-landed on a shell-cratered hill-side, where he was greatly relieved to hear soldiers speaking French in a nearby trench.

Ruth would soon learn of her husband's narrow escape, though not from him. After Tooey left for France, she had moved to New York to pursue her dream of becoming an actor, finding work with a touring theater troupe. A letter from Spaatz in the summer of 1918, suggesting through the veil of military censorship that he might soon be called back to Washington, spurred her to relocate to the capital. The country was then in the grip of the influenza pandemic. Ruth tried to volunteer as a nurse in an Army hospital, where the disease was taking a fearsome toll among patients and medical workers alike. But the chief nurse turned her down after learning that her husband was still in France. The Army would not risk both of their lives. So Ruth took a clerical job with the Department of Agriculture. She was reading the *New York Times* on her lunch break when she spotted a story about an American aviator who brought down "three planes, one his own and the other two Germans." The report did not name the officer, but it didn't have to—Ruth instinc-tively knew who he was.

"That must be Tooey," she thought.

Spaatz shipped home in October. He had barely settled into his new job at Air Service headquarters when the Armistice of November 11 was declared. After several short assignments—including one as com-mander of an aerial circus that toured the West to promote the sale of war bonds—Spaatz was named top deputy to Col. Henry H. "Hap" Arnold, the commander of the Air Service's Western Department, which was headquartered at the Presidio. (Spaatz and Arnold, who one day would lead U.S. Army Air Forces during World War II—again with Spaatz at his side—shared many attributes, but a love of flying was not one of them. One of the Army's first aviators, Arnold had grounded himself in 1912 after an unintentional spin that ended just short of disaster. "My nervous system is in such a state that I will not get in any machine," he wrote in a report to his commanding officer. He would not fly again for four years.)

Carl and Ruth Spaatz arrived in San Francisco in July of 1919. They loved their new assignment. More than sixty years later, Ruth would still speak fondly of the sweeping views from their hillside quarters, the officers' club with its adobe walls and deep casement windows, and the tiny airfield on the water next to the Palace of Fine Arts, the domed pavilion built for the 1915 Panama-Pacific Exposition.

———

Now Spaatz had a decision to make. A few days after Mitchell's September 18 telegram announcing the transcontinental race, Charles Menoher had decreed that it would be open only to military pilots "considered capable and reasonably certain of piloting their machine safely over the course." Spaatz more than met that standard, but why take the risk? Participation in the race was voluntary, and Army rules would prevent its winners from accepting any of the prizes—including automobiles and a Hendee-Indian motorcycle—offered by businesses seeking to cash in on the publicity surrounding the contest. Then again, prizes were not really the point. For Air Service pilots, the race would be the biggest operation—and their best shot at glory—since the war. Spaatz was not about to sit it out.

By the beginning of October, Menoher's office had approved more than sixty military pilots to fly in the contest. Except for a Marine and two foreigners—the French and British defense attachés, both decorated combat pilots—all were Army men. Ranging in age from twenty-one to forty-six, they were broadly representative of the nation's fledgling air force. Most, though by no means all, had gone to college, a few of them in the Ivy League. Some were career military officers, including several

The Presidio's waterfront airfield, with the Palace of Fine Arts in the foreground. *National Archives.*

West Pointers, who had come up through the cavalry or other branches of the Army. Many had fought in the air war at the Western Front, and several were bona fide aces—including Harold Hartney, the Canadian-born flyer who was now one of Mitchell's top aides and who would try to better his own performance in the New York–Toronto race. Others were unknowns who had finished their flight training too late to make it overseas. Most would soon return to civilian life, but for now, all were still on active duty, scattered among Air Service fields in the eastern half of the country and on the West Coast.

Orders went out from Washington directing them to proceed to the closest starting points—Mineola or the Presidio—and from there to the opposite coast. Each was granted an $8 daily allowance for travel expenses before and during the race.

9

"Sure Death If Motor Stops on the Takeoff"

Colonel Joseph C. Morrow, the Air Service regional commander in Chicago, wrote letters to the mayor and the chamber of commerce in Sidney, Nebraska, at the beginning of October. He told them of the race and appealed for their help. Among other things, he wrote, he needed to "locate a suitable field."

Sidney was one of twenty towns and cities that Billy Mitchell and his team had selected as mandatory refueling stops along the 2,700-mile route. Spaced at intervals that ranged in length from 56 to 180 miles, the control stops closely followed the transcontinental railroad built in the 1860s by the Central Pacific and Union Pacific Railroads. This was no accident. Besides following the lowest terrain, the railroad would serve as both a navigation aid—an "iron compass"—and a conduit for fuel, spare parts, and other supplies that would be needed at the control stops.

Like other western towns that would host the cross-country flyers, Sidney owed its existence to the railroad: It was founded in 1867 as a cavalry outpost to protect the men laying the track from Indian attack. Cowboys and miners soon followed, along with brothels, dance halls, and more than eighty saloons. By 1919, however, Sidney had mostly shed its brawling, disreputable image. It was now a prosperous farming and ranching community of about 2,800 people, with a new high school and a handsome public library built by the Carnegie Corporation. The Lincoln Highway had arrived in 1913, followed by gas stations and several car dealerships.

One thing Sidney lacked, however, was an airfield, at least in any formal sense. This was true of most stops along the route, because it was true of pretty much everywhere.

————

The rapid evolution of airplanes during the war had not been matched by the development of safe places for them to take off and land. For the most part, airfields of the day were nothing more than the name suggests. Pastures, croplands, racetrack infields, parade grounds, city parks, fairgrounds, the commodious lawns of country estates—almost any piece of flat ground would do, as long as it was big enough and free from ditches or obstacles.

The Army was among the first to recognize the need for better airfields. In 1916, it hired Albert Kahn, the industrial architect behind some of Detroit's most iconic automobile plants, to design one of the country's first purpose-built airfields, in Hampton, Virginia. The layout of Langley Field was dictated by the limitations of early aircraft. Most planes today are monoplanes equipped with a nose wheel and two main wheels, in a "tricycle gear" configuration. Most biplanes, by contrast, were "tail draggers"—they had tail skids instead of nose wheels,* which made them prone to swiveling like weather vanes when landing in a crosswind. To prevent the clumsy pirouettes known as ground loops, Kahn designed a square field that was a mile long on each side—large enough so that pilots could always land straight into the wind. The field was leveled, drained, and seeded; equipped with windsocks and hangars; and marked in limestone with a huge round circle so that it could be easily identified from the air. By the end of World War I, the Air Service had established twenty airfields around the country that were based on Kahn's design.

Because they were built primarily for training, many of the Air Ser-

————

* Some modern aircraft, especially those designed for use on rough fields, are still configured as tail draggers, but with tail wheels instead of tail skids.

vice fields were situated in the South and West, where the climate favored year-round flying. Flights generally began and ended at the same field. Longer cross-country trips remained a challenge. ("Next to his machine, the question of most interest to an aviator is the landing field," Belvin Maynard, the winner of the New York–Toronto race, later would write.) So the Air Service began promoting the development of not only airfields but also *networks* of airfields, arrayed along formal routes between cities and towns. Just weeks after the Armistice, a notice from headquarters announced a series of exploratory flights to "chart air lines," make maps, and "locate Sites for landing fields and airdromes." These fields would "become part of a great chain that soon would link every important community in the country from coast-to-coast." They also would serve as training centers for reservists in peacetime.

The Air Service had now committed itself to the same goal as the Post Office: to knit the country together by air. Unfortunately for both, Congress was not inclined to help; the skepticism toward government that was never far from the surface in American politics had only grown stronger amid the Red Scare triggered by the Russian Revolution of 1917. The advocates of a national system of airfields and airways would have to find another way to push it forward, betting that Americans eventually would back their cause once they grasped its potential to change the nature of commerce and travel. Otto Praeger already was trying to prove this point by cobbling together an airmail route between New York and Chicago. And now the Air Service was embarking on a parallel track, starting with exploratory flights that came to be known as "pathfinding" missions.

––––––

The first of these began even before Mitchell returned from France. On December 4, 1918, five Curtiss JN-4 trainers took off from Rockwell Field in San Diego. Their pilots and passengers—a photographer, a doctor, and three mechanics—were embarking on a voyage of discovery, tasked with mapping airfields and airways on a meandering journey from California to New York. Like nineteenth century sailing ships provisioned for a long voyage, the planes had been stuffed with spare propellers, spars, wheels, tail skids, engine parts, aircraft linen, and the clear lacquer known as dope, along with a five-day supply of food. The pilots followed a southerly route to Florida, then veered north along the East Coast, navigating by compass or with reference to natural and man-made landmarks—a method known as contact flying, or pilotage (each carried a Rand McNally road map). Along the way, they landed in farm fields, parade grounds, city parks, and—once—on a beach at Cumberland Island, Georgia, after one of the planes developed engine trouble. The pilots made many such unplanned stops, often because of poor-quality gasoline purchased along the route. Sometimes they departed a town with only a vague sense of where they would next set down. On reaching Raleigh, North Carolina, they circled the city for more than an hour before committing to what they deemed was a safe place to land. Though one plane dropped out along the way, four eventually reached Long Island, after thirty-three days and an odyssey of more than 4,000 miles. The leader of the expedition, Maj. Albert Smith, later compiled his notes into a kind of Baedeker's guide for pilots, providing details on navigational landmarks and the hazards of particular fields. "This field is an old meadow," he wrote of one such landing area in North Carolina, "and is suitable for any type plane and in wet weather, care being taken to avoid the old burned stumps which do not show very clearly from the air." As for navigation, Smith advised that following railroads was generally the safest course, because they tended to run through open country and "supplies may be obtained at practically every railroad town."*

Several more such missions would follow over the next nine months. Mapmaking aside, the pathfinding flights also had a publicity objective— to seed support for aviation in parts of the country where flyers rarely ventured. In Sweetwater, Texas, according to one account, townspeople poured into the streets at the sound of Army pathfinders overhead, then

---

* The pilots attempted a return flight to California, but only Smith managed to complete the round-trip journey. He was accompanied by a police dog named Flu, which he had acquired in New York while recovering from influenza.

surged across the train tracks to watch them land in an alfalfa field. Small boys watched, open-mouthed, as the pilots stripped off their gloves, lit cigarettes, and asked where they could get gas. "In some not very distant future," the anonymous author wrote, "the reports of these early exploration flights will make quaint and almost incredible reading."

In the meantime, Mitchell's training and operations group got to work on the nation's first national airways chart. Released in the spring of 1919, it showed a web of routes linking thirty-two towns and cities, scattered across the country from Boston, Massachusetts, to Bakersfield, California. Menoher wrote their mayors with a proposal: If they built proper airfields or airdromes—as they were sometimes called if situated in or near a city—the Air Service would supply war-surplus steel hangars at no charge. Like Congress, however, most local governments showed little interest in spending money to meet demand that was still mostly theoretical. Only a few communities took Menoher's deal, and some didn't bother to reply. Officials in Daytona, Florida, offered the use of the town's wide, hard-packed beach.

Mitchell kept at it, going so far as to propose an airdrome on a roof over the Central Park reservoir in Manhattan. He envisioned a structure of two levels, the top one for takeoffs and landings and the bottom for aircraft storage, like a giant parking garage. Planes would ascend to the rooftop runway by elevator. "In this way any unsightly material would not be in view and the entire structure could be made more or less attractive," Mitchell wrote the city's Board of Estimate. "An investigation on your part would be greatly appreciated." City officials were unreceptive to the idea.

———

The race lent urgency to Mitchell's crusade. It also gave the Air Service new leverage. In asking civic leaders in Sidney to "render all possible assistance" to the contest, Morrow, the regional commander in Chicago, appealed to their vanity, noting that the race would "attract world-wide attention . . . to every locality immediately connected with it."

It literally could put them on the map. In the days before the race, the

Air Service made it clear that designated control stops were auditioning for a place on a permanent New York–San Francisco airway. Each airfield was assigned an identification code, to be whitewashed on its surface in thirty-foot-high "commercial Gothic" letters and numbers. Emergency fields—including golf courses—were to be marked with white triangles. (An aide to Menoher acknowledged that not all such markings would be in place by the time of the race, citing "a lack of energy" on the part of some local authorities.)

Harold Hartney oversaw planning for the race. The Air Service's three regional commanders—in New York, Chicago, and San Francisco—were responsible for on-the-ground preparations. Less than a week before the start, Morrow embarked on a whistle-stop tour to scout the control stops along the central portion of the route. Hap Arnold made a similar excursion from San Francisco, traveling by rail as far east as Cheyenne.

For the most part, community leaders were happy to do their bidding. Municipal governments donated equipment and labor to prepare airfields, which often required the removal of vegetation and fences before they could be scraped smooth. Hotels offered free lodging and meals. Chambers of commerce arranged for the installation of temporary telephone lines between some airfields and nearby telegraph offices. Businesses loaned cars and trucks to the Air Service detachments at their stops. Local chapters of the Red Cross and the War Camp Community Service—established a few years earlier to offer wholesome entertainment to off-duty doughboys—set up canteens to serve coffee and sandwiches; in Cheyenne, the Red Cross stockpiled candy, cigarettes, and cigars, in addition to wool sweaters and balaclavas for flyers heading across the Rocky Mountains. "Cheyenne is going on the aviation map by leaps and bounds," boasted the *Wyoming State Tribune*, which a few days later reminded its readers, "Proudly take notice that Cheyenne, not Denver, is on the Route of the Transcontinental Flying Tournament."

Air Service leaders were delighted. "The civic authorities, Chambers of Commerce and other organizations are surpassing themselves," Menoher wrote Col. Gerald Brant, the Eastern Department commander, in early October. "The flight of the planes across the country will be in the nature of a triumphal reception for these airmen of the American Army who made such an excellent record on the Western Front."

More than patriotism was at work. Many local officials shared the view, expressed by the local newspaper in Rock Island, Illinois, that their inclusion on the contest route "practically assured" them of getting air-mail service in the near future. Some harbored even bigger dreams— as in Binghamton, New York, where boosters adopted a new municipal motto: "Air Gate to New York" (the Binghamton stop was actually in West Endicott, a few miles west of the city, on land borrowed from George W. Johnson of the Endicott-Johnson Shoe Company).

Omaha, for its part, was badly in need of an image makeover after a shocking incident of racial violence just weeks earlier. In late September, a white mob had besieged the courthouse in the city, where a black man named Will Brown was being held on suspicion of raping a white woman. Overwhelming police, the mob stormed the courthouse, dragged Brown outside, and hung him from a traffic tower before shooting him and burning his corpse. Omaha's mayor, Edward Smith, who had tried to prevent the lynching, was brutally attacked by the same mob and narrowly escaped with his life. He spent more than a week in the hospital, then departed for a spa in Missouri. The incident had made headlines across the country, and the Omaha Chamber of Commerce was eager to present a different face to the outside world. Pledging full cooperation to the Air Service, it rushed to prepare an airfield—in part by dynamiting several hundred trees—on land it had leased for the purpose several months earlier; the Omaha Athletic Club offered to put up flyers remaining in the city overnight or on Sundays. (Another lynching had occurred in Green River, one of three control stops in Wyoming, the previous December, when a black railroad porter named Edward Woodson, accused of shooting two white men, had been hauled from his jail cell and hung from a lamppost. His body was left for hours in full view of passing trains. No one was arrested or convicted for the crime.)

Final arrangements were overseen by Air Service "control officers" who arrived at each stop with small details of enlisted men, sometimes only forty-eight hours before the start. If the officers were lucky, supplies had reached their destination ahead of them. Each stop was to receive 2,000 gallons of gasoline, 300 gallons of motor oil, 300 gallons of castor oil, three tool kits, three fire extinguishers, six five-gallon fuel cans, three water cans, funnels, 100 yards of Manila rope, a blow torch, a wind cone, a medical kit, and fifty pounds of limestone for use in marking fields. The stops also required ample stocks of spare parts and aircraft materials such as spark plugs, wheels, tail skids, ailerons, hose connectors, propellers, linen, and dope.

At regional depots along the route, the supplies were loaded onto freight cars and shipped to the control officers in care of mayors' offices; delays prompted testy messages from Mitchell to the underlings he deemed responsible for the holdups. On October 4 he dispatched a subordinate in his office, Col. John F. Curry, to check on lagging preparations in the Midwest. Curry spent a day in Chicago trying to locate missing supplies, then borrowed a Curtiss trainer and flew through driving rain to inspect control stops further west. He ended his inspection tour in St. Paul, Nebraska, on October 9, the race already under way.

Even the length of the contest remained in flux until the last minute. Mitchell had puzzled over how aviators and their planes would return to their bases once they reached the opposite coast. On September 22, he proposed a "second transcontinental race" that would start around November 1. Because the weather was likely to worsen by then, the second competition would follow a southerly route through Arizona, New Mexico, and Texas. But the logistics of shifting the route were daunting, and Mitchell soon dropped the idea. In the end, he and Menoher decided on a single round-trip race along the original northern route—in effect, doubling the length of the contest to 5,400 miles. Not only would a round-trip contest help solve the problem of returning flyers and planes to their points of origin, it also would ensure that pilots starting on the East Coast would not be disadvantaged by prevailing winds, which tend to blow from the west. The schedule would be compressed. As a hedge against deteriorating fall weather, contestants who preferred to fly home instead of taking the train would have to complete their first crossing by

October 18. Menoher announced the decision on October 6, just two days before the start.

————

The Air Service and its local partners raced to meet the deadline. At Rochester, New York—home of the Eastman Kodak Company, whose new, nineteen-story headquarters dominated the city's downtown—flyers would land at Britton Field, a patch of high ground near the Genesee River that had a farmhouse, barn, and silo on one side. A barnstormer had begun flying a Jenny out of the field that summer, but it still needed lots of work. On the eve of the race, the control stop resembled a "circus lot," as carpenters banged together wooden cribs for fuel drums and soldiers applied limestone in a giant circle around the letter "R." A dump truck from the city's Department of Public Works deposited sledgehammers and stakes for tying down planes overnight. A sprinkler truck filled with water for replenishing aircraft radiators got stuck in the mud. Members of the Rochester Aero Club put up tents.

Some control stops required little preparation. On October 6, Mitchell's office had received "cheering news" of the "excellent pasture field at Sidney, big as all outdoors." And a few airfields on the route predated the race. The field in Bryan, Ohio, had been established months earlier by the Post Office for the New York–Chicago airmail service, complete with a 1,000-gallon underground fuel tank. In Cleveland, the Glenn L. Martin Company maintained a large field—"rolled to the smoothness of a blue-grass lawn"—next to its aircraft factory. The Curtiss Aeroplane & Motor Corporation loaned its narrow, single-axis field in Buffalo. Salt Lake City already had an airfield of sorts on the grounds of an old racetrack; just before the race, city workers screened the University of Utah's hillside logo—a large, white-painted "U" made of concrete—so that flyers would not mistake it for the airfield identifier. In Sacramento, flyers would land at Mather Field, a busy training facility established by the Air Service during the war.

The Rocky Mountain region posed the biggest challenge. The town of Rawlins, Wyoming, on the Continental Divide at an altitude of 7,000 feet, was the highest control stop on the route. (A town twenty miles to the east, Walcott, had initially been selected for the stop, but Arnold shifted it to Rawlins after visiting both during his inspection tour.) Its residents were on the older side, the Air Service officer assigned to the stop later wrote, and most had rarely "had occasion to leave its immediate vicinity during their lifetime." Only a few, he added, "had even seen an airplane prior" to the race. Moreover, a few months earlier, townspeople had raised $1,200 to hire a barnstormer from Denver to make an exhibition flight on July 4, but the aviator had failed to appear. His Curtiss JN-4 lacked the power to climb to Rawlins in the thin mountain air.

The experience had left a residue of skepticism. "The people of Rawlins did not believe it possible for any airplane to reach their town," the control officer wrote. So they had ignored Arnold's request to prepare a landing area on the infield of a horse-racing track near the Union Pacific roundhouse. When the control officer arrived on October 6 to find that nothing had been done, he sought help from the city marshal, who belatedly dispatched men and equipment to grade the landing area and remove a fence on one end. The field's identification code—WY 14—was hastily painted in white on the grandstand roof.

Despite those last-minute improvements, the Rawlins control stop left much to be desired. Alarmingly close to buildings and hills, it was situated in a hollow and often obscured by wood and coal smoke. Moreover, the landing area measured just 1,000 feet by 400 feet—too narrow to allow takeoffs and landings on more than one axis, which would pose a problem in crosswinds. "Worse field could not have been selected," one pilot later wrote. But there was no time to prepare an alternative on the scrub-covered plain east of town. The racetrack would have to do.

The control stop at Green River, 120 miles to the west, was at least as dangerous. Situated amid stunning, otherworldly rock formations, the small railroad town was woefully short of level ground. The only available landing area was on a narrow windswept bench called Hutton Heights, which was sandwiched between a sandstone butte and a cliff

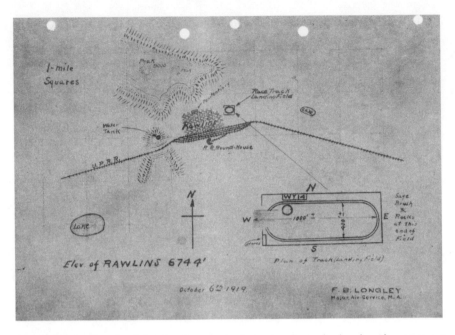

Hand-drawn sketch of the Rawlins control stop and nearby landmarks. *National Archives.*

that plunged 187 feet to the river for which the town was named. Shared with railroad tracks and a few ramshackle houses, the irregularly shaped field sloped gently upward to the northwest, into the prevailing wind. Pilots would have to take off uphill and pray they were flying by the time they reached the cliff. "Sure death if motor stops on the takeoff," one contestant would later report. A pilot who overshot the field while landing could meet the same fate. Even securing the planes overnight would prove a challenge. Because of the strong winds, ground crews would find it necessary to anchor them with ropes tied to thirty-inch bridge bolts driven deep into the earth.

The control officer, Lt. C. A. C. Tolman, arrived in Green River in the week before the race began. Through no fault of his own, he was mostly ignorant of his duties, his instructions having been sent to Green River, Utah, instead of Green River, Wyoming. But he was warmly received by the townspeople—a good thing, as he would need to rely on them to clear sagebrush from the field before any pilots could land. But then it started to snow.

By early morning on Monday, October 6, six inches of snow had fallen, and the ground was frozen solid. The landing area could not be prepared until the snow melted and the ground had thawed. Tolman, no doubt, was near despair. The first pilots were expected in two days.

PART II

The Reliability Test

10

"Interesting Happenings"

Billy Mitchell arrived early at Roosevelt Field on the morning of Wednesday, October 8, 1919, and commandeered a plane, ostensibly to check the weather. A few minutes in the air confirmed what anyone on the ground already knew: It was a perfect day for flying, with cloudless skies and a fifteen-mile-per-hour breeze blowing out of the northeast. The race would start at 9:00 a.m.

In the meantime, it was chilly on the field. Mechanics who had worked on engines all night warmed themselves over blazing fires. Aviators pulled on heavy sweaters, knowing it would be even colder aloft. Some wore belted leather flying coats over their extra layers and Army uniforms, while others favored one-piece coveralls with fur linings and collars.

As the sun rose over Long Island, spectators began arriving in motorcars, which they parked along a row of wooden hangars. By 8:30 a.m. or so a crowd of more than 1,000, some in fur coats, had assembled on the north side of the field. The spectators watched from a distance as senior military officers, politicians, and other dignitaries who had received engraved invitations to the event—Mitchell had sent out 600—mingled with flyers and mechanics making final adjustments for the long journey ahead (J. P. Morgan's secretary sent the financier's regrets, explaining that he was traveling in Europe). Young women in flowing white dresses—volunteers from War Camp Community Service—passed out

sandwiches and poured coffee from enameled pitchers. A brass band
from the Twenty-Second Infantry Division played.

Nearly fifty biplanes were parked in an uneven row with their noses
high and tails resting on the ground, like giant mechanical grasshoppers.
As the start time of 9:00 a.m. approached, Benedict Crowell, the assistant
secretary of war, shook hands with each of the flyers, wishing them well
on the long journey ahead. Those slotted for the first wave of departures
settled themselves in their cockpits, stowed their logbooks and maps, and
buckled their safety harnesses. They cracked open their throttles and
adjusted their spark settings, then signaled to enlisted men on the ground
to pull down hard on the wooden propellers. Engines coughed noisily to
life as blue exhaust smoke wafted over the field.

Mitchell turned to Col. Archie Miller, the commander of Roosevelt
Field, and issued a terse command.

"Let them go, Colonel," he said.

The ragtag fleet of airplanes lined up on the airfield that day had little in
common except a military pedigree. None had been designed for crossing a continent. They were warplanes, built for relatively short excur-
sions over the battlefield. The largest was a twin-engine Martin Bomber,
which resembled a flying bathtub and carried four men in two open cockpits. The smallest were single seaters, including French Spads, British
S.E.5s, an Italian-made Ansaldo S.V.A., and three German fighters—
Fokker D.VIIs decked out in lozenge-patterned camouflage and black
iron crosses—seized as war booty.

But one model outnumbered the others by far. It was the doughty
and familiar DH-4, which would account for forty-six of the sixty-three
aircraft that started the race on both coasts.

The only American combat aircraft with an actual war record over
the front, the DH-4 was a conventional-looking biplane, a little on the
spindly side, with room for two men, one each in front and rear cockpits. Its fuselage was long and tapered, and its slender, nearly translucent
wings—braced with a cat's cradle of wooden spars and stainless-steel

wire—measured forty-two feet, six inches from tip to tip. Despite its delicate construction, the DH-4 looked practical and businesslike, if not especially sleek, thanks in part to the massive twelve-cylinder engine on the nose. The "Liberty plane," as it was popularly known, would dominate Air Service flying fields through the 1920s, and some would be pressed into civilian service as airmail planes and crop dusters (they also were popular with smugglers during Prohibition).

The American DH-4 was the offspring of a rushed transatlantic marriage. The original was designed by the British aeronautical wizard Geoffrey de Havilland, manufactured by the Aircraft Manufacturing Company (Airco) of London, and powered by Rolls Royce engines. It was first flown into battle by the Royal Flying Corps—the aviation branch of the British Army*—in the spring of 1917. In August of the same year, U.S. military officials selected the Dayton-Wright Airplane Company as the first of several American firms to build a homegrown version of the aircraft—based on drawings provided by its British manufacturer—at a cost of $11,701.39 each ($214,878 in today's dollars).

The biggest difference in the Americanized DH-4 was its power plant, which was called the Liberty engine. Conceived and executed in extreme haste, it grew out of a belated effort by the War Department to boost the country's lagging aircraft industry by developing a standardized engine that could be used across a range of airframes. In the late spring of 1917, two of the country's leading automotive engineers, Elbert J. Hall and Jesse G. Vincent, roughed out the basic design in less than a week while huddled in a suite at the Willard Hotel in downtown Washington, D.C. The men drew heavily on concepts developed by French, British, and German manufacturers, including Mercedes. Nevertheless, the Liberty engine was revolutionary, widely considered the most important American aeronautical advance of the war. Unlike most aircraft engines, which were hand-built like fine Swiss watches, the Liberty was expressly designed for mass production, with interchangeable parts

---

* In 1918, the Royal Flying Corps merged with the Royal Navy's air arm to create the Royal Air Force.

that would make it easy to repair. With a rating of 400 horsepower, the twelve-cylinder Liberty was one of the most powerful aircraft engines yet developed—so big that starting it by hand required three men (one would swing down on the prop as the second pulled the first's belt or free hand, while the third did the same with the second). It was also very loud. Like all aircraft engines of the day, the Liberty had no muffler and ran at close to full speed even in level flight.

The Liberty engine was hustled into production at the Packard Motor Car Company and several other automotive firms; less than a year later, in April 1918, the first Liberty-powered DH-4s were crated and hoisted onto ships bound for France. Nearly 5,000 would be manufactured before the War Department terminated production in March 1919, though only a few hundred would actually make it into combat on the Western Front.

———

The DH-4 performed ably in battle dress. With a top speed of 124 miles an hour, it could outrun most German fighters and could carry cameras or 322 pounds of bombs. It was heavily armed with two Lewis machine guns mounted on a ring around the rear cockpit and a pair of lightweight Marlin machine guns in front of the pilot, who could fire them between the blades of the rotating propeller by means of synchronizing gears. Aviators praised the aircraft's stability and docile handling in flight.

But the DH-4 had some serious flaws. Its 88-gallon gas tank—in the fuselage between the front and rear cockpits—was an inviting target, easily pierced by bullets. And its fuel system was pressurized, rather than gravity fed, so that leaks from the gas tank or elsewhere would spray rather than dribble—an obvious fire hazard. Late in the war, a few aircraft models were fitted with rubber-coated fuel tanks designed to instantly seal after a puncture, but the DH-4 was not among them—hence its morbid nickname, "Flaming Coffin." The nickname found particular favor among the many critics of the government's aviation program, who cited it as evidence that taxpayers' money had been wasted on faulty planes.

This was not entirely fair; almost by definition, any wood-and-fabric airplane—even one with supposedly self-sealing tanks—was highly combustible. Still, there was a real problem with the DH-4's design: The gas tank was located immediately behind the pilot. Even in relatively low-speed crashes, the tank sometimes wrenched free of its wooden cage, crushing the pilot against the engine. Making matters worse, some DH-4s were poorly made, using soft pine instead of ash for the structural members, called longerons, that ran the length of the fuselage.

DH-4 pilots were keenly aware of their vulnerability in a crash. "A DH-4 as presently constructed gives the pilot an uneasy feeling in flying over rough country," Carl Spaatz wrote in an official report after the race. A solution of sorts was suggested by another contestant, who advised his fellow DH-4 pilots to kick the rudder at the last second before impact, so the plane would crash at an angle. The theory was that the fuel tank would then pass to one side of the cockpit, sparing its occupant.

There were other design flaws. With the gas tank between them, pilot and passenger sat about six feet apart, too far to hear each other over the roar of the engine. "The observer is a stranger to you and is so far-away it almost seems like flying alone," one DH-4 pilot observed. Pilots and observers communicated by hand signals. Landing was a particular challenge. The aircraft was nose-heavy—the Liberty engine weighed more than 800 pounds—and its wheels were too far aft, which gave it a tendency to dig in its prop and turn turtle when alighting on soft fields. Such mishaps rarely resulted in injury, except to the pilot's pride. But they contributed to a perception among flyers that the DH-4 was not entirely to be trusted.

None of this was news to higher-ups in the Air Service. "It was not a good ship," Mitchell told a congressional panel in June, when asked about the plane's performance in the war. "None of us liked it." To be fair to the DH-4, Mitchell had a political interest in painting the aircraft as obsolete and even dangerous to support his case for bigger procurement budgets. Still, there is some truth to Charles Menoher's claim, at the same hearing, that many pilots were "more or less afraid" of the DH-4. "There is a certain timidity, and that, to my mind, is a very important factor," said the Air Service chief. "If a plane gets a reputation among the flyers, it adheres to it, just like a ship that has a hoodoo"—a curse—"attached to it. Sailors do not like to go to sea in a ship that is hoodooed."

After the Armistice, the Air Service contracted with several manufacturers to improve the safety of its DH-4s by shifting the front cockpit behind the gas tank. Aviators welcomed the change, not only for the "greater intimacy" it afforded between pilot and observer, but also for the confidence it gave the pilot when flying over rough terrain, as he would now stand a better chance of surviving a forced landing. But only a handful of the rebuilt DH-4s—called "Bluebirds," or DH-4Bs—had been delivered by the time of the race. Most contestants would take their chances in the earlier version.

The gruesome death of one of the men entered in the race, just days before the start, only reinforced the DH-4's "hoodooed" reputation. At thirty-three, Col. Townsend F. Dodd was one of the most experienced aviators in the Air Service. An engineering graduate of the University of Illinois, he learned to fly at the Signal Corps Aviation School in San Diego in 1913, took part in Pershing's Mexico campaign as a member of the First Aero Squadron, and served under Mitchell at Air Service headquarters in France. After the war he was named commander of Langley Field.

On Saturday, October 4, four days before the start, Dodd and a mechanic departed Langley in an unmodified DH-4, planning to reach Mineola the same day. But clouds and rain delayed their progress, so they stopped for the night at the airmail field in Bustleton, Pennsylvania. By 1:00 p.m. the next day, the weather was not much better, but Dodd was impatient to resume his journey. He took off under low clouds and circled the field several times before deciding that the visibility was too poor to continue. After throttling back to land, he misjudged his approach and touched down in the middle of the field, with insufficient room to stop. The aircraft bounced twice and collided with a small tree. The front cockpit collapsed as the fuel tank, filled with more than 500 pounds of gas, lurched forward, pinning Dodd by his neck. He died of strangulation. His mechanic, seated behind the tank,

The wreckage of Colonel Dodd's plane in Bustleton, Pennsylvania. *National Archives*

suffered only a minor injury to his foot, which was jammed between the fuselage and the rudder bar.

The fatal crash was the second associated with the race, and it hadn't even begun. A day earlier, another senior aviator entered in the contest, Maj. Patrick Frissell, had lost his way in fog near Middletown, New York, descended to get his bearings, and flew into a treetop. His plane— one of the new Bluebirds—overturned, crushing Frissell beneath the engine and gas tank. The observer riding in the rear cockpit broke several ribs but managed to walk out of the woods on his own. The men had been flying from Indianapolis, where they were based, to Mineola.

Dodd's death in particular was a personal blow to Mitchell, who had worked closely with him in France and considered him a "gallant and talented officer." But Mitchell could not afford to dwell on the loss. Everyone knew that flying was dangerous, even in peacetime—during a single week in July, the Air Service had lost nine men in crashes around the country. Mitchell could only hope that the contest would go more smoothly than its prologue.

A lot was riding on the outcome. On the morning of Monday, October 6, two days before the start, Mitchell made another appearance on Capitol Hill, testifying yet again on the need for an independent air force and a prominent federal role in the development of aviation. A contest that proved the viability of airplanes for long-distance travel and commerce, starting with mail delivery, could only help his cause.

To underscore the point, the Air Service had arranged for pilots in the contest to carry letters from congressmen, senators, and other prominent people, to be dropped off at towns and cities along the route. Among the correspondents was William Fox, the movie producer and founder of the Fox Film Corporation (later 20th Century Fox), whose letters to company managers in Buffalo and Omaha announced "a new epoch in the delivery of moving picture films."

The airmail stunt was part of a larger publicity campaign. Army planes had been designated to carry cameramen aloft so they could film the start in New York and San Francisco for newsreels that would soon appear in theaters around the country. Photographs of contestants and their planes had been mailed to control stops for use by local newspapers. And Menoher had ordered control stop commanders to report "important and interesting happenings" to the American Flying Club, the Air Service veterans' group that had cosponsored the New York–Toronto race and was heavily involved in planning its successor. The club would distribute news of the flyers' progress to reporters in the nation's largest media market.

Now, with the race about to begin, Mitchell was determined to put on a good show. Caroline had packed his bags while he testified on Capitol Hill. After the couple ate lunch at home, she drove him to Union Station, where Mitchell caught the 3:00 p.m. train to New York.

The flyers got off to a faltering start. The British defense attaché, Air Commodore Lionel Charlton, had been granted the honor of taking off first from Roosevelt Field, but the engine of his Bristol Fighter developed carburetor trouble as he warmed it up. As a mechanic worked frantically to fix the problem, the next contestant in line—Air Service Lt. J. B.

Machle, in a DH-4—took off in his place, racing down the field as a timekeeper recorded the precise moment his wheels left the ground: ten minutes and five seconds past 9:00 a.m. Harold Hartney, in a Fokker, was the second to lift off.

Charlton was not the only pilot with mechanical troubles, and plans for an orderly series of departures, at precise two-minute intervals, soon fell apart. Instead, pilots took off in a ragged sequence that had been determined by lot. Some left within a few seconds of each other, others after minutes-long lulls. Once half had cleared the field, the takeoffs were paused until 2:00 p.m. to prevent a backup at the first refueling stop, in Binghamton.

Spectators got what they came for. Opening their throttles wide, flyers hurtled into the wind, toward the north side of the field, where three tents had been erected for dignitaries and race officials. Some pilots seemed to take a perverse delight in aiming straight for the tents, then yanking the stick back and zooming skyward at the last second. Of one such daredevil, the New York *Sun* reported, "it looked almost certain that he would score a clean hit on the tent pole."

No such disaster ensued, but another very nearly did. It involved none other than Benedict Crowell, the patrician, Yale-educated War Department official and one of Mitchell's closest allies in Washington. Over the summer, Crowell had led a delegation of aviation experts across the Atlantic to meet with their counterparts in France, Britain, and Italy. The American Aviation Mission, as it was called, returned with a strong endorsement of Mitchell's proposal for a cabinet-level department of aeronautics. Newton Baker, the secretary of war, had publicly disavowed the recommendation, but Crowell had continued to push Mitchell's cause, and he did so again at Roosevelt Field.

"It is beyond dispute the greatest aerial contest in the world," Crowell told reporters during a gap between takeoffs. "To watch these machines is to get an impression that there is more aerial activity in the United States than anywhere else in the world. But such, unfortunately, is not the case. America has lagged far behind the other nations in the development of aviation—the visit of the American Aviation Mission proves this. The transcontinental race, it is hoped, will awaken the people of the United States to take aviation seriously in national defense and commerce. America should lead the world in aviation."

What happened next only seemed to underscore his point, though not in the way he might have wished. Crowell decided he would like to take an airplane ride. He traded his overcoat and homburg for a borrowed flying jacket and helmet and lowered himself into the rear cockpit of a Curtiss R biplane. The pilot, Lt. Maurice Clearly, taxied into the wind and took off. Within seconds, the engine sputtered, caught again, then quit entirely. As Cleary swerved to avoid a building, the Curtiss pitched down, caught a wingtip on the ground, and overturned.

An ambulance was dispatched, chased by spectators who brushed past soldiers trying to keep them off the field. Amazingly, neither man was hurt. Cleary helped Crowell unbuckle his safety harness, and both crawled from beneath the inverted plane. "That's the shortest flight on record," the assistant secretary of war quipped. He gamely posed for a photograph with the mortified pilot but politely turned down an offer of another ride, pleading urgent business in New York.

———

Belvin Maynard—the Flying Parson—had risen early that morning, after less than a full night's sleep. He had only himself to blame. He had replaced the standard wire bracing of his DH-4 with streamlined "ribbon" wires, which boosted his speed by as much as twelve miles an hour. But the modification was against the rules. After the New York–Toronto race, Menoher had been irritated to learn that many pilots, Maynard included, had "mutilated" their machines to gain a competitive edge. A few days earlier, he had banned them from doing the same for the transcontinental race (though he allowed them to reduce weight by removing machine-gun mounts and bomb racks; in the rear cockpits of DH-4s, wicker seats replaced small rotating stools used by observers on combat missions).

Maynard was either unaware of Menoher's edict or chose to ignore it. As a result, his airplane had flunked a safety inspection on the eve of the race, for which he was "severely reprimanded." Skipping an awards banquet for top finishers in the New York–Toronto race, he stayed up past midnight restoring the plane's rigging to its original condition.

Maynard was in no hurry to resume his theological studies. He had scrapped his plans to return to Wake Forest College in the fall, using the excuse that he had been unable to find housing for his family. Now, he was determined to show the world that his victory in the New York–Toronto race had not been a fluke. On the morning of the race, there was no hint of the humble clergyman in his belted, double-breasted leather coat, riding breeches, and lace-up leather boots, nor in the jaunty name he had painted on his DH-4's nose: *"Hello Frisco."*

Maynard had been accompanied to the field by his wife and children as well as Trixie, his dog. As he waited in his cockpit, Trixie trotted to the airplane in a state of high agitation, leaping and barking furiously. Trixie had been ill after her long sea voyage from France, and Maynard spent several months nursing her back to health. The two had formed a fierce bond. After she recovered, Maynard often had taken her aloft, and Trixie—still a puppy at seven months old—apparently had no intention of staying on the ground while her master flew off on another adventure.

Much to the crowd's delight, Maynard climbed down from the plane, lifted Trixie into his arms, and deposited her in the rear cockpit with his mechanic, Sgt. William Kline. When Maynard soared into the sky a few minutes later, shortly after 9:30 a.m., Trixie was peering over the cockpit rim, "barking at the crowd for all she was worth." Maynard banked steeply to the west, and the plane soon disappeared from view.

Watching from the field, Lt. Daniel Brailey Gish was determined to catch up with him. He had finished third in the New York–Toronto race, a contest he claimed he would have won if not for a blinding rainstorm that damaged his prop. Even a serious physical handicap was not enough to deter him.

Gish was thirty-one, cocksure and garrulous, with a narrow, angular face and the slim-hipped build of a natural athlete. Competition was in his blood. A native of Indiana who grew up in the Pacific Northwest, he was a high school track star who set a national junior record in the javelin throw—144 feet—in Seattle in 1909. At the University of Washington, he was one of the fastest quarter-milers in the country and excelled at the shot put and broad jump. He dropped out after his sophomore year and competed briefly for the famed Irish-American Athletic Club in New York before moving to Washington, D.C., in 1911.

Gish prospered in the nation's capital. Within a few years, he had opened a garage, married, acquired a car dealership, and patented a gasoline filter for automotive use. He joined the Columbia Golf Club in Chevy Chase, Maryland, and made influential friends in Congress and the War Department. As competitive as ever, he was a five-handicap golfer and a star of the local auto-racing circuit, known for his fearlessness—the press called him "Daredevil Brailey"—and the unlit cigar clamped permanently between his teeth. On June 14, 1916, Gish drove a Haynes Six touring car between New York City and Washington, D.C., in seven hours and twenty-six minutes, breaking the previous record by more than an hour. "Excessive speed had to be maintained at all times and many chances were taken with the authorities in nearly every city and town en route," the *Washington Post* reported.

Aviation was an easy sell for a man so naturally drawn to risk. Not long after moving to Washington, Gish started a garage in partnership with a prominent young exhibition flyer, Paul Peck, who worked for an aircraft manufacturer at the Signal Corps' airfield in College Park, Maryland, where Gish learned to fly in 1911. Peck died in a plane crash the following year, but Gish kept up with his flying and in August 1917 volunteered for the Signal Corps' Aviation Section. He raced through his training and before long was teaching aerobatic maneuvers at an Air Service training field in Texas, even while technically still a cadet. In August 1918, with more than 500 hours of flight time under his belt, he sailed for France, where he was selected for one of the most dangerous flying jobs of the war—hunting German bombers at night.

But Gish would never get a chance to test himself in combat. As he sat in the cockpit of a Sopwith Camel fighter one night, waiting to take off on a practice flight with his new squadron, an unfamiliar Air Service captain appeared at his side. Claiming that Gish would see better in the dark without goggles, the officer snatched them from Gish's face before the startled pilot could even protest. Against his better judgment, Gish opened the throttle and bounded into the air, tears streaming from his wind-blasted eyes. He lost sight of the ground and crashed within seconds. The impact fractured his skull and injured his legs so badly that doctors wanted to amputate one. The onetime track star wouldn't let them.

Gish spent a year in hospitals in France and the United States, undergoing multiple surgeries to repair his shattered legs. In August 1919 he checked himself out of Walter Reed General Hospital in Washington to fly in the New York–Toronto race. He returned to the hospital, then checked himself out again on October 4 to fly in the transcontinental contest. He wore metal braces on both legs and carried crutches in the cockpit of his DH-4.

Gish was thrilled to be back in the arena, though he wished he had a different passenger. He had wanted to fly with a mechanic, in part because he worried that he would not be able to service his airplane with his damaged legs. But Mitchell, in a gesture of Franco-American solidarity, had insisted that he fly with Guy De Lavergne, a French Army captain and decorated aviator who served as the French defense attaché in Washington.

Whatever Gish's reservations, there was no denying that the injured veteran and his French passenger, a striking figure in his scarlet breeches and horizon-blue jacket, made a glamorous pair. As the men waited their turn to depart, several elegantly turned-out women from Larchmont, New York, gathered around their plane, presenting them with kid gloves and handkerchiefs to bring them good luck. Both got a kiss on the cheek. They took off at 10:34 a.m.

———

In contrast to the carnival in New York, the start of the race in San Francisco was a low-key affair. Low clouds and fog put a damper on the mood, as did the hour. Because of the three-hour time difference, pilots

Braily Gish and Guy De Lavergne (standing in the rear cockpit) shortly before starting the race at Roosevelt Field. *Library of Congress*

were supposed to leave San Francisco at first light, or as close as possible to the 9:00 a.m. start on the East Coast. A small crowd—including city officials, reporters, photographers, and relatives of the flyers—had braved the clammy predawn chill to gather at the edge of the Presidio's waterfront airfield.

Some of the flyers were based in Sacramento and San Diego and had only flown in the day before, not entirely without incident. Tricky winds caused one pilot to ground loop and another to hit a hay bale and a ditch, though neither mishap caused any damage. Aviators spent the afternoon preparing their machines and hobnobbing with reporters, veterans, and others who had turned out to watch. News photographers snapped pictures of the men—Carl Spaatz in his Army tunic, riding boots, and jodhpurs, others in oil-stained coveralls—next to their planes.

Hap Arnold took the opportunity to give the flyers a pep talk. He told them that he wanted a "Western Department man" to be first across the country, but not at any price. "Safety first," he admonished, urging them to baby their engines over the mountains, where a mechanical failure could be catastrophic. He advised them to wait until Cheyenne before opening their throttles wide.

The men agreed they would have an easier time of it than their rivals back East, who lacked their experience in mountain flying. They were glad to know that on their first crossing, at least, the most challenging part of the journey—over the Sierra Nevada and the Rocky Mountains—would come at the beginning, when their airplanes were in top condition. Spaatz calculated that if he avoided course deviations and lingered no more than the required thirty minutes at each control stop, he would reach Long Island by sundown on Friday, after three days of flying.

Lt. Edward V. Wales shared that sense of confidence. A 26-year-old former movie actor from Spokane, Washington, he had enlisted in the Army three years earlier and earned his wings at Scott Field near St. Louis. In the summer of 1918, the young officer was grounded for twenty days after stunt-flying over the city at a "dangerously low altitude," but the infraction apparently caused no lasting harm to his career. He recently had been placed in charge of aerial forest patrols operating out of Mather Field in Sacramento.

His personal life was also looking up. In Sacramento he had fallen in love with a young woman named Jesse McKenzie. The two had planned to marry on Saturday, October 4, but postponed the ceremony so that Wales could prepare for the race. He promised they would exchange vows as soon as he got back to California. To accompany him on the round-trip flight, he drafted a friend, Lt. William Goldsborough, who was assigned to forest-patrol duty in Washington State, to ride in the rear cockpit. As they worked on their plane at the Presidio, the two were in high spirits, with plans to see a Broadway show in New York.

––––––––

The first pilot was sent on his way at 6:54 a.m., just as the skies began to brighten, and the rest quickly followed. Soldiers removed wheel chocks, and the airplanes took off in rapid sequence, spitting blue exhaust flames and trailing whirlwinds of dust. The planes banked sharply to the east, over San Francisco Bay, and soon disappeared into the mist. Some crossed the water at 400 feet, just low enough that pilots could still make out the ghostly outlines of ships, which helped to keep them oriented and reassured them about the possibility of rescue should the need arise. Spaatz preferred to stay even lower, where the visibility was better. He skimmed the bay at just fifty feet until he reached clear air on the other side. By the time the sun rose at 7:11 a.m., all but one of the sixteen planes—an S.E.5 with misfiring cylinders—had left the field.

Jesse McKenzie had arrived at the Presidio at the last minute, hoping to bid her fiancé goodbye. She was heartsick to learn that she had just missed him. She hastily scratched out a note and handed it to another pilot, asking him to pass it along to Wales should he overtake him along the route.

———

Back on Long Island, the crowd was in need of a lift after Benedict Crowell's narrow escape. Or so Billy Mitchell believed. In a bid to "relieve the tension," he borrowed an S.E.5 and zoomed aloft, dazzling spectators with loops, spins, and barrel rolls. If nothing else, it helped to bleed off steam. The race was under way, and there was nothing more he could do. That night he returned to Washington to follow its progress from there.

11

No Parachutes

Around lunchtime, people in the village of Deposit, New York, heard the sound of an airplane and stepped outside to take a look. It seemed to be descending. A moment later, they heard a loud bang.

The plane was a DH-4 Bluebird emblazoned with the racing number "4." A little more than ninety minutes earlier, it had departed Roosevelt Field bound for the first control stop near Binghamton, some forty miles to the west of Deposit. Gerald Brant, the colonel and former cavalryman who ran the Air Service's Eastern Department, had elected to fly the plane from the rear cockpit while his mechanic, Sgt. William Nevitt, rode up front. (Though designed to be flown from the front, both modified and standard DH-4s could be piloted from the rear cockpit using a spare control stick that was intended for emergency use and normally stored in a bracket.) The men were nearing Deposit at 4,000 feet when an oil line broke. The engine lost oil pressure, and the tachometer registered a drop in revolutions as the plane began to lose altitude. Both men recognized the problem at once. Nevitt released his safety belt. With the prop blast tearing at his clothes, he pulled himself out of the cockpit and shimmied up to the engine.

He was hardly the first to attempt an in-flight repair. In Texas during the war, an Air Service trainee named Ormer Locklear had astonished his flight instructor by leaving his cockpit to replace a radiator cap that had fallen off and was dangling by a chain (Locklear subsequently worked as a professional wing-walker and Hollywood stuntman until his death in a plane crash in 1920). Another pilot in the race would later claim to have made a similar excursion that very morning, after losing power on the same leg to Binghamton. According to an interview he gave to the *Rochester Herald*, Lt. Ross Kirkpatrick straddled the engine to repair a broken throttle rod with his trouser belt, then returned to his cockpit and roared to safety, missing treetops "by a hand."*

But Nevitt did not have enough time. By one account, he was still clinging to the nose as Brant began spiraling down to land on a field near the West Branch of the Delaware River. The Bluebird was in a shallow bank when the oil-starved Liberty engine quit completely. The plane dropped a wing and dove thirty feet to the ground.

The first men on the scene found the plane inverted and broken in half, with its occupants trapped underneath. Brant, with four cracked ribs but no grave injuries, was quickly freed. "What has happened? What have I done?" he moaned, as the rescuers worked to pull his unconscious mechanic from beneath the engine. It took them fifteen minutes. The sergeant's legs were broken and his chest was crushed. Both Brant and Nevitt were taken to a nearby home, where Nevitt died within minutes. The control officer in Binghamton soon learned of the death and telegraphed the news to Washington.

Reports of other, less-consequential mishaps trickled in to Mineola throughout the day. Lionel Charlton, the British defense attaché, dropped out of the race after colliding with a fence in a forced landing. Lt. Russell Maughan ran short of fuel in his Spad and would spend the night in Scranton, Pennsylvania. Lt. William R. Taylor, in an Ansaldo S.V.A., put down in Nicholson, Pennsylvania, to repair a broken oil lead. Another DH-4 pilot and his mechanic spent the night in Ringtown, Pennsylvania, after their spark plugs fouled. And Kirkpatrick, the pilot who claimed to have fixed his throttle with his belt, never made it to Binghamton; bedev-

---

* Kirkpatrick's story should be taken with a grain of salt. Dorian Walker, a filmmaker and vintage-plane enthusiast who has restored and flown a DH-4, told me that the cowling hood would have prevented any access to the throttle control rod while the plane was in flight.

iled by a faulty compass, he landed many miles to the north and then returned to Mineola. He would restart the following day with a working compass.

Brailey Gish and his passenger, Guy De Lavergne, the French defense attaché, also faced a setback, one that nearly cost them their lives. Almost since leaving Long Island, the men had been plagued by an air leak in the DH-4's fuel system, which was pressurized by means of hand pumps in each cockpit. Now, over the Finger Lakes region of upstate New York, the problem had become critical. If the fuel tank lost too much pressure, the engine would stop. Gish began pumping air into the system and yelled at De Lavergne to do the same, but his words were lost to the slipstream. Gish pumped until his arm went numb but could not keep up with the leak. As the pressure dropped, the engine backfired, igniting fuel in the carburetor.

A sheet of flame rolled back from the engine.

———————

Gish and his passenger were living every aviator's worst fear. It was bad enough when a plane caught fire on the ground, after a crash. But fire aloft was another matter entirely, at least for airmen who did not yet fly with parachutes.

The Air Service's failure to equip its aviators with a proven lifesaving device is something of a mystery. The parachute was hardly a new concept. Leonardo da Vinci first sketched one in the fifteenth century, and in 1797 a Frenchman named André-Jacques Garnerin successfully jumped from a hydrogen balloon 3,200 feet over Paris. More recently, in the years leading up to World War I, parachutists made hundreds of descents from balloons at exhibitions and fairs on both sides of the Atlantic. A U.S. Army captain, Albert Berry, made the first successful jump from an airplane in 1912.

The parachute shed its novelty status in the war. Under constant threat from German fighters, Army observation balloonists—"balloonatics," as they were affectionately known—went aloft with silk parachutes in canvas bags attached to the sides of their baskets. The chutes inflated when the observers jumped over the side, yanking them out of the containers. These "aerial life preservers" were virtually foolproof, saving the lives of 116 balloonists and failing only once, when a canopy was ignited by flaming balloon fabric. But they were too bulky and cumbersome for use in airplanes.

Germany solved this problem with a compact thirty-pound seat pack, which was attached to flyers with a harness. When an aviator jumped out of a cockpit and began to fall, his chute was jerked out of its pack by a "static line"—a thin cord attached to the plane, designed to separate from the chute as it opened. The so-called Heinecke chute—named for its inventor, Otto Heinecke—made its first appearance over the battlefield in early 1918 and was credited with saving several lives, including that of German ace Ernst Udet. In Britain, meanwhile, a railway engineer named Everard Calthrop developed a parachute that deployed in a similar way, though it was carried in a fuselage compartment instead of a seat pack. The Royal Flying Corps eventually ordered twenty, with their canopies dyed black, for dropping spies behind enemy lines at night.

Nevertheless, neither Britain nor its allied partners saw fit to share this critical safety advance with aviators. "It is not general practice to employ parachutes in airplane work," said the Army's *Manual of Military Aviation*, published in 1917. The manual gave no explanation, though several were offered after the war. Samuel T. Moore, an Army balloon commander, blamed "old-timers" who believed that "parachutes might encourage pilots to become careless with government property." In a vivid World War I memoir—published in 1968 and aptly titled *No Parachute*— Royal Flying Corps and Royal Air Force veteran Arthur Gould Lee pointed a finger at military higher-ups who believed that "occupants of a stricken airplane should dive to their deaths with a stiff upper lip, in the manner of the captain of a sinking ship." Another factor, he wrote, was "sheer ignorance," especially among those with no flight experience, who argued that parachutes were unreliable or that flyers would not have the time or presence of mind to use them in an emergency.

Aviators in burning airplanes might have welcomed a chance to test that claim. In the absence of parachutes, they often were faced with a choice between incineration or jumping to their deaths. More than 200 British airmen chose to jump, though Raoul Lufbery, a top American ace, advised against it. "If your plane catches fire, don't jump," he told new combat pilots. "Stick with it and you may have a chance." But in May 1918, while engaging with a German two-seat observation plane, Lufbery failed to follow his own advice when his Nieuport burst into flames. He either jumped or fell from his cockpit. His body was found impaled on a picket fence. Some pilots carried revolvers to give themselves a third option.

In the summer of 1918, as its losses mounted in Europe, the Air Service belatedly began testing parachutes for aviators at Wright Field in Dayton, but its sense of urgency dissipated after the Armistice. Not until 1923 would the Army require its pilots to fly with parachutes.

In their absence, aviators faced a mortal threat from engine fires that spread to the fuselage or wings. In May 1919, the Air Mail Service had lost one of its best pilots, Frank McCusker, when his DH-4 caught fire shortly after taking off from Cleveland. As smoke trailed from his aircraft, McCusker fought the flames with a Pyrene fire extinguisher—it was later found empty—then jumped from an altitude of 200 feet. He died instantly when his head and neck struck the horizontal stabilizer. Prompted by the loss of his valuable cargo—McCusker had been flying with $63,000 in checks and drafts—the Post Office soon announced plans for asbestos-lined mail compartments, which would protect their contents if not pilots.

Scientific American, for its part, promoted the idea of detachable fuel tanks that could be jettisoned in flight. "The obvious thing to do with a flaming fuel tank is to drop it overboard," the magazine wrote in its September 1919 issue.

Billy Mitchell shared the aviator's obsession with fire. In July, he had written Charles Menoher to request a modification to the Liberty engine—an "outside air intake"—that "absolutely eliminates the danger of fire." He asked that it be put it into "immediate production."

———

Any such change would come too late for the transcontinental race. Over upstate New York, the flames streaming from Gish's engine seared his face and briefly ignited his leather helmet. He shielded his eyes with his left arm, closed a petcock valve to cut the gas supply, and switched off the ignition. Then he slammed the plane into a dive. Just as he had hoped, the sudden rush of air had the same effect as blowing on a candle. Gish pulled out of the plunge near treetop level and aimed for a shallow ravine on the side of a steep hill. A few feet above the ground, he eased back on the stick until the wings stalled. The DH-4 "pancaked" to a hard landing, then overturned. Remarkably, both he and De Lavergne emerged with only bruises. The Frenchman later said he had never witnessed a greater feat of flying.

The men hitched a ride to Britton Field in Rochester, where Gish checked in with the control officer and basked in the attention of spectators and reporters, for whom he could not resist inflating his war record. "Believe me, I saw some fighting in France, and I took one spill that I'll never forget," Gish said, though he had never served in combat. "But I'm here by the grace of a kind Providence to remark that nothing I saw or felt over there compares with the experience we had this afternoon.

"I would not have given a nickel for either of our lives right then."

The duo then went off in search of a "nice cozy hotel" and the next morning parted ways. De Lavergne resumed the race as a passenger in the Martin Bomber; piloted by Capt. Roy Francis, it was passing through Rochester and happened to have an empty seat. Gish took an express train back to Mineola and secured another DH-4.

He apparently did not think much of his latest plane, which he named *Junk*, painted in bold white letters on its fuselage. But this time, at least, he found a mechanic to ride in the rear cockpit.

Gish appears to have shrugged off the fire and the crash that followed. But such near-death experiences could leave deep psychological wounds. Hap Arnold, who had grounded himself for years after a near-fatal spin, knew this as well as anyone. Mitchell, too, seems to have had an appreciation for what today would be called post-traumatic stress disorder; as a combat leader in France, he made a practice of granting extra leave to pilots who showed signs of extreme stress. Though ground commanders sometimes resented this special treatment, Mitchell understood that aviators who were less than fully focused on their jobs were a danger both to themselves and their comrades.

For some pilots in the race, the war was not yet over. One of them was Russell Maughan, the 26-year-old lieutenant whose Spad had run short of fuel near Scranton. As a scout pilot in the Meuse-Argonne campaign, he had participated in some of the most intense aerial combat of the war, returning home with a Distinguished Service Cross and classic symptoms of PTSD. "He was during this period always under tense strain, and the slightest sound or event out of the ordinary would startle, and sometimes upset him," a medical report noted. After taking a break of several months, Maughan resumed flying in April 1919 with one of the Victory Loan squadrons touring the country. A few weeks later he flew into a tree while attempting to take off in Cooperstown, New York. Though Maughan was not injured, his psychiatric symptoms returned with a vengeance. "His sleep was filled with an almost continuous nightmare (living over the crash)," the medical report continued. "He states he went to pieces completely as far as his nerves were concerned."

After weeks in a military hospital that specialized in treating traumatized airmen, Maughan was granted permission to return to his hometown of Logan, Utah, for thirty days of medical leave. Mitchell turned down his request to compete in the race, on grounds of disability. Maughan then appealed the decision to Menoher, who overturned it shortly before the start.

————

The first day of Carl Spaatz's journey went smoothly. The red-haired aviator reached Mather Field in Sacramento in less than an hour, waiting impatiently as the control stop commander signed his logbook and his plane was replenished with gas and oil. After thirty minutes on the ground, he took off for the next control stop at Reno, across the snow-capped wall of the Sierra Nevada. Over the foothills, he noticed that his engine was running hot, so he throttled back and circled for twenty minutes, until it had cooled enough to allow his climb. He crossed the mountains at 12,000 feet, with Lake Tahoe sparkling in the sunshine off his right wing. Instead of following the railroad tracks, he had chosen to fly by compass, on a direct line, which saved him precious minutes. After Reno came stops in Battle Mountain, Nevada, and Salduro, Utah, where a temporary field had been laid out on the blinding white flats of the Great Salt Lake Desert. He touched down at Buena Vista Field in Salt Lake City at 1:40 p.m.

Spaatz was the third pilot to reach the control stop, just minutes behind Capt. Lowell Smith and Lt. Emil Kiel. There was plenty of day-light left and the men were eager to continue, betting they could make Rawlins or even Cheyenne by nightfall. But then the control stop com-mander at Salt Lake City, Capt. T. S. Voss, delivered some frustrating news: They would fly no farther that day.

The field at Green River, Wyoming, 137 miles to the east on the far side of the Wasatch Range, was not yet open for business—though not for lack of effort on the part of the townspeople or the harried control stop commander, Lt. Tolman. After waiting for the snow to melt and the ground to thaw, he had rounded up 150 volunteers and twenty teams of horses to clear and level the field. But it still needed time to dry, as Tolman explained to his counterpart in Salt Lake City. Voss reluctantly made the decision to hold contestants overnight.

Throughout the afternoon, planes approached the control stop in clear skies from the west, along the southern shoreline of the Great Salt Lake. The ninth was number 66, a DH-4 piloted by Maj. Dana H. Crissy, which arrived over Buena Vista Field at 5:15 p.m. In accordance with the rules, Crissy made one complete circuit of the landing area, giving his fellow aviators on the ground a merry wave. His mechanic, Sgt. Virgil Thomas, stood up in the rear cockpit and did the same. Crissy had no need to guess at the wind direction, taking his cue from an indicator on the ground— a portable, fifteen-foot "landing T" made of white-painted boards (pilots lined up with the shaft of the T, landing toward the cross arm).

He chopped the power and began his final turn to the right. Every-thing seemed fine.

Crissy was a popular, highly regarded Air Service officer but a relatively inexperienced pilot. After graduating from West Point in 1909, he had spent most of his career in the Coast Artillery before transferring to the Signal Corps' Aviation Section in 1917. He had never served overseas and spent the war in administrative jobs, first as the head of the Air Service ground school at Princeton University, then at headquarters in Washington. More recently he had been placed in charge of Mather Field. Only in May had he completed the training requirements for the rating of Junior Military Aviator.

Even for the most seasoned pilots, crossing the continent was a perilous undertaking—one reason, perhaps, that Crissy's wife had pleaded with him to skip the contest. But Crissy had insisted, and his wife, from a prominent San Francisco family, had seen him off that morning at the Presidio. Now her worst fears would be realized.

As Crissy steepened his bank on his final turn toward the field, the DH-4 "seemed to quiver as if wounded"—the sign of an incipient stall. Sure enough, the aircraft dropped a wing and entered a spin. At an altitude of about 150 feet, Crissy had no time to recover. The plane plunged into a shallow pond.

Spectators who had been cheering Crissy's arrival suddenly fell silent. A few began running toward the wreckage, where they found the unconscious aviators trapped in a tangle of wood and wire. For five minutes they held the flyers' heads above the water until a mechanic arrived with tools to cut them free. Thomas's eyes briefly fluttered open, then closed. Both men died before reaching the hospital.

———

Crissy had committed a classic aviation blunder. If a pilot loses too much airspeed, the wings will cease to produce lift—the condition known as a stall. (Because stall speed increases with the angle of bank, an airplane is more likely to stall during a turn.) Often, one wing will stop flying before the other, causing it to drop. The aircraft has now entered a spin. To recover, pilots are taught to neutralize their ailerons and apply rudder in the opposite direction of the plane's rotation. But a spin at low altitude is often fatal. There simply isn't time to get the plane flying again before it hits the ground. All it takes is a moment's inattention to the airspeed.

Such "stall-spin" accidents were, and remain, a scourge of aviation. Spaatz, who was on the field at the time of Crissy's crash, had no doubt as to its cause. "Ninety percent of the accidents which have come under my observation in France and the United States," he later wrote, "have resulted from a pilot's attempt to turn close to the ground." Even today, unintentional stalls account for nearly 25 percent of all fatal airplane crashes in the United States. As in Crissy's case, they typically occur in the final phases of flight, as planes are maneuvering near the ground at low speeds.

Modern aircraft are equipped with stall-warning horns and gyroscopic instruments, such as turn-and-slip indicators, that can help pilots avoid such lethal mistakes. But pilots in 1919 had little more than airspeed indicators and their senses. To keep their turns coordinated, and thus less prone to a stall, they took their cues from their buttocks—too much pressure on one side indicated that an aircraft was slipping toward the inside of a turn, on the other, that it was skidding toward the outside of a turn (hence the expression "flying by the seat of the pants"). Such knowledge only came with experience, and even experienced pilots needed regular practice to stay sharp. Flying is a perishable skill.

The deaths of Crissy and Thomas brought to three the number of men killed on the first day of the race. The next morning, the toll was reported prominently in newspapers across the country. "Corpses Mark Trail of Aerial Derby," read the headline on the front page of the *Atlanta Constitution*.

It was not the kind of publicity that Mitchell was seeking. Much to his relief, however, carnage was not the only story of the day.

12

"God's Given Children"

Perhaps because he was one, Billy Mitchell believed that good athletes—especially horsemen, tennis players, and golfers—made the best pilots. His opinion was widely shared. A Royal Air Force (RAF) report that emerged from the war argued that the best aviators, like the best riders, were distinguished by the quality of their "hands"—an admittedly nebulous concept that referred to deftness and sensitivity of touch. "The horse-rider with good hands is able to sense the mentality of a horse by the feel of the reins and also to convey his desires accurately to his mount," the authors wrote. "In the same way the pilot with good hands senses unconsciously the various movements of his airplane, and rectifies any unusual or abnormal evolutions almost before they occur. The skillful pilot appears to anticipate 'bumps.' He is invariably a graceful flyer, never unconsciously thrown [*sic*] an undue strain on the machine, just as a good riding man will never make a horse's mouth bleed." German aviators, most of whom came from the cavalry, shared the same bias.

Horsemanship aside, it was generally accepted that pilots should be reasonably well educated as well as young—flying skills were said to slip after thirty-five—and single, lest they suffer from an "increased sense of responsibility," as the RAF study put it. (Mitchell added a racist qualifier, typical for the day, suggesting that European origin conferred an advantage.) Personality traits were important, too. The ideal pilot, the authors of the study wrote, is "alert, cheerful, optimistic, happy-go-lucky, generally a good fellow, and frequently lacking in imagination." That women could fly as well as men—as a few already were—did not enter the conversation.

But the truth is that no one could predict with certainty who would succeed as a pilot. Some candidates who looked good on paper proved hopeless in the cockpit, and the opposite, of course, was also true. Among themselves, aviators addressed the matter in almost mystical terms, distinguishing between "natural" pilots, who flew by instinct, and "mechanical" ones, who slavishly followed the rules. "Natural flyers thought they were God's given children," Carl Spaatz would later say, including himself in the category.

Belvin Maynard's place in that hierarchy was clear. The winner of the New York–Toronto race flew like he was born to the task, with verve and an almost mathematical precision. On takeoffs he would bank steeply almost as soon as his wheels left the ground, on occasion nearly scraping a wing. ("He may be a parson," said a mechanic who watched his stylish departure from Roosevelt Field, "but he certainly flies like the devil.") When setting up to land, he would lose altitude by slipping the plane vigorously to one side and then the other, a tricky, cross-controlled maneuver that made it look as if the aircraft were fishtailing. But Maynard stopped short of rashness. He had an unerring feel for aerodynamics and the performance limits of his plane. In that sense, he embodied Mitchell's belief that the best pilots were bold without being reckless. There was no place for timidity in the cockpit, just as there was no place for foolish risk-taking. Maynard could walk right up to the line without crossing it.

But there was a lot more to flying—or "airmanship"—than manipulating an airplane on the three axes known as pitch (controlled with the elevator), yaw (controlled with the rudder), and roll (controlled with the ailerons). A good pilot also needed an eye for the weather, a solid grasp of engine mechanics, and an aptitude for finding his way over unfamiliar terrain. And Maynard, from all the evidence, was an airman of the first order.

His first task after taking off from Roosevelt Field was to find the control stop at West Endicott, New York, 142 miles to the west of Mineola near the small city of Binghamton. This was harder than it sounds. In the days before radio beacons and satellite-navigation systems, pilots relied on maps and compasses to find their way. Each had serious drawbacks. Early airplane compasses were poorly dampened, and the needle tended to swing wildly, especially during turns. Not only that, but a pilot following a compass bearing had to correct for wind direction and velocity, using visual cues such as the movement of an airplane's shadow across a field. A crosswind required flying at a steady angle to the desired course. It was tricky.

As for maps, they, too, were problematic. Very few had been designed for aviators.

———

Flyers had long recognized the need for charts that depicted the world in three dimensions instead of two. Ideally they would show not only rail lines, towns, and other landmarks readily identified from above, but also airfields as well as topographic features such as mountains and ridges. Some of the first such maps were published in 1916 and 1917 by the Sperry Gyroscope Company, a manufacturer of aircraft instruments in Brooklyn. The Sperry maps covered a portion of the Eastern Seaboard and a route from New York to Chicago. It was around that time that Mitchell, then the acting head of the Signal Corps' Aviation Section, pushed for the production of ten-inch-square "aerial navigation maps" that could easily be handled in a cockpit. But the effort was delayed by the war, and it wasn't until early 1919 that the Air Service embraced Mitchell's goal in a systematic way, when it charted roughly thirty routes linking training fields around the country. These maps foreshadowed, in crude form, the aeronautical charts of today, with colors used to differentiate between forests (green), water (blue), and mountains, ridges, or hills (brown).

Neither the Air Service nor any other organization, however, had developed aeronautical charts that covered the rest of the country—which is to say, most of it. In their absence, mail pilots had begun flying with Post Office maps designed for terrestrial use and reformatted as eight-inch-wide strips that could be rolled onto spindles and unfurled as a flight progressed. For the transcontinental race, Mitchell ordered that each contestant receive a set of these maps, covering its entire path. The maps were displayed on government-issue aluminum devices that typically were hung from the side of the cockpit. Though reasonably accurate, they omitted many prominent landmarks and showed only roads and railroads used to carry the mail. Nor did they show terrain, a significant shortcoming on a route that traversed two major mountain ranges. ("The issued maps were very good except for the lack of mountains," one contestant later observed.) Largely for that reason, some pilots in the race also carried Rand McNally state maps, which did show the contours of the land, at least in crude form. Some pilots folded the maps into smaller squares showing the line of flight and secured them with large paperclips, to keep them from blowing open in the cockpit.

Despite their limitations, the maps were essential, especially for pilots who preferred contact flying—navigating with visual reference to the ground—to flying by compass. For American aviators on the Western Front, contact flying was the favored method. They rarely ventured far from their home airfields, and there were plenty of roads, railroads, and villages to serve as landmarks. The downside was that they had to fly low enough to see them, which brought them within range of enemy guns. And contact flying was only possible when pilots could see the ground. In one notorious incident, an entire Air Service squadron got lost above the clouds and landed in Germany after running out of fuel. Its twelve pilots and observers—including the squadron leader, Maj. Harry M. Brown— were promptly captured, along with six undamaged Bréguet Bombers. Several days later, according to one possibly apocryphal report, a German pilot dropped a note on an American airfield. "We thank you for the fine airplanes and equipment which you have sent us," it read, "but what shall we do with the Major?" Mitchell, disgusted, later wrote that Brown was "better off in Germany than he would have been with us."

For pilots flying in clear skies during the transcontinental race, following the railroad was a reliable navigation method, especially in the uncluttered spaces of the West. But its tracks did not always follow a straight line between control stops. For that reason, Maynard and others preferred to navigate by compass, glancing at their postal-route maps periodically to confirm their positions. Maynard found that lakes and rivers made the most reliable landmarks.

As another aid to navigation, control officers at each stop were ordered to post simple, hand-drawn maps showing the location of the airfields to their immediate east and west. Pilots copied them into notebooks before they took off.

Nevertheless, flyers in the race often had a hard time distinguishing control stops from surrounding fields, especially in bad weather or fading light. To guide them in, soldiers fired flares from Very pistols, set gasoline ablaze, or generated smoke with smudge pots or fires made with wet leaves. The most effective beacons—used at Buffalo and a few other stops—were truck-mounted searchlights borrowed from the Army's Coast Artillery branch.

A few pilots struggled even to locate the first control stop. As he approached Binghamton, on the north bank of the Susquehanna River, Maynard passed one plane "several miles off course to our left." A short while later he saw another aircraft, its pilot "apparently lost," flying in circles over the city.

Then there was Lt. John Marquette, who missed the first control stop by such a wide margin that he never got there at all. His troubles began near Port Jervis, New York, about halfway between Mineola and Binghamton, when he noticed that his compass had "ceased functioning." He wagged his wings to jog the device and seemed to get it working again. Forty-five minutes later he realized that he had no idea where he was. He came to a river and followed it to Jersey Shore, Pennsylvania, where he landed his DH-4 for the night. After filling his gas and oil tanks the next morning, he resumed his journey and followed a rail line to Towanda, Pennsylvania. The town was on the Susquehanna but well southwest of his goal. Reversing direction, he followed a compass heading that he thought would take him back to Binghamton, but the needle "pulled to the left" and instead directed him to Keuka Lake sixty miles to the northwest. By now thoroughly rattled, he landed nearby to ask directions, took off, and flew back in the direction from which he had come. A short while later he reached the Susquehanna for the second time that day, but he was not sure whether Binghamton was upstream or downstream. Hoping to "ascertain my position," he set down on what he wrongly thought was an unobstructed field, taking out fifty feet of wire fence. The accident damaged his right wing and landing gear and forced him to drop out of the race.

————

Maynard had no difficulty finding the field at West Endicott, on a fertile plain between the river and a low ridge. He was the third to land, just after Harold Hartney, and was greeted by a cheering crowd of several hundred people held back by police. He and Kline, his mechanic, grabbed a snack at the Red Cross canteen, where Trixie was treated to boiled ham after turning up her nose at bread. Thirty minutes later the trio were on their way again.

As he followed his compass toward Rochester, Maynard flew fast—faster than some pilots thought prudent. They worried that if they pushed their engines too hard, vibration would cause parts to fail or come loose. But Maynard had an exceptional feel for engines, perhaps because he had dismantled so many as a teenager. He knew, counterintuitively, that the Liberty's thundering twelve cylinders ran more smoothly at close to full throttle. He covered the 125-mile distance to Rochester in just sixty-two minutes, for an impressive average speed of 121 miles an hour.

The crowd was even bigger than the one that had greeted Maynard and his companions at Binghamton. Cars were parked along both sides of the field, and small boys perched on tree limbs to get a better view.

Hartney's arrival minutes earlier had elicited a collective gasp, as spectators caught their first glimpse of the "hated black cross of the Boche" emblazoned on his Fokker. The plane was one of forty-five Fokkers that had been delivered to German forces in the village of Fleury in northwestern France and seized days later, still in their crates, when Fleury fell to the Americans. There was no small irony in Hartney's choice of aircraft. The D.VII was widely considered the best fighter of the war, with its Mercedes engine, steel-tube construction, and internally braced wing, which cut down on drag by eliminating the need for flying wires. It easily outclassed the Spad XIIIs flown by Hartney and the men under his command, many of whom died in contests with the German fighter. It was so effective a weapon that the Allied powers required Germany to turn over all its D.VIIs as part of the Armistice agreement. Now Hartney was flying one through the American heartland.

Maynard and Hartney were now vying for the lead among the westbound flyers, but not for long. Mechanics were unfamiliar with the German fighter and struggled to fill its hard-to-access gas and oil tanks. Hartney could only watch in dismay as Maynard took off ahead of him at 12:50 p.m., after thirty minutes and thirty seconds on the ground (timekeepers recorded arrivals and departures at each control stop, clicking their stopwatches each time a contestant's wheels touched or left the ground). Hartney left five minutes later.

Throughout the afternoon, Maynard extended his lead. He covered the fifty-six miles to Buffalo in sixty-two minutes, then set out for the next stop at Cleveland. He followed a compass line over Lake Erie. It would have been safer to fly along the shoreline, where he could have landed after an engine failure, but Maynard had faith in his Liberty. He had no trouble finding the Glenn L. Martin Company's well-groomed field on the outskirts of Cleveland, where police held back the large crowd. Glenn Martin came out to greet him, and factory mechanics fussed over his plane.

Hartney, meanwhile, made a tactical error in choosing to fly over Lake Erie at a relatively high altitude. It gave him an extra margin of safety, but at the cost of headwinds that slowed his progress and raised his fuel consumption. The Fokker was designed for sprints, not marathons; it could barely fly ninety minutes on a tank of gas. Realizing that he would not reach Cleveland before his engine quit, Hartney made an unplanned fuel stop in Pennsylvania, where minor mechanical trouble delayed his getaway by another hour and a half. He did not reach Cleveland until 4:21 p.m. By then he had been overtaken by several other flyers, and Maynard was long gone.

A dozen planes lingered at Buffalo. Their pilots wanted to press on, but the control officer stopped them, on the grounds that they would not be able to reach Cleveland by sunset. Pilots later complained that he had forgotten the one-hour time difference between Buffalo and the next stop.*

Examining his engine at Martin Field, Hartney was annoyed to find that his porcelain spark plugs had cracked after less than a day of flying. He installed replacements, but by the time he finished it was nearly sunset, too late to proceed. Instead he took a quick test flight, throwing in a flew loops and spins for the benefit of the crowd. He was pleased to find that the Fokker flew faster with the new plugs, boosting his hopes of catching Maynard the next day. He planned to get away at first light.

———

Maynard would be the only pilot to reach Chicago that day. After a mandatory stop at the Post Office field in Bryan, Ohio, he landed at Ashburn Field, sixteen miles west of the city, at 5:53 p.m. local time. It was a remarkable achievement. He had covered the 810 miles from Mineola in a record-breaking six hours and forty-five minutes of flying time, for an average pace of 120 miles an hour. Even allowing for time on the ground, the journey took just nine hours and twenty-nine minutes—half the time of the Twentieth Century Limited express train between New York and Chicago. Maynard's speedy performance carried obvious implications for the future of travel, perhaps best captured by a front-page story in the next morning's *Chicago Tribune*. "Breakfast in Long Island," it began. "Dinner in Chicago."

By Maynard's account, the Air Service personnel at Ashburn Field were surprised to see him; they had not expected any flyers until the next day. But a few hundred curious citizens had turned out just in case. So had a delegation from the Aero Club of Illinois, which had maintained

———

* Actually, there was no time difference. Cleveland switched from central to eastern time in 1914. However, railroads lagged in making the change on their schedules, which probably explains the confusion.

the field since taking it over from the Signal Corps a few years earlier. On the edge of the large four-way field was a steel observation tower and a steel hangar that had been converted into a dormitory for contestants staying overnight at the stop.

The long day of flying had taken its toll. "I'm tired," Maynard told a *Chicago Tribune* reporter after climbing down from his cockpit. On the other hand, he said, "It was a beautiful day for flying. That old Liberty motor batted out mile after mile without one complaint. It was a long, hard grind, but we're going to win this race."

At the first opportunity, Maynard and his mechanic slipped away to the temporary sleeping quarters in the hangar, where they flopped down on mattresses stuffed with hay. Maynard had declined the Aero Club's offer of more comfortable accommodations in downtown Chicago, knowing it would only delay his getaway the next morning.

It was not a peaceful night. The mattresses left much to be desired— Maynard later joked that their contents would have made a good meal for his father's Jersey cows—and in the middle of the night he and Kline were hauled out of bed by news photographers belatedly sent to take their pictures for the morning papers.

Then a storm blew in. For the rest of the night, pilot and mechanic tossed and turned as rain rattled on the metal roof.

13

"Snow Hurricane"

Weather forecasting in the United States had come a long way since the mid-nineteenth century, when the Smithsonian Institution established the first national network of weather observers. Scattered across thirty-one states, the observers kept daily records of temperature, barometric pressure, rainfall, and other data. They telegraphed their reports to Smithsonian headquarters in Washington, D.C., where the data were compiled into a crude daily weather map. But describing the weather was one thing; predicting it was another. In 1870, the U.S. Weather Bureau (now the National Weather Service) was created to do just that.

Signed into existence by President Ulysses S. Grant, the bureau initially relied on the Signal Corps, in partnership with civilian meteorologists, to generate its daily forecasts. Its first efforts dealt mainly with storms threatening the Great Lakes and the Gulf and Atlantic coasts. Forecasts for major cities soon followed, and in 1879 the bureau began publishing a daily national weather map that looks strikingly similar to its modern-day counterpart. Lines called isobars delineated areas of high and low pressure; arrows predicted the movement of storms. Closely spaced isobars indicated steep pressure gradients, which translate into higher winds. The weather maps were posted in hotels and railroad stations and published in newspapers across the country.

For obvious reasons, early aviators were eager consumers of the data furnished by the Weather Bureau, which had been taken over by the

Department of Agriculture in 1891. Basic forecasts of surface winds and visibility at least gave them some way to plan ahead. But as airplanes flew higher and over longer distances, pilots recognized the need for forecasts tailored to the unique challenges of traveling through the atmosphere. Where could they expect clouds, and at what altitude? What about headwinds? Ice? Fog? Thunderstorms? Much depended on humidity levels and temperatures at various altitudes. Aviation forecasts would need to capture all of these variables and more.

The field of "aerology"—the study of the atmosphere—long predated powered flight. In the United States, it arguably can be traced to 1752, when Benjamin Franklin famously flew a kite in a thunderstorm to prove the link between lightning and electricity. The field expanded during the nineteenth century with the use of manned balloons to hoist scientists and their instruments aloft. But the method was impractical for daily samplings, so the Weather Bureau began experimenting with kites to carry its equipment. Starting in 1915, daily reports from a kite observation station in Drexel, Nebraska, were telegraphed to Weather Bureau meteorologists in Chicago and Washington, D.C. The data informed the bureau's daily forecasts, but it only covered a portion of the Midwest and fell far short of aviators' needs.

As with so many other aspects of flying, World War I made the quest for trustworthy forecasts more urgent. After the United States entered the conflict in 1917, the Signal Corps trained more than 500 men, many of them physicists and engineers, in the gathering and interpretation of weather data for both air and ground forces. Some members of the Army's new Meteorological and Aerological Service were assigned to aviation units in France, while others remained in the United States to supply forecasts at training airfields. One of their most useful tools was the sounding balloon. Released to travel freely through the sky, it was tracked from the ground with a device called a theodolite, similar to a surveyor's transit, revealing cloud heights as well as the speed and direction of winds aloft. Billy Mitchell considered this information so critical that he ordered sounding balloons sent aloft "every hour, night and day" while running air-combat operations on the Western Front.

Civilians followed the Army's lead. On December 1, 1918, just weeks after the Armistice, the Weather Bureau began issuing daily aviation forecasts for the New York–Chicago airmail route. "Good flying weather today," read one from the period. "Generally clear sky and good visibility, moderate varying winds surface and aloft." By the summer of 1919, the bureau was making daily observations at kite stations in North Dakota, Oklahoma, Texas, Georgia, Indiana, New York, Michigan, and Washington, D.C.

The military continued to play an important role. In July 1919, the Air Service's chief meteorologist began using Weather Bureau data to produce thirty-hour aviation forecasts covering the entire country, as part of the organization's effort to boost commercial flying. Charles Menoher was careful to note that the Air Service was not "assuming any responsibility for accuracy."

––––––

Mitchell had given careful thought to providing pilots in the transcontinental race with accurate weather information. Before the start, his office arranged with a Weather Bureau meteorologist in Washington, a Mr. Bowie, to telegraph local forecasts to each control stop twice a day. Bowie's forecasts would supplement the weather observations made by the officers in charge, whose reports on surface winds and visibility were supposed to be transmitted by phone or telegraph to adjacent control stops daily at 8:00 a.m., 12:00 noon, and 3:00 p.m. At least in theory, flyers would then have some inkling of the conditions that awaited them at their next destination, if not along the route itself.

One important piece of missing data was the speed and direction of winds at various altitudes, which could affect navigation as well as fuel consumption between stops. The only exception was along a portion of the route through the Midwest. During daylight hours, meteorologists at the Fort Omaha Balloon School kept tabs on the winds aloft by means of a captive balloon fitted with an electric anemometer; their findings were transmitted three times a day to the Omaha control stop and to the control stops on either side of it: Des Moines, Iowa, to the east and St. Paul,

Nebraska, to the west. Over most of the route, flyers had to rely on Bow-ie's forecasts, which predicted the direction of winds aloft but not their altitude. For that, pilots could only make an educated guess.

The system had other gaps. The aviation forecasts issued by the Weather Bureau in Washington often failed to anticipate all but the big-gest storms or got the timing wrong when they did. "Weather forecasts, in my opinion, are useless on a trip of this nature," one pilot wrote after the race. The firsthand observations from control stops were helpful—but only when they were available and current. In many cases, pilots took off without knowing the weather at their next destination, either because of faulty communication between stops or lapses on the part of their commanders—many of whom, a pilot later complained, "did not seem to realize the importance of obtaining accurate weather reports before day-light about the weather conditions at the two adjoining control stations."

Even if the control officers were diligent in their reporting, they could provide only a snapshot of the weather, which often changed quickly. Destinations that one minute were reported clear might be blanketed in fog by the next. Without radios, pilots would have no advance warning. During overnight stays at control stops, at least one pilot made a habit of visiting the local Weather Bureau office, if he could find one nearby, to scan the national weather map for clues to the flying weather ahead.

If he did so on the second morning of the race, he might have felt his stomach lurch. Issued in Washington at 8:00 a.m., the weather map for Thursday, October 9, painted a worrying picture. Isobars showed low pressure dominating the country from coast to coast. In addition, a shaded gray zone covered roughly a thousand miles of the route from Pennsylvania to Nebraska. Another gray zone was draped over the north-ern Rockies, where it intersected with the route in Utah and Wyoming. The gray areas indicated precipitation, which would come in the form of rain (symbolized by the letter "R") in the East and Midwest and snow ("S") in the mountain states. The map also predicted that temperatures in the West would drop well below normal for early fall, to 20 degrees Fahrenheit in some areas. It didn't take an expert to know that both groups of aviators—eastbound and westbound—were in for a rough day.

———

Mr. Bowie, at the Weather Bureau, was the first to sound the alarm. On Wednesday, October 8, he had stayed late at his office in Washington, reviewing the latest telegraphed reports from field stations around the country. He was especially worried about conditions in the West. At 10:30 p.m. eastern time, he sent an ominous telegram to the control stop commander in Rawlins, Wyoming:

AVIATION FORECAST SALT LAKE CITY TO CHEYENNE ON THURSDAY FLYING WEATHER WILL BECOME BAD PERIOD   WINDS NEAR SURFACE WILL BECOME STRONG NORTHWEST WEATHER BECOME CLOUDY WITH RAIN OR SNOW AND MUCH COLDER PERIOD   DANGEROUS CONDITIONS IN MOUNTAINS

Thursday morning at 11:00 a.m., Bowie underscored the warning with another telegram to Rawlins. "Bad flying weather low clouds snow in the mountains," it read. "Strong shifting winds probably northwest gales aloft dangerous conditions in Wyoming."

Bowie's forecast was timely and accurate. Few paid it much attention.

———

Nine of the fifteen planes to leave San Francisco had successfully completed the trip to Salt Lake City, where they had been grounded overnight on orders of the control stop commander. Flyers were eager to be on their way. They had agreed to depart the Utah capital at the same intervals by which they had arrived, to preserve their positions in the race at the end of the first day. Capt. T. S. Voss, the control stop commander, was still worried about the condition of the field at Green River, Wyoming, one stop to the east. Early Thursday morning, after consulting with headquarters, he told pilots they could skip Green River and fly direct to Rawlins, though if they did so they would need to add thirty minutes to their elapsed time over the route.

Control officers had the authority to hold contestants if they thought it was too dangerous to proceed. Given his evident concern for safety, Voss's failure to do so on the second morning of the race is puzzling. Perhaps he never received Bowie's forecast. Or perhaps he did but was skeptical of its accuracy. After all, forecasts were often wrong. On the other hand, even if he believed the forecast, how would it look at Air Service headquarters—and especially to Billy Mitchell—if he held up the entire contingent of eastbound flyers? Grounding pilots every time the weather was less than perfect would undermine one of the main reasons for the contest, which was to demonstrate the viability of long-distance air travel.

Moreover, these were military flyers, accustomed to taking risks. They had volunteered for the race and could exercise their own judgment on whether to continue. No one was forcing them to fly.

At Salt Lake City, at least, there was no obvious reason to delay. The weather was fine. In keeping with the gentlemen's agreement reached the day before, Lowell Smith, who had been the first to reach Salt Lake City, would also be the first to take off. At twenty-seven, the former auto mechanic from California was an experienced pilot who was considered a top contender in the race. His aviation résumé dated to 1915, when Pancho Villa, the Mexican revolutionary, hired him to maintain his tiny air force, before Pershing's troops crossed the border. The job, like Villa's three planes, didn't last long, but it did give him a taste for flying. He joined the Air Service in 1917 and spent the war as a flight instructor in Texas.

Smith lifted off at 7:33 a.m., followed by Emil Kiel at 7:51 and Carl Spaatz at 8:04. The soon-to-be-married Edward Wales, with his friend William Goldsborough riding in the rear cockpit, departed the field half an hour later. One by one, the four pilots turned east and began to climb toward the vaulting peaks of the Wasatch Range, expecting to reach Cheyenne in plenty of time for lunch.

What they didn't know is that flying conditions on the other side of the mountains already had deteriorated. Just as Bowie had predicted, winter had come early to Wyoming. At 8:00 a.m., the control stop commander at Rawlins, Maj. Francis B. Longley, sent a telegram to his counterpart at Green River warning of dangerous conditions at the field.

"Snowing with gradual increase in density," Longley wrote, noting that the control stop's limestone markings already had been "rendered invisible." He advised the Green River commander to hold the eastbound flyers at that stop until the snow had abated.

The men who had just departed Salt Lake City would never get that message. Taking their cue from Voss, they had decided to fly past Green River rather than risk a landing on its waterlogged field. At some point during the morning, Voss got word of the treacherous conditions at Rawlins, perhaps after it was relayed from Green River. But by then it was too late.

———

Spaatz and Sgt. Emmett Tanner, his mechanic, crossed the Wasatch peaks at 12,000 feet, shivering in the frigid air, the shutters on the nose of the DH-4 closed to keep its radiator from freezing. As usual, Spaatz flew by compass to save time, crabbing to the left to compensate for a strong northwest crosswind. The flight to Rawlins would take about two and a half hours. Despite lowering skies, visibility along the route was good. Near Rawlins, he flew through a snow flurry, but he had no trouble finding the control stop at the town racetrack, which was easily identified by its grandstand and other nearby structures.

Spaatz circled the field and turned back into the wind to begin his final approach. As the aircraft settled toward the snow-covered landing area, he craned his neck over the side of the cockpit to get a better view, like the engineer of a steam locomotive rounding a bend—standard practice for DH-4 pilots, who otherwise could not see where they were going with the biplane's long nose raised for landing. He touched down at 10:34 a.m., behind Smith and Kiel.

Smith had had a difficult flight to Rawlins, having flown through adverse weather that the others somehow avoided. He landed with his wings and fuselage caked in what he estimated was 200 pounds of ice. Much to his irritation, soldiers at the field had not been waiting to receive him, and he wasted precious minutes thawing oil over a fire before it could be poured into his engine. "No markers visible at Field, snow on ground," Smith wrote in his logbook as he waited on the ground. "A very poor Field that I don't believe a takeoff is possible."

But Smith, eager to preserve his lead, quickly overcame his misgivings. After clearing his DH-4 of its frozen crust, he and his observer, Lt. Francis W. Ruggles, departed the field at 10:42 a.m., eight minutes after Spaatz's arrival. Kiel took off at 11:08, and Spaatz took off at 11:16, following a twelve-minute delay in servicing his plane caused by the cold.

The three were now the front-runners among the eastbound pilots, separated by just a few minutes. If they had not already been fierce rivals, they were now.

The most dangerous conditions were still to come. After a nerve-wracking departure from Rawlins—with a full load of fuel and its climb performance diminished by the thin air, his plane had barely cleared nearby hills—Spaatz turned toward Cheyenne, 115 miles to the east on the far side of the Medicine Bow Mountains. At heights of nearly 12,000 feet, the mountains were daunting enough on their own, but now they were capped by dense gray clouds. He could see that it would be folly, and perhaps suicide, to fly the compass line to Cheyenne.

Reluctantly, Spaatz decided to follow the railroad. Though it would add about seventy-five miles to his route, flying along the tracks would avoid the highest terrain.

But it wouldn't keep him out of the snow. Minutes after he took off from Rawlins, a blizzard—Spaatz called it a "snow hurricane"—enveloped his plane, reducing visibility to 200 or 300 yards. Spaatz feared that he might lose sight of the ground and descended to just fifty feet above the tracks, swerving to avoid water towers that appeared suddenly out of the swirling snow. After skirting Elk Mountain to the north, the tracks turned southeast and entered a series of narrow canyons between Laramie and Cheyenne. With clouds forming a barrier overhead, he had no choice but to thread his way through the treacherous maze, banking sharply with every twist and turn of the rails. It took all his concentration and skill.

Much to his relief, Spaatz exited the last of the canyons into clear skies. Just ahead lay Cheyenne and the big landing field at Fort D. A. Russell. The only threat now was the wind, which howled out of the north at between fifty and sixty miles an hour. As Spaatz touched down at 12:43 p.m., a gust rocked his plane so violently that a wing skid broke against the ground.

Smith and Kiel also had followed the railroad to Cheyenne. "It was snow and blow all the way," Smith told a reporter the following day, adding with a touch of melodrama, "Death was at our elbow."

Wales and Goldsborough, in the fourth plane to leave Salt Lake City that morning, landed at Rawlins at 11:05 a.m., while Spaatz and Kiel were still on the ground. At this point none of the men had any reason to doubt the hazards that awaited them just to the east. Snow was falling nearby, and Bowie's warning had been telegraphed to the control stop at Rawlins the night before. Nevertheless, after talking through the risks, Wales and Goldsborough rejected the safer option. They would follow their compass instead of the railroad.

Their reasoning is easy enough to grasp. Everyone understood that the race's official name—the "Reliability and Endurance Test"—was a little misleading. As Mitchell himself had acknowledged in a letter to Arnold in late September, the contest was "really a race," and the Air Service had treated it as one from the beginning. The *Air Service News Letter* of October 8 called it "a sporting event." The Air Service Information Group in Washington tracked flyers' progress on a nine-foot-wide "score board" showing their arrival and departure times—down to the second—at each control stop. Control stop commanders, who provided the data by telegram, sent duplicates to the American Flying Club in Manhattan, which passed it on to the press. Newspapers obliged with banner headlines and urgent, horse-race-style coverage, including agate lists of flyers and their times between stops.

Inevitably, the emphasis on competition pushed flyers to take risks they might otherwise have avoided—as one contestant later put it, "the human element is anxious to get there first." As they waited on the ground at Rawlins, Wales and Goldsborough knew they were near the front of the pack, with a fair chance to take the lead. And they wanted to get there first. They took off from Rawlins at 11:39 a.m., just twenty-four minutes behind Spaatz.

———

In better weather, the direct route would have posed no great challenge, but the DH-4's few instruments were of little help in the blinding snowstorm that Wales and Goldsborough encountered some twenty minutes after leaving the control stop. Now, as they approached Oberg Pass, they faced the consequences of their gamble.

Wales had been flying low to keep the terrain in sight. His aircraft was only about 150 feet off the ground when he tried to turn away from the side of Coad Mountain, glimpsed too late through the veil of snow. Like Crissy the day before, he stalled the plane and tipped it into a spin, with no time to recover. The DH-4 spiraled to the ground, coming to rest with its fuselage mostly intact but its wings broken and askew.

For a few minutes all was quiet save the muffled sounds of mountains in snow. Wales slumped motionless in his cockpit, wedged between the gas tank and the engine, blood pouring from a ragged hole in his fore head. Goldsborough, too, was unconscious, but his injuries were superficial and he soon recovered his senses. He extricated himself from the wreckage and then did the same for Wales. Despite the snow and piercing cold, he pulled off his clothing and tore strips from his underwear that he used to bind Wales's wounds. He covered the pilot with his flying coat, built a small fire with wood salvaged from the wreck, and propped up a broken aileron as a wind break. Then he stumbled off through the blizzard, his remaining clothes splotched with Wales's blood.

His plan was to find the ranch house he had seen from the air shortly before the crash. But Goldsborough was disoriented and set off in the wrong direction. Desperate and underdressed, he half-ran, half-skidded down the slope of Coad Mountain, skirting boulders and clumps of lodgepole pine. Sometimes he slipped and fell in the snow. Eventually he spotted another ranch house, in a basin about five miles from the

The wreckage of Wales and Goldsborough's DH-4 near the top of Coad Mountain. *National Archives*

downed plane. A rescue party was quickly organized. Cowboys saddled their horses, loaded them with blankets and coats, and headed back up the mountainside.

They had no difficulty following the trail made in the snow by Goldsborough's footsteps and the impressions of his body where he had fallen. But the rescuers arrived too late. Wales had been dead for hours.

14

Rain

On the other side of the country, pilots heading west also reckoned with deteriorating weather on the second day of the race. As in the mountain states, some learned of its arrival too late.

Pushed by a warm front, the storm that had passed through Chicago on the night of October 8, disrupting Maynard's sleep at Ashburn Field, continued its eastward march. Three flyers who spent the night in Bryan, Ohio, the last stop before Chicago, woke up to a downpour that foiled their plans to get away at sunrise. Rain also was falling at Martin Field in Cleveland. At 5:00 a.m. on October 9, the commander of that stop, Lt. W. H. Rice, sent a telegram to his counterpart one stop to the east in Buffalo, where eighteen aircraft had been staked down for the night. He warned the commander, Lt. A. B. Pitts, that it would not be safe for them to continue until the weather had improved.

Pitts never received the message, perhaps because of a "very, very poor Western Union operator" in Cleveland. The Weather Bureau only added to the confusion. Its forecast that rain would not arrive at Buffalo until nightfall was off by about twelve hours. By early morning, squalls and gusty winds already were sweeping across upstate New York.

As storm clouds gathered over Buffalo, some flyers grumbled that it was too dangerous to proceed. But Pitts, under pressure to keep the race on schedule, dismissed their concerns. Between sunrise and 8:30 a.m., when he finally conceded the obvious and ordered a halt to fur-

ther departures, fourteen aviators in eight planes—seven DH-4s and an
S.E.5 fighter—lifted off from Curtiss Field. "I was sent out of the Buffalo
Control Stop at sunrise before the weather report from Cleveland had
been received and against my desire," Lt. William C. F. Brown later
complained.

And with good reason. Minutes after taking off, he flew into a violent
storm.

———

Pilots could stay reasonably dry in their open cockpits. They sat deep
in the fuselage, protected by glass or celluloid windscreens that deflected
the slipstream and whatever moisture it might carry. But the rain could
have a dire effect on aircraft performance, mostly because of what it
did to propellers. Shaped from laminated hardwoods such as walnut or
mahogany, propeller blades whirled at speeds close to 400 miles an hour
at the tips. At that velocity, raindrops might just as well have been ball
bearings—which is why some manufacturers protected their props with
fabric or copper, at least along the leading edge. Others were simply var-
nished. Even a few minutes in rain could cause them to fray and start to
splinter. Longer exposure could whittle them down by inches, to the point
where they would stop generating sufficient thrust to keep an airplane in
the sky. One westbound pilot would replace his propeller four times by
the time he reached San Francisco.

The rain between Buffalo and Cleveland was accompanied by high
winds and at times was mixed with hail, which caused even more damage. Brown and three other DH-4 pilots decided that it was too risky to
continue. They set down in a field near Girard, Ohio, and took refuge in
a farmhouse, where their host served them a meal and cider. After the
skies cleared, the men resumed their flight to Cleveland, landing with
chewed-up propeller blades and wing fabric that had been torn away
in places. "The nastiest day I've ever seen for flying," one of the pilots
remarked.

Another flyer who had left Buffalo that morning, Lt. H. G. Norris,
landed on a field at the edge of Lake Erie, a few miles short of Cleveland,

A DH-4 propeller, its fabric covering in tatters, after flying through a storm.
National Archives

after his propeller was badly "feathered" by the rain. He motored to Martin Field to fetch a new one and completed the leg just before sunset.

Capt. John O. Donaldson, flying an S.E.5, had taken off among the same group at 7:54 a.m. Though not as maneuverable as some, the sturdy little fighter had a reputation for speed and easy handling; it was so "beautifully balanced" that one contestant wrote letters on his knee as he flew, glancing now and then at the compass and nudging the rudder bar with his toe if the plane started to wander off course. The fighter was propelled by one of the more reliable engines to emerge from the war, the lightweight, 180-horsepower Hispano-Suiza, or Hisso, which was designed by the Spanish automobile company of the same name and manufactured under license in the United States and elsewhere. It had a blunt nose that—at least in Donaldson's mind—conveyed a certain dourness of aspect. He had named the aircraft *Gloomy Gus*, painted in big yellow letters on the fuselage. Now he and *Gus* were in trouble. Rain and fog blanketed the route, and he flew at just 250 feet to keep the ground in sight. Before long he could sense that the S.E.5 was struggling to stay aloft, as the rain gnawed away at its propeller.

A more cautious—some might say prudent—pilot might have joined his comrades on the ground short of Cleveland. But Donaldson was used to pushing his luck. In fact, he was already famous for it.

———

At twenty-two, Donaldson was one of the youngest pilots in the race, though in photographs he looks even younger, with smooth cheeks and an inscrutable demeanor. The son of an Army general, he was born at Fort Yates, North Dakota, and spent much of his youth in South Carolina, while his father was serving in the Philippines. In 1916 he entered Cornell University to study engineering. After the United States declared war on Germany in 1917, he volunteered for the Signal Corps' Aviation Section—soon to become the Air Service—which sent him to Canada and Texas for flight training. He was subsequently attached to the Royal Air Force, one of about 300 Americans who flew for Britain during the war (most volunteered independently, before the United States entered the conflict). In the spring of 1918, Donaldson shipped out for England, where he completed his training with a course in pursuit tactics.

The young Air Service officer so impressed his British instructors that they selected him as one of the first ten Americans to fly the S.E.5, one of Britain's most advanced aircraft, in an RAF squadron at the front. "I am in the pool for France," he exulted in a letter to his aunt in June, while awaiting his transfer at a dreary outpost on England's northeast coast. It could not come soon enough. "This is a rotten place," he complained. "Food here is bad, there is no big town near here, it is cold all the time, you have to work like the dickens and worst of all you can't fly."

Donaldson got his wish in early July, when he traveled to Planques Aerodrome near Amiens to join the RAF's No. 32 Squadron. On July 22, he scored his first aerial victory, diving on a formation of twenty Fokker

D.VIIs with machine guns blazing. One of the enemy planes spiraled to the ground in flames; seven more would follow over the next five weeks.

Donaldson's flying skills were as unconventional as they were deadly. Among his fellow pilots, he was known as "the man who fought upside down," for his habit of attacking his German foes while inverted. The idea was to trick the enemy into thinking that *he* was the one flying upside down, causing momentary confusion that Donaldson could then exploit. (The S.E.5's rudder bars were fitted with metal stirrups to keep its pilot's boots in place during extreme maneuvers.) In the transcontinental contest, as in France, he was a contact flyer who rarely looked at his compass. "Unlike Lieutenant Maynard, he flies solely by instinct, traveling as near the ground as possible, picking out land marks and checking these up on his map," noted one account.

Donaldson would emerge from the war with a Distinguished Service Cross and formal recognition as an ace. But he was even more celebrated for his exploits on the ground, after he was shot down and taken prisoner.

His adventure began with what would turn out to be his last aerial engagement, on September 1. Alone against three enemy aircraft near the French town of Valenciennes, he maneuvered behind one of them and opened fire at close range—then followed its smoke trail to earth when his own plane was riddled with bullets. He crash-landed behind enemy lines, unhurt, and watched as the German pilot "burnt to death in his plane," as he later wrote matter-of-factly to his parents. He was captured minutes later.

Donaldson immediately set to plotting his escape. On his third night in captivity, he and another American airman, Lt. Oscar Mandel, jumped out a second-story window of a temporary prison in the French town of Condé-sur-l'Escaut on the Belgian border. Still in their Army uniforms, they walked for several hours until they came to a German airfield. They were trying to push a two-seat observation plane out of its hangar—"I was sure that I could fly it," Donaldson later wrote—when they were confronted by a German sentry, who bayoneted Donaldson in the back. Mandel clubbed the German with a flashlight and the two fugitives fled. Donaldson's wound was not serious and was bandaged with help from a French family. The men were recaptured a few days later while trying to ford a stream between German and British lines.

The story might have ended there, if not for Donaldson's persistence. Two weeks after their return to another prison near Belgium, he and Mandel got their hands on a saw blade and used it to cut a hole in the roof. The next night they and three other prisoners—two American pilots and a British noncommissioned officer—escaped through the opening and set off on foot, crossing into Belgium at dawn. Their plan was to walk across the occupied country to the Netherlands, which had remained neutral in the war.

Two of the escapees—Mandel and the Briton—were recaptured in Brussels after a few days. But Donaldson and the others slipped the German net and kept moving, aided along the way by Belgians who provided them with food, shelter, and civilian clothes. After twenty-eight days and more than 200 miles on foot, they reached a village near the Dutch border, where a man hid them in his home. The border was protected by German soldiers and a 5,000-volt electric fence. On the night of October 23, after procuring a pair of rubber-handled wire cutters, Donaldson and his companions wriggled to the fence on their bellies and escaped into the Netherlands in a shower of sparks.

———

Donaldson returned home as something of a celebrity. He wrote a lengthy account of his escape for *Harper's Monthly*, made a speech at the New York Aeronautical Exposition, and opined in newspapers on the future of aviation, for which he had lost none of his zeal. He was particularly enthralled by the prospects for flying as a sport, predicting in the *New York Herald* on March 16, 1919—a day after the exposition closed—that airplane races would soon become more popular than contests between automobiles or boats. "The boat of the air," wrote Donaldson, whose flying skills perhaps exceeded his literary ones, "will win thousands of sportsmen who have found no joy in the races of water craft."

Donaldson went on to propose a new kind of contest—an "aerial steeplechase"—in which pilots would perform aerobatic maneuvers at designated points along a course. "The thrill to the spectators when a horse comes a cropper is as nothing compared to seeing a plane fall into a tailspin when coming out of a loop," he declared.

Donaldson competed in the New York–Toronto race, also in an S.E.5, but dropped out because of a cracked crankcase (a mechanic had forgotten to fill the crankcase with oil). Now he had another chance. So he flew on through the rain, landing at Cleveland at 9:23 a.m. that morning of October 9. Only then could he inspect his propeller. The rain had chewed two inches from the tips and an inch from the leading edge.

The close call did nothing to diminish Donaldson's confidence in himself or his storm-battered fighter. "She's some sweet little bus," Donaldson told reporters at Martin Field, predicting that he would be among the first of the westbound flyers to reach California.

In the meantime, though, he was stuck on the ground, waiting impatiently for his propeller to be replaced and for Rice, the control stop commander, to lift the hold on departures from the field. At 12:59 p.m., with the visibility somewhat improved, Donaldson was allowed to take off. He reached Chicago just before sunset.

Bad weather continued to stymie the progress of westbound pilots who lagged behind. One of them was Brailey Gish, the brash former track star with the shattered legs whose DH-4 had caught fire near Ithaca the day before. Soon after starting the race at Mineola for a second time, he flew into heavy rain. At Binghamton, Gish found four other stragglers, who called themselves the "Hoodoo Quartet" because they also had been delayed for one reason or another. Now they were grounded because of the weather. Gish joined the other pilots in the Red Cross tent, where they swapped stories and snacked on pie and sandwiches to the scratchy accompaniment of a Victrola gramophone. Late in the afternoon on October 9 the men stepped outside to check the sky, hoping they might still get away before sunset. Then the airfield commander sent word to the contrary, and the pilots filed disconsolately back to the tent. They would remain in Binghamton overnight.

Harold Hartney, in Cleveland, also lost a day of flying, though he made good use of the delay. With morning departures on October 9 stalled by rain, he wired Billy Mitchell for permission to install a makeshift nine-gallon fuel tank behind the pilot's seat of his Fokker. Such modifications technically were against the rules, but Hartney argued that he would need the extra gas to safely cross the Rocky Mountains. After Mitchell approved the new tank, Hartney spent the day supervising its installation by workers from the Martin factory.

By late afternoon on October 9, the rain at Buffalo had stopped, though the winds remained fierce. Lt. Fred Nelson and his observer decided they still had time to make it to Cleveland. Other pilots tried to dissuade them from leaving, but Pitts, the control stop commander, apparently did not intervene. The two men took off at 4:40 p.m. Battling gale-force headwinds, they flew west for thirty-nine minutes before turning back to Curtiss Field, where searchlights guided them to a safe landing.

Accidents forced several westbound pilots from the race. Col. C. C. Culver, flying one of the three Fokkers in the race, had departed Rochester against his own better judgment, after the local commander told him, "No orders to stop." Within minutes, Culver flew into heavy rain. The engine of his Fokker started sputtering. He set down on a field and smashed his wings and undercarriage. Lt. H. D. Smith, who departed Rochester an hour behind Culver, got lost in the rain near Buffalo. He landed his DH-4 to ask directions, then tried to take off again. A gust blew his plane into an apple tree.

Among the westbound pilots, Lt. Alexander Roberts and his observer, Lt. Marion Elliott, had perhaps the narrowest escape of the day, though it had nothing to do with the weather. They were fighting through the rain from Buffalo to Cleveland when their throttle control rod broke. This was an emergency in the best of circumstances, but especially so when flying several miles off the shore of Lake Erie. The DH-4 rapidly lost altitude, and Roberts prepared to land in the water. In hopes of a quick rescue, he aimed the nose toward a Canadian steamer several miles distant.

But the men still had a last card to play. As the aircraft "volplaned"—

glided—toward the steamer, Elliott climbed out of the rear cockpit and gingerly stepped forward onto the lower wing, using struts and bracing wires as handholds. If he could work his way to the engine, he might be able to open the throttle by hand and keep the plane aloft. Buffeted by the slipstream, he began a precarious shuffle along the wing root. He never reached the engine. With the water fast approaching, Roberts yelled at him to get back to his seat.

Seconds later the plane splashed into the lake, its nose slightly down. The aircraft lurched to a violent stop, then righted itself and bobbed on the surface. Roberts and Elliott stood on the wreckage for forty minutes, until they were rescued by the steamer.

Sunset on October 9 brought a grim accounting. Wrecked or disabled planes were strewn across the countryside from New York to Chicago, and the picture was little better in the West, where Wales had died on Coad Mountain and others had dropped out of the contest after damaging their planes in forced landings. One pair of aviators had been reported missing in a snowstorm east of Salt Lake City, though they later turned up unharmed after landing their DH-4 in the sagebrush near Bitter Creek, Wyoming. On both sides of the country, some pilots had yet to progress beyond the first or second stop. And more bad weather was in store.

Wales's death raised the body count in the competition to four. The "world's greatest air race," less than forty-eight hours old, was starting to look like a tragedy tinged with farce. Not that Mitchell needed reminding; he had begun the second day of the race by crossing the Potomac River to Arlington National Cemetery, where he attended the funeral of his old friend Townsend Dodd, killed days earlier in Pennsylvania while flying to Long Island to start the contest. Caroline spent part of the week consoling Dodd's widow at the Mitchells' home.

After the funeral, Mitchell returned to the Munitions Building for an afternoon of office work, some of which probably involved drafting a statement issued by the Air Service that evening. "The recent deaths in connection with the great transcontinental race clearly point out the great necessity of municipal landing fields," it read. "Landing fields have been hastily laid out at several control stops along the continent, but had each city along the route had a permanent landing field it might have avoided several of the accidents which have occurred."

No one disputed the need for more airfields, but the Air Service's implication—that the fatalities could have been avoided if only cities had been wise enough to heed its earlier pleas to build them—was disingenuous. The accidents had little or nothing to do with landing facilities. Few, in any case, were buying the Air Service's claim. Some began to question why the race was being run in the first place.

In an editorial prompted by Wales's death in Wyoming, the *Buffalo Express* wrote:

> Without the stimulus of a great race, this man would not have been trying to cross the mountains under such weather conditions. Even if he had been at the front in the great war, it would not have been thought worth the risk to send him aloft in a snowstorm. Four deaths already have occurred since the race began. This peacetime test of machines is becoming almost as deadly as the air-campaigning over the German lines. Is the game worth such sacrifices? Could not the qualities of airplanes be adequately tested without contests that involve the lives of so many brave men?

Mitchell could only hope for better news in the days ahead.

15

Time and Space

Belvin Maynard and William Kline rose early on the morning of Thursday, October 9, after their restless night in Chicago. Neither felt much like eating, which was probably just as well. Not long after taking off from Ashburn Field at 7:09 a.m., Maynard was nearly airsick for the first time in his life, as his plane was tossed around by a gusty south wind. He later called it "the roughest weather I have ever flown in."

At least the flight to the next stop, at Rock Island, Illinois, was relatively short. Maynard flew low to stay beneath lingering clouds. Among the first to learn of his imminent arrival—from an Associated Press bulletin reporting that Maynard had left Chicago—was a reporter for the *Rock Island Argus*. The newsman dashed to the field nine miles east of the city, ahead of the control officer, and rousted four enlisted men from their tent. They were still positioning the landing T when Maynard came "roaring in from the east." He circled the field once and swooped in for a landing, nearly "knocking the chimney off the school house across the road," or so the reporter claimed.

"I'm a little late," Maynard told the *Argus* man. "It was a mighty rough passage."

The reporter had to shout his questions; Maynard had been temporarily deafened by the Liberty engine's earsplitting roar. After a few minutes on the ground, his hearing returned along with his appetite, and he asked if he might get breakfast. Alas, Red Cross volunteers had not yet turned up to open the canteen. He and Kline took off for Des Moines on empty stomachs.

The near-gale that had made their passage from Chicago so unpleasant had become a headwind that slowed their ground speed to just ninety miles an hour. As Maynard was all too aware, the same wind would boost the speed of planes flying in the opposite direction. He began to have "visions" of Lowell Smith, Carl Spaatz, and Emil Kiel sweeping past him on their sprint to the East Coast. His hopes of being the first man across the continent began to fade.

Finally he spotted the gold dome of the Iowa state capitol in Des Moines. On landing at Herring Field, on the outskirts of the city, he found "lots of good things to eat and a fine corps of fair women reporters from the local press." Maynard resumed his journey in calmer winds and a better mood.

Clouds covered much of the leg to Omaha. Maynard flew above them, his map all but useless now. Like a mariner on the open sea, he navigated by dead reckoning, estimating his position on the basis of course, speed, and time measured from a previously known "fix." Near Omaha the clouds began to part, and Maynard caught glimpses of ridges, hardwood forests, and low hills, "which seemed to be there to give us a little foretaste of what was coming."

The public was by now fully engaged with the race between Maynard and his eastbound rivals. About 200 people, including photographers and "every newspaper reporter in Nebraska," turned out to watch Maynard's arrival at Omaha. After circling the field at low altitude, he coasted in for a perfect three-point landing, touching down simultaneously on his main wheels and tail skid. He and Kline had a quick lunch and then were on their way.

Maynard flew west above a rippling ocean of corn. Since leaving Chicago that morning, the farm boy and seminarian from North Carolina, who in all likelihood had never traveled west of the Mississippi, had been struck by both the monotony and the bounty of the flat midwestern landscape. He marveled at the huge grain farms with their "large and commodious outbuildings" and a land so rich that "a retired farmer is considered nothing unusual."

Maynard was slowly gaining altitude as he headed across the Great Plains toward the Rockies. Rectangular fields gave way to grasslands dotted with cattle and sheep, neither of which seemed to have much experience with airplanes. Cattle, he observed, would scatter at the sound of his engine, while "sheep hundreds strong would huddle together" in a woolly ball, "the whole mass revolving like the disk of a gramophone."

But sightseeing was a secondary concern. By the time he reached St. Paul, Nebraska, the next stop west of Omaha, the pressure of competition was beginning to show. "I don't need any lunch," Maynard barked from his cockpit, moments after shutting down his engine. "Give me forty gallons of gas!" He turned down an offer of coffee—Maynard had never touched the stuff and didn't intend to start now—though he gratefully accepted a glass of milk.

The crowd, though smaller than the one at Omaha, was no less dazzled by his presence. "When did you leave New York, lieutenant?" asked the editor of the St. Paul *Phonograph*, though he surely knew the answer. "Here we were halfway across the continent from New York," the newsman subsequently wrote, "and yet a real live man, a human being, telling us he had left New York yesterday morning!"

The next stop was North Platte, Nebraska, at an elevation of 3,000 feet on the river of the same name. The air grew colder as Maynard gained altitude. After landing, he and Kline found their way to a tent where they could warm themselves next to an oil heater.

A moment later, Lowell Smith joined them in the tent, having just flown in from Sidney to the west. The two leaders in the race had a brief, friendly chat, then hustled back to their planes, determined to make the most of the remaining daylight.

———

Spaatz and Kiel were not far behind. Kiel landed at North Platte at 4:45 p.m., while Smith was still warming his engine; Smith took off four minutes and thirty seconds later. He had barely cleared the field when Spaatz touched down. Their three-way contest could not have been much closer.

At least for the time being, Smith would preserve his narrow lead among the eastbound flyers. Tired and hungry, their faces reddened by wind and cold, Spaatz and Kiel reached the next stop, at St. Paul, shortly before sunset, too late to continue. Townspeople were delighted to host the two flyers, who reluctantly accepted an invitation to a church festival. ("That's hardship on a couple of tired men," Spaatz said later.)

Meanwhile, Smith pressed on toward Omaha in the dwindling light. Soldiers at the control stop, alerted to his departure from St. Paul, readied Very pistols to send up flares at the sound of his engine, but the aviator managed to locate the field on his own. He landed at 7:20 p.m. central time. Since leaving Salt Lake City in the morning he had covered 852 miles, for a total of 1,460 miles over two days.

It was not enough to catch Maynard. After a quick flight from Sidney in western Nebraska, Maynard landed on the rough, hastily prepared field at Fort D. A. Russell in Cheyenne at 6:22 p.m. mountain time, just two minutes after Smith touched down at Omaha. Despite the headwinds along his route, he had flown 866 miles—slightly more than Smith—and was ahead of him by more than 200 miles, having logged 1,696 miles since leaving Long Island. Maynard's closest pursuer from the east, Capt. Harry Drayton, was still in Des Moines, nearly 600 miles to his east.

One of the many aeronautical advances to emerge from World War I was the ability to operate at night. Germany led the way by launching bombers after dark, which reduced their vulnerability to anti-aircraft fire. Allied forces countered with squadrons of fighters whose pilots were schooled in the tactics of "night pursuit," a subject on which Harold Hartney had written a manual.

Still, night flying remained a dangerous business, even apart from the threat posed by the enemy. Navigation was all the more difficult when landmarks were cloaked in darkness. Landing was the biggest challenge.

Airfields were haphazardly lit by searchlights or fires, if they were illuminated at all. To see the ground as it approached, pilots relied on parachute flares or sometimes flares attached to the wingtips, which were triggered mechanically from the cockpit. Both had drawbacks, including the risk that wingtip flares would set fire to fabric-covered wings if an airplane overturned. The Air Service recently had begun experimenting with a safer alternative, automobile headlights rigged to landing gear.

But night operations remained a rarity in peacetime and were banned entirely for pilots in the race, who were supposed to land by sunset. Both Maynard and Smith had broken this rule—by twenty-five minutes in Smith's case—prompting speculation in the press that one or both would be disqualified. A few days hence, another pilot would be tossed from the race for the arguably less serious offense of failing to circle the field at Battle Mountain before landing.

In this case, however, an exception would be made. Billy Mitchell was jubilant over the performance of the two front-runners, and of Maynard in particular; in a news release, the War Department boasted that Maynard had "annihilated time and space" between North Platte and Sidney, having covered the 112-mile distance in just fifty-eight minutes. Mitchell was not about to end this duel just as it was getting interesting. The American Flying Club put out a statement hailing both frontrunners for their "remarkable performances." Speaking with reporters in Washington, D.C., Air Service officials explained that the sunset rule "did not contemplate penalizing a flier when it was necessary for him to continue for a short time in order to reach a control station."

Maynard had pushed hard to make Cheyenne, and now he was exhausted and starving. "All I want is sleep and to get started at sunrise tomorrow," he told a reporter. After dismounting their plane, he and his mechanic were shown to the Red Cross tent, where they dined on steaming bowls of oyster stew made with heavy cream. Nothing had ever tasted so good.

Before retiring to their sleeping quarters at Fort D. A. Russell, pilot and mechanic tended to their plane, covering the cockpit with canvas and draining the radiator to prevent it from freezing overnight.

———

Mitchell could only have been gratified by the press coverage of Maynard's speedy progress toward the Pacific, which eclipsed the grim news of the previous day. The minister's arrival in Cheyenne would be reported the next morning on front pages across the country, vying for prominence with the Cincinnati Reds' victory over the Chicago White Sox in the final game of the World Series at Comiskey Park. In the meantime, an enterprising editor at the *San Francisco Examiner* had telegraphed Maynard at Cheyenne, asking him to "put on the wire for us tonight a signed story of the interesting points in your remarkable flight as far as Cheyenne."

It was rather a lot to ask of a pilot at the end of a grueling day, but Maynard obliged with a one-sentence dispatch that appeared under his byline the following morning. "I hope to make San Francisco by sunset tomorrow," it read.

16

Hungry Hogs and a Telegraph Pole

John Donaldson was low on gas. *Gloomy Gus* did not have a fuel gauge, but he knew how much its fuel tank held—thirty-one gallons—and could estimate how much he'd burned since filling it at Rock Island that morning of Friday, October 10. There couldn't be much left. The distance from Rock Island to Des Moines was 158 miles, and he'd been bucking a headwind the whole way. Now, after flying for almost two hours, he'd arrived over the Iowa capital near the limit of the fighter's range.

He was still some distance from the airfield when his engine sputtered to a stop. Donaldson was a glider pilot now. He dropped the nose to maintain flying speed and urgently scanned the ground for a place big enough to land. There were not a lot of options.

———

Any pilot with more than a few hours of experience had made at least one forced landing, and often many more. Engines routinely failed, sometimes for mechanical reasons, sometimes because of contaminated gas, or sometimes—as in Donaldson's case—simply for the lack of it. At other times, aviators were forced to land because of a sudden turn in the weather or because they were lost and needed to ask directions. Even if a flight were going smoothly, a prudent pilot made a habit of scanning the terrain for suitable landing areas within gliding distance, and fretted in their absence. The practice persists today, especially among pilots of single-engine planes. Because you just never know.

A true emergency was a test of discipline and skill. Separate and apart from the question of where to land, a pilot had to stay focused on flying the airplane. As soon as the engine stopped, he had to match the airspeed indicator to the most efficient glide speed—about seventy miles an hour in a DH-4—so the aircraft would not descend more quickly than necessary. Only then could he pick out a place to land, and commit to it. This required keen judgment, especially when the choices were few. "Fields of rocks, boulders, brush, high corn and other vegetation should be avoided whenever possible," advised the Army's *Manual of Military Aviation*.

Unfortunately, that wasn't always possible. Many an aviator had stalled and spun in while trying to "stretch" a glide to more favorable terrain beyond the reach of his stricken airplane. Even when a landing area was well within gliding distance, the pilot of a disabled aircraft had to set up the approach with extra care, so as not to overshoot or undershoot. Without a functioning engine there would be no opportunity for a "go-around," or second attempt. Finally, a pilot had to remember to switch off the ignition to reduce the risk of fire.

Aviators who kept their heads usually walked away from forced landings with little or no damage to themselves or their planes. Setting down on a cultivated field was not much different than landing at a designated airfield, especially if it were shorn of crops (and if it wasn't, the pilot or his employer could expect a bill from a farmer to cover the damage). Controlled landings on rougher ground were more challenging but rarely fatal, even if they sometimes ended with a pilot suspended upside down in his safety harness. With a little luck, a good flyer could survive a landing in a tree. The trick was to dissipate forward momentum by stalling just a few feet above the highest branches—the method known as pancaking, which also came in handy when setting down on hillsides or other inhospitable terrain.

Once an aircraft was no longer flying, a pilot still had to bring it to a stop—an especially urgent need on small fields fringed with trees or fence posts. Complicating matters was that airplanes of the day had no brakes, which would not come into widespread use until paved runways made them necessary in the 1930s. Until that day, flyers who needed to stop in a hurry sometimes resorted to desperate measures. On October 9, the second day of the transcontinental race, Lt. E. M. Manzelman had arrived over Chicago near dusk and could not find the control stop at Ashburn Field. Rather than keep flying after dark, he landed on the baseball diamond at Washington Park. The plane touched down and rolled toward a clump of trees—and would have hit them if not for Manzelman's civilian mechanic, Max Goodnough, who climbed out on the wing and dragged his boots along the ground like a "human anchor," as the *Chicago Tribune* put it the next day. Manzelman did not understand how the aircraft had stopped until he looked to one side and saw Goodnough clinging to a strut. (Hoping to find the control stop before sunset, Manzelman took off, got lost a second time, and returned to the same park for the night. He reached Ashburn Field the next morning, after phoning the *Tribune*'s newsroom for directions.)

The press could not get enough of these stories. In fact, to anyone following newspaper coverage of the race, it might have seemed that pilots landed more frequently *between* control stops than *at* control stops. The consequences were rarely serious, except perhaps for the airplanes. After his water pump failed over the Sierra Nevada, Maj. Henry Abbey, Jr., pancaked his DH-4 onto a rocky hillside, hitting a small pear tree and breaking his propeller and landing gear. Lt. Hiram W. Sheridan landed his DH-4 on a "bald hill" near Ithaca—his third forced landing of the race—after its radiator developed a leak; though he had switched off the ignition, the engine was still so hot that it kept firing and "pulled us through a small fence." He then swerved to avoid a ravine, completing the job of wrecking his airplane. Lt. G. B. Newman, the only Marine in the race, turned turtle in mudflats near Salduro after landing with an ignition problem.

Often a forced landing was a prelude to another ordeal. Lt. H. E. Queen and his mechanic "slept in a snowdrift" after they landed near Laramie, Wyoming, to wait out a blizzard. Lt. Robert S.

Worthington, who landed his S.E.5 in similar conditions, spent the night in a sheep wagon. Another pair of flyers, whose DH-4 went down with engine trouble in Nevada, had to push it across the desert to a road two miles distant so it could be dismantled and loaded onto a truck. The sand was so soft that they and two enlisted men sent from Reno had to lay planks in front of each wheel, removing and replacing them with every few feet of progress.

In the Midwest, pilots frequently set down on farms, where they generally could expect a hearty meal and perhaps a bed if they needed to stay the night. But they still had to worry about their planes. Early in the race, a DH-4 that landed near Stillwell, Indiana, in the midst of a rainstorm was set upon by hogs with a taste for aircraft linen. They gnawed two holes in the rudder before they could be driven away.

Human beings—especially those inclined toward the popular pastime of souvenir hunting—also posed a threat. Lt. Col. John Reynolds and Lt. Ralph Bagby, who landed on a rye field in Buchanan, Michigan, after losing their way in fog, were so worried that someone would steal something off their DH-4 that they spent the night with it, one standing guard while the other tried to sleep (the farmer who owned the field later billed the Air Service $100 for damage to his crop). Souvenir hunters could be remarkably brazen; during a stop at Rochester, a westbound contestant observed a youth with a lit cigarette leaning over his gas tank while casually removing a couple of small parts. Another pilot flew bare-handed across the Wasatch Range after a souvenir hunter stole his mittens.

————

Donaldson did not have the option of landing on a farm. In fact, he could hardly have picked a worse place to run out of gas. Below him was Highland Park, a bustling neighborhood in north-central Des Moines. Landing in such a congested area risked injury not just to himself but also to people on the ground.

After hasty consideration of his choices, he settled on one of the few open spaces within gliding distance—a small, informal baseball field. Bisected by a stream, it was flanked on three sides by houses and trees, and on the fourth by a twenty-foot-high fence; Donaldson later compared it to a "back yard." Nevertheless, it would have to do. He banked toward the tiny field and set up for his approach. Paying careful attention to his glide path and rate of descent, he floated in over the fence, just above stall speed, and touched his wheels on the grass. The fighter "rolled gently over the diamond, through the stream, and stopped within ten feet of a telegraph pole."

Donaldson was down, with no damage to himself or his airplane. He quickly found someone to supply him with enough gas to reach Herring Field and prepared to take off—an even bigger challenge than landing. If he tried to take off normally, he would not leave the ground in time to clear the trees. So he drafted three men to hold the plane's wings while he ran the Hisso up to full power. Then, on his signal, they released the plane, which fairly "leaped" into the air. It cleared the trees by two feet.

Donaldson was leapfrogging ahead of the competition. That morning of October 10, he had woken up at Ashburn Field, the Chicago control stop, which now resembled a "lake" after intermittent heavy rains. Of the four pilots who had spent the night there, he was the only one to get away from the control stop that day; two pilots flying heavier planes—DH-4s—tried to do so but nosed over in the muck as they taxied into position for takeoff. At Rock Island, he had passed another contestant, leaving only Belvin Maynard and Harry Drayton in front of him.

His emergency landing in Des Moines caused only a short delay. After reaching the city's control stop at Herring Field and adding another twenty-eight gallons of gas to his tank, he departed the airfield for Omaha, where his nimble little fighter alighted "like a dragonfly on a thistle top."

Donaldson was by now "a bundle of nerves and anxiety," desperate to close the gap with his rivals to the west. "Here, don't touch that!" he snapped at one of the soldiers tending his plane at Omaha. He hurried to the control officer's tent, where he presented his logbook for signing and reviewed a map showing the location of the next stop at St. Paul, making a rough sketch to take with him. He grabbed a roast beef sandwich, smeared his throat with Vaseline—for protection against the cold—and resumed his flight to the west.

The weather back East was not much better than that the day before. After his second night in Cleveland, Harold Hartney took off at dawn on Friday, October 10, under low clouds threatening rain. He had determined that the next stop, at Bryan, Ohio, was well within range of his Fokker, so he had not bothered to fill his new emergency fuel tank to capacity, adding only a couple of gallons to ensure that it functioned properly. But strong headwinds slowed his progress. About twenty miles short of his destination, he ran out of fuel. He landed in a field and sent a farmer to buy ten gallons of gas, then completed his flight to Bryan—"a cold dreary, dismal place"—in driving rain. Hartney had little hope of continuing that day. To pass the time, he and several other pilots attended a high school football game.

The weather was a little better the next morning, Saturday, October 11, with fair visibility and a 2,000-foot ceiling. Five pilots took off for Chicago before noon. But Hartney was not among them. It was still raining lightly, and he did not want to risk his propeller. Fokker parts were in short supply, and he feared he would not be able to replace it. He finally got away at 3:08 p.m. and reached Chicago ninety minutes later. After snacking at the Red Cross canteen, he started for Rock Island—only to make his second forced landing in as many days, after his main fuel tank lost air pressure. The problem was easily fixed, but by then it was dark; Hartney had no choice but to accept a farmer's invitation to spend the night. He completed the leg to Rock Island the next morning, resigned to the knowledge that he would be stuck there until the following day, because Mitchell had barred flying on Sundays. (The prohibition had less to do with the Sabbath than with pilots' need to rest and tend to their machines.)

That night Hartney attended a service led by Billy Sunday, one of the nation's most famous evangelists, who invited him and a few other pilots to join him on the platform of his tabernacle. It was small compensation for the delay.

———

Brailey Gish trailed the front of the pack by an even wider margin, but as he readied his plane at Binghamton on Friday morning, he did not seem the least bit discouraged. "I'm going out to overhaul the Martin Bomber and reclaim my passenger, Captain De Lavergne," he bragged to a reporter, "and then do my damndest to win!"

Or perhaps not. Gish was barely a third of the way to Rochester when he made his second forced landing of the race, this time because of an oil leak. He borrowed a farmer's phone to contact the Thomas-Morse Aircraft Corporation factory in nearby Ithaca, which dispatched a mechanic with a can of oil. The leak was plugged with a six-penny nail and the oil reservoir refilled. Gish flew on to Rochester, then to Buffalo's Curtiss Field, where he landed at 3:42 p.m. He still expected to make Cleveland by sunset, so it must have been a bitter disappointment to learn that Pitts, the control officer at Buffalo, had put a stop to any departures. With gale-force headwinds from the west, Pitts was worried about planes running out of gas over Lake Erie.

Gish had been on the ground for less than ten minutes when another DH-4 descended toward the muddy landing path, where soft spots were marked with red flags. Maj. A. L. Sneed was nearly out of gas after flying for three hours from Rochester against a strong headwind. Just before his wheels touched, spectators observed what to most was an extraordinary and baffling sight: Sneed's mechanic, having unfastened his safety belt, stood up in the rear cockpit and slid back onto the fuselage, which he straddled as if it were a horse.

It looked like an ill-considered stunt. In fact, it was a common practice inspired by the DH-4's well-known tendency to nose over on rough or soggy fields. The idea was to hold down the tail. If the man in the back thought the plane was at risk of nosing over, he levered himself onto the fuselage and slid back toward the vertical stabilizer, or tail fin, where he remained until the aircraft stopped rolling. The day before, Maynard's mechanic, William Kline, had done the same thing while landing on the soft field in Des Moines. "This is the only 'movie stuff' we pulled off on the entire trip," Maynard later wrote.

Kline had at least waited until the wheels were on the ground. At San Francisco on the day before the race began, Emil Kiel's mechanic, Sgt. Frank McKee, had exited the cockpit while Kiel was still airborne. He had not anticipated that Kiel would come in high and abort the landing. Blasted by the slipstream, "clinging for dear life," he remained on the fuselage with his back pressed against the tail fin as Kiel circled the field for a second attempt. Kiel landed successfully, but there was no denying the risk. On the fourth day of the race, Harry Drayton was riding in the rear seat of his DH-4 while his observer, Lt. Lester Sweeley, took a turn at the controls. The engine began acting up, and Sweeley decided to land on a plowed field near Lovelock, Nevada. Just before the plane touched down, Drayton left his cockpit and slid back on the fuselage, but his weight was not enough to keep the tail on the ground. The aircraft tipped on its nose and catapulted him over the wings.

Drayton was lucky: He landed, unhurt, in the soft loam, and the plane did not turn over completely, suffering only a bent radiator. The damage was easily repaired, and Drayton later found humor in the incident. "I recommend that in the future all pilots wear spurs so they will not be thrown off the tail of their ship," he wrote in an official report.

Sneed's mechanic, Sgt. Worth McClure, would not be so fortunate. Buffeted by the strong wind and trying to avoid the red flags just in front of him, Sneed landed much too hard, bouncing the airplane to a height of about fifty feet. Now in real trouble, he gunned the engine to slow his descent, but a gust knocked the plane out of balance. The right wing hit the ground, and the DH-4 tipped onto its nose, launching McClure from his perch on the fuselage "like a stone flung from a slingshot." He landed on his head and shoulders, breaking his neck.

As McClure lay unconscious, a Red Cross ambulance raced onto the field. He died on the way to the hospital.

Gish, who likely witnessed the accident, would spend the night in Buffalo, hoping for a better day ahead. But for that, his luck would have to change. As one newspaper put it the next morning, "It appears that John L. Hoodoo is still pursuing him."

Gish had hoped to log as many miles as possible before the required layover on Sunday. But he did not get away from Buffalo until afternoon on Saturday, October 11, during a break in the rain. Even then he had to fly just 200 feet above the ground because the visibility was so poor. By the time he landed at Cleveland at 3:26 p.m., the rain had started up again, dashing his hopes of further progress before sunset.

The only consolation was that his DH-4 already was in need of repair. At least now he would have time to work on it.

———————

In Cheyenne on the morning of Friday, October 10, Maynard remained comfortably in the lead among the westbound pilots, and he was determined to keep his promise to reach San Francisco by sunset. He and Kline had risen at Fort D. A. Russell before dawn. Now, as the sun crept over the eastern horizon, he sat in his cockpit and warmed up the Liberty engine, watching the temperature gauge and listening to the familiar percussive clatter of valves and rocker arms. Everything seemed fine. Then, with no warning, the temperature jumped alarmingly, followed by a loud pop. A cloud of smoke blew in Maynard's face. Fearing the Liberty had caught fire, he switched off the ignition, scrambled to the ground, and joined his mechanic at the nose.

As smoke billowed from beneath the cowling, Kline stared at a puddle of water on the ground. "You have burst your radiator," he said. "It can't be anything else."

Maynard was baffled and dismayed. To prevent this very outcome, they had drained the radiator the night before, refilling it in the morning. But it didn't take long to solve the mystery. Water in the overflow pipe had frozen overnight, forming a plug that prevented the water in the radiator from expanding. So it had found another way out.

The day had started with promise. After a comfortable night at the Army post, Maynard rose at 5:30 a.m. He had every reason to believe that he would reach the Pacific coast by sunset, just as he had promised the readers of the *San Francisco Examiner*. His route would cover 842 miles, slightly fewer than he had flown from Chicago the day before, and the weather, at least in southeastern Wyoming, looked favorable, with clear skies and a moderate breeze blowing out of the southwest. He and Kline headed out to the field with plans to get away by the time the sun rose at 7:06 a.m.

Now Maynard could feel his lead slipping away. He helped Kline get started on removing the radiator, then telegraphed the control stop commander at Rawlins to inquire about the status of a DH-4 that had been damaged during a botched landing the day before. Was the aircraft, which had started in San Francisco, out of the race? And if so, could the radiator be salvaged and driven to Cheyenne? Told that the damaged plane was being repaired and that its pilot planned to continue, Maynard realized that he would have to solve the problem on his own.

He took the radiator to a garage in Cheyenne and watched anxiously as a mechanic filled it with water to find out where it had ruptured. To Maynard's relief, the mechanic found only one hole, which was quickly sealed. Maynard raced back to the field, stopping once so his driver could change a flat tire. By now it was late morning and a crowd had gathered, including an Indian chief who approached Maynard to offer his greetings and ask for an airplane ride. Maynard politely demurred. The radiator was reconnected and bolted into place. After a quick bowl of oyster stew, Maynard took off at 12:20 p.m., more than five hours behind schedule.

Just ahead was the layered, imposing rampart of the Medicine Bow Mountains. Before Maynard departed Cheyenne, the control stop commander had counseled him against flying straight across the range to Rawlins, urging him to follow the safer but longer route along the Union Pacific tracks. With the death of Edward Wales fresh in his mind, the officer repeated his admonition so many times that Maynard was reminded of his first days as a preacher, when he "would stand in the pulpit and tell the same story over and over again because I could think of nothing else to say."

Still, Maynard took the warning seriously and departed the field with every intention of heeding it. His resolve crumbled, however, when he took a careful look at his map and realized that following the tracks would add seventy miles to his flight. "When you are racing every mile counts," he recalled. "I changed my mind and headed out across the mountains."

It was, in the end, an uneventful crossing. The storm clouds of the day before had dissipated, and the air over the mountains was smooth. Maynard was awed by the beauty of the high peaks with their mantle of glistening snow. Occasionally, he passed above isolated mining settlements where children spilled from tiny schoolhouses, waving and staring with upturned faces. Maynard guessed that their teachers had declared recess at the sound of his engine. He reached Rawlins at 2:10 p.m. and departed after forty-three minutes.

The next leg was long, cold, and even lonelier than the one that preceded it. Maynard had decided to fly direct to Salt Lake City, skipping the stop at Green River, Wyoming; though the field had mostly dried, it was dangerous in a crosswind, and he saw no reason to risk a landing there. But the longer trip would push the limit of his fuel supply, especially because he would be battling a quartering headwind from the northwest. He could take no comfort from the terrain. The flight across southwestern Wyoming seemed interminable as the DH-4 droned above barren mountains and high desert plateaus empty of human beings and even livestock. A forced landing, Maynard knew, would mean "a long walk at least." The air was frigid; he and Kline were grateful for the wool sweaters and balaclavas that the Red Cross man had given them in Cheyenne.

Finally, after two and a half hours of flying, Maynard crested the Wasatch Range and caught his first glimpse of the Utah capital, with the Great Salt Lake gleaming in the distance. He descended along roughly the same route followed by Mormon pioneers in 1847, emerging over the foothills northeast of the city just as the mountaintops were turning purple in the late-afternoon light.

Maynard's plane dropped "like an arrow" toward Buena Vista Field, prompting cheers from a crowd of several thousand. "Lookit 'im come!" exclaimed one of the enlisted men assigned to the stop. Another was more colorful: "That boy sure is some throttle bustin', sky jazzin', aviatin' baby!"

Maynard could not have cut it any closer. As he approached the field, his engine ran out of gas. He had just enough altitude to glide to a safe landing.

Trixie was, perhaps, even more relieved than her master to finally be on the ground. Almost as soon as the airplane stopped rolling, she scrambled from the cockpit and scampered off. Meanwhile, the crowd swarmed the plane, pressing in close to get a glimpse of this unconventional, leather-clad hero. Numb with cold, Maynard smiled and waved, then climbed from the cockpit to chase down his dog and check in with the control officer.

The strain of the journey was beginning to show on pilot and mechanic alike. Their eyes were red-rimmed and inflamed from dust and dry air, and their hearing had been damaged, perhaps permanently, by the engine's ceaseless thunder. "The roar of the motor is awful," Kline said later, "especially when you hear it ten and twelve hours a day. I would wake up in the night and start to fix something before fully awakening. All night long I would be traveling in my sleep." Mechanics at Salt Lake City had to shout to make their questions heard. But there was no question of stopping now, not while there was just enough daylight left to make Salduro.

The crowd cheered them on. Just before Maynard took off, a man yelled out, "Parson, the sinners are with you."

17

Spaatz vs. Kiel

Flying between 200 and 600 feet, Carl Spaatz hugged the shoreline of Lake Michigan, following it southeast from Chicago in rain and fog. In a few minutes he reached Gary, Indiana, where the lakeshore started to curve north. He crossed the shoreline and flew inland toward Bryan, Ohio. A short time later he realized he was lost.

The skies had been clear when Spaatz took off from St. Paul, Nebraska, early that morning of Friday, October 10, with Emil Kiel just thirty seconds behind. Their rivalry was in the open now. Kiel was a 34-year-old former schoolteacher who had spent the war stateside as a flight instructor. Now he pushed his Liberty engine hard, overtaking Spaatz on the short, 118-mile "hop" to Omaha, by one account waving as he passed. He landed at the Chamber of Commerce's Ak-Sar-Ben Field—Ak-Sar-Ben is Nebraska spelled backwards—minutes ahead of Spaatz, with Frank McKee once again serving as a human counterweight on the tail.

On the ground, Spaatz and Kiel had a brief, tense exchange. "If I don't beat you into Mineola," Kiel said, "I will break my neck trying."

They caught up with Lowell Smith at Rock Island, Illinois. After spending Thursday night in Omaha, Smith had made good time to Des Moines and then Rock Island, where he landed at 10:43 a.m. But he'd been stuck at Rock Island for almost two hours. With Ashburn Field in Chicago under several inches of water, Air Service officials had shifted the Chicago control stop to Grant Park, on the lakefront at the edge of the city's central business district. But Grant Park was now blanketed in fog. The control officer at the field had closed it temporarily, informing Rock Island by telegram.

Spaatz, whose low-key style was not to be confused with patience, was having none of it. After landing at Rock Island at 12:32 p.m., ten minutes behind Kiel, he got on the phone to Colonel Morrow, the head of the Air Service's Central Department, and challenged the control officer's decision. Morrow didn't need much persuading. "Do all you men know how to find Grant Park?" he asked. "Yes," Spaatz replied. "Come on then," Morrow said. The control officer at Rock Island later complained of Spaatz's "over-bearing attitude," noting that Smith had accepted the delay without complaint, even though it had cost him his lead.

The trio left Rock Island within three minutes of each other, in the order in which they had arrived. It was raining along the route to Chicago, and Spaatz was grateful that his plane had been equipped with one of the new copper-tipped propellers. After a flight of less than ninety minutes, he and the others landed in "quick succession" at Grant Park, a long rectangular greensward opposite the Blackstone Hotel and other prominent buildings. Spaatz dropped off a letter he had carried from the mayor of San Francisco to the mayor of Chicago, then resumed his journey just behind Smith, with Kiel trailing by eighteen minutes.

"Squally weather" was reported from Chicago all the way to New York. After leaving the lakeshore about fifteen miles northeast of Gary, Spaatz began following what he thought was the compass course to Bryan. But the visibility was poor, even at low altitude. Spaatz meandered above the checkerboard farm country of northeastern Indiana, hoping to spot an obvious landmark that might confirm his position. Finding none, he landed in a field to ask directions and learned that he was two miles south of the town of Hamilton. He also was stuck in the mud. Fortunately for Spaatz, an airplane in a field could always be counted on to draw a crowd, and he had no difficulty finding six men to help him push it free. He took off after thirty minutes on the ground.

Billy Mitchell next to plane emblazoned with his personal insignia, which his mechanic copied from a dollar bill. *Library of Congress*

Harold Hartney at the controls of a single-seat SE-5, the same type he flew in the New York–Toronto race in August 1919. *National Archives*

At Roosevelt Field just before the start, Billy Mitchell (right) stands in front of a DH-4 with its pilot, Lt. Ross Kirkpatrick, along with Benedict Crowell, the assistant secretary of war, and Col. Archie Miller, the commander of Roosevelt Field. Kirkpatrick's mechanic, Sgt. E. J. Bruce, sits on the rim of the rear cockpit. *Library of Congress*

Belvin Maynard (standing) and his mechanic, William Kline, pose with Trixie, the German police dog that accompanied them across the country and back. *Library of Congress*

Right: Air Commodore Lionel Charlton, the British defense attaché in Washington, prepares to start from Mineola in a Rolls Royce–powered Bristol Fighter. *Library of Congress*

Below: Captain Roy Francis, on left with hand on propeller, with the crew of the Martin Bomber. *Library of Congress*

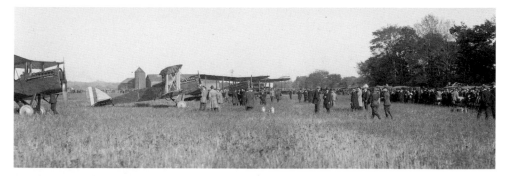

Spectators and race planes on the pasture known as Britton Field, which served as Rochester's control stop during the contest. *From the Albert R. Stone Negative Collection. Rochester Museum & Science Center, Rochester, New York*

In the days before the race, the Air Service dispatched an officer and eight enlisted men to each of the eighteen control stops between New York and San Francisco. These men were assigned to Rochester. *From the Albert R. Stone Negative Collection. Rochester Museum & Science Center, Rochester, New York*

Ground personnel servicing a DH-4 at Rochester. *From the Albert R. Stone Negative Collection. Rochester Museum & Science Center, Rochester, New York*

At Rochester and a few other control stops, mobile searchlights borrowed from the Army's Coast Artillery branch served as beacons for pilots trying to find airfields in poor weather or fading light. *From the Albert R. Stone Negative Collection. Rochester Museum & Science Center, Rochester, New York*

Mechanics swarm over Harold Hartney's Fokker D.VII, its German insignia visible on the tail, during its stop at Rochester on the first day of the race. In the background is the DH-4 flown by Belvin Maynard, who will take off ahead of him and steadily extend his lead. *From the Albert R. Stone Negative Collection. Rochester Museum & Science Center, Rochester, New York*

The Martin Bomber, seen here after reaching Binghamton on October 8, carried a crew of four and was the largest plane in the race. *National Archives*

As Charles Menoher looks on, Maynard shakes hands with Lt. Gen. Hunter Liggett, commander of the Army's Western Department, after reaching San Francisco on October 11, 1919. *National Archives*

Unidentified contestant landing on the Presidio's dirt airfield after crossing the country from New York. *Library of Congress*

After landing in near-darkness at Roosevelt Field, an exhausted Carl Spaatz shakes hands with Col. Archie Miller, the commander of Roosevelt Field. Standing next to him are his mother, sister, and mechanic, Sgt. Emmett Tanner. *Library of Congress*

Brailey Gish (right) and his mechanic, Sgt. George Pomeroy, during their stopover in Rochester after Gish restarted the race in a new plane, to replace the one that caught fire on the first day. *From the Albert R. Stone Negative Collection. Rochester Museum & Science Center, Rochester, New York*

Major John Bartholf in an SE-5 fighter, the same type flown by John Donaldson, after completing his flight from San Francisco to New York. *National Archives*

Brailey Gish's DH-4, with its name—"Junk"—visible on the fuselage, at the Cheyenne control stop during its flight west. *National Archives*

This DH-4 overturned after running off the end of the landing area at the Rawlins control stop, which pilots considered one of the most dangerous because of its short length, high altitude, and gusty winds. Neither occupant was hurt but the plane had to be shipped to California for repairs. *National Archives*

On his return trip from San Francisco, Brailey Gish overshot the landing area at Rawlins and nosed over, causing damage that took a day to repair. *National Archives*

After completing his round-trip journey, Lowell Smith signs the logbook at the Presidio with Hap Arnold looking on. *Library of Congress*

Spaatz reached Bryan at 5:46 p.m., joining Smith and Kiel. He was desperate for a room and a hot bath. Told that none was available in the small Ohio town, he reconciled himself to another night of austere lodging at the field. In the morning, they would begin the final sprint to Long Island.

18

Salduro

Even in clear weather, flying in mountains can be dangerous. Wind swirls and eddies as it flows across irregular terrain, like water tumbling over a rocky streambed. One of the most common threats is called mountain wave. As wind crests a mountaintop and descends its opposite side, it can form downdrafts or rotating currents called rotors. In severe form, rotors can cause airplanes to break apart or collide with terrain. Mountain wave has been blamed for a number of fatal accidents over the years, including the breakup of a Boeing 707 near Fuji in Japan in 1966, which killed all 124 passengers and crew (the pilot is believed to have diverted from his route so that passengers could get a better view of the mountain). As awareness of the threat has grown, so have the means to avoid it. Among other things, pilots are taught to look for the lens-like lenticular clouds that can form over mountaintops in the presence of dangerous air currents. They also learn to approach ridges and mountains at a 45-degree angle, which makes it easier to turn away in a downdraft.

The hazards of mountain flying were only dimly understood in 1919. To the extent that anyone addressed the subject, it was only to advise that pilots flying over high, rugged terrain should keep as much distance as possible between them and the ground. "Air currents are much more violent and active near the earth, due to the deflection by the irregularities of the earth's surface," wrote C. Lamar Nelson, a former Air Service pilot, in the *Salt Lake Telegram* on the second day of the race. "The higher the safer." This was only common sense, in part because it would give pilots an extra margin of safety if an engine failed.

But John Donaldson rejected this wisdom. With questionable logic, he reasoned that if his engine quit it wouldn't matter how high he was, because he probably was going to crash anyway. "As long as it was impossible to get a good landing place in case of motor trouble I thought, 'What's the use of wasting time by flying high?'" he recalled. So he took the opposite approach. In the treacherous high country west of Cheyenne, he skimmed through mountain passes just twenty-five feet above rocks and trees, telling himself that he was avoiding headwinds at higher altitudes. "I sought the protection of every hill, coming down again on the other side," he later said.

Donaldson was lucky. When he crossed the Medicine Bow Mountains and the Wasatch Range on Saturday, October 11, the air was relatively calm, and his biggest complaint was the bitter cold—24 degrees below zero Fahrenheit, or so he later claimed (it's not clear how he would have known this, as airplanes of the day typically lacked thermometers to measure ambient temperature).

The airfields at Rawlins and Green River posed a bigger threat. Both were rough, short, and topographically challenging, especially when considering the effect of high altitude on aircraft performance. After landing at Rawlins, Donaldson watched as a DH-4 piloted by Lt. Lewis S. Webster rose from the small racetrack infield, then entered a tight climbing spiral to avoid hitting houses and a hill. Donaldson's S.E.5—light in weight, with a powerful engine—climbed more quickly, but even so, he had to "jump straight up" to clear the same obstacles.

Donaldson caught up with Webster at Green River, where both had chosen to land now that the winds had dropped. Once again, he watched Webster begin his takeoff run—then looked on in horror as Webster's DH-4 plunged off the cliff at the end of the field. Donaldson and others sprinted to the edge, expecting to see a pile of wreckage on the rocks nearly 200 feet below. But a gust of wind, forced upward by the cliff, caught Webster's wings; just in time, his plane began to climb. Some pilots who attempted to land at Green River only touched their wheels and then zoomed skyward, deciding at the last second they would not be able to stop before running off the edge of the cliff—or take off successfully later if they did.

Donaldson made it through the Rockies unscathed. He touched down at Buena Vista Field at Salt Lake City at 3:46 p.m., then departed for Salduro 100 miles to the west.

———

Salduro—an amalgam of Spanish words that means "hard salt"—was a small mining town on the ancient lake bed known as the Bonneville Salt Flats. Named for the Army officer who explored the region in the 1830s, the flats were an important source of potash, a mineral used in fertilizer, and lately had attracted a new activity, that of daredevils chasing speed records in powerful automobiles. The unobstructed white surface also made for a wide-open airfield that had required little in the way of preparation, other than the marking of its corners in black so that pilots could see it from above (the landing T also was painted black). Still, it could be devilishly hard to control an airplane on the slick, hard-packed salt, especially in a crosswind. "The flyers, on landing, skated around like drunken sailors," Donaldson recalled, "spinning on one wing and then another, and sometimes skating backwards."

Donaldson did not land so well himself. Temporarily blinded by oil that had coated his goggles and gotten in one eye, he hit so hard that he snapped one of his wooden landing-gear struts and cracked the other. With more than two hours of daylight left, he would have liked to press on to Battle Mountain, Nevada, but that was not an option now. He consoled himself with the thought that he could make repairs the next day—Sunday—without losing any more time.

19

Hello Frisco!

Fog and smoke blanketed the Presidio on the afternoon of Saturday, October 11. In a state of high anticipation, a large crowd of military personnel and civilians waited at its waterfront airfield, peering through the murk to catch a first glimpse of Belvin Maynard's plane. They expected him to come from the east, over San Francisco Bay, and were facing that direction when they heard the faint sound of an aircraft engine. Confusion momentarily reigned. As the engine grew louder, it seemed to be coming from another direction entirely—from the south, over the San Francisco Peninsula. As the watchers turned toward the sound, a DH-4 broke through the ceiling and sank toward the field.

Late on the previous afternoon, Maynard had reached Salduro, Utah, where he made the first less-than-perfect landing of his journey west. He touched down smoothly enough, but as his speed diminished, so did the air pressure on his rudder, which cost him the ability to steer. After rolling for what seemed like miles, *"Hello Frisco"* inscribed a few leisurely circles on the salt, then came to an awkward stop.

Maynard was lucky—the ground loops caused no damage. After a hot bath and a restful night, he got away from Salduro early on Saturday morning, this time with a little extra cargo: The manager of a local salt-mining company had given him two bags of salt for a business associate in San Francisco.

With only 518 miles to go, Maynard expected to reach San Francisco by 2:00 p.m., and had promised as much in another dispatch for the *San Francisco Examiner*. The weather on the first part of his trip augured well. In clear skies and light winds, he flew over desert mountains to the stop at Battle Mountain, Nevada, finding the town easily because it was the only place for miles with any trees. Reno, obscured by a low haze, proved more of a challenge. As residents stepped outside and craned their necks from windows, he puttered above the city for twenty minutes before he finally located the airfield. Later he would joke of Reno's thriving divorce industry, noting that he and William Kline departed the control stop "without the usual loss of wife."

Maynard crossed the Sierra Nevada at 13,000 feet, so dazzled by the views that he almost forgot the savage cold. He was especially struck by Lake Tahoe, which he would recall in terms that might have been lifted from one of his sermons ("amid the tallest of the Sierras with their peaks of silver white, as if some Divine hand might have placed it there with a thought of perfect beauty"). Before long he was descending over the thick pine forests of the western slope. As the atmosphere warmed, he kept a close eye on his temperature gauge, lest the engine overheat. It was always a fine balance. At higher speeds, the Liberty engine's valves glowed cherry red and could warp from cooling too quickly if the engine were abruptly throttled back.

The final leg, after a thirty-minute stop at Sacramento, went smoothly until Maynard reached San Francisco Bay. With the city shrouded in fog, he crossed the water until he could make out the peninsula shoreline, then turned south in what he thought was the direction of the Presidio. In fact, it was to the north. Maynard realized his mistake after five minutes and reversed course. Soon he spotted tall buildings through rifts in the overcast. He descended toward the Presidio, stunned by his first glimpse of the crowd. "It seemed as though the whole city were out to welcome us."

Even after Maynard's plane appeared over the field, some doubted it was him until they saw the "31" painted on his fuselage. The field erupted in joy.

Maynard arrived with his customary flair, banking steeply toward the field and sideslipping twice to bleed off his remaining altitude (like

Maynard's plane, *"Hello Frisco,"* seconds after touching down in San Francisco. *National Park Service*

all biplanes of the day, the DH-4 was not equipped with wing flaps—standard equipment on modern airplanes—to slow and steepen its descent). He slipped at such a steep angle that some in the crowd cried out in alarm, certain "the machine would skid to the ground." But he straightened at the last second and settled gently onto the dirt at 1:12 p.m., nearly fifty minutes ahead of schedule.

———

No human being had ever made a faster journey across the continent, by airplane or any other means. Maynard's total elapsed time of three days, six hours, and forty-seven minutes bested by roughly half a day the fastest trains from New York to San Francisco. His flying time—twenty-five hours, sixteen minutes, and forty-eight-and-a-half seconds—worked out to an average speed of 108 miles an hour. His closest westbound competitors would not reach the Presidio until Monday.

As he coasted to a stop, the crowd enveloped Maynard's plane. Trixie was the first to alight, pawing her way out of the cockpit as Maynard and Kline unbuckled their safety harnesses. Well-wishers practically pulled them from their seats. Hap Arnold shouldered his way forward and led Maynard to a group of senior officers—including Charles Menoher, who had just arrived in San Francisco by train—offering handshakes and congratulations. Reporters and photographers swarmed. Smiling "until my cheeks became cramped," Maynard posed with Trixie in his arms and gamely fielded questions on his journey. "It was a great trip," he said, while acknowledging that he was still a little deaf. "I enjoyed it immensely." He credited his success to his Liberty engine, which "ran almost wide open most of the way."

Maynard was soon whisked off to the Palace Hotel, on the corner of Market and New Montgomery Streets, which had agreed to host flyers in the contest free of charge. He retired briefly to his room to wash the grime from his face, then reemerged, still in his "dusty and bedraggled uniform," for a celebratory lunch with Menoher and other dignitaries. He'd brought an extra uniform but didn't take time to change. Later in the afternoon, he dashed off another dispatch for the *San Francisco Examiner*, in which he claimed, with no apparent irony, "Flying is a safe means of travel and it is a lot of fun."

For Billy Mitchell, Maynard's arrival on the West Coast was the second piece of good news in less than twenty-four hours. On Capitol Hill the previous afternoon, he had told the Senate Military Committee of his ambitious plans to expand air routes from the continental United States to Alaska, Cuba, Panama, and, eventually, Asia. The panel responded by voting an additional $15 million for the Army to fund the construction of new aircraft. Mitchell got word of Maynard's achievement after a morning of bird shooting. He dashed off a telegram to Arnold. "Convey to Lieutenant Maynard sincere congratulations of entire A.S. on his remarkable transcontinental flight," he wrote. "The manner in which he has cared for his motor and other equipment in this long test is indeed wonderful."

Similar messages poured in from friends, relatives, and admirers. "Congratulations upon your marvelous feat," read a telegram from "your parents and the people of Sampson County, North Carolina." Maynard replied, "It shows that the east is only three days from the west and if I chose I could be back with you in three days. San Francisco reminds me of our God's country of the east. My comfort and happiness at reaching here cannot be expressed."

Maynard's wife, Essie, learned of his arrival late Saturday afternoon at Roosevelt Field, where she'd been waiting for the first eastbound flyers. "The children and I are very happy to know you landed safely in San Francisco," she wrote in a telegram that reached Maynard a day or two later. "We are so proud of you."

But Essie's relief was tinged with fear. She'd been shocked by the death toll in the race and closed her message with a heartfelt plea. "I hope so much you will not try to fly back," she wrote. "Letter following. Much love."

Maynard shrugged it off. "I had heard that before I left home," he told a reporter. "It was not news to me."

20

Roosevelt Field

In the headquarters tent at Binghamton, New York, on Saturday, October 11, the control officer pleaded with Carl Spaatz and Emil Kiel. "I think the best thing for you both to do is to stay over," Capt. C. C. Mosely said. "You'll never have the luck to get over the mountains in this storm. It's sure to result in a mishap."

The flying weather could not have been much worse. Rain fell in sheets, slanting down from clouds so low they obscured the tops of nearby ridges and hills. Moreover, though Roosevelt Field was still reporting clear skies, the storm was moving east. It would likely cover most if not all of their route by the time they reached Long Island— assuming they even got that far. "They'll both be killed if they dare to start," said one elderly woman, part of a large crowd that had braved the elements to welcome the first of the flyers from San Francisco. "They ought not to let them go."

There was general agreement that no sensible person would take off in such foul conditions. Spectators began drifting toward their motorcars.

Not for the first time that afternoon, Spaatz stuck his head out of the tent and scanned the menacing sky. He made up his mind. Turning to Mosely, he clasped his hand and said, "We'll start." Mosely tried to argue—"I wish you'd reconsider"—but Spaatz cut him off. "We'll get there all okay."

And with that he and Emmett Tanner, his mechanic, returned to their plane at the edge of the rain-soaked field. Kiel and Frank McKee soon followed. It was late in the day and they didn't have much time.

In Bryan, Ohio, the night before, Spaatz, Lowell Smith, and Kiel had gone to bed knowing they still had a chance to beat Maynard across the country. It was 560 miles to Mineola—only forty-two more than the distance from Salduro to San Francisco—and because of the time difference they would be able to start earlier than the westbound leader. Determined to make the most of their advantage, they rose at 4:30 a.m. on Saturday and got away from Bryan minutes after the sun rose at 6:40 a.m.

Not that there was any sign of it. Patchy rain and fog covered the route from Bryan to the next stop at Cleveland. Spaatz followed his compass, flying at 1,000 feet or below to keep the ground in sight. It was raining heavily by the time he caught sight of Martin Field, where he landed at 8:16 a.m. Kiel touched down eighteen minutes later.

Smith, curiously, was nowhere to be seen. The first to take off from Bryan, he had reached Cleveland in good time. But once he was over the city, he could not locate the field northeast of downtown, perhaps because he needed the map that had blown out of his cockpit while he was taking off from Bryan. After circling aimlessly for several minutes, he landed on a field south of the city, intending to ask directions. His plane hit a ditch and nosed over, breaking its propeller as well as a strut. The erstwhile eastbound leader found a ride to the Glenn L. Martin Company plant and retrieved the necessary parts. He and Francis Ruggles, his observer, spent the next several hours repairing their machine, then made the short hop to the airfield.

The pair finished the day in Rochester, then found a ride to the Hotel Seneca, where bellhops and desk clerks looked on in speechless wonder as the two weary flyers, still in their oil-stained coveralls, signed their names in the register. Smith knew he had lost any chance of beating his rivals to Long Island. Ruggles tried to lift his spirits. "It's just fisherman's luck," he said. "One fellow gets it and the other doesn't. There is no other explanation."

———————

Spaatz and Kiel surged ahead. The two raced neck-and-neck to Buffalo under low clouds, their compass routes taking them over Lake Erie. Reporters at the *Buffalo Times* learned that Spaatz had reached their city when his plane whipped past their office window "at a terrific rate of speed." He circled for several minutes before he found the field, where Pitts, the control officer, had ordered the searchlight switched on. Spaatz landed less than three minutes behind Kiel and made a beeline for Pitts, brusquely asking how quickly he could be supplied with gas and oil.

The control officer had some disappointing news. He was not letting any planes take off from Buffalo, on account of the dismal weather. Spaatz protested, arguing that "the visibility was not so bad after the machine got in the air." A short time later, Pitts relented after receiving instructions from Washington, D.C.—it's unclear whether Spaatz had a hand in this—to let the men proceed. Spaatz got away at 12:40 p.m., after forty-nine minutes on the ground. Kiel, delayed by a minor repair, followed half an hour later. After another stop at Rochester, they flew through more rain to Binghamton.

Spaatz, who landed first at 2:51 p.m., had but one thing on his mind. "Where is Lieutenant Maynard?" he asked as soon as he had shut down.

"The Flying Parson left Sacramento at 12:19," came the reply.

Spaatz quickly found Mosely, the control officer. "If you give me permission to clear, I'll start just as soon as I am fueled. I've still got a chance of winning."

Mosely was aghast. "It would be foolhardy, major, to think of taking off under such adverse conditions."

Spaatz pushed back. "The rain doesn't bother me in the least," he said. "I've been in it for a third of the distance clear across the country. In fact haven't seen the sun since we left Salt Lake."

A short while later, Spaatz heard the sound of an approaching aircraft. "That's Lieutenant E. C. Kiel and Sgt. Frank McKee," said the red-haired aviator, whose excitement, perhaps, had rendered him more talkative than usual. "He's a splendid flier. I can't see him but

I know the voice of his machine. He was right behind us all the way clear across the country, flying like a bat up Sixth Street in Lucifer's well-known town."

Mosely ordered soldiers to light a fire and shoot flares from Very pistols. Kiel, who had been searching for the field for ten minutes, saw the flares glowing through the rain and made a safe landing at 3:45 p.m. He was now nearly an hour behind his rival. If Spaatz took off right away, he would have at least a thirty-minute head start, as Kiel waited on the ground in accordance with the rules.

But Spaatz, appearances to the contrary, did not have a death wish. By this point he must have known, or at least surmised, that Maynard had beaten him to the coast. He also knew that conditions might improve if he delayed his departure. So he offered his challenger a deal. "I'll admit the present weather conditions are mighty bad," he said. "It'll be hard right now to get over the mountains. One or both of us are very liable to crash into them." He proposed that both wait for at least thirty minutes, at which point Spaatz would be free to take off. Kiel would follow him by ten minutes. Spaatz made it clear that if Kiel did not agree to the arrangement, he was prepared to leave immediately.

Spaatz may have been bluffing, but if not, Kiel could give up any hope of beating him to Mineola. He took the deal. "I'll be right on your tail," he said with a smile. "I've hung to you all the way from Frisco. I'm not going to quit now." In a magnanimous gesture, Spaatz then told the other pilot that he could follow him by five minutes instead of ten.

Mosely, the control officer, had no part in these negotiations. He was outranked and out of arguments, especially after a telephone call from Col. Archie Miller, the commander at Roosevelt Field, reporting clear conditions at Mineola and urging the flyers to proceed. Mosely could only watch and hope for the best as Spaatz and then Kiel opened their throttles, bounced across the muddy field, and vanished into the murk.

––––––––––––

There was no question of flying the compass line. The flight over southeastern New York would cross hilly terrain just south of the Catskill

Mountains. Because of the low overcast, the men would have to find a way through the hills instead of over them.

Each took a slightly different path. Following his map, Spaatz flew south along the Susquehanna River, then lost "considerable time" as he searched for the pass that would take him east along the Erie Railroad to the Delaware River. After finding the pass and then the river, he followed it south to Port Jervis, where the ceiling was higher and he was able to climb to 2,000 feet. Kiel chose a slightly more northerly route, flying as low as fifty feet so he could read the names of towns on railroad station signboards. After reaching the Hudson River near West Point, he turned south. By the time he reached Long Island Sound he had nearly caught up with Spaatz.

About 300 people waited at Roosevelt Field, eagerly searching the sky. Earlier in the afternoon, the crowd had been bigger, prompting Miller to post guards to keep the landing area clear. But as the hours dragged on with no sign of the flyers, some had grown restless and headed home. Then word filtered out from Miller's tent that Spaatz and Kiel were on their way.

As the men neared their destination, the weather, which had been glorious all afternoon, took a sudden turn. Dark clouds rolled in, raindrops spattered on the ground, and a brisk, chilly wind swept the field. Lt. George C. McDonald, an early dropout in the race, flew out to meet the two flyers but was beaten back by the approaching storm. The light was fading quickly. Speculation grew that the aviators had been forced down short of their goal.

Then came a shout—"Here they come!"—and the crowd finally got its reward. Two dots, "moving like the wind," were barely visible against the tumultuous magenta sky. There was a faint whir of aircraft engines, which faded and then returned at increasing volume. Spaatz had beaten Kiel to Mineola, though not by much. And he was about to lose his lead. The Air Service originally had named Hazelhurst Field, adjacent to Roosevelt, as the terminus for the West-to-East race, then switched the finish line to Roosevelt Field. But pilots never got the word. Now, as Spaatz coasted to a stop at Hazelhurst Field, soldiers rushed to the side of his DH-4, shouting that he had landed in the wrong place. After seconds on the ground, he gunned his engine and returned to the air. He gained a little altitude and banked toward Roosevelt, where a circle of gasoline had been dumped on the ground and set alight. Kiel followed the beacon and touched down on Roosevelt Field at 6:35 p.m. and ten seconds. Spaatz landed twenty seconds later.

Spaatz was unaware Kiel had landed first. "Anyone else here?" he yelled to an approaching officer, as soon as he had shut down the engine.

"Yep, he just landed," the officer replied. "It will take a Dutch lawyer to fix your time at Hazelhurst."

Not that it really mattered. Each man could claim victory, depending on how it was defined. Despite landing at the wrong airfield, Spaatz still had the faster elapsed time from coast to coast, having departed San Francisco three minutes and five seconds later than his rival. And Kiel recorded the faster flying time, twenty-six hours and seventeen minutes. That was seventeen minutes better than Spaatz's time. At that moment, though, neither much cared. They were glad just to be on the ground. In the flickering light of the burning gasoline, the two pilots and their passengers clambered from their cockpits and exchanged handshakes with each other, like tennis players after a doubles match. They were quickly surrounded by high-ranking officers and other dignitaries, as well as spectators who broke through a cordon of soldiers. Among the well-wishers were Spaatz's mother, father, brother, and sister, who had traveled from Pennsylvania to greet him. His mother threw her arms around his neck.

"I'm awfully dirty," Spaatz said, trying to duck her kisses.

"I don't care how dirty you are!" she replied.

The exhausted flyers retreated to Miller's command tent, where they faced reporters in the light of two oil lamps and a dozen candles. "How do I feel?" Spaatz asked, repeating a question. "To be perfectly frank, I feel like a drink of whiskey." He then acknowledged that he was "rather tired" and in no particular hurry to make the return flight. "I could, I think, undertake it, but I don't want to just now."

––––––

It appeared he would get plenty of rest. After Maynard's arrival in San Francisco that afternoon, the Air Service had announced that the second crossing of the continent would not begin until October 20, which was more than a week away. The idea was to allow stragglers to catch up and ensure that all would start their return trip at the same time. Forty-four of the sixty-three planes that started the race—thirty-seven from New York and seven from San Francisco—remained in the contest, though only three had reached the opposite coast. Seventeen of the westbound planes had yet to pass Chicago, and four of those were still at Buffalo. What's more, pilots would have to wait until Monday, October 13, to start making up ground, since no flying was permitted on Sunday. Twenty planes had dropped out because of crashes or mechanical trouble.

For some near the back of the pack, any sense of urgency had dissipated. Among the flyers killing time at Buffalo on Sunday were Lt. J. G. Williams and his observer, who had endured a series of setbacks that included a forced landing in a thunderstorm two days earlier. In an interview with a reporter who caught up with him at Curtiss Field, Williams sounded resigned. "We have been pursued by a jinx," he said. "Out of the race now? It looks that way, but we'll meander along and make a sightseeing tour of it." Three days later, in western Iowa, Williams would drop out of the race entirely after wrecking his DH-4 in a landing forced by heavy fog.

Billy Mitchell and Charles Menoher were committed to finishing what they had started, but others were having second thoughts. Among them was Charles J. Glidden, the wealthy Bostonian and former Air Service publicity officer who had first proposed the contest back in August. Now, in a telegram to Newton Baker, the secretary of war, Glidden accused the Air Service of botching its preparations for the race and called for ending it as soon as possible. In the future, he wrote, "men taking part in a strenuous event of this character should go into training as men do for prize fighting." A day later, on Sunday, October 12, the *Denver Post* weighed in with an editorial cartoon. It showed a grieving Uncle Sam with an aviator standing before him, one hand frozen in a salute and the other holding a sheet of paper listing the names of those killed. "An awful price to pay—for what?" read the caption.

In New York on Saturday evening, just a few hours after Spaatz and Kiel reached Long Island, members of the American Flying Club's contest committee were asking themselves the same question. In a meeting with Air Service officials, some argued for calling off the return journey or at least shifting the route to the south, where the weather presumably would be better.

No announcement was forthcoming, but pilots also had a choice. Kiel made his known within a few hours of landing at Roosevelt Field. "No one can make me race back to California," he said during an appearance that night at the flying club's headquarters in Manhattan. "It was a wonderful trip, but the train will be good enough for me."

PART III

Triumph

21

Donaldson and Hartney

Battle Mountain in Nevada had long been welcoming travelers. In a wide basin between two mountain ranges, the town had been part of the nation's transportation network for nearly a century—first as a way station for westbound wagon trains, then, since 1869, as a stop on the transcontinental railroad. Now it was a small but industrious community surrounded by copper mines, sheep ranches, and alfalfa farms irrigated by the Humboldt and Reese Rivers. There were several good hotels, one with an elegant restaurant whose French-born chef had worked in New York and San Francisco. A new power plant supplied electricity to homes and businesses seven nights and one full day a week. Townspeople were especially proud of their handsome new grammar school and its four large classrooms, marble bathrooms, and hallways floored in maple, although the school was closed to Native American children, who took their lessons in the one-room schoolhouse it had replaced.

Battle Mountain had jumped at the opportunity presented by the race. After it was selected as a control stop, the local government spent $2,000—roughly $30,000 in today's dollars—to scrape and level a 2,000-foot-long oval in the sagebrush half a mile south of town. That Lowell Smith had briefly lived in Battle Mountain before the war—while his father, a mining engineer, worked nearby—only added to the town's enthusiasm.

Once the race was under way, the arrival of any flyer could be counted on to draw a crowd of eager locals, whose curiosity sometimes got the better of them. "At some stops, notably Battle Mountain, the crowds around the airplane were thick, and all spectators found it necessary to handle the plane, much to the annoyance of the pilot," complained Harry Drayton, who had passed through the stop on the afternoon of Saturday, October 11, a few hours behind Maynard. "This is an extremely bad feature as a flight of this kind is apt to make pilots irritable."

But John Donaldson was charmed by this "rip-roaring Western town." He landed at Battle Mountain at 8:34 a.m. on Monday, October 13, just three minutes behind Lewis Webster, the pilot who had nearly come to grief while taking off from Green River a few days earlier. Waiting at the airfield was a sizable crowd, among them grizzled ranchers in open-topped "flivvers"—motorcars—fitted with rifle pockets, and a group of Native Americans who descended from nearby hills. One of the ranchers wanted to know if a plane could be fitted with a rifle pocket, and Donaldson assured him that it could. The Indians were more reticent, except for an elderly, bent-over woman who approached to touch a wing. "She gave a scream, and jumped back as though she had been hurt," Donaldson recounted. He took the opportunity to try out a few words of Sioux, which he presumably had picked up as a child in North Dakota. The Indians responded with blank stares.

Donaldson was confident of reaching San Francisco that afternoon. On Sunday, he had used his layover at Salduro to tend to his S.E.5, cleaning his spark plugs in a bucket of kerosene and repairing his broken landing struts. One he replaced with a pine board, and the other he bound with fabric and aircraft dope. A piece of cable and a turnbuckle completed the job. Donaldson was proud of his handiwork, which would last the rest of his journey.

By midday Monday, after a stop at Reno, he was over the Sierras, skimming the mountaintops with his usual disdain for altitude. He was dumbstruck by the scenery and mused about the possibilities of seaplanes landing tourists on Lake Tahoe. He landed at the Presidio at 2:49 p.m., and soon checked into the Palace Hotel, joining Maynard and two other pilots who had reached San Francisco from the East.

Harold Hartney would not get there for days. Near dusk on Thursday, October 16, he and his German fighter limped into Reno. His radiator was patched with tin, and oil streaked his fuselage. Way back in Nebraska, Hartney had stripped off the tattered remnants of the fabric that protected his laminated wooden propeller. Now, with San Francisco nearly within reach, the prop was scarred and "dangerously" warped, its layers starting to separate. He despaired of where he might find a new one.

The past four days had been trying ones. On the morning of Monday, October 13, after his layover in Rock Island, Hartney had finally gotten a break in the weather, taking off under clear skies. But the respite didn't last. Not long after leaving Omaha, he lost his way in fog. He meandered above the cornfields until he spotted a DH-4 circling near Center City, then made the mistake of following it. After realizing that the other pilot was just as lost as he was, he landed in a field to get his bearings, took off again, and followed railroad tracks that he thought would lead to the control stop at St. Paul. He soon realized that the tracks were taking him in the wrong direction and set down in the field he had just left. Eventually, he sorted out his position and found St. Paul, where he scribbled in his logbook, "This was a terrible trip."

Fog and rain—"my greatest bugbear"—kept him on the ground for more than two hours, and conditions weren't much better on the leg to North Platte. He covered the distance at such a low altitude, he wrote in his logbook, that he had the "unique experience" of detecting cooking smells wafting up from houses on the ground.

The weather got even worse. After reaching Sidney, Nebraska, where he spent the night in a hotel, Hartney woke up to a dismal brew of rain, snow, and fog on Tuesday. One DH-4 pilot, Lt. French Kirby, managed to get away at 4:15 p.m. Hartney attempted to follow thirty minutes later. He flew into a snowstorm and after twenty minutes returned to Sidney, where he resigned himself to spending a second night.

The visibility was better on Wednesday morning, though the air was bitterly cold. After covering his radiator to keep it from freezing, Hartney took off for Cheyenne and his first encounter with serious mountains. It did not inspire confidence. Though agile and easy to fly, the Fokker with its 160-horsepower engine performed poorly at higher altitudes (one reason that later models had been equipped with 180-horsepower engines). Getting off the ground in Cheyenne seemed to take an eternity; departing Rawlins, 1,000 feet higher, was even more of a challenge. Seeking every advantage, Hartney drafted several soldiers to hold his wings, then ran the engine to full power and signaled them to let go. He bumped along the racetrack infield and staggered into the air, barely clearing nearby chimney tops. The only consolation was that his engine consumed about 20 percent less fuel than at lower altitudes.

Hartney had just enough time to make Green River before dark. The small, windswept airfield posed less of a challenge for him than it did for some other pilots. Because of its unusually thick airfoil, the Fokker could fly so slowly that it required only a few hundred feet to land, or even fewer in a moderate headwind (its stall speed was just forty miles an hour, compared with forty-nine for the DH-4).

Townspeople were delighted by the arrival of the famous ace and his exotic German biplane. After working so hard to prepare the airfield, and delegating a Boy Scout troop to patrol it during the day, they had been disappointed that so many pilots had skipped the stop. Hartney was one of several pilots who spent that night in Green River, where they were treated like princes. In the absence of any hotels, the men put up with the Couzens family, who made "the most wonderful dinner of wholesome food, including real thick Jersey cream and made us happy that we had stopped there for the night."

Hartney took off on Thursday morning under clear skies, after a short delay caused by a leaky fuel tank. He followed his compass over the Wasatch Range—"a very delightful trip"—to Salt Lake City, where he impressed the crowd with a perfect three-point landing. His arrival at Salduro was not so elegant. Like many others, he ground-looped on the hard-packed salt, though without any damage to his wings or landing gear.

Shortly before sunset, he made it into Reno, where he took stock of his damaged propeller. ("The Germans evidently did not know much about wood lamination," he later sniffed.) But his worries soon vanished. To his surprise and delight, Hartney learned that a brand-new Fokker propeller—one of only a few in the entire country—had been shipped to Reno from McCook Field in Ohio. Installing it on Friday morning caused a five-hour delay, after which he took off on the penultimate leg to Sacramento.

Even with its new propeller, the Fokker struggled to make the steep climb over the Sierras, heaving and bouncing in turbulence that Hartney found "most unpleasant." It took forever to gain altitude. Foothills and then snow-covered mountaintops passed beneath his wings at a crawl. Finally, Hartney crested the range and began the steep descent to Mather Field in Sacramento.

The last leg to San Francisco was "most delightful." At 1:49 p.m. on that Friday, October 17, Hartney's underpowered "lightning bug"—as the *San Francisco Chronicle* described it—touched down at the Presidio. A full week had passed since Maynard completed the same journey. Another eighteen planes had followed in the intervening days. Hartney had made a total of five forced landings since leaving New York, most because of fuel starvation. Nevertheless, he felt a keen sense of accomplishment, as well he should have. He not only had completed the coast-to-coast journey but also was one of the few who had done it alone, without the advantage of a passenger to help him navigate or tend to the airplane at control stops.

"I arrived there happy in the fact that I was the only Fokker to get across the continent," he recalled. Now all he had to do was fly back.

22

"The Man of a Hundred Wounds"

Junk, **as Gish had christened** his DH-4, was living up to its name. He and his mechanic, Sgt. George C. Pomeroy, had gotten only as far as the first control stop at Binghamton before the plane's bracing wires lost tension, causing its wings to sag. Before they could safely continue, "it was necessary to practically rerig the machine," Gish recalled. The engine also was giving them trouble. Its water pump and radiator leaked, and the contact points of the distributor, which routed electricity to the spark plugs, required cleaning at nearly every stop. During their layover in Cleveland on the night of Saturday, October 11, through Sunday, October 12, Gish and Pomeroy replaced the radiator, changed the spark plugs, installed an air pressure gauge on the gas tank, and secured gas, oil, and water connections. It wasn't until Sunday night that the overhaul was complete.

At a few minutes past seven on the morning of Monday, October 13, Gish continued his journey west. The press and the public cheered him on. Though far behind, Gish had emerged as one of the most colorful and prominent pilots in the race, in part because of the cumbersome metal braces he wore on both legs. After he landed in Chicago later that morning, the sight of him hobbling from his plane prompted someone to call for the ambulance on the field (Gish waved it off). On Tuesday morning, the *Chicago Tribune* would marvel at his courage in attempting the race despite crippling injuries suffered "in a night bombing attack in France a year ago." That false claim—Gish had crashed on a training flight—was part of an expanding mythology surrounding his wartime service, some of which Gish had encouraged. Other newspapers reported that "the tail of his plane was shot off," credited him with downing multiple German planes and balloons, and attributed scars on his wrists to machine-gun bullets, calling him "the man of a hundred wounds."

But there was no denying his grit. After reaching Omaha's control stop that Monday the 13th at 4:22 p.m.—guided by flares in dense fog—Gish encountered yet another spell of low ceilings and heavy rain that kept him on the ground until the following afternoon. He took off into more fog, which forced him to fly to St. Paul below 200 feet. With sunset near, he attempted to make North Platte, but by then the visibility was so poor that he had to turn back. Along the way, he landed in a field to refill his new radiator, which already had sprung a leak. Bad weather held him at St. Paul for two nights, until Thursday morning, October 16, when he took off for North Platte.

There was more trouble ahead—in Gish's case, there was always more trouble ahead. A blizzard delayed his departure from North Platte by ninety minutes, and at Salt Lake City the next morning, he lost more time as his leaky radiator and water pump were repaired. Then, hurrying to get off the ground, he turned too quickly into the wind to begin his takeoff run, breaking his right wheel. Gish waited impatiently as a new one was fitted to the landing strut. After stops at Salduro and Battle Mountain later that Friday, October 17, he landed at Reno two hours before sunset, but fog over the Sierras prevented further progress. He used the extra time to have his engine oil changed.

Finally, in the late morning of Saturday, October 18, Gish reached San Francisco. He was one of five to make it to the West Coast that day, which Mitchell had set as the deadline for pilots who wished to return to their points of origin. It might have been a moment to celebrate, had Gish not managed to crash.

It happened on his second landing attempt. On his first one, he had come in too high, aborted his approach, and circled around for another try. There was nothing wrong with that; then as now, pilots were taught that there is no shame in a go-around, which is almost always a better option than trying to force a landing after a sloppy approach. On his second attempt, Gish again came in too high. But this time, instead of going around, he decided to risk a landing—with insufficient room to stop. As the DH-4's wheels grazed the dirt, Pomeroy, in the rear cockpit, scrambled onto the fuselage to hold down the tail in hopes of slowing the aircraft. His weight broke the tail skid, but they were carrying too much speed. About halfway down the field, the plane began veering to the left, toward a row of small buildings. Gish tried to straighten the plane by stepping on the right rudder bar and adding a little power, but the correction came too late. The DH-4 plowed into a shack at the end of the row. Pomeroy was tossed from the fuselage but, remarkably, neither he nor Gish was hurt. Among those who witnessed the accident were Gish's parents, who had traveled from their home in Seattle.

The Presidio control officer attributed the crash—the only serious accident to occur on his watch—to pilot error; Gish blamed a flat left tire. Either way, the plane would not fly again. "Derby Airplane Named 'Junk' Is Just That Now," read the headline in the *San Francisco Chronicle* the next morning.

It seemed that Gish, too, was out of the contest. After walking away from two serious crashes in ten days, to say nothing of the one that had nearly killed him in France, how could it be otherwise? But anyone who asked that question did not know Brailey Gish.

23

Homeward Bound

Maynard was trapped between two snow squalls, with no obvious path to safety. He was once again over the Medicine Bow Mountains in Wyoming, this time heading east. Ahead, he knew, were mountain peaks that rose above his flight path, but he could not see them through the snow. A dense layer of clouds prevented him from climbing any higher. He could only hope that he would find an opening—a crack in the ceiling, a cleft in the terrain—before it was too late. Only Trixie, nose in the wind, was oblivious to their peril.

Maynard's departure from San Francisco had come much sooner than he would have liked. After reaching the Presidio on Saturday, October 11, he had been delighted by the news that the second half of the race—the return journey—had been put off for more than a week. The opulent, nine-story Palace Hotel, which had opened a decade earlier after the original was destroyed in the earthquake of 1906, seemed like heaven after the stress and discomforts of his flight. Maynard spent the rest of his weekend reading congratulatory telegrams, making appearances at two of the city's biggest Baptist churches, and tooling around the city's hilly streets in an automobile that had been provided for his use (William Kline spent most of his time "resting and sleeping"). He delivered the bags of salt he had carried from Salduro and mailed a stamped letter from Archie Miller, the commander of Roosevelt Field, to a friend of Miller's who lived on Vallejo Street. The Flying Parson was the toast of San Francisco, flooded with invitations to dinners and luncheons—including one from King Albert of Belgium, a wartime ally who was visiting the city as part of a nationwide victory tour.

But Maynard would have to decline the king's offer. On Sunday night, the Air Service announced a change in plans, transmitted to control stops by telegram over Charles Menoher's name. Pilots who wished to fly round-trip would have to begin their return journey within two to four days of completing their first crossing. Though the Air Service gave no reason for the change, it likely was driven by concerns about the approaching weather. Maynard swallowed his disappointment and began making preparations to leave.

"If the Air Service says, 'Fly back,'" Maynard told reporters, "Sergeant Kline and myself will try to be ready."

Maynard planned to depart the city on Tuesday, October 14, at 1:12 p.m.—precisely the time he had landed at the Presidio three days earlier. It was the earliest he could do so under the new rule, which exempted Sunday from the two- to four-day layover period.

———

On Monday, October 13, Maynard stopped by the Presidio to prepare for his flight back to Long Island. He was pleased to see that *Hello Frisco* was in fine shape; its wings and fuselage had been soaped and rinsed and its propeller sanded and shellacked. Kline had seen to the Liberty engine. After taking the aircraft aloft for a trial "jazz," Maynard pronounced it ready to go. He visited the hospital for a quick physical exam, which rendered a similar verdict, and checked in with Trixie, who had been quartered at the base and spoiled on a diet of roast chicken.

Maynard expected the second crossing to be easier than the first. This time, the prevailing wind would be with him, and by now he was familiar with the locations of the airfields along the route. He was so confident that he would reach his goal by Friday that he made arrangements to dine with his wife and children that night at the Ritz Carlton in New York. Not only that, but he already had secured permission to embark on a *third* crossing of the continent—to San Diego via Dallas—soon after his return to the East

Coast. This time he would fly alone, in a DH-4 fitted with an extra gas tank in the rear cockpit. The extra range, he told reporters in San Francisco, would allow him to complete the crossing in just two days.

At the Presidio on Tuesday, Maynard and Kline completed their final preparations before a large audience of civilians and military personnel. Only Trixie seemed less than pleased, whimpering and resisting efforts to nudge her toward the plane. Mechanics finally wrestled her into the front cockpit, where she would ride with Maynard for at least the first leg, to Sacramento. Maynard could not resist putting on a final show. After taking off at 1:23 p.m.—eleven minutes behind schedule— he banked so steeply over San Francisco Bay that the DH-4 seemed to stand on its wing, its landing gear pointed straight at the Golden Gate. Kline waved at the cheering throng, and in three minutes the airplane was out of view.

Left behind were John Donaldson, Harry Drayton, and four other pilots who had reached the Presidio the day before. It was hard to see how they could catch the Flying Parson; under the rules, none could begin the return flight until the following day. As for the Western Department flyers, those who had reached Long Island were still on the ground, with no word on when they would start their return flights. The race, it seemed, was Maynard's to lose.

———

Battle Mountain was ready for him. After taking off from the Presidio and an easy flight over the Sierras and across the Nevada desert, he reached the lively mining town under scattered clouds at 5:47 p.m. Townspeople had turned out in force, cheering wildly as he touched down at the sandy field. A feast had been prepared at the new schoolhouse. Maynard and Kline gave short speeches and were presented with a gold nugget and three arrowheads symbolizing their role as "pioneers." The auditorium was then cleared for a dance, at which point the two honored guests excused themselves. They spent a comfortable night at the Nevada Hotel, which was built in 1872 and recently had acquired a billiards table along with a telephone, steam heat, electric lights, and hot and cold running water.

The next morning, Wednesday, October 15, Maynard and Kline were "up before the chickens." Pushing the rules, they took off six minutes before sunrise and climbed above the jumbled desert mountains of eastern Nevada. The air was still and the sky clear, though ground fog filled the valleys, like milk in a bowl. Soon only mountaintops were visible. With no railroads or towns as reference points, Maynard paid careful attention to the gimbaled brass-and-steel compass in the center of his instrument panel. The Liberty engine, at least, showed no sign of distress. Like all pilots, Maynard dreaded the prospect of engine failure over terrain he could not see, knowing that a descent through zero-visibility conditions could end in disorientation and an unrecoverable spin.

Still, he was disappointed that the fog had lifted by the time he reached Salduro; with plenty of fuel in the tank, he would have liked an excuse to skip the control stop with its treacherous surface. But this time Maynard managed to land without ground-looping.

At Salt Lake City, the airfield was partially shrouded in smoke, and Maynard was above the Wasatch foothills before he realized he had overshot it. After circling back and landing, he was told he would have to wait a while, because of snowstorms over southwestern Wyoming. Irritated by the delay, Maynard complained that "he had a dinner engagement" in New York on Friday evening, but the control officer at the field— Lt. J. G. Hall, who had taken over from Capt. T. S. Voss—was unmoved.

With time to spare, Maynard accepted an offer to fly a civilian airplane—a Curtiss JN-4—accompanied by a newspaper reporter "who did not much care for his life." The short flight nearly ended in disaster. The underpowered Curtiss struggled to get off the ground with its full load, running off the airfield and onto a road before it hit a bump and staggered weakly into the air. Maynard skimmed over fences and ditches, banking sharply to avoid a tree. After much effort, the Curtiss reached an altitude of about 1,000 feet above the ground, where Maynard cautiously performed a few maneuvers for the crowd. He landed after fifteen minutes in the air, feeling "shaky all over."

Shortly after that near-calamity, Hall lifted his hold, and Maynard took off for Green River, where he landed at 1:35 p.m. He and Kline lunched on steaks while their plane was serviced, then departed for Rawlins, which they reached in less than an hour. But the weather didn't favor them for long.

Storms were building over the Medicine Bow Mountains. As Maynard flew the compass course toward Cheyenne—once again eschewing the safer path along the Union Pacific railroad—he threaded his way among snow showers until they converged to the point where he could no longer see the mountains ahead. Then he spotted "a narrow opening of light"—a gap in the clouds—that offered a possible escape. Just as he passed through it, a mountainside loomed. Maynard pulled back on the stick, clearing the peak by 150 feet. Later he would realize how lucky he had been. The mountain was just a few miles from the pass where Wales had died a week earlier.

At least he was making good time. Pushed by a fierce tailwind, Maynard completed the 133-mile leg from Rawlins to Fort D. A. Russell in just fifty-seven minutes, for an astonishing average groundspeed of 140 miles an hour. At this rate he would easily beat his record on the flight west. Though it was late in the afternoon, and snow was falling lightly, Maynard was determined to press his advantage. He apologized to civic leaders who had expected him to spend the night and prepared an elaborate reception in his honor. "The ninety-three miles from here to Sidney might just be the margin that would prevent me from reaching New York before sunset Friday," he explained.

After half an hour on the ground, and another bowl of oyster stew, Maynard was on his way again. He took off to the west, into the wind, then banked so steeply toward his eastbound course that a wingtip nearly brushed the grass. He reached Sidney in less than an hour, though he lost a couple of minutes searching for the control stop, which was covered in snow that made it hard to distinguish from surrounding fields. He landed at 5:54 p.m.

Maynard was feeling good about his progress. The mountains and their myriad threats were behind him. That night he and Kline headed into downtown Sidney to see a movie, *The Woman on the Index*, at the sparkling new U.S.A. Theatre.

24

A Telegram from Omaha

On the same afternoon that Belvin Maynard reached Sidney, Billy Mitchell was back on Capitol Hill, publicly disparaging his boss.

He was testifying before a House subcommittee investigating wartime spending on aviation. After recounting his experiences in France, Mitchell was asked about the wisdom of placing ground commanders in charge of aviation, as the War Department had done in selecting an artilleryman—Charles Menoher—to run the Air Service. His answer was characteristically blunt.

"It has been proved beyond a measure of doubt," he told the panel, "that unless you have a flying officer commanding, you cannot do anything."

A congressman then asked: "You have got to have a man who from his own experience and knowledge knows the game from the ground up?"

"Yes," Mitchell replied. "He cannot know it any other way."

Mitchell's testimony prompted no apparent reaction from the Air Service chief, who once again showed remarkable forbearance toward his impertinent second-in-command. Then again, Mitchell was at that point close to untouchable, protected by his war hero's halo as well as his allies in Congress, where his plans for an independent air force—and a bigger aviation budget—appeared to be making headway.

Both were linked to the transcontinental race, which also had taken a promising turn after the mayhem of its opening days. Belvin Maynard's arrival in San Francisco on October 11 had triggered an avalanche of favorable press. Now the Flying Parson was on his way home, and a dozen more pilots had arrived on the coasts; more than twenty others were positioned to complete their first crossing in the next couple of days. Moreover, the weather predicted for much of the route looked promising, at least for now. Mitchell finished his testimony at 5:20 p.m. on that Wednesday, October 15, then went to the movies with Caroline.

––––––––

He may have gotten the news later that night, in a telephone call from headquarters. In any case, by the time he left for work on Thursday, October 16, it was all over the morning papers: The contest had claimed two more lives.

Late on the previous afternoon, French Kirby and his observer, Lt. Stanley C. Miller, had taken off from Green River, Wyoming, and headed west toward the next stop at Salt Lake City. By some reports it was snowing along the route, though the weather appears to have had little bearing on what happened next. As the men passed over a ranch near Castle Rock, Utah, near the Wyoming border, their engine stopped. Cowhands watched the biplane glide into a turn as Kirby set up for an emergency landing. But like others before him, he failed to maintain sufficient flying speed to compensate for the bank angle. The DH-4, named *Defender*, stalled and spun, plummeting about 200 feet to the ground.

By the time the cowboys pulled the two men from the wreckage, Kirby was already dead. Miller died about ninety minutes later, before the arrival of a doctor who had been summoned from Castle Rock. The manager of the ranch telephoned Salt Lake City with the news, which was relayed from the control stop to Washington, D.C., by telegram. Both men were married, and Kirby left behind a nine-year-old daughter. A day after the crash, Kirby's father boarded a train in Washington, D.C.—Kirby's hometown—and began the journey to Utah to retrieve his son's body.

The trickle of second-guessing that had begun a few days earlier now became a torrent. The Associated Engineers of Spokane, Washington, said in a statement that the race "is doing more in the public mind to injure legitimate aviation than perhaps anything so far attempted." An aviator who recently had left the Air Service to join the Curtiss Aeroplane & Motor Corporation derided the contest as "a mere sporting event that put a premium on speed and therefore induced carelessness."

No one was more caustic in his judgment than Fiorello La Guardia, the diminutive, sharp-tongued Republican congressman from New York City, which he would later serve as mayor. An Air Service veteran who had flown Caproni Bombers on the Italian Front, La Guardia was one of the country's most influential voices on aviation policy and a strong backer of an independent air force. Unlike Mitchell, though, he thought the best way to achieve that goal was to starve the Air Service of funds, as a means of pressing the War Department to support the new air arm. He believed, like many of his wartime comrades, that the United States had squandered its billion-dollar investment in aviation, a failure he blamed on unscrupulous contractors and "incompetent officers." As he saw it, the transcontinental race belonged on the same continuum of ineptitude, hubris, and disregard for the welfare of military airmen that had plagued the nation's aviation program since 1917.

He unleashed his broadside during a visit to New York:

> The recent transcontinental race is a most pathetic display of selfish interests. The toll of death is beyond all expectation of the percentage of casualty necessarily involved in an undertaking of this kind.
>
> The same gang that disregarded war in order to develop and help their own industries now send boys across the continent with an obsolete discarded machine in a vain hope to save their face.

La Guardia went on to claim, wrongly, that "ninety percent of the fatalities would not have happened" if aviators had been flying in aircraft other than the unmodified DH-4, given the risk it posed to pilots seated in front of the gas tank.

Newspaper editorials were scarcely more charitable. The *Chicago Tribune* accused the Air Service of "rank stupidity." The *San Francisco*

Chronicle called the deaths "rather a high price for a race across the continent merely to demonstrate that the journey could be made." The *Buffalo Express* dryly observed that the contest had "done little to strengthen the public's faith in the safety of the heavier-than-air-machines." In Salt Lake City, the *Deseret Evening News* carried an editorial beneath the headline, "Death Rides with the Airmen." It read in part, "The men whose lives have been lost have not died for any great principle, nor have they even advanced the cause of science or contributed to the store of human knowledge or welfare." The *New York Times* was a rare exception, attributing most of the deaths to adverse weather that the Air Service could not have foreseen, as October is generally dry and clear.

————

The Air Service was thrown on the defensive. Harold Hartney, who had led the planning for the contest, ungenerously deflected blame to his fellow aviators. "The entrants were cautioned to be careful and the rules governing the contest were so drawn that there would be little chance of an accident," he told a reporter during his stopover in Reno on October 16, on the way to San Francisco. "But the men forgot the rules and forgot the safety-first slogan and tried to make a race out of it." Maynard, he added, "should have been disqualified" for flying after sunset.

Hartney's criticism was a little disingenuous. It should hardly have come as a surprise that aggressive, high-spirited young men who flew airplanes for a living would try to outrun one another in a contest judged by speed—even Mitchell had acknowledged that it was "really a race." At the same time, Hartney had a point: Many pilots in the contest *did* behave recklessly at times—and they continued to bend the rules even after so many of their comrades had died.

One of the more brazen offenders was Lt. J. P. Roullot, who arrived in San Francisco on Friday, October 17. An inspection of his DH-4 revealed that he had tuned his wings to reduce their upward angle to a barely perceptible half a degree. By flattening the so-called angle of incidence, he had gained a little speed, but at the cost of climb performance. It was later revealed that his DH-4 could fly no higher than 9,500 feet—

its standard operating ceiling was 14,000 feet—and had barely made it through the mountainous West. The control stop commander at the Presidio, Lt. H. A. Halverson, told Roullot that before he could begin his return journey, the wings would have to be restored to the proper angle, as required by the rules. Roullot ignored him. On his fourth day in San Francisco, he waited until Halverson left the field for a few minutes, then took off for Sacramento. Halverson, on his return, was livid. He called Mather Field and ordered that Roullot be sent back to the Presidio. If he wouldn't play by the rules, then he could damn well ride the train to New York.

Roullot was so angry he had been disqualified that on his short flight back to San Francisco, he deliberately overtaxed the Liberty engine, damaging its crankshaft. The engine was knocking audibly when he landed. He was then "heard to say that he had put his ship in such condition that nobody else could fly it if he could not," as Halverson put in a telegram to headquarters.

Roullot's spiteful vandalism paled in comparison to an act of sabotage that could have cost another contestant his life. Lt. Robert S. Worthington was the fifth contestant to reach Mineola from the West, landing his S.E.5 at Roosevelt Field on Monday, October 13. Three days later, while inspecting his plane in preparation for his return journey, he was shocked to discover that someone had punched three small holes in his fuel tank. The holes had jagged edges that suggested they had been made with a nail. Worthington had the holes patched and the tank filled up with gas. But a few miles out of Binghamton the next day, the fighter's engine went dead. Worthington coasted to a successful landing, narrowly clearing telephone wires along one side of the field. His fuel tank—which normally held thirty-one gallons, more than enough to make the short flight from Mineola—was empty. Worthington speculated that someone had drained it before he took off. After landing at Buffalo the next day, he telephoned Mineola to report the tampering, but no culprit was ever identified.

Mitchell had little to say on the subject of competitive pressures for which he was at least partly responsible. In a memo to Menoher on October 24, he blamed most of the deaths on "bad flying on the part of the pilots," the solution for which was better training. He also noted that all but one of the men had died in unmodified DH-4s, "which should all be retired from the service as soon as practicable." He did not address the question of why, if he thought the biplane was fatally flawed, he had allowed his men to fly it across the country in the first place.

Now two more aviators were dead. Mitchell had barely had time to digest that loss when, on the afternoon of October 16, a telegram from Omaha delivered more bad news. Maynard was down with engine trouble in Nebraska.

25

Buffalo

Carl Spaatz was in no hurry. He was worn out from his flight to Mineola and ambivalent, at best, about repeating the journey in the opposite direction. He told Archie Miller, the commander at Roosevelt Field, that if he did choose to fly back to San Francisco, he would "take his own time" and fly a different route. Spaatz had had his fill of snow, rain, and bone-chilling cold. He planned to follow a southerly path through Texas, New Mexico, and Arizona to San Diego, at which point he would track the coast north to San Francisco. It would take him out of the running, but Spaatz told himself he didn't care.

He and Emmett Tanner, his mechanic, attended to their machine. In a hangar at Roosevelt Field, they replaced their DH-4's propeller and an exhaust pipe that had cracked from vibration and installed a new wing skid to replace the one they had broken while landing at Cheyenne. The Liberty engine needed only routine maintenance. Spaatz later would sing the praises of its Splitdorf Mica spark plugs, marveling that they had not needed cleaning or replacing even after crossing the continent.

By Wednesday, October 15, the plane was ready to go, but Spaatz continued to drag his feet. He planned to start his flight home the next morning. Then he learned that Lowell Smith was preparing to take off for San Francisco.

After laying over in Rochester on Saturday, October 11, Smith finally had reached Roosevelt Field late in the morning of Monday, October 13. The weather had turned colder and he was deeply chilled; water leaked from a hole in his radiator that had been plugged with corn-meal during his stop at Binghamton. But Smith had lost none of his competitive zeal. One of the first things he did after landing was to file a formal complaint that he had been intentionally delayed—at Salt Lake City, Rawlins, and Rock Island—for the benefit of Spaatz and Emil Kiel. It was a questionable charge at best, but his frustration was understandable. If not for the holdups, Smith probably would have beaten both men to the coast. And his logbook showed an unofficial flying time of twenty-four hours and thirty minutes—twenty minutes faster than that of the headline-grabbing Belvin Maynard (Smith's offi-cial flying time was considerably longer, because it included the hours he lost after damaging his plane short of the control stop in Cleveland). Smith confidently told reporters that he could still win the race and prepared to leave for San Francisco within forty-eight hours, just as soon as the rules allowed.

Spaatz would beat him into the air by three minutes. After saying goodbye to his parents, he took off Wednesday at 2:28 p.m. He had aban-doned his plan to take the southerly route and was once again back in the race.

Though not, it seemed, with any real conviction. Spaatz climbed through hazy skies to 3,000 feet, then throttled back to 1,450 rpm—well below normal cruise speed. After crossing the Hudson River, he contin-ued at a stately pace, taking in the view of lakes, farms, and forests tinged with autumn gold. Despite his head start, he reached Binghamton thirty minutes behind Smith, who had overtaken him along the way. "We hope to show a few of the boys what we can do on the way back to Frisco," Smith said at the control stop, where he anxiously scanned the horizon for any sign of his rival. "In fact, we expect to be the first ones to reach the Golden Gate."

By the time Spaatz's wheels touched the ground at Binghamton, Smith's biplane already was vanishing over the hills to the west. Spaatz climbed from his cockpit looking "tired and worn." He claimed that his engine was misbehaving, and he didn't want to push it too hard.

He was also reluctant to push himself. Spaatz finished his day at Rochester, where he landed at 6:14 p.m., while Smith made it to the next stop at Buffalo. Leaving his DH-4 in the care of mechanics at Curtiss Field, Smith headed into the city, presumably in search of a good meal.

What followed is a plot twist worthy of O. Henry. While Smith was enjoying himself in Buffalo, the mechanics flushed the oil tank of his plane with what they thought was kerosene. In fact, it was gasoline, which is far more volatile. The fumes were ignited by a kerosene lamp, and in seconds flames spread from the engine to the fuselage. Smith returned to the airfield to find his plane reduced to a charred hulk. The following day, the Curtiss Aeroplane & Motor Corporation, which operated from the field, offered to loan Smith another airplane—an Oriole, the company's latest model—with which to complete the contest. Charles Menoher granted permission for the switch, though in the meantime, rain had moved in, preventing any departures.

By the next morning—Friday, October 17—the skies had cleared. But then another telegram arrived from Menoher, rescinding his approval on grounds that the Curtiss was not a government machine. He ordered Smith to return to San Francisco by train. Smith, it seemed, was out of the race for good.

Or perhaps not. Spaatz had spent an extra night in Rochester because of the rain. When he finally reached Buffalo on Friday morning, Smith approached him with a bold request. Would he be willing to drop out of the race and turn over his DH-4 to him?

At first, Spaatz wouldn't hear of it. But it didn't take long for Smith to change Spaatz's mind. After fifteen minutes of cajoling, he decided there was little to be gained—for himself, the Air Service, or aviation—by completing the round-trip. Smith, on the other hand, still had something to prove. "I wanted to fly bad, and he was simply good enough to give me the ship and his chance," he explained to a reporter. Tanner agreed to occupy the rear cockpit in place of Francis Ruggles, who also was glad of an excuse to drop out. After a telegram from Pitts, the control stop commander, reporting that "all parties concerned are agreeable" to the swap, Menoher gave his approval.

Smith was back in the running, but his troubles were not behind him. The engine of his borrowed plane gave out at Cheyenne, where he lost two days swapping it out for one salvaged from a wreck; then, on the leg to Salt Lake City, he was knocked unconscious by a chunk of ice that detached from his radiator (Tanner flew the plane until he recovered his senses). But on the morning of October 21, six days after he left Long Island, Smith landed in San Francisco, the first pilot from the West to complete the round-trip journey.

For part of his return trip, Smith was pursued across the country by Emil Kiel, who days earlier had been the first to land at Roosevelt Field. After a few days of rest, and perhaps a little peer pressure, Kiel had changed his mind about returning to California by rail. Like Spaatz, however, he displayed no particular enthusiasm for his second flight across the continent. He delayed his departure as long as possible, as his wing fabric and struts were repaired. He finally left Mineola on Thursday, October 16, nearly twenty-four hours behind his two rivals. It was probably with some relief that he dropped out of the race three days later, after smashing his landing gear in a forced landing in western Nebraska.

Spaatz was only too happy to put such adventures behind him. After wishing Smith good luck, he hopped on a train to Chicago, where he met up with Ruth for five days of leave.

26

The Mechanic

Whipped by an icy wind, snowflakes danced across the prairie as Belvin Maynard and William Kline readied their plane at Sidney in the pre-dawn hours of Thursday, October 16. They had been hoping, as always, to get away at dawn, a prospect that now seemed unlikely. A message from North Platte, one stop to the east, had reported similar conditions there. The control officer at Sidney had put a hold on any departures until the flying weather improved.

Maynard was dismayed. With victory seemingly within his grasp, every wasted minute felt like torture. Impatiently he searched the eastern horizon for any sign of an improvement.

It was not long in coming. Around sunrise, the clouds began to break up, and the Sidney control officer lifted his hold. Maynard took off at 7:14 a.m.

Flying skills alone did not account for Maynard's lead. He also had been lucky, avoiding the mechanical or weather problems that had caused long delays or worse for so many other contestants. If he needed a reminder of his good fortune, he got one later that morning at North Platte, where he met up with seven pilots who had started with him in Mineola eight days earlier—including Brailey Gish—and still were working their way west. They had been held for two days at St. Paul—Maynard's next stop east—because of fog. Maynard gave them advice on crossing the Rockies then took off after thirty minutes on the ground.

Maynard could almost allow himself to relax. The day had turned beautiful, and his confidence in the Liberty engine, whose virtues he never tired of promoting, was absolute. "I believe it is in better condition than when we hopped off on the race," he had claimed after reaching San Francisco. "We had absolutely no motor trouble coming across and did not have to replace a single spark plug." With more good weather ahead, he and Kline were now all but certain that they would be the first to complete the round-trip journey. They expected to make Bryan, Ohio, by sunset, and Mineola on the following day. After climbing away from St. Paul, Maynard leveled off at 2,500 feet, admiring the board-flat farm country stretching in all directions. "A plane never carried two more jubilant spirits than old *Hello Frisco* carried away from St. Paul that day." His comeuppance soon followed.

Airplane engines rarely failed without warning. A temperature jump, a loss of oil pressure, a change in rhythm or pitch—all were signs that something was amiss, and pilots ignored them at their peril. Now and again, however, an engine would quit without the courtesy of a heads up, instantly transforming a routine flight into an emergency.

Maynard was about thirty miles west of Omaha—close enough that he would have seen the city and a bend in the Missouri River just beyond—when it happened. Without so much as a stutter or a cough, the big Liberty engine simply shut down. "Our hearts just about did the same thing," Maynard said later. In place of the engine's roar, there was only the oceanic hiss of wings and wires cleaving the air. Instinctively, Maynard lowered the nose to maintain flying speed. As the propeller windmilled uselessly, he ran his eyes over his instrument panel in search of an obvious explanation. Finding none, he focused on his next task, which was to get the airplane safely on the ground.

He was glad he was over Nebraska and not the mountains he had crossed a day earlier. With no shortage of options, he chose a stubbled cornfield on the outskirts of the town of Wahoo. He coasted in over tele-phone wires and a fence, touching down smoothly and with ample room to spare.

Utterly confounded, Kline scrambled from his cockpit even before Maynard could turn around to look at him. The mechanic climbed onto the wing so he could inspect the engine, while Maynard dismounted and walked to the nose. Somewhat optimistically, he suggested that the igni-tion system might be faulty—a relatively minor problem that could easily be repaired. But when Kline pulled off the distributor cap, he could find nothing wrong.

It didn't take long to arrive at a diagnosis. "Turn the propeller," Kline said. As Maynard tugged down on one of the blades, Kline could detect no movement of the camshafts, which lift and close the cylinder valves. Not a good sign. He jumped down from the wing and turned the propeller a few times himself. Just as he had feared, it rotated without resistance. That could only mean one thing.

"We have broken the crankshaft," Kline declared. There was not much more to say. It was akin to a death sentence.

"Well, I guess we are through," Maynard replied. "There is not another motor this side of Chicago." He laughed a little and tried to lighten the mood, saying that at least they could get some rest and a good meal.

Then Maynard remembered something. Somewhere along the way—probably during his stopover in Sidney the night before—he had seen a newspaper report about the Martin Bomber, the lumbering twin-engine biplane piloted by Capt. Roy Francis. A few hours before May-nard left the Presidio, Francis had taken off from Des Moines and flown into heavy fog near Omaha. He lost his bearings and attempted an emer-gency landing near Yutan, Nebraska, a few miles west of the control stop. The bomber was snagged by telephone wires and plowed into a field. Francis and his three crew members escaped serious injury, though the aircraft was damaged beyond repair. (Guy De Lavergne, the French air-man who had hitched a ride on the Martin Bomber at Rochester, had dropped out in Des Moines, after his superiors called him back to Wash-ington, D.C.)

Out-of-focus photo of the Martin Bomber after its crash near Omaha. *Library of Congress*

But what about the two engines? They were identical to the Liberty engine on the nose of Maynard's DH-4. If he could somehow recover one and install it on his own plane, he would still have a shot at winning the race—though he would have to complete the task within forty-eight hours, the time limit on layovers between control stops. It was a tall order. Even in a fully equipped maintenance hangar, swapping out an engine was a big job that would normally take a couple of days.

Still, it was worth a try. Maynard had landed around noon. He quickly found a farmhouse with a telephone and called the control officer at Omaha, who told him that the bomber was only about twelve miles distant. Not only that, but the engines were undamaged and were to be removed by a salvage crew that very day. Then Francis got on the line and "told me I was welcome to one as far as he was concerned," advising him on which of the two was in better shape. Maynard asked the control officer to wire headquarters for permission, then waved down an automobile and persuaded its driver to take him to Yutan; Kline stayed with the DH-4.

Maynard arrived in Yutan to find an Army detail from Omaha already working to unship the Martin's engines. They loaded one of them onto a truck supplied by the Fort Omaha Balloon School, and Maynard accompanied it back to Wahoo.

The quality of Air Service mechanics was uneven at best. One pilot in the race would later remark that an incompetent one was "more useless than a sandbag because he had to be wakened in the morning." Another pilot was delayed when a mechanic accidentally filled his oil reservoir with gasoline. But Maynard had been shrewd in his choice of passengers. A 27-year-old sergeant from Harrisburg, Pennsylvania, the stocky, handsome Kline had served with Maynard in France, impressing him as one of the best mechanics in the Air Service. Now his resourcefulness and expertise would be put to the test as never before.

Kline had been busy during the few hours that Maynard was away. With help from a mechanic who lived nearby—and happened to have worked on Navy seaplanes during the war—he pushed the DH-4 next to a tree and rigged a block-and-tackle from a limb. They hauled out the old engine soon after Maynard arrived with the new one. In the meantime, Charles Menoher had telegraphed his approval of the plan.

"I am still in the race," Maynard told a reporter late that afternoon, "and I will make up the lost time as soon as I can take to the air." He made time to send a telegram to Essie, assuring her that he was okay.

After the new engine was lowered into place, the real work began— bolting it to wooden rails, mating fuel and oil lines, and reconnecting engine instruments, switches, and ignition wires. Darkness complicated the task. Maynard and the two mechanics worked feverishly in the glow of automobile headlamps, a bonfire, and a portable Delco lighting system. By 9:00 p.m., Maynard felt confident enough of their progress to tell a *New York Times* reporter who reached him by telephone that the work would be completed before daylight.

A couple of hours later, he excused himself to sleep at nearby farmhouse. He would need some rest if he was going to fly the next morning.

Kline and his helper kept working. After a short and restless night, Maynard returned to the cornfield before dawn on Friday, as the mechanics were taking the final step of fitting the propeller onto the driveshaft.

They tightened the last of the bolts. "O.K., warm 'er up," Maynard said.

Red-eyed, grimy, and unshaven, Kline climbed into the front cockpit and adjusted the spark and throttle settings. The engine was started without difficulty, to everyone's immense relief. Kline let it idle for a few minutes, watching the engine gauges and listening carefully to satisfy himself that nothing was amiss. Then he joined Trixie in the rear cockpit.

The trio was soon on its way, stopping first in Omaha so that Maynard could complete the leg he had started the day before. If it were up to him, he would have returned to St. Paul to restart the leg to Omaha, so that the time he lost replacing his engine would not count against his flying time. But Menoher had turned down his request.

Kline was bone tired. Oblivious to the wind and the engine's roar, nestling with Trixie for warmth, he slept most of the way to Chicago.

Remarkably, Maynard had lost only half a day of flying. For the moment, his closest competitor was Lt. Alexander Pearson, also in a DH-4, who had started with him in Mineola and had departed San Francisco less than twenty-four hours after him. By the morning of Friday, October 17, as Maynard resumed his journey in Nebraska, Pearson had closed to within 400 miles (Lowell Smith, who led the pilots returning from Long Island, was still in Buffalo trying to secure a replacement for his incinerated plane). Then, as Pearson flew between Sidney and North Platte, a bearing in his engine burned out. He managed to make the airfield in North Platte, but the Liberty engine was ruined. Taking a cue from Maynard, he got permission from headquarters to replace it with the Martin Bomber's remaining engine. But the engine had to be shipped to North Platte by rail, and he would not be able to resume his journey until three days later, on Monday, October 20. "We're going to stick it out if we have to borrow an engine from a flivver," Pearson said on reaching Omaha that afternoon. But only one other pilot had a hope of catching Maynard now.

John Donaldson had been "royally entertained" in San Francisco. The youthful war hero toured the city in a friend's high-powered automobile—later he would remark that "driving such a car through San Francisco was more dangerous, in my opinion, than flying my S.E.5 over the Sierras"—and luxuriated in the five-star comforts of the Palace Hotel, where he got his boots shined and charged taxis to his room. (The Air Service would be billed $16 for charges run up by Donaldson and other flyers, who apparently did not realize that the hotel's courtesy extended only to lodging and meals. The sum might well have been larger had its popular bar not been closed with the advent of Prohibition.)

Meanwhile, as Donaldson swanned around the city, mechanics at the Presidio saw to *Gloomy Gus*, replacing its tachometer and other parts and gluing a protective layer of linen to the leading edge of its propeller.

It seems they botched the job. At 3:41 p.m. on Wednesday, October 15, after two nights in San Francisco, Donaldson took off from the Presidio to begin his return journey. He had not even reached Sacramento, a short 75-mile flight, when *Gloomy Gus* began shaking violently. The linen had separated from one blade of the propeller, throwing it out of balance. Donaldson set down in a field, stripped off the remaining cloth, and returned to the air. He did not reach Sacramento until shortly after 5:00 p.m., too late to attempt the leg over the Sierras.

On Thursday, Donaldson made it to Rawlins, just one stop behind Pearson, whom he would soon overtake. Heavy snow on Friday morning made for a difficult crossing of the Medicine Bow Mountains, but after Cheyenne "nothing startling happened." Nevertheless, by the time he reached Omaha that afternoon, his hopes of catching Maynard were fading fast. "I'm willing to bet $10 I'll never make New York," he told a reporter, who was struck by the parallel between Donaldson's mood and the name painted on his plane. "My motor is wearing out and needs attention now." Mechanics at the field agreed, shaking their heads as he flew away.

But the Hisso held up and so did the weather. Heavy fog in Des Moines that morning had lifted by the time he landed there at 4:20

p.m. In good visibility under high, thin clouds, Donaldson completed the next leg to Rock Island in just under two hours, having covered 844 miles since leaving Rawlins that morning. It was a remarkable showing, approaching a single-day distance record in the race. But it would not be good enough to catch the Flying Parson.

27

Victory

Belvin Maynard had slept more than William Kline, but not by much. Now his weariness was starting to show. Moments after taking off from Omaha on Friday, October 17, with his newly installed engine, he realized he'd forgotten to display the proper map in his cockpit. The one in front of him covered the route he had just flown. The map he needed, showing the route ahead, was in a small suitcase stowed beneath Kline's wicker seat. Reluctantly, he turned back to the field to retrieve it, then departed Omaha for the second time that morning.

That was not the end of his troubles. About halfway to Des Moines, with Kline nodding off in the back seat, his famous navigation skills failed him for the first time in the race. Following his compass as always, he could find no obvious landmarks to confirm his position. He set down in a field to get his bearings and took to the air a few minutes later, reaching the Des Moines control stop, which was partially shrouded in smoke, at 10:13 a.m.

But if Maynard was fatigued, the crowds along his route provided a welcome source of renewal. Their excitement seemed to mount with every stop. After a bumpy flight from Des Moines, Maynard grinned broadly as he taxied to a halt on the sandy soil at Rock Island, where hundreds looked on as he was welcomed by the city's mayor along with Billy Sunday, the evangelist, and his wife Helen, and Homer Rodeheaver, Sunday's music director and a prominent composer of gospel songs. After providing Maynard and Trixie with lunch, the Sundays sent him on his way with a blessing and a photograph of Billy, on the back of which was written, "To Lieutenant Maynard—he leads, others follow."

That reception was dwarfed by the one at Grant Park in Chicago, where an estimated 3,000 people watched Maynard's steep, fishtailing descent toward the field. It took less time than a long shallow approach and always gave the crowd a thrill.

Once he was on the ground, reporters peppered him with questions.

"Don't you get awfully tired?"

"No, I don't get as tired as some of them. One aviator whom I met on the way to the coast looked like a corpse."

"Which side of the country would you recommend to cross-country flyers?"

"Well, I'd recommend the West if they want to see pretty country."

A newsreel cameraman asked, "Lieutenant, would you mind picking up your dog again?"

Maynard obligingly scooped up Trixie, who licked his nose.

But there were limits to his patience. Ever since he left Long Island, reporters had been badgering him about whether he would return to the pulpit after leaving the Army. His inconsistent answers made it clear that he was still struggling to make up his mind. By now he was heartily sick of the subject, which came up again in Chicago. "I can't tell you whether I'll go back to church again or not—please don't talk of it," he snapped at a reporter. "I'm tired. No sleep at all last night."

Maynard's departure was no less memorable than his arrival. Taking off into the wind, the safest option, would have required him to taxi into position down the field, at a cost of precious time. So instead, he simply gunned the engine and raced down the turf at a right angle to the wind, pushing the stick to one side to deflect the ailerons and keep the wings level. He skimmed the ground for a hundred yards to gain speed, then climbed so steeply that it seemed certain the plane would stall. In moments he was over Lake Michigan, flying far offshore on a direct line to the next stop at Bryan, Ohio. There he chatted briefly with Lowell Smith, who earlier in the day had resumed his journey west in the plane he had wheedled from Carl Spaatz in Buffalo.

Maynard finished the day on Friday in Cleveland, where he spent a comfortable night in the grand family home of an Air Service buddy whose father was the publisher of the *Cleveland Plain Dealer*. After dinner with his hosts, Maynard turned in early, brimming with confidence. Only 503 miles to go. Earlier in the day, he and Kline had agreed on a motto: "Mineola by two o'clock."

They would make it with ten minutes to spare. The weather map issued in Washington, D.C., at 8:00 a.m. on Saturday, October 18, showed high pressure dominating the entire route. Except for ground fog at Binghamton, which would soon burn off, the visibility was ideal. Maynard's main worry now was his engine. He'd been pushing it hard, as he always did, and any little hiccup was cause for concern. It took some doing to start the engine at Cleveland and again at Buffalo, where he was delayed by 14 minutes, but once airborne, the Liberty engine seemed to run fine. Still, he later acknowledged, it wasn't until he was within gliding distance of Roosevelt Field that he finally allowed himself to relax.

With Donaldson hundreds of miles behind, and his victory all but assured, Maynard's final sprint evoked a ball player trotting around the bases after smacking one over the fence. Each stop celebrated his achievement in its own way. As Maynard approached Buffalo over Lake Erie, ships and locomotives blasted their steam whistles, and thousands watched his DH-4 descend toward Curtiss Field in sparkling sunshine. "Welcome back, ace," said the control officer at Rochester, where amateur and news photographers alike surrounded Maynard and his companions, clicking their shutters "until not an idea for a picture remained." At Binghamton, the self-proclaimed Air Gate to New York, Maynard was formally welcomed by Boy Scouts and clergymen, who presented him with cut flowers. "No nervous hurrying, no boastful statements, no semblance of a pose marked the man whose aerial achievement, for speed and endurance and everything else, is unequaled," the Rochester *Democrat and Chronicle* gushed the next morning. "He just munched roasted chestnuts and played the modest man."

At Roosevelt Field that Saturday, about 1,000 people waited and watched for a first glimpse of *"Hello Frisco."* Shouts arose when it finally appeared as a tiny dot high in the sky, "moving at great speed, with a heavy blue haze trailing behind." Once over the field, Maynard raised the nose to a near-stall and descended in an oscillating "falling leaf" maneuver. He sideslipped to complete the descent, then straightened and settled gently onto the dirt.

As *"Hello Frisco"* rolled to a stop in front of the headquarters tent, an official recorded the time its wheels touched the ground: five seconds past 1:50 p.m.

Essie and their two small children had been waiting anxiously at the edge of the landing area. All were smartly dressed—Essie in a pleated skirt and flat-brimmed hat, the girls in matching capes and bonnets. Each child held a big red apple that they had brought as a gift for their father. As officers cleared a path through the surging crowd, mother and children made their way to the plane, where Trixie rested her paws on the cockpit rim, barking and slapping Kline in the face with her tail.

After his propeller had shuddered to a stop, Maynard stiffly climbed down and embraced his wife, giving her a long kiss as the girls hugged his legs. He scooped them up in his arms and kissed them as well.

"I knew you would do it," Essie said, tears of happiness in her eyes.

"Kiss her again, parson," a cameraman yelled.

Maynard laughingly obliged.

In anticipation of their finish, Maynard and Kline had scrubbed the grime from their faces, probably during their stopover at Binghamton, and they both looked remarkably fresh, though Maynard seemed a little thinner than he had at the start. The two men beamed as they were surrounded by dignitaries and spectators, who competed to pump their hands and pound their backs amid shouts of "Atta boy!" and "Oh, you Maynard!" It was all a bit overwhelming for Trixie, who soon took refuge in the front seat of a nearby automobile. Reporters inspecting Maynard's plane noticed that its rudder was covered in names and addresses that had been scribbled by admirers at stops along the route.

After their initial welcome, Maynard and Kline were ushered into the headquarters tent, where newsmen scratched furiously on their notepads as Maynard gave a detailed account of their trip that would be carried verbatim in the next day's papers. Each credited the other for their success. Maynard called Kline "the best mechanic in the Air Service," and Kline returned the compliment, saying, "I would not want to fly with anyone except Lieutenant Maynard. He is a natural born flier and the greatest in the Air Service today." Mindful of the publicity aspects of the race, Maynard promoted both American engineering ("I think the Liberty motor is unsurpassed") and the prospects for aviation in general ("The airplane is built just as safe as the Brooklyn Bridge").

He also claimed to have made up his mind about his future. "I am going back to the ministry after getting out of the Army," he said.

Billy Mitchell learned of Maynard's success in Washington, D.C., where he had spent part of the afternoon horseback riding with his children. But he also found time to write a lengthy statement on Maynard's achievement that was released that night to the Associated Press. "The air distance covered is 5,402 miles, in less than 50 hours of actual flying time," it read in part. "It is as far from Constantinople to New York, from Berlin to Denver, from Tokyo to San Francisco, and twice the distance from Europe to America. From a military aspect there no longer can be any doubt that a complete control of the air by any nation means military control of the world."

He added, "As an individual performance Maynard's record stands second to none in the annals of the air in time of peace. His judgment, ability, grit, and determination exhibit the quality shown by our pilots in the European war and are typically American."

Maynard's job was done. After reporters had finally run out of questions, he retreated with his wife, daughters, and Trixie to their small cottage at Mitchel Field, where they celebrated that night with a chicken dinner and a "victory cake." The next morning he took a long walk by himself.

As Maynard was flying toward the finish line in New York on Saturday, John Donaldson was at Grant Park in Chicago, cursing his "pilot's luck." It was shortly after 9:00 a.m. Earlier that morning, he'd left Rock Island in good weather, his motor running more smoothly with eight fresh spark plugs. But he was already working on his excuses. "Pilot's luck breaks both ways, and that preacher had the good I had the bad," he told a reporter from the *Chicago Tribune*. "I think I can fly faster than the parson's big D-H. This ship of mine certainly knocks off the miles—it's a scout plane, a battle plane, and his is a great big old oil can that was built for bombing purposes." But Maynard, he said with a touch of bitterness, had consistently been favored by the weather. "It was uncanny. The storms were always just ahead or just behind him."

Donaldson was not wrong. His rival *had* been favored by the weather, especially at the outset, when an early departure from Mineola allowed him to leap ahead of the rainstorms that grounded flyers, including Donaldson, who left a bit later. At the same time, his comments revealed a sensitive ego. The clergyman's flying had been nearly flawless (for that matter, so had Donaldson's, notwithstanding his preference for hugging the ground). But Donaldson could not bring himself to say that. So he made excuses instead.

At the very least, Donaldson hoped he would reach Mineola on the same day as Maynard, but as he flew across Ohio and upstate New York it became clear that he would fall short. He got as far as Binghamton, just 142 miles short of his goal, when darkness curtailed his progress. Because of the rule against Sunday flying, he would not be able to complete his journey until Monday morning. He flew the last leg—the worst of the entire trip, he later said—in rain, fog, and biting cold. Maynard was among the few who turned out to greet him when he touched down at Roosevelt Field at 10:03 a.m. The next day, Donaldson's second-place finish was noted in a single paragraph on page nineteen of the *New York Times*.

The press and the public had moved on, but the race was far from over. Twenty-nine of the sixty-three airplanes that started the contest had completed the first crossing by Mitchell's deadline of October 18. Seventeen pilots ultimately would attempt to fly back to their starting points, though by Monday night only Maynard and Donaldson had succeeded in completing the return trip. The remainder were on their way or soon would be.

28

Flying Blind

A pilot who trusts his senses to guide him through bad weather or a dark night is asking for trouble. Deprived of visual cues—the horizon or the ground—the brain falls back on other biological mechanisms. The most important of these, the vestibular system, is situated in the inner ear. When the head moves, so does fluid in the vestibular system, displacing tiny filaments that alert the brain to changes in spatial orientation. This generally works fine on the ground. Under certain conditions of flight, however, the fluid and the filaments can interact in ways that send the wrong signal. The pilot might sense that his plane is turning left when it's turning right, climbing when it's descending, accelerating when it's slowing down—or even that it's inverted when it's flying right side up. Trying to correct for the illusion only makes things worse. One of many possible bad outcomes is called a "graveyard spiral."

A disoriented pilot is living on borrowed time. In 1954, researchers at the University of Illinois recruited twenty inexperienced pilots to fly with a flight instructor in simulated zero-visibility conditions. The subjects were told to execute a 180-degree turn, as if they had inadvertently flown into a cloud. None succeeded, losing control of the aircraft in an average of two minutes and fifty-eight seconds. Today, spatial disorientation accounts for between 5 and 10 percent of all general-aviation accidents. Ninety percent are fatal, famously including the crash that claimed the lives of John F. Kennedy, Jr., his wife, Carolyn, and her sister, Lauren

Bessette, while Kennedy was piloting a small plane on a hazy night off the coast of Massachusetts in 1999.

With proper training, modern pilots can safely fly in poor visibility by means of gyroscopic instruments such as the attitude indicator, which displays an aircraft's pitch and bank angle relative to the horizon. Sperry and other companies were already developing such instruments by 1919. But the Air Service was slow to adopt the technology, and it wasn't until the late 1920s that it began to work seriously on the problem of "blind flying." An Army reservist named James H. "Jimmy" Doolittle—remembered today as the leader of the bombing raid against Japan in 1942 that was immortalized in the book and movie *Thirty Seconds over Tokyo*—played a key role in that effort. On September 29, 1929, Doolittle took off from Mitchel Field with his head beneath a leather hood that prevented him from seeing outside the cockpit. Aided by radio direction-finding equipment and an early version of an attitude indicator, he circled back to the field and landed successfully. It was the first completely blind flight.

But the instrument panels of 1919 were unchanged since World War I. Besides a few engine gauges, they usually included a compass, an altimeter, an airspeed indicator, and sometimes a turn indicator, a crescent-shaped device that worked on the same principle as a carpenter's level, with a bubble to show the angle of bank. Pilots trapped in clouds or fog banks flew mostly by the seat of their pants. They did not train for instrument flight, and the Army's flying manual had little to say on the subject, other than that clouds "should be entered with caution."

———

Harold Hartney had been delayed by engine repairs in San Francisco. But at 9:22 a.m. on Tuesday, October 21, four days after his arrival on the West Coast, he began his journey home.

After an uneventful crossing of the Sierras, he raced across the Nevada desert to Salduro, where he managed to land without ground-looping, perhaps because of the jackknife he had lashed to his tail skid to give it more purchase on the hard-packed salt. He then flew to Salt

Lake City, where he would spend the night, and departed on Wednesday morning. Other than a close call at the infield-turned-airfield of Rawlins's horse-racing track, where a stiff crosswind nearly blew him into the grandstand, his second day also went smoothly. He reached North Platte before dusk, surely pleased with his progress.

But the weather was about to get much worse. By the time Hartney woke up Thursday morning, a dense blanket of fog, drizzle, and snow had settled across the Great Plains. He took off anyway, which proved to be a mistake. After covering just twenty-five miles, he lost his way in heavy fog and landed in a field to recover his bearings. He decided that it would be foolish to continue and returned to North Platte.

He would be stuck there for the next four nights, waiting for the weather to improve, but at least he would have some company. A day after his abortive departure, Hartney was joined at the stop by another pilot and a mechanic, who were making the return flight from San Francisco in a DH-4.

Lt. Ralph Bagby had not begun the race, or for that matter his flying career, as a pilot. A cheerful, mandolin-playing Missouri native with a mischievous smile and an engineering degree from MIT, "Baz," as his friends called him, flew on the Western Front as an observer. It was dangerous, vital work. Nine days before the end of the war, he and a pilot he paired with decided, on their own, to fly a reconnaissance mission in heavy fog that had grounded the planes on their field. Under intense ground fire, they flew deep into enemy airspace, taking photographs and strafing German targets on the ground, including an airfield and truck convoys, until Bagby's machine gun ran out of bullets. They returned with valuable information on the disposition of German troops and the condition of bridges over the river Meuse. Bagby finished the war with a Distinguished Service Cross and a French Croix de Guerre. Still, he chafed at what he perceived as the second-class status of observers. He yearned to be a pilot. After the Armistice, he was assigned to occupation forces in Germany, where he learned to fly in his spare time. He liked it so much that he changed his plans to seek an immediate discharge when he got home.

Bagby, now twenty-six, started the air race as an observer in a DH-4 flown by Lt. Col. John Reynolds. On the trip west, he occasionally took over the controls as Reynolds fiddled with his maps or goggles. Once the DH-4 "flew herself" for a full minute because each man thought the other was handling the stick. The two had complete trust in one another—while Reynolds did most of the flying, Bagby was "the boss" on matters of navigation—and never argued. Nevertheless, once they reached San Francisco, Reynolds decided that he would prefer to ride the train back home. Bagby's moment had arrived. He and the mechanic who had agreed to replace him in the rear cockpit, Sgt. L. M. Parrish, departed the Presidio on the morning of Monday, October 20.

Bagby was in no hurry—in a letter from San Francisco on Palace Hotel stationery, he had assured his mother that he would "take the return trip slowly"—and on the leg to Sacramento deviated from his route so that Parrish could drop a letter over the town where his family lived. Late in the afternoon, he bent an axle in a hard landing at Salduro. He spent the next day getting it repaired, finally reaching North Platte on the morning of Friday, October 24.

Three days would pass before the control officer judged the flying conditions safe enough to allow Hartney and Bagby to continue. What he and the aviators didn't know is that portions of the route, especially near St. Paul, were draped in an icy, nearly impenetrable fog—ideal conditions for disorientation and loss of control. After departing the field on the morning of Monday, October 27, Bagby climbed to 2,800 feet, but sleet and deteriorating visibility forced him to descend. He completed the last minutes of his flight at just 100 feet, skimming trees and rooftops in a dense fog, guessing at his airspeed because his indicator had frozen. He landed at St. Paul with his wings coated in ice.

Hartney, who followed a more southerly path, fared even worse. After he had covered about two-thirds of the distance to St. Paul, he flew into sleet and heavy fog. He could not see the ground, the horizon—anything beyond the nose and wings of the aircraft. He might as well have been blindfolded. "I lost all sense of direction," he recalled. Urgently, he scanned his instruments to glean what little information he could. Noting that his airspeed indicator registered sixty miles an hour—on the slow side—he dropped the nose to keep the plane in level flight. But the indicator, as he discovered only later, wasn't working properly—the slender, forward-facing *pitot tube* that measured the velocity of the plane's movement through the air was partly clogged with ice. Already disoriented by the fog, Hartney thought he was flying slower than he was and kept pushing on the stick to gain speed.

He plunged out of the soup in a vertical dive, heading straight for the gunmetal surface of the South Loup River just a few hundred feet below. Reflexively, he yanked on the stick and leveled off, avoiding catastrophe by a few seconds. He completed the leg at such a low altitude that he could see the startled expressions of people on the ground. At times, he recalled, they seemed to "step back to avoid the swift plane," which "zigzaged [*sic*] across country to avoid obstacles in the driving freezing mist."

By the time he landed, Hartney's plane, too, had picked up a load of ice. Neither he nor Bagby flew any farther that day.

The race, for them, was over. Their only goal was to reach Mineola before sunset on Friday, October 31, the official end of the contest. Mostly, it seems, because they enjoyed each other's company, they agreed to complete the journey together, sometimes flying in formation; Bagby had to throttle back because the DH-4 was faster than the Fokker. By Tuesday they had reached Chicago, from which they departed early the next morning, believing they could "easily" make New York by the end of the day. To their frustration, however, they were delayed at various control stops, where Bagby detected a lackadaisical attitude on the part of the Air Service troops who were starting to break camp. "In cold weather the oil is stiff as molasses and they wouldn't bother to warm it up," he complained to his mother. They finished the day at Binghamton, engaging in a brief mock dogfight—Hartney "put it all over me," Bagby reported—just before they landed. They assumed they would fly the final leg in the morning.

In fact, they would barely make the Friday deadline. Overnight, low clouds moved in, grounding them for the entire day on Thursday. "We used to fly in France in worse weather but there was more reason for it then," Bagby wrote his mother. With time on their hands, Hartney and Parrish, Bagby's mechanic, accepted an invitation to the weekly Kiwanis Club lunch at the Hotel Bennett, where Hartney promoted Mitchell's plan for an independent air arm.

They finally reached Mineola on Friday afternoon, just a few hours before sunset. It was an anticlimactic finish, barely noticed except by the men working at Roosevelt Field. By mutual agreement—and in deference to Hartney's higher rank—the Fokker's wheels touched down first.

29

Three Horses

By the time Brailey Gish approached Rawlins on the morning of Thursday, October 23, this time from the west, the small horse-racing track that served as its temporary airfield was well established as one of the most dangerous in the race. Pilots departed the stop in a state of high anxiety, as they strained to clear nearby hills and buildings in the thin air. Altitude aside, the field was raked by strong, unpredictable winds, which already had caused several crashes. The latest had occurred only minutes earlier. Lt. Thomas V. Hynes, an eastbound rival, was taking off when a gusty crosswind pushed his DH-4 to the north side of the field, where its landing gear clipped a fence top. The plane slammed to the ground, breaking its propeller, damaging its radiator and wings, and snapping four of its longerons. The aircraft could not be repaired with the limited parts on hand and would have to be shipped by rail to Mather Field in Sacramento.

With Hynes's accident fresh in his mind, Francis Longley, the control stop commander, was understandably concerned that Gish would meet a similar fate. The 35-mile-per-hour crosswind was far above the safe threshold. As Gish descended toward the field, the control officer tried to wave him off, signaling that he should proceed to the next stop at Cheyenne. Gish either misunderstood or failed to see him. He circled the field three times, gauging the wind as best he could, and lined up for his final approach.

———

Gish had wasted no time in finding a replacement for the plane he wrecked while landing at San Francisco on Saturday, October 18. As committed as ever to completing the round-trip flight, he persuaded Hap Arnold, the Air Service's Western Department commander, to assign him another DH-4, this one with "38" painted on its fuselage. Its pilot had just completed one flight across the continent and had no wish to repeat the experience. Soon after daybreak on Wednesday, October 22, Gish and George Pomeroy, his mechanic, took off from the Presidio and headed east in Gish's third plane of the race.

By now, Gish was known far and wide as the intrepid but unlucky pilot who was always just a hairsbreadth away from catastrophe. He had not even crossed San Francisco Bay when his engine started missing. But the Liberty engine settled down, and except for a tense moment at Salt Lake City—where Gish narrowly missed telephone wires that stretched across one end of Buena Vista Field—most of the day went smoothly. He landed for the night at Green River, where he found lodging with the ever-hospitable Couzens family, and took off early on Thursday morning. In Washington, D.C., Bowie, the Weather Bureau forecaster, had predicted snow over the mountains, but Gish apparently had little difficulty finding his way to the next stop at Rawlins.

Landing was another matter. The stiff south wind was blowing straight across the axis of the narrow landing area. As he sank toward the dirt with the engine throttled back, Gish pushed the joystick to the left, toward the wind, to lower the wing on that side and prevent the aircraft from drifting. At the same time, he worked his rudder bars to keep the plane aligned with his landing path. But the airfield was short at just 1,000 feet. In the absence of a headwind to check his ground speed, Gish overshot the landing T, which not only indicated the wind direction, but also was positioned alongside the optimal spot for touching down. Gish ran out of room. With no brakes to slow it down, his DH-4 rolled onto the rough ground at the west end of the field, tipped onto its nose, and lurched to a halt with its tail pointing skyward. Neither Gish nor his mechanic was hurt, but the same could not be said for their plane. The propeller was splintered. The radiator was smashed. A wheel had given way, snapping the rubber cords that served as shock absorbers. Worst of all, there was damage to the leading edges of the upper and lower left wings.

It was another setback, and a major one at that, but Gish had not come this far to give up now. With help from the Rawlins ground crew, he and Pomeroy immediately set to work. A new propeller and other parts were retrieved from stocks kept at the field, while a radiator and wing sections were salvaged from a wreck. They rebuilt the wings and completed the job with linen and dope. They would have resumed their journey on Friday, but storm clouds blew in, and Longley ordered them to wait.

————

For Gish, the race was no longer a test of speed but of stamina. He was now in second-to-last place, his only goal to complete the round-trip journey before the clock ran out on Friday, October 31. On the morning after his accident in Rawlins, the *New York Tribune* ran an editorial praising the "sheer pluck and grim determination" of the ill-starred airman. "The whole country will watch his progress," it concluded. "His matchless spirit demands success, but should he fail his cup of glory is already filled to the brim. Some uplifting influence seems to be in the upper reaches of the air. It feeds the eagle spirit and makes men more than men."

Having patched up his plane, Gish hoped to get away early on the morning of Saturday, October 25, after his second night in Rawlins. But the weather, once again, foiled his plans. By 8:30 a.m., more than three inches of snow had fallen, and conditions to the east were not much better. A bulletin from Washington forecast "continued bad weather along entire Transcontinental route except near the Pacific Coast."

Early that afternoon, Gish finally was permitted to take off from the snow-covered field, after better visibility was reported at Cheyenne. But getting there was a painful ordeal. To avoid snowstorms along the route, Gish climbed high above the Medicine Bow Mountains, where he and Pomeroy "suffered severely" in the intense cold. The radiator froze, and the engine temperature dropped to 45 degrees Fahrenheit—far below normal—as indicated by the gauge on the instrument panel. By the time he reached Cheyenne at 2:27 p.m., the wings and fuselage were coated with ice.

Gish lingered on the ground for an extra twenty-nine minutes while a hole in his radiator was soldered closed. He then took off for Sidney. Despite ground fog and drizzle, the westernmost stop in Nebraska had advised that "there was a possibility of getting thru." Gish made it to within thirty-three miles before giving up. He banked into a 180-degree turn and flew back to Cheyenne.

The following day was Sunday, which meant more time on the ground. Gish could not afford many more delays. Only five flying days remained until the end of the race. In the meantime, he was stuck in Cheyenne at least until Monday morning. With time on their hands, he and Pomeroy saw to their plane. They installed a new propeller, soldered—again— his chronically leaking radiator, installed a new distributor, changed the oil, cleaned the spark plugs, and tightened the stagger wires on his wings.

It was now more obvious than ever that Billy Mitchell had taken a big risk by extending the contest into late October. The weather, bad enough in the first days of the race, was now an unrelenting foe. On Monday morning—October 27—Gish took off early at Cheyenne, only to be forced back to Fort D. A. Russell a second time by fog and snow. He tried again at noon and made it as far as North Platte before dark, for a pathetic daily gain of 205 miles.

Mechanical problems caused further delays. On Tuesday morning, Gish was stalled by yet another radiator leak and did not take off from North Platte until 10:29 a.m. By the time he reached Des Moines at 3:01 p.m., not only was his radiator leaking again, but also his wheels needed attention. Reluctantly, he stopped for the night.

Gish must have wondered at times if he would not do better on horseback. At Rock Island on Wednesday, he again was delayed by weather—mist and low clouds—though flying conditions were not so bad that they prevented him from taking the Rock Island mayor's secretary on a brief sightseeing flight. He did so as a favor to Harold Hartney, who had passed through Rock Island the day before. The secretary, Miss Velma Hickman, had been delegated to help the control stop with its paperwork, and Hartney had proposed the joyride as a way of thanking her.

Public relations were all well and good, but the race would end in not much more than forty-eight hours. Given the weather, it was going to be tight. Gish had hoped to leave Rock Island in the afternoon, after taking Miss Hickman aloft. But rain kept him on the ground overnight and again the next morning. He did not take off until 1:21 p.m. on Thursday, October 30.

The daily weather map showed clouds across the entire Midwest, but visibility, it turned out, was the least of Gish's problems. Less than thirty miles from Chicago, the Liberty engine began to sputter. Gish correctly diagnosed the problem as low air pressure in the fuel tank. Unfortunately, he was flying at just 200 feet, to stay under the low ceiling, so he did not have time to try the hand pump (not that it would have mattered; later investigation would reveal that the air line was clogged with grease). The only option was to land immediately.

The DH-4 touched down on a plowed wheat field, sank to its wheel hubs in mud, and tipped briefly onto its nose before settling back onto its tail skid. The propeller was spared but not the radiator, which was spewing water and cracked beyond repair. Gish made his way to a telephone and informed the control stop at Grant Park that he was down near the town of Naperville. Help was promptly dispatched. A new radiator was installed, and the air line was unclogged. After the plane was pulled from the muck by three horses, Gish was finally able to continue. He reached Chicago later that afternoon and took off early Friday morning, expecting to make Mineola by sunset.

It was not to be. Within minutes of leaving Grant Park, the Liberty engine started missing badly, forcing Gish to return to the field. The carburetor was cleaned, the gas lines blown out, and the fuel tank drained so that it could be purged of mud and brass filings. A broken intake valve was replaced. Gish took off again, but the Liberty engine still wasn't running properly. He circled back to Grant Park, where mechanics found pieces of rubber in the carburetor and gas line. They reassembled the carburetor and started the engine, which ran beautifully for all of a minute. Mechanics replaced the carburetor, then tried to start the engine again. This time it failed even to catch. There was a short in the electrical system. Mechanics fixed that, too.

But Gish was out of time. At 1:35 p.m., he made his third departure of the day from Grant Park. Mineola was 810 miles to the east. He could not possibly get there by sunset and would have to settle for spending the night in Cleveland. The transcontinental air race was over.

Gish must have been bitterly disappointed, but in one sense, at least, he was able to finish what he started. On November 3, after a detour to Bolling Field in Washington, D.C., he completed his round-trip journey at Roosevelt Field. It had taken him twenty-six days.

PART IV

Foundation

30

A Sour Parting

A few days after Belvin Maynard completed the race, a brief controversy erupted in the press. The question was whether he actually had won. Solely on the basis of flying time, it was clear that he had not. The fastest pilot by that standard was Alexander Pearson, who had completed the round-trip journey in forty-eight hours and fourteen minutes, not counting time on the ground. Maynard had covered the distance in fifty hours and thirteen minutes at the controls, though his official flying time was much longer, because it included the time he lost replacing his engine in Nebraska. Lowell Smith had completed the race with the second-fastest official flying time, at fifty-four hours and fourteen minutes.

But the controversy, to the extent that there was one, faded quickly—it was an intramural dispute among aviators. As far as the public was concerned, "Maynard is the winner and will always be so considered," declared the *Reno Evening Gazette* on October 23. "Maynard was the first man to see New York harbor and San Francisco bay within four days time. He was the first man to fly across the continent in open competition and he was the very first man to fly from the Atlantic to the Pacific and back to the Atlantic. There is no getting away from that fact. Elapsed time, waiting time, penalties—all these may interest the technicians, but from the point of view of achieving a set object in the quickest time there is only one man to be considered and he is Maynard." The *New York Times* agreed, praising Maynard for his "skill, pluck," and "perseverance."

The Flying Parson was now one of the most famous pilots in America. In early November, with Charles Menoher's blessing, he took a victory lap in his home state of North Carolina, accompanied by William Kline and Trixie, in the same DH-4 that had borne them across the country and back. He spoke to civic groups and churchgoers, attended the dedication of a new airfield near Winston-Salem that was named in his honor, and buzzed a waiting crowd at Wake Forest with Governor Thomas W. Bickett riding in the rear cockpit (he tried to land on a golf course but aborted at the last second because the wind was blowing from the wrong direction). In his hometown of Clinton, he was the marquee attraction at the Sampson County fair, where he put on an aerobatics display for a crowd estimated at 25,000—"the largest assembly of people ever attending a fair in North Carolina," according to the Raleigh *News & Observer.* The mayor of Clinton presented him with a silverware service. He made it back to New York in time to deliver a speech at the American Flying Club's Armistice Day bash, though the ballroom at the Hotel Commodore was so noisy that few could make out his words.

———

His fall was not long in coming. For all his celebrity, Maynard remained a guileless country boy. He also had a censorious streak that now became evident. In a sermon on November 30 at the Brooklyn Methodist Church, he declared himself "shocked by the lack of clothes worn by women at receptions I have attended in New York City." Having been "raised in the peace, security and modesty of country life," he continued in the same priggish vein, "I could not but be displeased by the costumes of women whose dresses are cut so low in the back that one can count every vertebra from the waist up."

The parson was just warming up. In a statement solicited by the Anti-Saloon League, one of the main groups behind Prohibition, he dropped a bombshell—on aviators, on the Air Service, and ultimately on himself. "I have seen men who never flew unless they were half intoxicated," said the statement, which the league released to the press on December 8. "I have seen some who always took a drink before flying. I have seen

others who flew with a hangover from the night before." He then leveled
his most incendiary charge, suggesting that alcohol might have caused
some of the accidents in the race: "The secret of the failure of some of the
pilots in the recent transcontinental race can be attributed to too much
booze: If all of them had been as sober as myself, I probably would not
have been the winner."

It's true that many pilots liked a drink. Flyers on the Western Front,
Billy Mitchell very much included, were prodigious consumers of alcohol, which was seen as a useful antidote to stress. "It appears necessary
for the well-being of the average pilot that he should indulge in a really
riotous evening at least once or twice a month," reported the same Royal
Air Force study that had posited a link between horsemanship and flying skill. The authors saw nothing wrong with this, so long as pilots did
their imbibing *after* they were done flying for the day. Not surprisingly,
some failed to observe this rule. In a report on the medical aspects of the
transcontinental race, the Air Service's chief flight surgeon, Col. Albert
E. Truby, acknowledged the possibility that a few contestants might have
tried to calm their nerves with "an ill-advised 'bracer' or two," though
he offered no evidence that alcohol had contributed to any crashes. Nor
had Maynard provided any.

Mitchell was furious at what he perceived to be an insult to the memories of the men who had died in the race, to say nothing of the Air
Service's reputation. A few hours after reading of Maynard's claim in
the *Washington Post*, he released a blistering public rebuke. "This is not
only not true, but, if given out, constitutes a statement unbecoming an
officer and a gentleman," he declared. He listed each of the dead aviators by name and challenged Maynard to prove his charge. There was
talk of convening a board of inquiry that could lead to a court martial.
The mortified champion was summoned to Washington, D.C., to explain
himself. Resorting to a familiar dodge, Maynard claimed in a meeting
with Menoher that he had been misquoted. He repeated that claim to the
press, accusing the Anti-Saloon League of "juggling" his words to "create
a sensation." This was patently false, and the league had Maynard's typewritten statement to prove it. But Menoher was inclined to take Maynard

at his word, if only to avoid further embarrassment to the Air Service. Maynard returned to Long Island to ponder his future.

A letter from a stranger would point the way. "I am an old man of eighty," it read. "When I was young, a man who was then as old as I am today told me not to make a fool of myself. I now pass that advice on to you. Go back to your pulpit and give up your flying and newspaper fame." Maynard showed the letter to Essie, who could not have said it better herself. Her husband made up his mind. On December 21, he announced at the West Side YMCA in Manhattan that he would resign from the Air Service and "go back to my preaching" in North Carolina as soon as possible.

It was a long, unhappy goodbye. Maynard had hoped to shed his uniform in January of the new year, but the Army would take months to process his discharge, leaving him in an uncomfortable limbo. His plan for a third transcontinental flight—the one he had announced in San Francisco—was canceled without explanation. Even more humiliating, he was ordered to repay $825 that he had been awarded by the American Flying Club as the winner of the race (Menoher had sent conflicting signals on prizes before deciding belatedly that Army rules against accepting them would stand). Maynard already had spent part of his winnings, but he managed to repay the sum after the Air Service threatened to dock his paycheck.

In February, Maynard embarked on his last mission for the Air Service, a recruiting tour of the Southeast in *"Hello Frisco"*, this time accompanied by an Army photographer instead of Kline. Trixie, too, stayed behind, having recently given birth. Crowds still gathered for a glimpse of the Flying Parson and his well-traveled DH-4, which by now had "the appearance of a trusted war horse after many hard knocks." But Maynard seemed to take little pleasure in his duties; he was tired and off his game. He broke a propeller taking off from a muddy field, got lost over the Smoky Mountains, and was forced down in Hot Springs, North Carolina, after running out of gas. He pushed his luck in ways that he hadn't in the past. During a flight with a reporter from the Raleigh *News & Observer*, Maynard terrified his passenger with extreme maneuvers—

at one point diving on a crowd gathered on a baseball diamond—that caused the aging DH-4 to groan and shudder. On landing he sheared off the crown of a cedar tree, part of which was still dangling from his tail skid when he touched down.

The reporter, Ben Dixon MacNeill, was struck not only by Maynard's reckless flying but also by his prickliness. Gone was the bashful, smiling clergyman who had bewitched the American public with his daring and resourcefulness. Now he seemed angry, even bitter—"not a gracious hero," MacNeill wrote many years later. "He was pretty blunt with those who would touch the hem of his garment, very nearly as surly as Lindbergh."

It's a wonder he made it back to Mineola. Maynard's DH-4 was powered by the same engine that had been salvaged from the wrecked Martin Bomber during the race. Not only that, but mechanics who examined the plane at Mitchel Field found nine cracked wing ribs and a broken horizontal stabilizer. All its wires were loose, and the cowling was split and knocking against the propeller. *"Hello Frisco"* was deemed unsafe and unceremoniously scrapped. It was said that no other plane in the Air Service had logged as many flying hours.

In May, the Flying Parson finally left the Air Service, surely relieved to begin writing a new chapter in his life.

31

The Woodrow Wilson Airway

The Air Service, too, was moving on. In late September 1919, Billy Mitchell had floated the idea of a *second* transcontinental race, this one open to civilians, to start on November 15—but only if the first contest proved successful. There was no more talk of that now. Instead, Mitchell and his aides busied themselves with loose ends: tracking down a missing DH-4, writing thank you notes to community leaders and businesses, reimbursing farmers for crop damage from forced landings, settling bills from merchants (such as the grocer who supplied $358.99 worth of food to supplement the meager Army rations sent to the Omaha control stop). In one case, Mitchell had to personally intervene when the owner of the field used as the control stop at Rock Island accused the government of stiffing him on rent. "All I ask is a square deal," W. J. Franing wrote in a letter to Air Service headquarters. Mitchell replied that the city had offered the use of the field, which the city sublet from its tenant, and that if the owner had a problem he should take it up with the tenant.

The most important task was to glean whatever lessons could be learned from the race. Working from logbooks and reports written by pilots and control officers, the Air Service Information Group produced a 35-page document summarizing the contest and its implications for the future of flight. For the most part, it was a sober, thoughtful piece of work that frankly acknowledged the many problems exposed by the race. There were sections on the DH-4 ("there is no question but that the

landing gear should be advanced to relieve the observer from the dangerous practice of sliding down the tail upon landing"); flight instruments
("certain speed indicators were found to freeze up"); and the need for
advances in radio technology, both for communication and navigation
("the *sine qua non* of successful long distance cross-country flying"). In
particular, the report urged the widespread adoption of radio direction-
finders, later known as localizers, which would allow pilots to navigate
in fog and clouds by homing in on an audible signal, as Jimmy Doolittle
would demonstrate in 1929.

None of this was especially revelatory. The shortcomings of the
DH-4 were well known before the race. So was the need for more and
safer landing fields, improved weather forecasting, and solutions to the
problem of blind flying. Nor was there anything new about radios in
airplanes. The first wireless signal from an airplane to a receiver on
the ground was transmitted in 1910, during a demonstration at Sheeps-
head Bay, Brooklyn. Soon after the outbreak of World War I, British
artillery spotters in planes equipped with radio telegraphs began tap-
ping out grid coordinates in Morse code. Radios that could carry the
human voice were used by the French over Verdun in 1916 and later
by the Air Service, which deployed hundreds of the wireless devices
in the last months of the war. Similarly, the technology behind radio
direction-finders had been around since the late nineteenth century; a
practical version had been patented by two Italian engineers, Ettore
Bellini and Alessandro Tosi, in 1909. The device was called a "radio
compass." During their attempt to cross the Atlantic in the spring of
1919, Navy aviators used radio compasses to home in on ships along
the route, though electrical interference from engines limited their use-
fulness. Seen in that light, the transcontinental race merely added an
exclamation point to the obvious.

That's not to say it didn't yield some useful practical data. Among
other things, the contest established the life span of a Liberty engine at
fifty hours if run hard, revealed the tendency of certain types of oil to foul
spark plugs, and demonstrated the need for luminous instrument dials for
pilots flying after dark. Pilots' complaints about the safety of the DH-4, a

recurring theme in their contest postmortems, spurred the Air Service to accelerate its program to modify the aircraft by relocating the gas tank.

But the price of these insights had been high, even in mundane financial terms that ignored the loss of nine men, seven in the race and two who died while flying to the start of the contest in Mineola. Fifty-four planes had crashed, many of them damaged beyond repair. After accounting for these and other costs, the final bill for the contest was estimated at $500,000 (about $7.7 million today), roughly ten times more than anticipated. The figure would have been even higher if it included the $10,000 benefit paid to the families of the dead.

Aviation boosters tried to put the best face on the outcome. Despite the death toll, Harold Hartney claimed that there was "less danger in aeroplaning than in fast or careless automobiling." Glenn Martin, the aircraft builder, echoed that argument with a tortured comparison to the country's most famous auto race. In an article for the November 1919 issue of *U.S. Air Service* magazine, he noted that the death rate in the transcontinental contest, at least on a per-mile basis, was far lower than that of the Indianapolis 500. Technically, this was a true statement: In the lineup of thirty-three vehicles entered in the Indianapolis 500 that year, crashes killed two drivers and a mechanic who was riding with one of them. But it was hard to see why anyone should have taken comfort from the comparison, which was a little like saying that juggling with knives is safer than juggling with hand grenades.

The efforts of Hartney and Martin notwithstanding, the race did nothing to change public perceptions that flying was dangerous. The death rate, based on the seven men killed during the contest itself, worked out to one fatality for every 180 hours of flying time (the death rate for general aviation in the United States today is about one fatal accident per 100,000 hours flown). On the basis of that statistic, at least, it was hard to see the race as anything other than a setback for commercial aviation, and especially for Otto Praeger's plans to extend the airmail route to San Francisco. The New York *Sun*, extrapolating from the toll, estimated that three to four mail pilots would die along the route every month. To proceed on that basis, the newspaper editorialized, was "homicidal insanity."

———

Praeger ignored the naysayers. For all the doubts that the race might have created, he was as determined as ever to realize his vision. And in one important respect, the transcontinental race had made his job easier: It had sparked a surge of interest in municipal airfields, especially in towns and cities along the trail it had blazed.

The "Woodrow Wilson Airway"—a marketing ploy coined by the Aero Club of America in 1917—was no longer just a concept or a line on a map. The race had made it real. Even before the contest was over, communities large and small started lobbying for a place on it. On October 13, 1919, a jeweler in Ogallala, Nebraska, named Robert A. Goodall alerted the Air Service to the town's new municipal airfield. "You will note the field is located directly in the path over which the aviators in the recent Transcontinental Race have been passing," Goodall wrote in a letter to one of Menoher's aides that included a rough map. "It is located just south of the Lincoln Highway, and north of the south Plate [sic] river and Union Pacific Railway, one mile and a quarter due west of Ogallala." A hangar already had been erected at the field, and there were plans to add a telephone line and a small repair shop. Its surface, meanwhile, had been "dragged with a blade machine which cuts off all small bumps of any kind."

The Air Service moved to capitalize on the moment, urging towns and cities that had served as control stops to upgrade their hastily prepared fields. "Your field will be satisfactory for emergency landing and a very limited amount of air travel," wrote Lt. Col. H. M. Hickam, the chief of the Air Service Information Group, in a form letter sent in November to the mayors of North Platte, Sidney, and several other control stops. "But what of the future? The airplane is here to stay." Local officials, for the most part, agreed. In December, the city council in Rochester authorized the purchase of Britton Field as a "municipal aviation station," with hangars soon to follow.

No one was more gratified by the response than Praeger. "As this race has progressed the Post Office Department has received many urgent appeals from cities along the line of flight asking that the air mail be established as soon as possible," Praeger said on October 20, while the contest was still under way. "Thanks to the activity and initiative of the army, we have obtained the necessary information as to meteorological conditions, landing fields, and, more than all, as to the intense interest of the people."

Praeger's exaggerated claim—it's hard to see how the Air Service could have imparted "necessary information" that it had not even started gathering for itself—was aimed squarely at Congress. To expand airmail routes to the West Coast and elsewhere, the Post Office was seeking to more than triple its annual airmail budget, to $3,000,000. But it faced stiff political headwinds from Republicans who recently had taken control of the House and Senate. They had little interest in supporting the Wilson administration's Progressive goals, especially one that envisioned an expanded government role in commerce. At a hearing of the House Post Office Committee in December, Praeger tried to assure skeptical lawmakers that the government would turn over the airmail to private contractors as soon as the service was up and running. The committee rejected his appeal, but Praeger had better luck in the Senate, which approved a budget increase of $1,375,000—the number that Congress ultimately approved when it passed the Post Office appropriations bill in June 1920. Though short of what Praeger had sought, it was enough to keep the mail planes flying and allow him to proceed with his plans.

—————

The logistical and technical challenges were daunting. It was hard enough flying the mail over the 775 miles between New York and Chicago. Now Praeger was proposing to extend the service for nearly another 2,000 miles, across the same mountains that had claimed several lives in the coast-to-coast race. And that was in October. The mail pilots would cross over the same terrain in winter. Moreover, unlike the military men who had preceded them along the route, they would attempt to keep a daily schedule, regardless of the weather, as reliably, or nearly so, as the train. Between Chicago and San Francisco, they would stop at half a dozen of the same towns and cities that served as control stops in the race, along with Iowa City, Iowa, Rock Springs, Wyoming, and Elko, Nevada. Airfields would need to be improved or relocated, as in Chicago, where the airmail station at Grant Park was shifted to the nearby suburb of Maywood, which was less susceptible to fog and wind off Lake Michigan.

The Post Office's meager airmail budget made no allowance for building or improving airfields. Following the example set by the Air Service during the transcontinental contest, Praeger and his team would leave that job to cities designated as stops along the route, betting that most would jump at the opportunity. Praeger was mostly right, though some required a little persuasion. For that he once again turned to "Colonel" John A. Jordan, the civil engineer who had helped establish the New York–Chicago service. And just as it had before, sweet talk worked wonders, especially when combined with subtle extortion. Meeting with local officials in Cheyenne, Jordan made it clear that if they did not agree to provide a suitable airfield and hangar, the Post Office might have to shift its airmail station to Laramie, which he claimed was eager to have it. The city agreed to spend $15,000 on the new facility. Jordan used a similar approach with Reno and Salt Lake City. Elected officials in Salt Lake City, who had feared losing airmail service to nearby Ogden, later claimed that Jordan had bamboozled them with a pledge that the federal government eventually would reimburse the city for its expense. Six years later they were still trying to recover the money.

As Jordan chatted up the locals, James Edgerton, the Air Mail Service's talented operations chief, focused on communications. The race had underscored the need for reliable links between airfields, both to provide pilots with up-to-the-minute weather observations and also to report on their comings and goings. The Air Mail Service already operated radio stations at several of its fields in the eastern half of the country. Praeger had ordered Edgerton to set up seven more along the transcontinental route, and another at St. Louis. Edgerton completed the task on a budget of just $20,000, buying surplus transmitters and receivers intended for use on ships. The network included a new radio station on the top floor of the Post Office headquarters in downtown Washington,

D.C., where a huge antenna had been erected on the roof. Praeger literally "rubbed his hands in glee" as he inspected the new facility, then scribbled out a note of congratulations that was translated into dots and dashes and broadcast to airfields from coast to coast.

Choosing the right planes posed another challenge. The DH-4s used by the Air Mail Service—reconfigured with a mail compartment behind the engine and the pilot seated behind the gas tank—were safer than the version used in the race. But Praeger wanted better performance. He had high hopes for a new, purpose-built mail plane powered by two Liberty engines and built on the DH-4 airframe by the L.W.F. Engineering Company of New York City. It would carry more mail, and the second engine would add a margin of safety over the mountains. The Post Office ordered fifteen.

Almost from the moment the new planes entered service in August 1920, it was obvious that Praeger and his colleagues had made a costly mistake. The Twin DH—"a dreadful abortion of a plane," in the words of one pilot—climbed poorly and was prone to alarming and unpredictable vibrations. A mail pilot attempting to land one in Chicago felt a structural member snap while attempting a turn seventy-five feet above the ground. He crash-landed and avoided serious injury. Another pilot experienced a similar failure at 2,000 feet. With the left wing drooping, he spiraled downward, caught a wingtip on the ground, and overturned. Somehow he, too, walked away. The new planes were grounded.

Praeger also had been captivated by a bold new design from the German aeronautical engineer Hugo Junkers and sold in the United States by John A. Larsen, a Danish-born industrialist. Clad in corrugated aluminum, with an all-metal frame, the Junkers-Larsen 6, or JL-6, was a sleek low-wing monoplane that made its competition look like antiques. It was conceived as an airliner, with a partially enclosed cockpit—it had a roof but no side windows—and room for four passengers in a heated cabin. Safety was one of its biggest selling points. "These metal machines," Larsen claimed, "eliminate the aviator's greatest fear—fire." The plane received glowing reviews from, among others, Harold Hartney, who took one for a test flight at Bolling Field in Washington. After the Army and

Navy bought six of them, Praeger needed no further evidence, approving the purchase of eight JL-6s at $25,000 each.

But the JL-6, like the Twin DH, was plagued with troubles from the start. During test flights that August, pilots made nine forced landings in the planes, mostly because of radiator or fuel leaks. Nor was the JL-6 impervious to fire, as Larsen had claimed. On August 31, Wesley L. Smith and a copilot, Edward M. Haight, were flying from Chicago to Cleveland at 8,000 feet when flames from a fuel leak burned through the cockpit floor. The flames engulfed Smith's leather boots and spewed from the left side of the engine. Smith sideslipped to blow the flames away from the engine, then extinguished them by pushing the plane into a dive. He leveled the plane in time to land in a cornfield, escaping with serious burns to his face. Haight, unhurt, waved down a car to take them to the nearest town.

Max Miller would not be so lucky. The Norwegian-born pilot had started flying for the Post Office in 1918, after wartime service as a civilian flight instructor. Tall, blond, and blue-eyed, he was a true prince of the skies, widely admired for his airmanship and dedication to his job. No one thought more highly of him than Praeger. On September 1, 1920, a day after Smith and Haight's narrow escape, Miller and Gustav Rierson, a mechanic, were flying near Morristown, New Jersey, when their JL-6 started backfiring and losing altitude. A moment later, witnesses on the ground saw flames erupting from the engine. Someone, probably Rierson, began tossing mailbags from the plane.

They could save the mail but not themselves. The aircraft dove into the ground, exploding into a ball of fire. The bodies of Miller and Rierson were burned beyond recognition. "Max Miller was the best pilot who ever sat in a plane," a heartbroken Praeger told reporters. Miller had only recently gotten married. The accident was painfully ill-timed, with the transcontinental airmail service set to begin in just one week.

———

Early on the morning of September 8, as a mist hung over Hazelhurst Field on Long Island, a postal truck pulled up next to a DH-4. Canvas bags filled with 400 pounds of mail were unloaded. Not all the mail would fit in the fuselage compartment, so the pilot, Randolph Page, transferred the overflow to a suitcase and strapped it to a wing. Then he warmed his engine and took off.

The plan was to fly the mail in relays, Pony Express–style. Pilots would land each night and turn over the mail to another man, who would take off the following morning. And that is more or less what happened, though not precisely on schedule. The flyers were supposed to cover the distance to San Francisco in fifty-four hours, including time overnight on the ground. In the end, after a series of mundane and entirely predictable delays, it took four men eighty-three hours to complete the journey. But complete it they did. At 2:30 p.m. on September 11, Air Mail Plane No. 151 descended through the fog over San Francisco and touched down on the new airmail field that had been prepared on the waterfront just a few blocks south of the Presidio. As newsreel cameras whirred, its pilot, E. E. Moulton, an Air Service veteran, was greeted by San Francisco postmaster Charles Fay, Mayor James Rolph, and Colonel Jordan, who barked orders as seven mailbags were hastily unloaded and transferred to trucks. "C'mon, this is government mail," he urged, no doubt mindful that reporters were within earshot. "We must hurry it into the wagons." In one of the mailbags was a film, *The Restless Sex*, sent from a studio in New York. It was said to be the first such delivery of its kind.

In the aviation press, at least, the opening of the first coast-to-coast airmail service was greeted as the historic achievement that it was. *Aerial Age* magazine hailed it as an "epoch-making event," and *Flying* magazine commissioned a poem by Alice Hunt Bartlett, a prominent socialite and writer ("Then off with hats, to cheer this famous day. Transcontinental Air Mail's here to stay"). But for the rest of the country, the arrival of the first mail plane in San Francisco was something of an anticlimax. Certainly there was nothing like the hoopla sparked by Belvin Maynard's landing in the same city just eleven months earlier. The *New York Times* noted Moulton's arrival in four paragraphs at the bottom of page one. The extraordinary was fast becoming the routine.

Billy Mitchell would later claim a big share of the credit for the extension of the airmail route. The race "established the first airway for such
a distance—about 2500 miles—ever established in the world," he said
in a speech a few years later to the National Aeronautic Association.
"This had a succession of landing fields connected by radio telegraphy, telephony, and ground telegraphy, had a weather service, had fuel
for the airplanes, had mechanics and the necessary transportation for
supplying them. . . . This same airway grew into an avenue for the carrying of the airplane mail between New York and San Francisco." On
another occasion, he declared that the race "led to the establishment of
the airmail system."

Mitchell's claim, echoed through the years by some admiring writers
and historians, contains a kernel of truth. There's little question that the
air race helped seed the ground for transcontinental airmail, hastening
the development of at least some of the airfields along the route that
would be used by the mail planes. But was it critical to the effort? Almost
certainly not. William Leary, among the nation's foremost aviation historians until his death in 2006, admired the military flyers for their gump-
tion and tenacity, but he took a skeptical view of what they actually had
achieved. "Associating the Army flyers with such a milestone in the history of aeronautics might sanctify to some degree the lives lost during the
race, but, unfortunately, a careful study of the evidence does not support
this conclusion," he wrote. "The presence of the railroad was the key factor, not the efforts of the Air Service."

It's hard to argue with his logic. Because the railroad followed the
friendliest terrain in the West and simplified the dispatch of fuel, spare
parts, and ground personnel, it was the natural route for the transcontinental airmail, just as it had been for Mitchell's contest. Praeger and his
team, in other words, didn't need the Air Service to point out what they
surely would have figured out for themselves.

Nevertheless, pilots in the race deserve their reputation as pioneers.
They were the first to fly the route in its entirety, several completing

the journey in less than four days. That in itself was a remarkable feat, and one that arguably changed the way that Americans thought about aviation. True, there was no shortage of competition in that era, including the flights across the Atlantic the previous spring; the first nonstop aerial crossing of the continent in 1923; the first aerial circumnavigation of the globe, led by Lowell Smith, in 1924; and Lindbergh's solo flight to Paris in 1927, the most dazzling feat of airmanship the world had ever seen. Each underscored the rapid advance of airplane technology and flying skill. But the transcontinental race—with its dozens of pilots and planes, complex logistics, and reliance on a formal air route, however crude—was something different. It showed Americans what an air transportation system would actually *look* like. Some might argue over details, but no one who followed the contest could seriously doubt that the airplane would soon join the passenger train, the steamship, and the automobile as a practical feature of everyday life. Mitchell's "greatest air race" was not just a spectacle. It was the first iteration of a new age. As the *Rockford Morning Star* put it in an editorial on October 23, 1919, a few days after Maynard and several others completed their round-trip journey, "The successful journey of the racers means that airplane journeying is right here at our doors. It isn't going to be very long before people . . . get into the habit of buying a ticket and taking a seat with a suitcase just as calmly as ever they do now on the local for the next town." After the race, the control officer in Binghamton reported that public libraries in Binghamton, Endicott, and Johnson City had been unable to meet demand for aeronautical books, many of them checked out by schoolchildren. The phenomenon surely was repeated elsewhere, as Americans contemplated a future that was taking shape before their eyes.

––––––

Much sacrifice lay ahead. Just days after the first mail flight across the country, another JL-6 burst into flames and dove into a clover field in Ohio, incinerating both its occupants. Two more men died in separate accidents over the next several weeks. And just as predicted, flying the mail across the mountainous West proved nearly as dangerous as it had for pilots in the transcontinental contest.

The accidents did nothing to improve Praeger's relations with Republicans in Congress, who gained more power after the election of Warren G. Harding as president in 1920. The change in administrations meant that Progressives in government, Praeger among them, were on their way out.

But Praeger had one last point to prove. In February 1921, shortly before he left his position as second assistant postmaster general, he orchestrated a demonstration by a team of pilots who relayed a load of mail from San Francisco to New York in just thirty-three hours, a third of the time it took to cover the same distance by rail. Several of the pilots had flown at night for the first time, proving the viability of round-the-clock operations. It was an important breakthrough that made headlines across the country and helped cement Praeger's reputation as a visionary, if sometimes a merciless one.

His legacy, if not the Air Mail Service itself, would endure. The service began night operations in 1923, on a route made safer by the installation of a lighted path—acctylene beacons at three-mile intervals—on the prairie between Omaha and Cheyenne (mail stations along the route were equipped with rotating electric beacons, not so different than the ones atop modern control towers). The following year, President Calvin Coolidge, another Republican, signed a law that allowed the Post Office to transfer its airmail operations to private companies, making good on Praeger's long-ago promise. The U.S. Air Mail Service completed its last flight on September 1, 1927.

The awarding of mail contracts to private carriers was a pivotal moment in the history of commercial aviation. Backed by a flood of new investment, contractors soon began carrying passengers along with the mail. Among the first of these was Colonial Air Transport, a Connecticut-based company that flew people, letters, and freight between New York and Boston in twelve-seat Ford Trimotors. In 1929, Colonial and several other contract carriers were acquired by a Delaware-based holding company, the Aviation Corporation, as part of an industry-wide consolidation driven by stock mania on Wall Street. The Aviation Corporation, or AVCO, was an unwieldy giant with investments across the field, including manufacturing. In early 1930, AVCO spun off its airlines into a single entity called American Airways. That company is known today as American Airlines. Other contract carriers followed a similar arc, evolving, like American Airlines, into some of the most dominant airlines of the twentieth century. Among them were United Airlines, Eastern Airlines, Northwest Airlines, and TWA. Consider that history, and Hap Arnold's assessment—that the transcontinental contest was "the foundation" of commercial aviation in the United States—does not seem quite so far-fetched.

If not the foundation, it was at least a rough sketch.

EPILOGUE

Fifty miles off Virginia's Cape Charles, Billy Mitchell peered over the side of the DH-4 he had christened *Osprey*, his eagle crest painted on the fuselage and a blue squadron leader's pennant trailing from the tail. Below was the immobilized hulk of the *Ostfriesland*, a captured German battleship that measured 548 feet at the waterline. Nearby was a Navy transport ship, the USS *Henderson*, its deck crammed with admirals, generals, politicians, War Department officials, foreign military attachés, and reporters. As blimps and planes carrying cameramen circled overhead, the audience waited for what promised to be Mitchell's biggest show yet. Or perhaps his biggest stumble. Months earlier, in February 1921, Mitchell had publicly challenged the Navy to a test of air power, after claiming that "we can destroy or sink any ship in existence today." Navy leaders had scoffed at the idea—"I would be perfectly willing to be on board," one anonymous high-ranking official told reporters—but relented after months of public goading from Mitchell and his allies in Congress and the press. On July 20, Navy and Army bombers had damaged the *Ostfriesland* before storms forced them to retreat. Now, a day later, they would get another chance. As Mitchell watched eagerly from his cockpit, eleven Army bombers—eight Martins and three British-made Handley Pages— approached the battleship in formation, each carrying a 2,000-pound bomb. Seven bombs were dropped. Though none scored direct hits, several detonated close to the ship, including one that glanced off its armor-plated side. The blasts generated concussion waves that ruptured seams below the waterline. Mitchell watched in awe as the once mighty warship slowly turned turtle, hissing and bubbling as it slipped stern-first beneath the surface. The whole thing was over in minutes.

The sinking of the supposedly unsinkable battleship—even one that was undefended and already taking on water from the previous day's attack—was a personal triumph, a blow to the Navy's prestige, and a powerful symbol that warfare had entered a new age. After a victorious, wing-wagging flyby of the *Henderson*, Mitchell returned to Langley Field in Hampton, where he was greeted by cannon blasts and carried from his cockpit on the shoulders of cheering aviators. The *Ostfriesland*'s demise made the front pages of newspapers across the country. It was Mitchell's proudest moment, fueling talk he would soon be made the next chief of the Air Service.

But Mitchell would never achieve that long-cherished goal. Many military leaders, including Charles Menoher, were by now thoroughly fed up with Mitchell and his ceaseless grandstanding. In June, more than a month before the battleship test, Menoher had petitioned the new secretary of war, John W. Weeks, to fire his obstreperous deputy. Though Menoher was unsuccessful, and subsequently transferred to a ground command, Weeks named Mason Patrick, who had run the Air Service under Pershing in France, to take his place.* In the meantime, Mitchell's crusade for an independent air force had lost momentum, and the Air Service had continued to shed men and airplanes, of which only 754 remained in the inventory by 1924.

Mitchell also was fighting battles at home. He was drinking heavily and spending as recklessly as ever, fanning tensions with Caroline that now threatened their marriage. Noisy quarrels escalated into violence. In September 1920, after a particularly ugly fight, Caroline suffered a superficial gunshot wound to the chest from a .38 caliber revolver. She accused Michell of shooting her accidentally while he was drunk; he claimed she had tried to kill herself. Mitchell moved out of the house shortly before the *Ostfriesland* test. A few months later, Caroline pulled strings at the War Department to force him to undergo a psychiatric evaluation at Walter Reed, a humiliation for which Mitchell never forgave her. The two were divorced in September 1922. The following year, Mitchell married Elizabeth Trumbull Miller, a stylish, blue-eyed 31-year-old who came from a

---

* Soon after his reappointment, Patrick, who was well aware of Mitchell's view that only pilots should run the Air Service, learned to fly at the age of fifty-eight.

wealthy family in Detroit and shared Mitchell's love of riding and hunting. The couple eventually would have two children of their own.

Mitchell hung on for several more years as the chief of training and
operations. Though he traveled frequently, he remained an outsize presence in Washington, D.C., where he spent much of his time in budget
fights with the Navy. When he failed to make much headway, he appealed
directly to the public in speeches as well as newspaper and magazine articles that now appeared under his own byline. This was a clear breach of
War Department policy, verging on insubordination, but Mitchell would
not be silenced. "He had more brass than a monkey," one contemporary
recalled.

War Department officials—backed by President Calvin Coolidge,
who also regarded Mitchell as a liability—would get their revenge.
Mitchell had expected to be reappointed as assistant air chief in March
1925, when his term was due to expire. Instead, he was transferred to an
aviation command in San Antonio and reverted to the rank of colonel.
Unchastened, he persisted with his public broadsides against the military
establishment, until one day he pushed his luck too far.

On September 5, 1925, Mitchell summoned reporters to his office in
San Antonio after the crash two days earlier of the *Shenandoah*, a Navy
dirigible that had broken up in a thunderstorm over Ohio with the loss
of fourteen men. The airship had been on a publicity tour—in Mitchell's
view an unnecessary mission and a reckless one, as the *Shenandoah* was
based on an outdated design and said to be in poor repair. The calamity
had closely followed the loss of a Navy seaplane on a flight to Hawaii. To
Mitchell, the accidents were further evidence of military leaders' neglect
of aviation across the board and their careless disregard for the lives of
the nation's airmen. (It apparently didn't occur to him that many had
said the same thing about the transcontinental race.) Now he went public
with his fury, using words that were sure to inflame. "These accidents are
the direct result of the incompetency, criminal negligence, and almost
treasonable administration of the national defense by the Navy and War
Departments," he declared, reading from a 6,000-word statement.

The reaction in Washington was predictably outraged, but Mitchell refused to back down, openly daring his superiors to court-martial him. It was a challenge they were glad to accept. The resulting seven-week trial, held in a nondescript Army warehouse near the Capitol, was among the most sensational of the decade. With some success, Mitchell and his attorneys sought to turn the proceeding into a forum on air power, calling as friendly witnesses Carl Spaatz, Hap Arnold, and Eddie Rickenbacker, among others. But there was never much doubt about the verdict. On December 17, a military jury found Mitchell guilty of insubordination and related charges, firing him from his command and stripping his rank and pay.* He resigned from the Army on February 1, 1926.

Billy and Betty retired to their estate near Middleburg, Virginia, where Mitchell bred horses and dogs and churned out a steady stream of magazine articles, along with several books. He died of heart disease in 1936, at the age of fifty-six. Not until 1947, more than a decade later, would Congress finally authorize the creation of the U.S. Air Force he had sought for so long. By then the transcontinental air race, and Mitchell's role in it, were all but forgotten.

———

To the men who flew in it, the transcontinental race brought no fortune and only fleeting glory. Menoher, though ruling out cash prizes, had allowed top finishers to keep "personal souvenirs," such as the shotgun presented to Belvin Maynard by Abercrombie & Fitch, the sporting goods store. They also earned a place on the Mackay Trophy, a silver cup on a tiered mahogany base that is named for Clarence Mackay, a financier and aviation enthusiast who first presented it (to Hap Arnold) in 1912. For more than a century, the trophy has been awarded annually to recognize achievements by flyers in the Air Force and its predecessors. Winners' names are engraved on silver medallions affixed to the base of the trophy, which is displayed in the National Air and Space Museum in Washington. Under "1919," Belvin Maynard's name appears at the

———

* President Coolidge approved of the guilty verdict but softened the punishment by partially restoring Mitchell's pay.

top, followed by nine other winners in various categories. Among them are Carl Spaatz, the first man to reach Long Island from San Francisco, as well as John Donaldson, Harold Hartney, and Ralph Bagby, who shared honors in the "endurance" category (because they completed the round-trip journey without changing engines). Brailey Gish, though he failed to complete the race, was awarded a place on the trophy for his "spirit of pioneer endeavor," as one of Menoher's aides put it in a commendation letter.

Spaatz was one of the few contestants who would make his career in the Army, though not entirely by choice. In 1925, after command jobs in Texas and Michigan, he decided that he, too, was ready to return to civilian life. He saw no future in a peacetime Air Service hollowed out by budget cuts. So he and an Air Service buddy made plans to purchase a ranch in California's Imperial Valley, imagining a new life as cowboys. Only a shortage of funds prevented them from going through with the deal.

It was probably just as well. Spaatz continued to thrive in the Air Service and its successors, the Army Air Corps and then the Army Air Forces. In 1929, he set a world endurance record as commander of a Fokker Trimotor that remained aloft for more than six days (gas was transferred through a hose from a Douglas biplane). He and Ruth had three daughters, who followed him to prestigious assignments in Washington and elsewhere. In 1944, Spaatz took command of U.S. Strategic Air Forces in Europe under Hap Arnold, the country's top aviation commander. He orchestrated the bombing campaign against Germany and later commanded strategic forces in the Pacific, where he oversaw the dropping of nuclear bombs on Hiroshima and Nagasaki. (If Spaatz had any qualms about the use of atomic weapons, he never said so in public, though David R. Mets, his biographer, noted that Spaatz insisted on written, rather than verbal, orders to launch the missions, probably "to emphasize that the moral choice was not his.") No one was particularly surprised when President Harry S. Truman chose him as the first Air Force chief of staff in 1947.

Spaatz retired the following year, settling with Ruth in Alexandria, Virginia, across the Potomac River from Washington. After turning down lucrative offers from industry, he took a job as a military-affairs columnist for *Newsweek*, a job he thoroughly enjoyed. In the late 1950s, Ray L. Bowers, the young Air Service officer who wrote his master's thesis about the transcontinental race, stopped by Spaatz's *Newsweek* office in Washington to interview him for the project. In keeping with his reputation, Spaatz was "very tight-lipped," Bowers recalled when I spoke with him in 2017. But Spaatz did share a vivid memory of Belvin Maynard, recalling his habit of removing and polishing his spectacles whenever he climbed down from his cockpit.

Spaatz died in 1974 at the age of eighty-three. He is buried at the U.S. Air Force Academy in Colorado Springs.

———

Harold Hartney had not lost his zeal for competition. In 1920, while still in uniform, he piloted a Thomas-Morse biplane to a second-place finish in the Pulitzer Trophy Race, held on a closed 32-mile course on Long Island. The following year, he left the Army for more promising opportunities in civilian life, determined to give "my whole enthusiasm to the building of air consciousness on the part of the public." That goal was nearly derailed in October 1921, when he crashed near Omaha during the second Pulitzer race. But Hartney recovered from his injuries and went on to a prominent role in commercial aviation, taking jobs with—among others—the Sikorsky Aircraft Corporation and a passenger airline that operated between New York and Detroit. In 1935, with the strong endorsement of Billy Mitchell, he went to Capitol Hill as an adviser to a Senate subcommittee on air safety. "I considered Hartney at the time of the Armistice the best pursuit commander on the front in any service," Mitchell wrote in recommending him for the job. Hartney subsequently worked as an adviser to the Civil Aeronautics Administration, precursor to today's Federal Aviation Administration.

In 1945, Hartney died of a heart ailment in Washington at the age of fifty-seven. He was buried at Arlington National Cemetery, where he would soon be joined by his eldest son, Harold Jr., an Army fighter pilot who had been killed in action over Germany. In 1968, another son, James

C. Hartney, also a military aviator, was shot down over North Vietnam. His remains were returned to the United States in 1989.

––––––––

After the race, Brailey Gish served briefly on Mitchell's staff, then left the Air Service in February 1920 to resume his business career. He sold Hendrick automobiles, started a company to manufacture the gas-filtering device he had invented before the war, and worked as the Washington representative for the company that made Thompson submachine guns. During World War II, he ran a company in Massachusetts that made parts for airplane engines and submarines. Gish divorced and remarried several times. In the 1950s, he and his latest wife retired to Fort Lauderdale, where they owned a house with a swimming pool. Between rounds of golf, Gish wrote cranky letters to the local newspaper complaining about taxes and promoting flogging as a punishment for teenage miscreants. He spent much of his last years in a fruitless battle with the Air Force to correct trivial discrepancies in his World War I military records. His letters to high-ranking officials—including Vice President Lyndon Johnson—became increasingly grandiose and paranoid. Eventually, an Air Force official informed him that his queries would no longer be answered.

Gish died of heart disease in 1963 at the age of seventy-five.

––––––––

John Donaldson left the Air Service within months of the race, hoping to make his fortune in the Texas oilfields. But Donaldson missed flying. By the late 1920s, he had moved north to run a flight school at Newark Metropolitan Airport in New Jersey. He competed in airplane races and frequently flew in aerobatic shows. The last was on September 7, 1930, at an airfield in Philadelphia. Stunting before a crowd of 40,000, he put his Travel Air biplane into a spin, but failed to recover in time. The aircraft plunged into tall weeds at the edge of the field. Donaldson was extricated from the wreckage and rushed to a local hospital, where he died a short while later. He was thirty-two.

————

Ralph "Baz" Bagby, the MIT-educated observer-turned-pilot who served as Hartney's wingman on the return flight from San Francisco, remained in the Air Service long enough to take part in some of the bombing tests that preceded the sinking of the *Ostfriesland*. By then, however, Bagby was newly married and ready to move on. After leaving the Air Service in mid-1921, he took an engineering job in Cedar Rapids, Iowa, and a few years later settled outside Chicago, where he started an engineering firm under his own name. He and his wife, Anne, had four children. In 1942, at the age of forty-nine, Bagby returned to active duty as a senior staff officer. He helped plan the invasions of North Africa and Italy, then moved to Allied headquarters in London, where he assisted with preparations for D-Day. He couldn't bear the thought of sitting out the invasion. In the predawn hours of June 6, 1944, without bothering to ask permission, Bagby talked his way onto a transport plane filled with airborne troops and parachuted into occupied France. It was his first jump. After stumbling around in darkness amid grazing cows and wrecked gliders, he made his way back to the English Channel and then London, where a young war correspondent named Walter Cronkite wrote a story about "this little bald, red-faced colonel who was AWOL more than 48 hours." Bagby was reprimanded and awarded a medal.

He resumed his engineering career after the war. In June 1961, at the age of sixty-eight, he was killed in a car accident while driving to a reunion of World War I aviators in Ohio.

————

Belvin Maynard never did go back to the pulpit or even to Wake Forest College to finish his degree. Essie, who knew her husband better than he knew himself, was disappointed but not surprised. She knew he could never stop flying. "I don't see how he ever is going to get that bee out of his thoughts," she had admitted to a reporter soon after Maynard's victory. "He is intensely interested in aviation, both from a professional and sporting standpoint, and I can't imagine him settling down to his theological studies again." In the summer of 1920, after leaving the Air Service, Maynard attempted to monetize his fame by embarking on a speaking tour with a canned address titled "The Motor Troubles of Society." He then took a job at the Brooklyn YMCA while he tried to establish an aerial-photography business. In the meantime, he purchased a small house for his family in Queens. The house sat directly on an airfield—the Queens Village Airdrome—where several pilots had set up a business offering rides in surplus Jennies. Maynard found his own plane—a surplus Nieuport 28—on Coney Island, where a photographer had been using it as a portrait backdrop in his studio. The Nieuport was badly in need of refurbishment, but the price was right. Maynard worked on it in his spare time and eventually got it flying again.

But something had changed since he won the transcontinental race. The carelessness he had displayed during his final unhappy months in the Air Service had followed him into civilian life. Maynard was no longer the meticulous pilot who had flown with such precision and flair, first in France and then back home in competition. He'd gotten sloppy, perhaps through overconfidence. Fellow pilots were alarmed at the condition of his patched-up Nieuport, with its sagging fabric and wings braced with mismatched wires and turnbuckles.

In the late summer of 1922, the owner of a flying circus hired Maynard for a temporary job performing stunts and giving rides at a fair in Rutland, Vermont. Maynard took the train to Rutland, where there was high demand for time aloft with the famous pilot. A British trainer   a two-seat Avro—had been reserved for his use. To bring in more money, Maynard replaced the single seat in the rear cockpit with a makeshift wooden bench that could accommodate two passengers.

At 1:00 p.m. on September 7, Maynard took off on a test flight with a pilot and mechanic who worked for the flying circus. He climbed to 2,000 feet, performed a few stunts, then tipped the plane into a spin—a routine maneuver he had performed countless times. The Avro never recovered. As fairgoers watched in horror, the biplane spiraled into a field at the edge of the fairgrounds. An investigation would reveal that the bench Maynard had rigged in the rear cockpit had broken under the weight of the two passengers, interfering with control cables running underneath. The two men in the rear cockpit died instantly. Maynard was still breathing when he was pulled from the wreckage, but he died before reaching a hospital. He was twenty-nine.

A few days later, the Flying Parson was buried beneath four oak trees on the family farm in North Carolina. More than 3,000 people turned out for his funeral.

2019

The skies are clear and a light breeze blows from the north as I take off from Republic Airport, a busy corporate-jet center a few miles east of the original East Coast starting point at Roosevelt Field. Even with a full load of fuel, the plane climbs quickly in the cool morning air, rising above a dense suburban neighborhood of office parks and warehouses. In moments I can see the shining expanse of Long Island Sound and the shoreline of Westchester County, New York, and Connecticut on the opposite side. A controller in the Republic tower bids me good day and clears me to change frequencies. I tune my radio to New York Departure Control, which assigns me a transponder code so my plane can be tracked on radar, then cautions me to stay below 4,500 feet to stay clear of jetliners departing LaGuardia. It's a little nerve-wracking—I'm not used to such congested airspace—and I glance now and then at my instrument panel to check the position of nearby aircraft, which appear on a glowing screen as small black diamonds. (Tiny arrows indicate whether they are climbing or descending; if one were to get too close, the diamond would become a yellow dot, and an urgent warning—"Traffic! Traffic!"—would sound in my headset. But today there is no such drama.) Time to switch on the autopilot. I set the altitude to 3,000 feet and twist a knob until my course—indicated by a blue-green line on a moving map—intersects with my first stop at Binghamton. I release the stick and take my feet off the rudder pedals, then scan the engine instruments for signs of trouble. Oil pressure, fuel flow, voltage—everything looks good. As the Hudson River slides beneath my wings, I lean back in my seat and take a moment to enjoy the view. I am finally on my way.

––––––

I could not precisely retrace the flight path of the men who made the same journey a century earlier. Most of the airfields that served as control stops are long gone, having reverted to farmland or, more commonly, been subsumed by development of one sort or another. (Roosevelt Field is now a huge shopping mall of the same name.) For the most part, they have been replaced by modern municipal airports with paved runways and, if they are large enough, glass-and-concrete towers staffed by air traffic controllers. At smaller facilities such as Sidney and Rawlins, among others, I would be responsible for my own safety, using a common radio frequency to alert other aircraft to my position and intent. St. Paul does not have an airport of any kind. Neither does Green River, unless you count the waggishly named Intergalactic Space Port, a dirt airstrip on a mountaintop five miles to the south (Hutton Heights, the gusty plateau where pilots landed in 1919, is now a subdivision of modest ranch-style homes). And Salduro, on the western edge of the Great Salt Lake Desert, is a ghost town, abandoned after its potash plant closed in the 1940s. I overflew all three towns, just so I could connect the dots.

Rochester was one of the few stops along my route whose airport could trace its lineage to the transcontinental race, though I could find no hint of its humble origins. Britton Field is now Frederick Douglass Greater Rochester International Airport, which is served by several major airlines (the same is true of the control stop in Rock Island, Franing Field, known today as Quad Cities International Airport). When I landed at Rochester after the short flight from Binghamton, I taxied off the runway and parked in front of a sleek private terminal run by the airport's "fixed-base operator," or FBO, which provides services to noncommercial aircraft. Some of these FBOs are big businesses, geared primarily to corporate and private jets, and the sight of my tiny two-seater rarely failed to raise an eyebrow among the receptionists who took my orders for fuel ("It looks like a pregnant mosquito," said one). The larger FBOs are all pretty much the same. There are comfortable lounges with Wi-Fi and free coffee, televisions tuned to the Weather Channel or cable news. It was a far cry from an Army tent and a bowl of hot oyster stew.

So, too, with flying. Digital technology has added a layer of safety and awareness that would have been unimaginable in 1919 (or even in 1990). Thanks to the satellite-based Global Positioning System, finding my way from one stop to the next was as simple as entering an airport code on a touchscreen; the autopilot would do the rest, maintaining a constant altitude and correcting for any crosswinds. At the same time, satellites and ground-based stations supplied a constant stream of weather data in near real time. This was invaluable as I crossed the country in June, at the start of the summer convection season. On hot afternoons over the Great Plains, thunderstorms appeared on my instrument panel as red and purple blobs, long before they posed any threat. Most of the time I easily flew around them. The one time I couldn't, in Nebraska, I landed short of my destination and called it a day.

It helped that I wasn't in a race. Waking up to 1,500-foot ceilings after my first night in Rochester, I briefly considered pressing on, but thought better of the idea after a quick Google search for advice on "scud-running"—pilot slang for flying under low clouds—revealed a surfeit of good reasons for staying on the ground. What was the rush? I had budgeted up to six weeks for my round-trip journey, and Rochester, on the banks of the tumbling Genesee River, is a pleasant city dotted with some of the most distinguished American architecture of the early twentieth century. I spent the next two days doing research in the local library and exploring the city on the folding bike I'd brought with me on the plane in place of a passenger seat.

The air traffic control system was another source of comfort. Minutes after departing an airport on a new leg, I would contact the regional control center and request "flight following." Unless they are too busy, controllers invariably grant such requests. They assign you a transponder code, follow your progress, and warn you of approaching aircraft or other potential hazards, such as parachute jumpers or military activity (there are a lot of bombing ranges out West). I thought of them as guardian angels. Once, over the alkali badlands of western Utah, I lost radio contact with the controller who was tracking my flight from Salt Lake City. Unable to reach me directly, he relayed a message through the pilot of a nearby American Airlines jet, who informed me that I had entered an area without radar coverage and that I was now, effectively, on my own. The next hour was the loneliest of my entire journey, though in truth, I wasn't really alone. Interstate 80 snaked through the desert to my north, and I knew that if for some reason I did make a forced landing, I could easily summon help with the emergency satellite beacon I carried in my flight bag.

Stick-and-rudder skills still matter. Though some new aircraft can literally land themselves, my Flight Design CTLSi was not one of them, and it could be challenging to touch down safely, especially in higher winds that would not have posed a problem for larger planes. Before taking off from North Platte one afternoon, I called the 800 number for Leidos Flight Service, a contractor for the Federal Aviation Administration that provides weather briefings for pilots in the continental United States. The forecast was for clear skies and light winds at my destination, Sidney, 104 miles to the west, though it looked as if the wind would pick up later. The forecast was right about everything except the timing. Forty minutes or so into my flight, I called up the latest Sidney weather on a satellite receiver on my instrument panel. I was alarmed to learn that the winds already had jumped sharply—to fourteen knots gusting to twenty-five at forty degrees off the single paved runway. This was right at the edge of my airplane's performance limit, to say nothing of my own. I thought about diverting to another airport but the winds elsewhere were not much better. I decided to give it a try.

I crabbed toward the wind on final approach, but just as I straightened out over the asphalt, a gust caught my right wing. The plane rocked sharply, slamming down hard on the left wheel and rebounding into the air. It's tempting, at moments like these, to try to salvage the landing by adding a little power to soften the next touchdown. This is generally a bad idea, at least in a plane as small as mine. I did the right thing and shoved the throttle forward, executing a go-around and rejoining the traffic pattern for another attempt. My nerves settled. This time, when the gust came, I was ready for it. Both wheels stayed on the runway.

More than the wind or any other aspect of the weather, fatigue was my biggest challenge, impairing both judgment and reflexes. Three of my worst mistakes came on the same day, when I was more than halfway across the country and the strain of my travels had started to catch up with me. Landing at a satellite airport near Salt Lake City after a memorable flight over the steep forested canyons of the Wasatch Range, I skidded my turn to final approach and let my airspeed sink dangerously low. It was the same sort of low-altitude carelessness that had killed Dana Crissy and Virgil Thomas just a few miles away and a hundred years earlier, on the first day of the race. As my plane was refueled, I tried to collect myself in the FBO lounge, where I called up a sectional chart on my iPad to plan my exit through the complicated airspace around Salt Lake. I should have known better than to push my luck. A few seconds after my wheels left the asphalt, I could tell that the plane was not climbing normally, even for a hot afternoon at relatively high altitude. Then I glanced at the T-shaped throttle lever on my center console. I was horrified to see that I had failed to advance it fully. This was a serious lapse—like every other pilot who ever lived, I had been trained to take off at full power, leaving a hand on the throttle to ensure that it stayed wide open. Yet somehow I had neglected to follow this elemental rule. I shoved the handle to the firewall, cursing my stupidity. I didn't want to think about what might have happened on a shorter runway with tall trees at the end. My third mistake came at Battle Mountain, which I reached in the late afternoon. On final approach, I failed to compensate for hot air rising from the desert floor, came in way too high, and was forced to go around—twice. I finally succeeded on my third attempt, but only after extending full flaps to steepen my descent. Even then my wheels didn't touch the pavement until I was halfway down the ridiculously long, 7,300-foot runway.

These slipups gave me a new appreciation for Belvin Maynard and his peers, who sometimes flew ten hours in a day, blasted by wind and noise, with no autopilot to ease the strain. It's a wonder they didn't make more errors. I was shaken by my sloppiness and resolved never again to fly when I was tired.

Mountains turned out to be the least of my worries. With the death of Edward Wales very much on my mind, I opted not to fly the direct line across the Medicine Bow Mountains, between Cheyenne and Rawlins, but took the longer, safer route to the north of Elk Mountain. This time I didn't bother programming my GPS. I simply followed Interstate 80, which carved a path through wrinkled empty rangelands in roughly the same vicinity as the railroad tracks that Carl Spaatz and others had followed a century earlier. It was a pleasant, uneventful flight in stable air beneath high clouds. I flew most of the distance to Rawlins at 10,500 feet, the snowy summit of Elk Mountain—one of the highest peaks in the range at more than 11,000 feet—looming off my left wing.

Three days later I crossed San Francisco Bay.

————

I'm just a few minutes east of Rawlins when I catch my first glimpse of Oberg Pass. From a distance it doesn't look especially daunting. It's a wide saddle between two treeless peaks, with plenty of room to maneuver or turn back should the need arise. The pass spills onto a rolling high plain, green from recent spring rains. In the distance are more mountains, which form a dark, irregular barrier backlit by the rising sun. The weather is good—unlimited visibility, high thin overcast, the winds atypically light. Not much chance of a snowstorm today. As I approach the pass, I switch off the autopilot and pull the throttle back to idle. The plane sinks gently toward the forest and pasture at the base of Coad Mountain on the north side of the pass. Now on my return trip across the continent, I have overcome my misgivings and decided to fly the direct line across the Medicine Bow Mountains. I want to see the mountain where Wales died.

It was easy enough to find. A detailed story on the crash that appeared in a local newspaper, the Saratoga Sun, several days after it occurred provided me with solid clues to its location. So did Steve Wolff, an amateur historian and former professional pilot who has extensively researched the crash—as it happens, the first fatal aviation accident in Wyoming. He emailed the GPS coordinates before I left San Francisco.

After spending the night in Rock Springs, just east of Green River, I call Flight Service for a weather forecast. The briefer reports broken overcast at 12,000 feet or so, well above my planned cruising altitude of 9,500 feet, and light winds aloft. I follow his advice to leave early because of thunderstorms predicted for later in the morning. After passing Rawlins, I have no difficulty spotting Oberg Pass, in part because it's well within sight of Elk Mountain—an unmissable landmark in good visibility. With my engine throttled back, I descend to about 700 feet above the ground at the lowest point in the valley. I'm well south of the interstate now; with no signs of human habitation, other than a few dirt roads, the country under my wings looks pretty much as it did in 1919.

I pass below the 9,300-foot summit of Coad Mountain, whose tundra-like flank is creased with small ridges and ravines. It gives me a chill to think that Wales died on the same mountainside. With one eye on the airspeed, I coast for a minute or so above the treetops at the base of the mountain. I picture the pilot slumped senseless and bleeding in the cockpit of his wrecked DH-4. I see the blowing snow and Goldsborough's desperate, skidding descent in search of help that would arrive too late.

As a memorial to the men who died in the race, I can think of none better than that lonely knob of wilderness on the north side of Oberg Pass. In moments the gap is behind me. With mountains rising ahead, I shove the throttle forward, ease back on the stick, and resume my course on the direct line to Cheyenne.

ACKNOWLEDGMENTS

This book would not have been possible without the capable and conscientious staff at the National Archives in College Park, Maryland, where records of the transcontinental race are stored, along with many others relating to military aviation in the World War I era. Special thanks to Mitchell Yockelson and Eric S. Van Slander for pointing me in the right direction.

At the Library of Congress, John Buydos was an invaluable guide to one of the world's best collections of aeronautical books and publications. I am similarly indebted to Jennifer Lynch, the U.S. Postal Service historian, for aiding my research on Otto Praeger and the beginnings of airmail, and to Mary Ruwell, chief of special collections at the U.S. Air Force Academy's McDermott Library in Colorado Springs. Matthew J. Boylan, senior reference librarian at the New York Public Library, went far beyond the call of duty to find an answer to my question on how long it took to travel across the country by train in 1919—an important point of comparison with the transcontinental race. I'd also like to thank the researchers who assisted me with this project—Kyle Massey and Daphne Glover Ferrier in Washington, D.C.; George Cully and Randy Asherbranner at the Air Force Historical Research Center at Maxwell Air Force Base in Montgomery, Alabama; and Geoff Gentilini at the National Personnel Records Center in St. Louis.

During my flight across the country in 2019, I landed at most of the towns and cities that served as control stops during the race, where I discovered valuable information in public libraries and other archives. I could not have done so without local help. In particular, I am grateful to Roger Luther, the county historian in Binghamton; Jane Huffman and Denver Henderson of the Williams County Public Library in Bryan; Dave Mead, Brie Blasi, and Dick Blust of the Sweetwater County Historical Museum in Green River; Lori Price of the Cookhouse Museum in Battle Mountain; and Amanda Williford of the National Park Service archive at the Presidio in San Francisco. Steve Wolff, a retired professional pilot and expert on Wyoming's aviation history, shared his voluminous files on the crash that killed Edward Wales and pointed me to its exact location on the side of Coad Mountain. I am grateful, as well, to David and Susan Golden for hosting me during my four-day layover in San Francisco, and to Rone Tempest and Laura Richardson for putting me up in Salt Lake City on my return flight to the East Coast.

There is no one alive who even remembers the race, much less participated in it, but there are plenty of people with familial or personal ties to those who did. For sharing memories, family histories, and other material, I am deeply grateful to Tom O'Kelley, whose late wife, Sylvia, was Belvin Maynard's niece; Rose Ann Holoman and Helen Aanes, Maynard's granddaughters; Robert McMillan, an attorney in North Carolina who got to know Maynard's widow, Essie, in the 1960s; and Betty Goerke, Ralph Bagby's daughter, who was kind enough to send me copies of her father's logbook and letters he wrote during the race (some of this material appears in *A Broken Propeller*, a book she wrote about her father and the transcontinental race). Thanks, also, to Rebecca Abbott, Otto Praeger's granddaughter, for sharing his unpublished memoir.

Original research aside, I owe a major debt to the authors whose books provided crucial context for the transcontinental race. My portrait of Billy Mitchell benefited greatly from the work of Douglas Waller (*A Question of Loyalty: Billy Mitchell and the Court Martial That Gripped the Nation*); James J. Cooke (*Billy Mitchell*); and Thomas Wildenberg (*Billy Mitchell's War with the Navy*). Key details from Belvin Maynard's early life came from *First to Fly*, a history of early aviation in North Carolina by Thomas C. Parramore. *Master of Airpower*, by David R. Mets, was a rich source of material on Carl Spaatz. William M. Leary's *Aerial Pioneers* was essential to my depiction of Otto Praeger and the origins of airmail. *Flight in America*, by Roger E. Bilstein, filled in many of the blank spaces in my understanding of aviation before and during World War I.

For help with technical details, I tapped into the thriving community of vintage-airplane experts and pilots, among them Mike O'Neal, Glenn Peck, Brian Karli, John Weatherseed, Steve Ruffin, and Dorian Walker, the latter also a filmmaker whose documentary on the DH-4 will be shown on PBS in 2022 and who is one of the few men alive who has actually flown one of the planes (though not for long, unfortunately).* Steve and Dorian carefully reviewed the manuscript for accuracy, as did Roger Connor, aeronautical curator at the Smithsonian's National Air and Space Museum, and Jon Barrett, a volunteer researcher and photographer at the museum and the webmaster of the League of WWI Aviation Historians. All were extremely generous with their time and saved me from embarrassing mistakes; the responsibility for any that remain is entirely mine. My thanks also to the Smithsonian's Larry Burke and Carl Bobrow, the latter for walking me through the finer points of airplane radio technology as it existed in 1919.

This project would never have gotten off the ground, so to speak, without the patient, surefooted guidance of Howard Yoon, my agent at the Ross Yoon Agency in Washington, D.C. Long before I sat down to write a proposal, Howard pushed me to think hard about what I wanted to say and how I wanted to say it. I am extremely grateful for his efforts, which led not just to a book contract but also, I think, to a better book. I owe a similar debt to my editor at Liveright, Daniel Gerstle, for taking a chance on a first-time author and carefully shepherding my manuscript to completion. It was greatly improved by his shrewd questions and thoughtful comments. The final form of the book also owes much to managing editor Becky Homiski and the rest of the Liveright editorial and production team, including Christopher Curioli, Susan Sanfrey, Julia Druskin, Zeba Arora, and Sarahmay Wilkinson; thanks, as well, to Peter Miller, Cordelia Calvert, Carine Zambrano, and Nick Curley for their diligent work on publicity and marketing.

Several good friends were particularly helpful to me as I set about

---

* On May 2, 2020, Dorian was test flying a newly restored DH-4 when he experienced control problems caused by faulty rigging. He crash-landed on his home airfield in Bowling Green, Kentucky. He was not seriously hurt, but the DH-4 was wrecked.

the lonely business of writing this book. Over a glass of wine in her living room one evening, and many subsequent conversations, Cherie Burns demystified what to me was the alien world of book publishing, sharing insights from her own experiences as a successful author and boosting my confidence along the way. David Nathan believed in my idea from the start and badgered me on my progress, usually while holding me captive in his catboat as we tacked back and forth in Nantucket Harbor. I'm not sure I would have finished without his words ringing in my ears. And special thanks to Holly Weeks, whom I first encountered decades ago as a student in her English class during my senior year of high school. From start to finish, she was indispensable, listening patiently as I read passages over the phone, offering suggestions when I was stuck, and carefully reading a late draft for stylistic or other failings, of which there were more than one. I am deeply grateful for her encouragement and wisdom, and most of all for her friendship.

Finally, I want to thank my family—my children, Drew and Catie, for indulging my obsession these past five years, and especially my wife, Gail Walker, who raised her eyebrows but no objections when I revealed that my plan to write this book included buying a small airplane and flying it across the country and back. She has always allowed me to chart my own course, even if it's not one that she would have chosen. For that and so much more, I am forever in her debt.

NOTES

Unless otherwise noted, weather conditions, pilots' arrival and departure times, and their relative positions in the race are taken from original Army records at the National Archives and Records Administration in College Park, Maryland. These and most other documents relating to the contest can be found in Record Group 18, Records of the Army Air Corps, Office of the Chief of the Air Corps, "Correspondence Related to Transcontinental Reliability Test Flights, and to Station at Columbus, NM, 1919," NM-53, Entry 187, boxes 1–5. Individual pilot reports from the October 1919 transcontinental race referenced herein are contained in box 5.

Abbreviations

NARA (National Archives and Records Administration)
RG (Record Group)
NASM (Smithsonian National Air and Space Museum)
NPRC (National Personnel Records Center, St. Louis)

PROLOGUE

xi **The snow came on suddenly:** "Aviator Didn't Crash into Any Mountain Peak," *Wyoming State Tribune*, October 11, 1919, 1.

xi **Before leaving Rawlins:** "U.S. Military Airplane Wrecked Near Saratoga, Pilot Killed," *Saratoga Sun* (Saratoga, WY), October 16, 1919, 1.

xi **second thoughts:** Caption under photo of Wales's wrecked DH-4, Rawlins control stop final report, NARA, RG 18, "Reliability Test Flights," box 3.

xi **making good progress:** "Aviator Didn't Crash," *Wyoming State Tribune*, 1.

xii **isolated ranch house:** "He's Idol of Wyoming," *The Sun* (Baltimore, MD), November 30, 1919, 13.

xii **friendly wave:** "A Heroic Incident of Transcontinental Air Race," *St. Louis Post-Dispatch*, November 23, 1919, 87.

xv **"commercial aviation":** Henry H. Arnold, *Global Mission* (New York: Harper & Brothers, 1949), 92.

xv **$15 joyrides:** Martin Caidin, *Barnstorming* (New York: Bantam Books, 1991), 29.

x **the vicinity of Oberg Pass:** "Aviator Didn't Crash," *Wyoming State Tribune.*

x **Wales attempted to turn away:** "Aviator Didn't Crash," *Wyoming State Tribune.*

CHAPTER ONE: The Honeymoon Special

3 **biplanes performing . . . reinforcements:** Jack R. Binns, "First Air Exposition Opened Here with Martial Ceremony," *New York Tribune*, March 2, 1919, 11.

3 **fanciful tableau:** Manufacturers Aircraft Association, Inc., "Aeronautical Exhibition of 1919," *Aircraft Year Book 1920* (New York: Doubleday, Page, 1920), 140; Hathi Trust, http://hdl.handle.net/2027/umn.3195 1000924617d.

4 **more than thirty:** "Principle [*sic*] Specifications of All Aeroplanes at the Aeronautical Exposition," Smithsonian Institution, NASM Technical Reference Files, Drawer J1, Folder 1919-580-01.

4 **Caproni . . . DH-4:** Alexander Klemin, "Airplanes at the Aeronautical Exposition," *Aviation and Aeronautical Engineering*, March 15, 1919, 210; Hathi Trust, http://hdl.handle.net/2027/coo.31924060892050.

4 **Nieuport . . . Spad:** "Correct List of Exhibitors at the Aeronautical Exposition," *U.S. Air Service* magazine, March 1, 1919, 4; Hathi Trust, http://hdl.handle.net/2027/ucl.c2638493.

4 **Douglas Campbell:** "Aircraft Show Is Ready," *New York Times*, March 1, 1919, 4.

4 **Fokker D.VII:** "All War Aircraft to Be Shown Here," *New York Times*, February 23, 1919, 22.

5 **President Wilson had barred:** Bulletin No. 3, Air Service Bureau of Aircraft Production, January 28, 1919, NARA, RG 18, Central Decimal Files, 1917-38, box 9.

5 **reserving a Pullman:** Memorandum for the Director of the Air Service from Maj. Raycroft Walsh, administrative executive, March 10, 1919, NARA, RG 18, Central Decimal Files, 1917-1938, box 10.

5 **admiring young "adorables":** "Aero Show Opens in Burst of Glory," *New York Herald*, March 2, 1919, 7.

5 **every afternoon during the exposition:** "New Aircraft Shown in Garden," *New York Times*, March 2, 1919, 5.

5 **Images of gunnery practice:** "Correct List," *U.S. Air Service.*

5 **"A most important and valuable application":** Glenn L. Martin, *Souvenir Catalogue: Aeronautical Exposition, Madison Square Garden and 69th Regiment Armory, New York City, March 1st–15th, 1919* (New York: Carey Printing Co., 1919), 28; Hathi Trust, http://hdl.handle.net/2027/njp.3210 1048877359.

6 **also came in a transport version:** Eric J. Shaw, "Controls on Developing Technology: The U.S. Commercial Air Transportation System During the Interwar Period, 1919–1939" (PhD diss., Salve Regina University, 2000).

6 **a ride in one of the planes:** " 'Big Bomber,' Laden with Scribes, Flies over New York City," *New York Tribune*, March 11, 1919, 9.

6 **"a buffet arrangement":** "Novelty Aircraft Abound at Exhibit," *New York Times*, March 9, 1919, 27.

6 **Chummy Flyabout:** "Novelty Aircraft," *New York Times*, 27.

6 **The Loening Kitten:** Manufacturers Aircraft Association, Inc., "Aeronautical Exhibition of 1919," 146.

6 **five feet nine-and-one-half inches:** Mitchell's annual efficiency report, January 16, 1920, Douglas Waller Papers, Wake Forest University, ZSR Library Special Collections and Archives, MS 645, box 4 (hereafter cited as Waller Papers).

7 **eschewed red meat:** Douglas Waller, *A Question of Loyalty: Gen. Billy Mitchell and the Court Martial That Gripped the Nation* (New York: HarperCollins, 2004), 8.

7 **hunting wild boar:** Waller, *A Question of Loyalty*, 126.

7 **walking cane:** James J. Cooke, *Billy Mitchell* (Boulder, CO: Lynne Rienner, 2002), 61.

7 **"a charming quality":** Reminiscences of Jerome C. Hunsaker, 1960, p. 104, oral history collection, Rare Book & Manuscript Library, Columbia University (found in Waller Papers, box 4).

7 **Hazelhurst Field . . . "branches of aerial tactics":** Binns, "First Air Exposition."

8 **less than three-to-one:** Manufacturers Aircraft Association, Inc., "Aeronautical Exhibition of 1919," 81.

8 **More than eighty:** Martin, *Souvenir Catalogue*, 73–77.

CHAPTER TWO: Willie

9 **came from money:** Douglas Waller, *A Question of Loyalty: Gen. Billy Mitchell and the Court Martial That Gripped the Nation* (New York: HarperCollins, 2004), 63–64.

9 **outbid John D. Rockefeller:** James J. Cooke, *Billy Mitchell* (Boulder, CO: Lynne Rienner, 2002), 9.

9 **John Lendrum Mitchell . . . Mitchell was born:** Waller, *Question of Loyalty*, 63–64.

10 **fluent in French . . . U.S. Senate:** Isaac Don Levine, *Pioneer of Air Power* (New York: Duell, Sloan and Pearce, 1943), 12, 15.

10 **bright, curious . . . air rifle:** Waller, *Question of Loyalty*, 65–66.

10 **Racine College . . . better athlete:** Waller, *Question of Loyalty*, 67–68.

10 **"boisterous conduct":** Burke Davis, *The Billy Mitchell Affair* (New York: Random House, 1967), 13.

10 **"lots of fellows here":** Waller, *Question of Loyalty*, 68.

11 **some of the best horses:** Cooke, *Billy Mitchell*, 17.

11 **"letter is silent":** Waller, *Question of Loyalty*, 68.

11 **teenage Mitchell:** Waller, *Question of Loyalty*, 70.

11 **done so reluctantly:** Waller, *Question of Loyalty*, 71.

11 **same state militia:** Waller, *Question of Loyalty*, 71.

11 **just seven days:** Waller, *Question of Loyalty*, 71.

12 **Spain's formal surrender:** Waller, *Question of Loyalty*, 74.

12 **137 miles:** Waller, *Question of Loyalty*, 75.

12 **Luzon . . . daring night raid:** Waller, *Question of Loyalty*, 77–78.

12 **Mauser:** Cooke, *Billy Mitchell*, 34.

12 **work was going slowly . . . "hard as boards":** Brig. General William Mitchell, "Billy Mitchell in Alaska," *American Heritage*, February 1961, https://www.americanheritage.com/billy-mitchell-alaska.

12 **one of the most capable:** Waller, *Question of Loyalty*, 82.

13 **Caroline Stoddard . . . School of the Line:** Waller, *Question of Loyalty*, 93–99.

13 *Cavalry Journal* **. . . youngest officer:** Waller, *Question of Loyalty*, 98, 100.

13 **gracious townhouse . . . shopping:** Waller, *Question of Loyalty*, 101.

13 **borrowed from banks . . . appearances:** Waller, *Question of Loyalty*, 102–3.

13 **advise lawmakers . . . temporary command:** Waller, *Question of Loyalty*, 103, 105.

14 **promotion . . . "What did I do wrong?":** Waller, *Question of Loyalty*, 105.

14 **unprepared for war . . . sailed for France:** Waller, *Question of Loyalty*, 104, 106.

CHAPTER THREE: The Western Front

15 **only 128,000 men:** Garrett Peck, *The Great War in America* (New York: Pegasus Books, 2018), 92.

15 **all but ignored . . . hard time believing:** Roger F. Bilstein, *Flight in America* (Baltimore: Johns Hopkins University Press, 2001), 14–15.

15 **Attitudes began to shift:** Bilstein, *Flight in America*, 15.

16 **the Army purchased:** Juliette A. Hennessy, *The United States Army Air Arm: April 1861 to April 1917* (Washington, DC: Office of Air Force History, 1985), 34; Hathi Trust, http://hdl.handle.net/2027/mdp.39015028456823.

16 **Patent disputes:** Bilstein, *Flight in America*, 28.

16 **laissez-faire economic traditions:** Walter A. McDougall, *The Heavens and the Earth: A Political History of the Space Age* (New York: Basic Books, 1985), 74–75.

16 **National Advisory Committee . . . volunteer:** Bilstein, *Flight in America*, 31.

17 **"This airplane business":** Bilstein, *Flight in America*, 38.

17 **backed by governments:** "NACA Origins (1915–1930)," NASA History, https://history.nasa.gov/SP-4406/chap1.html.

17 **"manifold and comprehensive":** A. F. Zahm, *Report on European Aeronautical Laboratories* (Washington, DC: Smithsonian Institution, 1914), 2; Hathi Trust, http://hdl.handle.net/2027/nnc1.cu55773982.

17 **Two French brothers:** Ben Mackworth-Praed, *Aviation: The Pioneer Years* (London: Studio Editions, 1990), 147.

17 **French government:** Walter J. Boyne, *de Havilland DH-4: From Flaming Coffin to Living Legend* (Washington, DC: Smithsonian Institution Press, 1984), 15.

18 **reconnaissance and artillery spotting:** Bilstein, *Flight in America*, 31.

18 **synchronizing gears:** Jack Harris and Bob Pearson, *Aircraft of World War I: 1914–1918* (London: Amber Books, 2010), 22–27.

18 **required to wear spurs:** "Spurs," *Air Service News Letter* (Washington, DC: War Department), January 25, 1919, 4.

19 **in pursuit of the Mexican revolutionary:** Julie Irene Prieto, *The Mexican Expedition 1916–1917* (Washington, DC: U.S. Army Center of Military History), https://history.army.mil/html/books/077/77-1/index.html.

19 **seventy-five miles an hour:** J Rickard, "Curtiss JN-3," History of War, July 21, 2020, http://www.historyofwar.org/articles/weapons_curtiss_JN3.html.

19 **delaminated in the dry heat:** Hennessy, *United States Army Air Arm*, 169.

19 **"51 were obsolete":** John J. Pershing, *My Experiences in the World War* (New York: Frederick A. Stokes, 1931), 27.

20 **American Radiator Company . . . French observation planes:** Douglas Waller, *A Question of Loyalty: Gen. Billy Mitchell and the Court Martial That Gripped the Nation* (New York: HarperCollins, 2004), 123.

20 **silver eagle:** Waller, *Question of Loyalty*, 119.

20 **French government cabled:** Alfred F. Hurley, *Billy Mitchell: Crusader for Air Power* (Bloomington: Indiana University Press, 1964), 27.

20 **20,474 . . . largest single-purpose appropriation:** Bilstein, *Flight in America*, 36.

20 **"darken the skies":** Ray Landis Bowers, "The Transcontinental Reliability Test: American Aviation After World War I" (master's thesis, University of Wisconsin, 1960), 1.

20 **150 per day:** Manufacturers Aircraft Association, Inc., *Aircraft Year Book 1919* (New York: Doubleday, Page, 1919), 53.

20 **such as spruce:** Memorandum, Bureau of Aircraft Production to Senator Thomas, May 31, 1918, NARA, RG 18, Records of the Bureau of Aircraft Production, Records of the Executive Department, General Correspondence (1917–19), box 1, NM-53, Entry 22.

21 **India . . . roughly 18-fold:** Bilstein, *Flight in America*, 36.

21 **about 10,000:** Bilstein, *Flight in America*, 36.

21 **other senior officers:** Waller, *Question of Loyalty*, 126.

21 **named an artilleryman . . . mollified:** James J. Cooke, *Billy Mitchell* (Boulder, CO: Lynne Rienner, 2002), 58.

21 **passed over:** Cooke, *Billy Mitchell*, 65.

21 **self-promoting loudmouth:** Benjamin D. Foulois, *From the Wright Brothers to the Astronauts* (New York: McGraw-Hill, 1968), 157.

21 **The antipathy . . . graciously conceded:** Burke Davis, *The Billy Mitchell Affair* (New York: Random House, 1967), 36–38.

22 **American doughboys:** Cooke, *Billy Mitchell*, 89.

22 **huge relief map:** William Mitchell, *Memoirs of World War I* (New York: Random House, 1960), 237.

22 **1,481 planes . . . fourteen airfields:** James J. Hudson, *Hostile Skies: A Combat History of the American Air Service in World War I* (Syracuse, NY: Syracuse University Press, 1968), 139.

22 **parked in hangars:** Brig. Gen. William Mitchell, "The Air Service at St. Mihiel," *World's Work*, August 1919, 360, http://hdl.handle.net/2027/njp.32101075886422.

22 **heavy rains:** Cooke, *Billy Mitchell*, 90.

22 **Mitchell had observed:** Waller, *Question of Loyalty*, 119.

22 **pursuit planes . . . horse-drawn wagons:** Hudson, *Hostile Skies*, 148–73.

23 **More than sixty:** Hudson, *Hostile Skies*, 186.

23 **repeated flights:** Cooke, *Billy Mitchell*, 92.

23 **forty Air Service aviators:** Mitchell Yockelson, *Forty-Seven Days* (New York: New American Library, 2016), 74.

23 **promotion to brigadier general:** Cooke, *Billy Mitchell*, 93.

23 **shortages of aircraft:** Cooke, *Billy Mitchell*, 99.

23 **Mitchell and ground commanders:** Waller, *Question of Loyalty*, 130.

23 **planning for bombing raids:** Hurley, *Billy Mitchell: Crusader*, 36.

24 **pampered life:** Cooke, *Billy Mitchell*, 90.

24 **740 American planes . . . another 319:** Hudson, *Hostile Skies*, 299–300.

24 **younger brother . . . cufflinks:** Waller, *Question of Loyalty*, 125.

24 **jubilant French aviators:** Davis, *Billy Mitchell Affair*, 45–48.

24 **"delightful chat":** Davis, *Billy Mitchell Affair*, 48.

24 **strutting the decks:** Davis, *Billy Mitchell Affair*, 3.

25 **"sick with excitement":** Caroline Mitchell diary, February 28, 1919, Douglas Waller Papers, Wake Forest University, ZSR Library Special Collections and Archives, box 15 (hereafter cited as Waller Papers).

25 **"At home at last":** Caroline Mitchell diary, March 2, 1919, Waller Papers, box 15.

CHAPTER FOUR: Aftermath

26 **"a little experiment":** Reminiscences of Reed M. Chambers, 1960, p. 56, oral history collection, Rare Book & Manuscript Library, Columbia University.

27 **"I got your resignation":** Reminiscences of Reed M. Chambers, 57.

27 **St. Nazaire:** Maurer Maurer, *Aviation in the U.S. Army 1919–1939* (Washington, DC: Office of Air Force History, 1987), 4.

27 **"shooting of wild fowl":** "Hunting in Airplanes Forbidden," *Air Service News Letter,* January 4, 1919, 16.

27 **Curtiss JN-4 trainers:** Henry Ladd Smith, *Airways: The History of Commercial Aviation in the United States* (New York: Knopf, 1942), 48.

27 **2,300 surplus Air Service planes . . . 30 million feet:** Maurer, *Aviation*, 10, 11.

27 **only about 1,300 officers:** Maurer, *Aviation*, 8.

28 **"esprit de corps":** Memorandum from Col. T. F. Dodd to William Mitchell, July 30, 1919, William Mitchell papers, Library of Congress, Manuscript Division, box 7 (hereafter cited as Mitchell Papers).

28 **a Civil War veteran:** Edgar F. Raines, "Menoher, Charles Thomas," American National Biography, February 2000, https://doi.org/10.1093/anb/9780198606697.article.0600432.

28 **"sweet tenor voice":** Menoher obituary, *The Association of the Graduates of the United States Military Academy Annual Report,* June 10, 1951, 235.

28 **more capable, mobile weapons:** Raines, "Menoher, Charles Thomas."

28 **military aviation academy:** Ray Landis Bowers, "The Transcontinental Reliability Test: American Aviation After World War I" (master's thesis, University of Wisconsin, 1960), 16.

29 **an independent air force:** Alfred F. Hurley, *Billy Mitchell: Crusader for Air Power* (Bloomington: Indiana University Press, 1964), 38.

29 **"marched back in good order":** Douglas Waller, *A Question of Loyalty: Gen. Billy Mitchell and the Court Martial That Gripped the Nation* (New York: HarperCollins, 2004), 137.

29 **erected in less than six months:** "'Temporary' War Department Buildings," National Park Service, July 18, 2017, https://www.nps.gov/articles/temporary-war-department-buildings.htm.

30 **The Navy:** Thomas Wildenberg, *Billy Mitchell's War With the Navy* (Annapolis, MD: Naval Institute Press, 2013), 39.

30 **two aircraft carriers:** Memorandum from Mitchell to Menoher, April 12, 1919, Mitchell Papers, box 7.

30 **13,000 planes:** Roger F. Bilstein, *Flight in America* (Baltimore: Johns Hopkins University Press, 2001), 42.

30 **furniture and speedboats:** Susanna Ray, "From Cloth to Carbon Fiber, a Timeline of Boeing's 100-Year Flight," *Seattle Times,* July 9, 2016.

30 **converted Farman F-60 Bombers:** Ben Mackworth-Praed, *Aviation: The Pioneer Years* (London: Studio Editions, 1990), 220.

30 **"U.S. Lags":** "U.S. Lags Far Behind Europe in Preparations for Air Transport," *U.S. Air Service* magazine, January 18, 1919, 1; Hathi Trust, http://hdl.handle.net/2027/uc1.c2638493.

31 **"intercity" biplane:** Manufacturers Aircraft Association, Inc., *Aircraft Year Book 1920* (New York: Doubleday, Page, 1920), 192.

31 **"Steadier than any Pullman":** Thomas William McFadden, "Building Industries: Collective Action Problems and Institutional Solutions in the Development of The U.S. Aviation Industry, 1903–1938" (PhD diss., University of Arizona, 1999).

31 **onetime professional baseball player . . . "upper stratas":** Joseph Corn, *Winged Gospel* (Baltimore: Johns Hopkins University Press, 2002), 40–41.

31 **"Lawson Air Liner" . . . smoked celluloid:** "First Liner of Air Reaches Washington with Fourteen Aboard," *U.S. Air Service*, October 1919, 29.

31 **green leather:** Richard Wightman, "Account of Flight Written on Board Air Liner," *Flying*, November 1919, 858; Hathi Trust, http://hdl.handle.net/2027/nyp.33433057646469.

31 **giant spoked wheels:** Interior photograph, *Flying*, October 1919, 756.

31 **"a good first attempt":** *War Expenditures: Hearings Before Select Committee on Expenditures in the War Department*, 66th Congress, 1st sess., October 15, 1919 (testimony of William Mitchell).

32 **"the Millionaire's Special":** Magazine advertisement, NASM Technical Reference Files, American Institute of Aeronautics and Astronautics collection, box 62.

32 **"aerial transport of prisoners":** "Prisoner Rides in Airplane: No Handcuffs On," *San Francisco Chronicle*, November 2, 1919, 7.

32 **"the longest airplane trip":** "Woman Makes Air Record," *New York Times*, October 8, 1919, 20.

32 **blue-eyed, and "golden-haired":** Marguerite Mooers Marshall, "Son Flies to School in Airplane," *Evening World* (New York, NY), Wednesday, October 8, 1919, 5.

32 **diverting to Cincinnati:** "Mother Brings Her Son Through Air to School in New York," *Flying*, November 1919, 846; Hathi Trust, http://hdl.handle.net/2027/nyp.33433057646469.

33 **"doesn't hurt my complexion":** Marshall, "Son Flies to School," 5.

33 **"threshold of a new age":** Editorial, *New York Times*, March 16, 1919, 31.

33 **forest fires:** Eldon Wilson Downs, "Contribution of U.S. Army Aviation to Uses and Operation of Aircraft" (PhD diss., University of Wisconsin, 1960), 100–103.

33 **photography techniques:** Capt. M. A. Kinney, Jr., A.S.A., "Broad Field for Commercial Aerial Photography," *Flying*, April 1919, 250; Hathi Trust, http://hdl.handle.net/2027/nyp.33433057646469.

33 **a grizzled old cavalry colonel:** Henry H. Arnold, *Global Mission* (New York: Harper & Brothers, 1949), 95.

33 **fresh oysters:** "Oysters via Airplane," *Air Service News Letter*, September 9, 1919, 7.

34 **"We ask for 1,050":** *Army Appropriations Bill: Hearings on H.R. 5227, June*

16, 1919, Before the Subcommittee of the Committee on Military Affairs of the United States Senate, 66th Congress (testimony of William Mitchell).

34 **"practically the only market":** Charles T. Menoher, "Memorandum for the House of Representatives and the Senate," July 30, 1919, NARA, RG 18, Records of the Office of the Chief of the Air Service, 1917–21, "Correspondence and Reports Relating to Air Service Policy, Organization, Programs, and Legislation, 1919–21," box 1, Entry 160.

34 **$25 million:** Maurer, *Aviation*, 44.

CHAPTER FIVE: The Flying Parson

35 **morning of August 25:** "Menoher Starts Planes," *New York Times,* August 26, 1919, 1.

35 **huge British dirigible:** "RC-34 Crosses Ocean, Lands Safely Here," *New York Times,* July 7, 1919, 1.

35 **summer colonies:** "Menoher Starts Planes," *New York Times,* 1.

35 **Wrigley's chewing gum:** Photograph from USAF Museum collection, CANAV Books, CANAV Books Blog, May 12, 2009, https://canavbooks .wordpress.com/2009/05/12/aviation-in-canada-the-formative-years -is-on-final/p019-2-2/.

35 **roughly 2,000:** "Menoher Starts Planes," *New York Times,* 1.

35 **thirty biplanes:** "Menoher Starts Planes," *New York Times,* 1.

35 **painted in vermilion:** "Menoher Starts Planes," *New York Times,* 1.

36 **Low clouds:** "Menoher Starts Planes," *New York Times,* 1.

36 **"sensational amusement":** Roger F. Bilstein, *Flight in America* (Baltimore: Johns Hopkins University Press, 2001), 25.

36 **$50,000 prize . . . eighty-four days:** William M. Leary, *Pilots' Directions: The Transcontinental Airway and Its History* (Iowa City: University of Iowa Press, 1990), 1–3.

37 **passengers and mail:** Bilstein, *Flight in America*, 25.

37 **rusty radiator water:** Manufacturers Aircraft Association, Inc., "NC-4 Transatlantic Flight," *Aircraft Year Book 1920* (New York: Doubleday, Page, 1920), 259.

37 **John Alcock . . . hit a tree:** Graham Wallace, *The Flight of Alcock and Brown* (London: Putnam, 1955).

38 **founded by Air Service veterans:** "American Flying Club Temporary Constitution," *American Flying Club Annual Report* (1920), 9; Hathi Trust, http://hdl.handle.net/2027/njp.32101071859225.

38 **$10,000 in prize money:** "The New York-Toronto Airplane Race," *Aviation and Aeronautical Engineering,* September 15, 1919, 80.

38 **"precisely, precisely":** William Mitchell, *Memoirs of World War I* (New York: Random House, 1960), 253.

38 **joined the British Royal Flying Corps:** James J. Hudson, "Harold E. Hartney: Pursuit Group Commander and Author," *Air University Review* (Maxwell AFB, AL: Department of the Air Force, 1963–1987), 81.

38 **"green pilots":** Harold E. Hartney, *Up and at 'Em* (London: Cassell and Company, 1940), 55.

39 **airplane ride:** Caroline Mitchell diary, September 6, 1919, Douglas Waller Papers, Wake Forest University, ZSR Library Special Collections and Archives, box 15.

39 **"encourage the industry":** Memorandum from Hartney to Mitchell and Menoher, July 23, 1919, NARA, RG 18, Central Decimal Files, 1917–38, box 719.

39 **civilian planes:** Telegram from Menoher to Lawrence Driggs, American Flying Club, August 1, 1919, NARA, RG 18, Central Decimal Files, 1917–38, box 719.

39 **at least thirty minutes:** Memo from Mitchell to commanding officer, Hazelhurst Field, Long Island, August 22, 1919, NARA, RG 18, Central Decimal Files, 1917–38, box 719.

40 **"shortest possible time":** Telegram from Menoher to commanding officer, Selfridge Field, Michigan, August 21, 1919, NARA, RG 18, Central Decimal Files, 1917–38, box 719.

40 **"the actual conditions":** "Menoher Starts Planes," *New York Times*, 1.

40 **"joyous throng":** "Menoher Starts Planes," *New York Times*, 1.

40 **dropped a handkerchief:** "Menoher Starts Planes," *New York Times*, 1.

41 **gale-force winds:** "Americans Fight Wind," *New York Times*, August 26, 1919, 3.

41 **no feeling in his left arm:** "New York-Toronto Race Commercial Flying Test," *Automotive Industries*, August 28, 1919, 434; Hathi Trust, http://hdl.handle.net/2027/njp.32101048984023.

41 **DH-4 into a stall:** Handwritten draft of telegram from Hartney to Menoher, undated, NARA, RG 18, Central Decimal Files, 1917-1938, box 719.

41 **Austin Crehore:** Jon Guttman, *Grim Reapers: French Escadrille 94 in World War I* (Reno, NV: Aeronaut Books, 2016), 79–80.

41 **thirty-two of fifty-three:** Unsigned editorial, *Aviation and Aeronautical Engineering*, September 1, 1919, 117.

42 **"The performance I consider":** Letter from Brant to Mitchell, August 29, 1919, William Mitchell papers, Library of Congress, Manuscript Division, box 7.

42 **seven hours, forty-five minutes:** "Liberty Engines Fastest in Race," *Automotive Industries*, September 1, 1919, 491; Hathi Trust, http://hdl.handle.net/2027/njp.32101048984023.

42 **electric-blue eyes:** Rosemary Ann Holoman (Belvin Maynard's granddaughter), interview by the author, January 1, 2019.

42 **polish his rimless spectacles:** Ray Landis Bowers, "The Transcontinental Reliability Test: American Aviation After World War I" (master's thesis, University of Wisconsin, 1960), 137.

43 **"selfishness and commercialism":** Thomas C. Parramore, *First to*

Fly: North Carolina and the Beginnings of Aviation (Chapel Hill: University of North Carolina Press, 2002), 252.

43 **mechanical hay press:** Frank G. Weaver, "From Pulpit to Cockpit— and Back Again," *Young Men* [YMCA magazine], Vol. 45, September 1919, 222; Hathi Trust, https://hdl.handle.net/2027/wu.89059432856.

43 **high-school sweetheart:** Parramore, *First to Fly*, 253.

43 **Remington Arms Company:** Maynard's draft registration card, Ancestry.com, https://www.ancestry.com/imageviewer/collections/6482 /images/005152208_03881?usePUB=true&_phsrc=dKW1&_phstart=suc cessSource&usePUBJs=true&pId=9128537.

43 **ground school in Ohio:** "More than Three Thousand Attend Funeral of Lieutenant Maynard," *Wilmington Morning Star*, September 11, 1922, 1.

43 **test-flying . . . a new world record:** Parramore, *First to Fly*, 253–54.

43 **never had an accident:** " 'Flying Parson' Skilled Airman," *Salt Lake Tribune*, October 11, 1919, 10.

43 **resume his theological studies:** Parramore, *First to Fly*, 254.

44 **a German police dog:** Belvin W. Maynard, "Blazing the Air Trail from Coast to Coast with Tar Heel Aviator in Army Race," *News & Observer* (Raleigh, NC), October 24, 1919, 1.

CHAPTER SIX: Praeger

45 **Praeger entered the office:** Otto Praeger, "Moss from a Rolling Stone" (unpublished memoir provided to the author by Rebecca Abbott, Praeger's granddaughter), 117–18.

45 **not a view to lift the spirits:** Praeger, "Moss from a Rolling Stone," 117–18.

45 **"Do you think that airplanes":** Praeger, "Moss from a Rolling Stone," 117–18.

46 **more than 400,000:** Rinker Buck, *The Oregon Trail* (New York: Simon & Schuster, 2015), 15.

46 **twenty-one-and-a-half days:** "Overland Mail to California in the 1850s," U.S. Postal Service, https://about.usps.com/who-we-are /postal-history/overland-mail.html.

46 **in about ten days:** "The Pony Express," U.S. Postal Service, https:// about.usps.com/who-we-are/postal-history/pony-express.pdf.

46 **almost instantly obsolete:** "The Pony Express," U.S. Postal Service.

46 **"big iron needle":** Simon Winchester, *The Men Who United the States* (New York: Harper Perennial, 2014), xiii.

46 **as few as 100 hours:** William M. Leary, *Aerial Pioneers* (Washington, DC: Smithsonian Institution Press, 1985), 182.

47 **6.5 million automobiles:** Pete Davies, *American Road: The Story of an Epic Transcontinental Journey at the Dawn of the Motor Age* (New York: Henry Holt, 2002), 1.

47 **Fisher would lead the way:** Davies, *American Road*, 13.

47 **Times Square to Lincoln Park . . . "seedling miles":** Davies, *American Road*, 13, 29–31.

48 **eighty-one military vehicles:** Davies, *American Road*, 6, 45.

48 **"military and economic asset":** *Report on the First Transcontinental Motor Convoy,* from Lt. E. R. Jackson to Col. L. B. Moody, Tank, Tractor and Trailer Division, Office of the Chief of Ordnance, War Department, October 31, 1919, https://web.archive.org/web/20101206123736/http://www.eisenhower.archives.gov/Research/Digital_Documents/1919Convoy/New%20PDFs/Report%20Jackson%20to%20Moody.pdf.

48 **barely a year old:** Richard Killblane, "70 Years of the Transportation Corps," U.S. Army Transportation Corps, https://transportation.army.mil/history/index.html.

48 **little more than a wagon trail . . . broke down:** Davies, *American Road*, 122, 125, 173.

49 **morning of September 6 . . . national highway bill:** Davies, *American Road*, 210, 215–16.

49 **stagecoaches, and cowboys:** Leary, *Aerial Pioneers*, 22.

49 **1,700-mile bicycle trip . . . hilltop palace:** Praeger, "Moss from a Rolling Stone," 20, 23, 25.

49 **his journalism career:** Devin Leonard, *Neither Snow nor Rain: A History of the United States Postal Service* (New York: Grove Press, 2016), 94.

50 **segregationist:** Leonard, *Neither Snow nor Rain*, 93.

50 **horse-drawn mail . . . 2,600:** Leary, *Aerial Pioneers*, 25.

50 **an aviation meet:** Leary, *Aerial Pioneers*, 15.

50 **written at his urging:** Leary, *Aerial Pioneers*, 26–27.

51 **The Army offered . . . did not have the range:** Leary, *Aerial Pioneers*, 30–32.

51 **humiliating pratfall:** Leary, *Aerial Pioneers*, 36–40.

51 **Subsequent efforts:** Leary, *Aerial Pioneers*, 45–50.

51 **"Neither snow nor rain":** "Postal Service Mission and 'Motto'," U.S. Postal Service, https://about.usps.com/who-we-are/postal-history/mission-motto.pdf.

52 **"Their hearts":** Leary, *Aerial Pioneers*, 46.

52 **Praeger hired . . . Praeger fired:** Leary, *Aerial Pioneers*, 51–64.

52 **Post Office could boast . . . New Orleans:** Leary, *Aerial Pioneers*, 62, 66.

52 **Praeger dispatched:** Leary, *Aerial Pioneers*, 58.

52 **a civil engineer . . . "Colonel":** "The Jordan Years and Hilldale Park," San Anselmo Historical Museum, https://sananselmohistory.org/articles/before-united-markets-3/.

53 **surplus DH-4s:** Leary, *Aerial Pioneers*, 66.

53 **Praeger was determined:** Leary, *Aerial Pioneers*, 66–67.

53 **morning of December 18:** Leary, *Aerial Pioneers*, 70–71.

53 **"All that remains":** Leary, *Aerial Pioneers*, 70.

54 **The next few days:** Leary, *Aerial Pioneers*, 71.

54 **a bleak period:** Leary, *Aerial Pioneers*, 75–76.

54 **$3,600 yearly salary . . . night flight:** Leary, *Aerial Pioneers*, 69, 39.

54 **trusted lieutenant . . . fourteen steps:** Leary, *Aerial Pioneers*, 78–85.

55 **The new route . . . "two-cent stamp":** Leary, *Aerial Pioneers*, 82–90.

55 **seven hours:** "Chicago Air Mail Linked with East," *New York Times,* July 19, 1919, 16.

55 **"pioneering venture":** Leary, *Aerial Pioneers*, 93.

55 **"Commercial aviation has arrived":** Leary, *Aerial Pioneers*, 95.

CHAPTER SEVEN: "The Greatest Airplane Race Ever Flown"

56 **frequent trips . . . dinner with friends:** Caroline Mitchell diary, various entries, summer 1919, Douglas Waller Papers, Wake Forest University, ZSR Library Special Collections and Archives, box 15.

56 **phalanx of mounted officers:** "Capital Pays Homage to Pershing and His Conquering Hosts," *Washington Post*, September 18, 1919, 1.

56 **wireless-equipped DH-4:** "Interesting Incident of the First Division Parade," *Air Service News Letter*, September 23, 1919, 2.

57 **A day after the victory parade:** Telegram from Mitchell to chiefs of Eastern, Central, and Western Departments, September 18, 1919, NARA, RG 18, "Reliability Test Flights," box 5.

57 **not an original idea:** "Air Derby Planned Across Continent," *New York Times,* August 19, 1919, 17.

57 **joined the Air Service:** "Charles J. Glidden Leaves the Army," *Boston Globe*, August 9, 1919, 6.

57 **a telegraph office:** "Charles J. Glidden Dead, Ill Long Time," *Boston Globe*, September 12, 1927, 1.

57 **telephone exchange . . . switchboard "operators":** "Charles Jasper Glidden." *Dictionary of American Biography* (New York: Charles Scribner's Sons, 1936); *Biography in Context*, http://link.galegroup.com/apps/doc/BT2310012737/BIC?u=loc_main&sid=BIC&xid=62cbdc7a.

57 **annual motorcar rally . . . 46,000 miles:** T. R. Nicholson, *The Trailblazers: Stories of the Heroic Age of Transcontinental Motoring, 1901–1914* (London: Cassell & Company, 1958), 152–53.

58 **"good eating":** "The World and Its People as Seen from the Motor Car," speech by Charles J. Glidden, New England Railroad Club, Boston, Massachusetts, May 11, 1909, NASM Technical Reference Files, Drawer CG, Folder 32000-01.

58 **flanged wheels:** Nicholson, *Trailblazers*, 161.

58 **balloon named *Boston* . . . "adjunct to country estates":** Charles J. Glidden, "The Balloon an Adjunct to the Country Place," *Country Life in America,* January, 1909, 253; Hathi Trust, http://hdl.handle.net/2027/umn.31951000739026j.

58 **"after the style":** "Birdmen in Match Race," *Boston Globe*, September 15, 1910, 1.

58 **commercial airline service:** James R. Morrow, "Skylarking in the
    Air," *Boston Daily Globe*, July 2, 1911, SM5.
58 **announced in New York:** "Fly from New York to San Francisco," *Boston
    Globe*, August 19, 1919, 3.
59 **"The course will be":** Telegram from Mitchell to chiefs of Eastern,
    Central, and Western Departments, September 18, 1919, NARA, RG 18,
    "Reliability Test Flights," box 5.
59 **Peary graciously wrote:** Telegram from Robert F. Peary to Menoher,
    September 23, 1919, NARA, RG 18, "Air Service 1917–1926," General
    Correspondence 1919–1921, box 14.
60 **Forecasters in the Weather Bureau . . . "maneuver problem":**
    Report on the First Transcontinental Reliability and Endurance Test (Washington,
    DC: Government Printing Office, 1919), 5–6; Hathi Trust, http://hdl
    .handle.net/2027/uiug.30112112405466.
60 **"the greatest airplane race":** Memorandum from William Mitchell to
    Charles Menoher, October 3, 1919, NARA, RG 18, Air Service 1917–1926
    (Administrative Group), box 8.

CHAPTER EIGHT: Spaatz

61 **Twilight was settling:** Ruth Spaatz reminiscences, United States Air
    Force Oral History Program, Washington, DC, 1981 (Montgomery, AL:
    Alfred F. Simpson Historical Research Center, Maxwell Air Force Base), 19.
61 **"strong as hickory":** Carl B. Ogilvie, "The 'Mad Major's' Escapades,"
    Flying and Popular Aviation, June 1939, 17, NASM Technical Reference Files,
    Drawer CS, Folder 796000-01.
61 **"I never learned anything":** James A. Parton, *"Air Force Spoken Here"*:
    General Ira Eaker and the Command of the Air (Maxwell Air Force Base, AL:
    Air University Press, 2000), 115; Defense Technical Information Center,
    https://apps.dtic.mil/sti/pdfs/ADA376708.pdf.
62 **liquor . . . ragtime:** David R. Mets, *Master of Airpower* (Novato, CA: Pre-
    sidio Press, 1988), 7, 19.
62 **Of German heritage . . . marching them off:** Mets, *Master of Airpower*,
    4–10.
62 **flight from Albany:** Mets, *Master of Airpower*, 10–11.
63 **infantry company in Hawaii . . . shipped out:** Mets, *Master of Air-
    power*, 11–23.
63 **aerial finishing school . . . building duckboards:** Mets, *Master of
    Airpower*, 24–25.
63 **ten airfields . . . Nieuport fighters:** Mets, *Master of Airpower*, 25–29.
64 **"no more rough landings":** Hiram Bingham, *An Explorer in the Air Ser-
    vice* (New Haven, CT: Yale University Press, 1920), 103.
64 **gun cameras:** Mets, *Master of Airpower*, 26.
64 **"reasoning powers":** Memo from Spaatz, April 6, 1918, NARA, RG
    18, World War I Organization Records, Air Service Orders, box 3409.

64 **one in twenty-five:** Statistical analysis provided by Mike O'Neal, managing editor of *Over the Front*, quarterly journal of the League of WWI Aviation Historians.

64 **venereal disease:** Memo from Spaatz aide to C.O. Headquarters Detachment, Third Aviation Instruction Center, August 8, 1918, NARA, RG 18, World War I Organization Records, Air Service, box 3384.

64 **Spaatz pleaded:** Mets, *Master of Airpower*, 30.

65 **first taste of combat . . . speaking French:** Mets, *Master of Airpower*, 34–35.

65 **theater troupe . . . an American aviator:** Ruth Spaatz reminiscences, United States Air Force Oral History, 14–16.

65 **"must be Tooey":** Ruth Spaatz reminiscences, United States Air Force Oral History, 14.

65 **an aerial circus:** Mets, *Master of Airpower*, 40.

66 **"My nervous system":** DeWitt S. Copp, *A Few Great Captains: The Men and Events That Shaped the Development of U.S. Air Power* (Joint Base Andrews, MD: Air Force Historical Foundation, 1980), 8–9.

66 **sweeping views:** Ruth Spaatz reminiscences, United States Air Force Oral History, 21.

66 **"reasonably certain":** Memo from Charles Menoher to commanding officers, Air Service airfields, September 22, 1919, NARA, RG 18, "Reliability Test Flights," box 1.

66 **Army rules would prevent:** "Menoher Frowns on Air Derby Prizes," *Washington Herald*, Monday, October 6, 1919, 10.

66 **Hendee-Indian motorcycle:** Letter to William Mitchell from G. V. Hass, Splitdorf Electrical Co., October 7, 1919, NARA, RG 18, "Reliability Test Flights," box 5.

66 **more than sixty:** *Report on the First Transcontinental Reliability and Endurance Test* (Washington, DC: Government Printing Office, 1919), 12; Hathi Trust, http://hdl.handle.net/2027/uiug.30112112405466.

67 **Orders went out:** Telegram from Charles Menoher to Mather Field, October 2, 1919, NARA, RG 18, Central Decimal Files, 1917–1938, box 2115.

CHAPTER NINE: "Sure Death If Motor Stops on the Takeoff"

68 **"suitable field":** Letter to Sidney Chamber of Commerce from Col. Joseph C. Morrow, Central Department commander, reprinted in *Sidney Telegraph* (Sidney, NE), October 3, 1919, 6.

68 **one of twenty:** *Report on the First Transcontinental Reliability and Endurance Test* (Washington, DC: Government Printing Office, 1919), 9; Hathi Trust, http://hdl.handle.net/2027/uiug.30112112405466.

68 **a cavalry outpost . . . eighty saloons:** "Lynchings, Legends, and Lawlessness," City of Sidney, https://www.cityofsidney.org/265 /Lynchings-Legends-Lawlessness.

68 **farming and ranching . . . car dealerships:** R. Laurie Simmons, Thomas H. Simmons, Mary Therese Antsey, and Nebraska State Historical Society, "Sidney Original Town Plat Intensive Historic Buildings Survey, 2015–16, 8–10, https://archive.org/details/SidneyOriginalTownPlatI ntensiveHistoricBuildingsSurvey.

69 **Pastures, croplands, racetrack infields:** Geza Szurvoy, *The American Airport* (St. Paul, MN: MBI Publishing, 2003), 10.

69 **Albert Kahn . . . twenty airfields:** Szurvoy, *American Airport*, 20–22.

70 **"Next to his machine":** Copy of typewritten manuscript for Belvin Maynard's race diary, provided to the author by Rosemary Ann Holoman (Belvin Maynard's granddaughter).

70 **"chart air lines":** Janet R. Daly Bednarek, *America's Airports: Airfield Development, 1918–1947* (College Station: Texas A&M University Press, 2001), 19.

70 **Curtiss JN-4 trainers . . . "every railroad town":** Memo from Major Albert D. Smith to the director of Military Aeronautics, Washington, D.C., February 14, 1919, NARA, RG 18, "Reliability Test Flights," box 5.

70 **a police dog named Flu [footnote]:** "Trans Continental Flight Returns," *Air Service News Letter*, February 8, 1919, 4.

71 **Sweetwater, Texas . . . "quaint and almost incredible":** "Pathfinders," anonymous author, NARA, RG 18, Records of the Office of the Chief of Air Service, 1917–21, Information Group, Records Relating to Aeronautics 1917–27, box 26.

72 **thirty-two towns and cities . . . steel hangars:** "War Department Air Service Announces Official Plans for Cooperation with Municipalities in Extension of Aerial Navigation and Establishment of Municipal Landing Fields," *Air Service News Letter*, May 3, 1919, 2, 4.

72 **Daytona:** Letter from Menoher to *Engineering News*, July 23, 1919, NARA, RG 18, Central Decimal Files, 1917–38, box 12.

72 **airdrome on a roof . . . "An investigation":** Letter from William Mitchell to Committee on Finance and Budget, Board of Estimate and Apportionment, New York City, October 18, 1919, NARA, RG 18, Central Decimal Files, 1917–38, box 1226.

72 **"render all possible assistance":** Letter to Sidney Chamber of Commerce from Col. Joseph C. Morrow, *Sidney Telegraph*, 6.

73 **"commercial Gothic":** Letter from Lt. Col. H. M. Hickam, chief, Air Service Information Group, n.d., NARA, RG 18, Air Corps Library, "U Stencils" 1919–1940, box 3.

73 **white triangles:** Ray Landis Bowers, "The Transcontinental Reliability Test: American Aviation After World War I" (master's thesis, University of Wisconsin, 1960), 77.

73 **"a lack of energy":** Unsigned memo "to all contestants" from Office of the Director of Air Service, September 27, 1919, United States Air Force Academy Archives, SMS 66, file for Drayton, Harry C.

73 **whistle-stop tour:** Letter from Col. J. F. Curry to Lt. Wells, control stop

commander, Omaha, October 6, 1919, NASM Technical Reference Files, "1919 Transcontinental Reliability and Endurance Test Omaha Control Stop Information," Acc. No. 2009-004, box 1.

73 **as far east as Cheyenne:** Lt. E. A. Clune, Cheyenne control stop final report, November 15, 1919, NARA, RG 18, "Reliability Test Flights," box 2.

73 **Businesses loaned cars:** Letter from Lt. J. MacEwan VanderVoort, North Platte control stop commander, to Department Air Service Officer, Central Department, October 29, 1919, NARA, RG 18, "Reliability Test Flights," box 5.

73 **War Camp Community:** Telegram from Laurence L. Driggs to Col. Harold Hartney, September 29, 1919, NARA, RG 18, "Reliability Test Flights," box 5.

73 **candy, cigarettes:** Lt. E. A. Clune, Cheyenne control stop final report.

73 **"Cheyenne is going":** Bowers, "Transcontinental Reliability Test," 75.

73 **"surpassing themselves":** Message to Brant from Menoher, October 6, 1919, NARA, RG 18, "Reliability Test Flights," box 5.

74 **"practically assured":** "Assures Rock Island Is Practically Certain to Be on Official Air Map," *Rock Island Argus* (Rock Island, IL), October 11, 1919, 5.

74 **"Air Gate to New York":** "Six Additional Man Eagles Leave West Endicott," *Morning Sun* (Binghamton, NY), October 11, 1919, 3.

74 **Will Brown:** Orville D. Menard, "Lest We Forget: The Lynching of Will Brown, Omaha's 1919 Race Riot," *Nebraska History* 91 (2010): 152–65, https://history.nebraska.gov/sites/history.nebraska.gov/files/doc/publications/NH2010Lynching.pdf.

74 **Omaha Chamber of Commerce:** Memo from Lt. Harold Wells, Omaha control stop commander, to Otto Praeger, November 1, 1919, NASM, "1919 Transcontinental Reliability and Endurance Test Omaha Control Stop Information," Acc. No. 2009-004, box 1.

74 **Omaha Athletic Club:** Memo from Wells to Department Air Service Officer, Central Department, October 25, 1919, NASM, "1919 Transcontinental Reliability and Endurance Test Omaha Control Stop Information," Acc. No. 2009-004, box 1.

75 **2,000 gallons:** Memo from Menoher to Commanding Officer, All Fields, September 22, 1919, NARA, RG 18, "Reliability Test Flights," box 5.

75 **testy messages:** Memo from Mitchell to Col. John F. Curry, October 4, 1919, William Mitchell papers, Library of Congress, Manuscript Division, box 7 (hereafter cited as Mitchell Papers).

75 **a subordinate . . . inspection tour:** Memo from Curry to Menoher, October 15, 1919, NARA, RG 18, Central Decimal Files, 1917–38, box 719.

75 **"second transcontinental race":** Memo from Mitchell to Menoher, September 22, 1919, Mitchell papers, box 7.

75 **first crossing by October 18:** Memo from Mitchell to Air Service Administrative Executive, October 17, 1919, NARA, RG 18, Air Service 1917–1926, "General Correspondence, 1919–1921," box 11.

76 **just two days before the start:** "Transcontinental Air Derby, Flying Classic, Brings Out 55 of the 'Who's Who' in Aviation," *Evening World* (New York, NY), October 7, 1919, 3.

76 **Britton Field:** Memo from Brant to Menoher, "Preparations for San Francisco–New York Race," October 2, 1919, NARA, RG 18, "Reliability Test Flights," box 5.

76 **"a circus lot" . . . tents:** "First of Transcontinental Fliers Are Expected Here Today," *Rochester Herald*, October 8, 1919.

76 **"cheering news":** Telegram from Menoher to Brant, October 6, 1919, NARA, RG 18, "Reliability Test Flights," box 5.

76 **underground fuel tank:** "Report of Field at Bryan, Ohio," from J. A. Bishop to Central Department, Air Service Officer, n.d., NARA, RG 18, "Reliability Test Flights," box 2.

76 **"a blue-grass lawn":** "Air Derby Flyers Land Here Today," *Cleveland Plain Dealer*, October 8, 1919, 1.

76 **Curtiss Aeroplane & Motor Corporation:** Lt. A. B. Pitts, final report, November 5, 1919, NARA, RG 18, "Reliability Test Flights," box 5.

76 **white-painted "U":** "Transcontinental Sky Race Is Twice Distance First Planned," *Salt Lake Telegram*, October 7, 1919.

77 **"its immediate vicinity" . . . lacked the power:** Rawlins control stop final report, "Reliability Test Flights," NARA, RG 18, "Reliability Test Flights," box 5.

77 **"The people of Rawlins" . . . WY 14:** Rawlins control stop final report.

77 **situated in a hollow:** Capt. J. O. Donaldson, pilot report.

77 **"Worse field":** Maj. A. H. Gilkeson, pilot report.

77 **a narrow windswept bench:** Author visit to Green River, Wyoming, in June 2019.

78 **187 feet:** "Donaldson Describes His Record-Breaking Flight," *Binghamton Press* (Binghamton, NY), October 23, 1919, 19.

78 **"Sure death":** Lt. Homer B. Chandler, pilot report.

78 **sent to Green River, Utah:** Telegram from Menoher to Lt. C. A. C. Tolman, Green River control stop commander, October 4, 1919, NARA, RG 18, "Reliability Test Flights," box 3.

79 **six inches of snow:** Air Service press release, October 9, 1919, NARA, RG 18, "Records of the Office of the Chief of the Air Service, 1917–21," "Records Relating to Aeronautics," Entry 117, box 27.

CHAPTER TEN: "Interesting Happenings"

83 **fifteen-mile-per-hour breeze:** "Aviators Are Off in Big Race from Coast to Coast," *Evening Star* (Washington, DC), October 8, 1919, 1.

83 **chilly on the field:** "Three Dead, Many Hurt, in Start of 2700 Mile Air Race," *The Sun* (New York, NY), October 9, 1919, 1.

83 **arriving in motorcars:** "Three Dead, Many Hurt," *The Sun* (New York, NY), 1.

83 **sent out 600:** Handwritten memo from Information Group officer to Hartney, NARA, RG 18, "Reliability Test Flights," box 1.

83 **Young women . . . A brass band:** "63 Fliers Start 5,400-Mile Race," *New York Times*, October 9, 1919, 1.

84 **a terse command:** "Three Dead, Many Hurt," *The Sun* (New York, NY), 1.

84 **"Let them go, Colonel":** "Three Dead, Many Hurt," *The Sun* (New York, NY), 1.

84 **a twin-engine Martin Bomber . . . Fokker D.VIIs:** *Report on the First Transcontinental Reliability Test* (Washington, DC: Government Printing Office, 1919), 12; Hathi Trust, http://hdl.handle.net/2027/uiug .30112112405466.

84 **forty-six of the sixty-three:** *Report on the First Transcontinental Reliability Test*, 12.

84 **Its fuselage . . . crop dusters:** Walter J. Boyne, *de Havilland DH-4: From Flaming Coffin to Living Legend* (Washington, DC: Smithsonian Institution Press, 1984), 11–12.

85 **popular with smugglers:** Roger Connor (aeronautics curator, Smithsonian National Air and Space Museum), email correspondence with the author, January 2, 2022.

85 **original was designed by . . . Dayton-Wright Airplane Company:** Boyne, *de Havilland DH-4*, 24–25, 35.

85 **$11,701.39:** "Monthly Report on AEF Air Service Liquidation and Demobilization, Nov. 1918–Mar. 1919," *Gorrell's History of the American Expeditionary Forces Air Service, 1917–1919*, NARA, RG 120, Records of the American Expeditionary Forces (World War I), 1848–1942, https://www.fold3.com /image/27516687.

85 **standardized engine . . . downtown Washington, D.C.:** Phillip S. Dickey III, *The Liberty Engine 1918–1942* (Washington, DC: Smithsonian Institution Press, 1968), 7, 14–15.

85 **The men drew heavily:** John Weatherseed (aircraft restoration specialist, Vintage Aviation Team, Caledon, Ontario, Canada), email correspondence with the author, February 19, 2021.

85 **designed for mass production:** Dickey, *Liberty Engine*, 9.

86 **required three men:** Glenn Peck, who has restored and flown a DH-4 (Peck Aeroplane Restoration, Maryland Heights, Missouri), telephone interview by the author, May 10, 2017.

86 **Packard Motor Car Company:** Dickey, *Liberty Engine*, 67.

86 **April 1918 . . . only a few hundred:** Boyne, *de Havilland DH-4*, 12, 13.

86 **top speed . . . docile handling:** Boyne, *de Havilland DH-4*, 101, 11.

86 **88-gallon:** Boyne, *de Havilland DH-4*, 44.

86 **fuel system was pressurized . . . faulty planes:** William M. Leary, "Billy Mitchell and the Great Transcontinental Air Race of 1919," https:// www.earlyaviators.com/emitchel.htm.

87 **gas tank was located:** Boyne, *de Havilland DH-4*, 11.

87 **soft pine instead of ash:** William M. Leary, *Aerial Pioneers* (Washington, DC: Smithsonian Institution Press, 1985), 71.

87 **"A DH-4 as presently constructed":** Maj. Carl Spaatz, pilot report.

87 **kick the rudder:** Lt. Cleveland W. McDermott, pilot report.

87 **"The observer is a stranger":** Lt. J. G. Williams, pilot report.

87 **more than 800 pounds . . . turn turtle:** Boyne, *de Havilland DH-4*, 31, 11.

87 **"not a good ship . . . hoodoo":** *Army Appropriations Bill: Hearings on H.R. 5227, June 16, 1919, Before the Subcommittee of the Committee on Military Affairs of the United States Senate*, 66th Congress (testimonies of William Mitchell and Charles Menoher).

88 **"greater intimacy":** Lt. J. G. Williams, pilot report.

88 **Col. Townsend F. Dodd:** "Death of Col. Dodd," *Liaison: The Courier of the Big Gun Corps* (Coast Artillery School), October 11, 1919, 174; Hathi Trust, https://hdl.handle.net/2027/uc1.c3113448.

88 **Dodd and a mechanic . . . rudder bar:** Accident report by Lt. Col. S. W. Fitzgerald, Aircraft Accident and Incident Reports, Air Force Historical Research Agency Archives, Maxwell Air Force Base, Alabama.

89 **A day earlier . . . out of the woods:** "Major Frissell Is Killed as 'Plane Flies into Tree," *Binghamton Press* (Binghamton, NY), October 6, 1919, 12.

89 **"gallant and talented":** William Mitchell, *Our Air Force: The Keystone of National Defense* (New York: E.P. Dutton, 1921), 100.

89 **lost nine men:** "Airplane Fatalities and Accidents at United States Flying Fields for Week Ending July 17, 1919," report to Menoher, July 18, 1919, NARA, RG 18, Air Service 1917–1926, "General Correspondence, 1919–1921," box 14.

90 **another appearance on Capitol Hill:** *Army Reorganization: Hearings Before Committee on Military Affairs*, U.S. House, 66th Congress, October 6, 1919 (testimony of William Mitchell).

90 **"a new epoch":** "Eleven Air Racers Pause," *Omaha World-Herald*, October 11, 1919, 1.

90 **Army planes had been designated:** Telegram from Menoher to International Film Company, New York, October 7, 1919, NARA, RG 18, "Reliability Test Flights," box 5.

90 **"interesting happenings":** Telegram from Menoher to Cheyenne control stop, October 9, 1919, NARA, RG 18, "Reliability Test Flights," box 5

90 **packed his bags:** Caroline Mitchell diary, October 6, 1919, Douglas Waller Papers, Wake Forest University, ZSR Library Special Collections and Archives, box 15.

90 **honor of taking off first:** "Col. Brandt's [*sic*] Plane Falls, Causing Observer's Death, *Evening World* (New York, NY), October 8, 1919, 1.

91 **Machle . . . the second to lift off:** "63 Fliers," *New York Times*, 1.

91 **two-minute intervals:** "Aces Start Today in Great Air Race," *New York Times*, October 8, 1919, 1.

91 **to prevent a backup:** "Three Dead, Many Hurt," *The Sun* (New York, NY), 1.

91 **Opening their throttles wide . . . "a clean hit":** "Three Dead, Many Hurt," *The Sun* (New York, NY), 1.

91 **Over the summer:** "Report of the American Aviation Mission," *Aircraft Journal*, August 23, 1919, 10; Hathi Trust, http://hdl.handle.net/2027/ucl .c2638494.

91 **publicly disavowed:** Statement of Nelson Baker in War Department press release, August 11, 1919, William Mitchell papers, Library of Congress, Manuscript Division, box 31.

91 **"It is beyond dispute . . . lead the world":** "63 Fliers," *New York Times*, 1.

92 **Crowell decided:** "63 Fliers," *New York Times*, 1.

92 **An ambulance . . . urgent business:** "63 Fliers," *New York Times*, 1.

92 **less than a full night's sleep:** "Two Miles a Minute Made by Maynard in Flight to Chicago," *New York Tribune*, October 9, 1919, 2.

92 **"mutilated":** Telegram from Menoher to commanding officer, Mather Field, October 2, 1919, NARA, RG 18, Central Decimal Files, 1917–38, box 1743.

93 **"severely reprimanded":** Belvin W. Maynard, "Blazing the Air Trail from Coast to Coast with Tar Heel Aviator in Army Race," *News & Observer* (Raleigh, NC), October 24, 1919, 1.

93 **Skipping an awards banquet:** "Two Miles a Minute," *New York Tribune*, 2.

93 **scrapped his plans:** "Maynard Describes Flight Twice Across Continent," *Sunday Star* (Washington, DC), October 19, 1919, 3.

93 **double-breasted leather coat . . . *"Hello Frisco":*** Photograph of Maynard and Kline after reaching Chicago on day one, Binghamton Press (Binghamton, NY), October 11, 1919, 1.

93 **high agitation:** "63 Fliers," *New York Times*, 1.

93 **Trixie had been ill:** Maynard, "Blazing the Air Trail," 1.

93 **seven months old:** Thomas C. Parramore, *First to Fly: North Carolina and the Beginnings of Aviation* (Chapel Hill: University of North Carolina Press, 2002), 256.

93 **Maynard climbed down . . . "barking at the crowd":** "63 Fliers," *New York Times*, 1.

93 **He had finished third:** "Real Sky Pilot Wins First Air Honors in International Race," *Washington Times*, September 1, 1919, 9.

93 **a narrow, angular face:** Photograph of Gish at track meet, "Famous Athletes at the A-Y-P," *Bonville's Western Monthly*, September 1909, 204; Hathi Trust, http://hdl.handle.net/2027/coo.31924087802215.

94 **national junior record:** "The Year in Sports," *Washington Post*, December 26, 1909, 4.

94 **one of the fastest quarter-milers:** "Irish-American A.C. Games," *New York Times*, August 13, 1911, 27.

94 **competed briefly . . . moving to Washington, D.C.:** "Washington C.C.C. Plans Dual Meets with Many Clubs," *Washington Times*, December 24, 1911, 10.

94 **acquired a car dealership:** Advertisement (Haynes Motor Cars), *Washington Post*, May 28, 1919, 19.

94 **patented a gasoline filter:** Brig. Gen. (ret.) Bradford Grethen Cynoweth, *Bellamy Park: Memoirs* (Hicksville, NY: Exposition Press, 1975), 89.

94 **Columbia Golf Club . . . influential friends:** Letter from Gish to Col. Carl M. Nelson, U.S.A.F., Congressional Inquiry Division, Office of the Legislative Liaison, Department of the Air Force, May 16, 1961, Gish's military personnel file, NPRC.

94 **"Daredevil Brailey":** "Gish Hupmobile Agent," *Washington Times*, December 21, 1916, 7.

94 **cigar clamped permanently:** "'Si' Writes 'Bo' of Holiday Trip," *Washington Herald*, July 9, 1916, 20.

94 **On June 14 . . . "Excessive speed":** "Sets New Auto Record," *Washington Post*, June 18, 1916, 14.

94 **started a garage:** "Burman Regains the Remy Trophy in Laurel Races," *Washington Times*, June 29, 1912, 12.

94 **worked for an aircraft manufacturer:** Advertisement for the Rex Smith Aeroplane Co., *Washington Times*, August 13, 1911, 13.

94 **learned to fly in 1911:** "Wounded Aviator in Grueling Race," *Washington Times*, October 8, 1919, 18.

94 **Peck died:** "Burial of Paul Peck," *Washington Post*, September 16, 1912, 12.

94 **raced through his training . . . more than 500:** Letters from Gish to Retired Activities Branch, Department of the Air Force, Washington (January 10, 1959, and September 7, 1959), Gish file, NPRC.

94 **hunting German bombers at night:** Letter from Gish to Lt. Col. Charlotte B. Wildbur, Chief, Retired Activities Branch, Department of the Air Force, August 15, 1960, Gish file, NPRC.

94 **sat in the cockpit . . . wouldn't let them:** Letter from Gish to Lt. Col. Charlotte B. Wildbur, August 15, 1960.

95 **multiple surgeries:** Letter from Gish to Lt. Col. Charlotte B. Wildbur, August 15, 1960.

95 **checked himself out:** "Chronological Statement of Service," Gish file, NPRC (shows that Gish was hospitalized at Walter Reed from October 22, 1918, to December 19, 1919).

95 **wore metal braces:** Letter from Gish to Gen. Nathan B. Twining, Air Force Chief of Staff, Washington, September 26, 1960, Gish file, NPRC.

95 **fly with a mechanic:** Letter from Gish to Gen. Nathan B. Twining, September 26, 1960.

95 **scarlet breeches and horizon-blue jacket:** "Thrilling Day for Fliers in Cross-Country Contest," *Rochester Herald*, October 9, 1919, 1.

95 **women from Larchmont, New York . . . kiss on the cheek:** "63 Fliers," *New York Times*, 1.

95 **Low clouds and fog:** "15 Flyers Start from S.F. Base for Atlantic Goal," *San Francisco Examiner*, October 9, 1919, 2.

96 **not entirely without incident . . . next to their planes:** "Great Coast-to-Coast Air Race Starts Tomorrow," *San Francisco Chronicle*, October 7, 1919, 2.

97 **The men agreed . . . sundown on Friday:** "Great Coast-to-Coast Air Race," *San Francisco Chronicle*, 2.

97 **former movie actor:** "Lt. Wales Dies of Injuries in Air Race," *St. Louis Post-Dispatch*, October 10, 1919, 1.

97 **grounded . . . Mather Field:** "Lt. Wales Dies of Injuries," *St. Louis Post-Dispatch*, 1.

97 **fallen in love:** "Lt. Wales Dies of Injury in Air Race," *San Francisco Chronicle*, October 11, 1919, 3.

97 **drafted a friend . . . Broadway show:** "He's Idol of Wyoming," *The Sun* (Baltimore, MD), November 30, 1919, 13.

97 **skies began to brighten . . . whirlwinds of dust:** "15 Flyers," *San Francisco Examiner*, 2.

98 **crossed the water at 400 feet:** Maj. John C. P. Bartholf, "From Pacific to Atlantic in an SE-5," *U.S. Air Service* magazine, November 1919, 14; Hathi Trust, https://hdl.handle.net/2027/mdp.39015024398896.

98 **Spaatz preferred:** Maj. Carl A. Spaatz, pilot report.

98 **Jesse McKenzie had arrived . . . asking him to pass it along:** "Lt. Wales Dies of Injury," *San Francisco Chronicle*, 3.

98 **zoomed aloft:** "63 Fliers," *New York Times*, 1.

CHAPTER ELEVEN: No Parachutes

99 **people in the village of Deposit . . . loud bang:** "Col. Brant Is Anxious to Enter the Race Again," *Binghamton Press* (Binghamton, NY), October 11, 1919, 7.

99 **racing number "4":** "Col. Brant Is Anxious," *Binghamton Press* (Binghamton, NY), 7.

99 **from the rear cockpit:** "Col. Brant Is Anxious," *Binghamton Press* (Binghamton, NY), 7.

99 **4,000 feet:** "Col. Brant Is Anxious," *Binghamton Press* (Binghamton, NY), 7.

99 **released his safety belt . . . shimmied up:** "Col Brant Plans to Continue Great Race," *Morning Sun* (Binghamton, NY), October 10, 1919.

99 **Ormer Locklear had astonished . . . plane crash in 1920:** Art Ronnie, *The Man Who Walked on Wings* (Cranbury, NJ: A. S. Barnes, 1973), 20, 275.

100 **Another pilot . . . "by a hand":** "Pilot Straddles Engine and Laces Up Tie Rod with Trousers Belt," *Rochester Herald*, October 11, 1919.

100 **still clinging to the nose:** "Col Brant Plans to Continue," *Morning Sun* (Binghamton, NY).

100 **The first men . . . "What has happened?":** "Col. Brant Is Anxious," *Binghamton Press* (Binghamton, NY), 7.

100 **control officer in Binghamton:** Telegram from Capt. C. C. Mosely to Menoher, October 8, 1919, NARA, RG 18, "Reliability Test Flights," box 1.

100 **Charlton . . . colliding with a fence:** "63 Fliers Start 5,400-Mile Race," *New York Times*, October 9, 1919, 1.

100 **Lt. Russell Maughan ran short of fuel:** Lt. Russell Maughan, pilot report.

100 **William R. Taylor . . . put down in Nicholson:** Binghamton control stop final report, Capt. C. C. Moseley, November 14, 1919, NARA, RG 18, "Reliability Test Flights," box 1.

100 **Another DH-4 pilot:** "'Flying Parson,' Far in Van, Reaches Cheyenne," *Morning Sun* (Binghamton, NY), October 10, 1919, 1.

100 **Kirkpatrick . . . faulty compass:** "Plane Thought Down Arrives After Dark," *Buffalo Courier*, October 9, 1919, 1.

101 **Almost since leaving Long Island . . . igniting fuel in the carburetor:** Letter from Gish to Maj. Sidney Ormerod, Directorate of Administrative Services, Department of the Air Force, Washington, December 29, 1960, Gish file, NPRC.

101 **sheet of flame:** "Flyer Tells How He Cheated Death in a Burning Plane," *Evening World* (New York, NY), October 9, 1919, 5.

101 **in 1797 a Frenchman . . . successful jump:** R. Ray Ortensie, "Development of Parachutes to 1945," Air Force Material Command History Office, January 5, 2021, https://www.wpafb.af.mil/News/Article-Display/Article/2462753/a-look-backat-the-development-of-parachutes-to-1945/.

101 **Army observation balloonists . . . 116 balloonists:** Office of the Director of Air Service, *Parachute Manual for Balloons* (Washington, DC: Government Printing Office, August 1919), 1–3.

102 **Ernst Udet:** Peter Hart, *Aces Falling* (London: Orion Books, 2008), 188.

102 **Everard Calthrop . . . dropping spies:** Arthur Gould Lee, *No Parachute* (London: Grub Street, 2013), 231 (originally published by Jarrolds Publishers, 1968).

102 **"It is not general practice":** Maj. Hollis Leroy Muller, *Manual of Military Aviation* (Menasha, WI: George Banta, 1917), 132; Hathi Trust, http://hdl.handle.net/2027/ucl.b3141330.

102 **"old-timers":** Ray Landis Bowers, "The Transcontinental Reliability Test: American Aviation After World War I" (master's thesis, University of Wisconsin, 1960), 5.

102 **"occupants of a stricken airplane":** Lee, *No Parachute*, 229.

103 **More than 200 British airmen:** Eldon Wilson Downs, "Contribution of U.S. Army Aviation to Uses and Operation of Aircraft" (PhD diss., University of Wisconsin, 1960), 141.

103 **"If your plane catches fire"** . . . **a picket fence:** Harold E. Hartney, *Up and at 'Em* (London: Cassell and Company, 1940), 139.

103 **Some pilots carried revolvers:** O'Brien Browne, "The Passion and the Fury: Mick Mannock," *Aviation History,* July 2007, https://www.historynet .com/edward-mick-mannock-world-war-i-raf-ace-pilot.htm.

103 **the Air Service belatedly began testing . . . 1923:** Downs, "Contribution of U.S. Army Aviation," 143, 160.

103 **McCusker . . . asbestos-lined:** William M. Leary, *Aerial Pioneers* (Washington, DC: Smithsonian Institution Press, 1985), 82–83.

103 **"obvious thing":** "Reducing the Fire Hazard in the Airplane," *Scientific American,* September 20, 1919, 1.

103 **"outside air intake":** Memo from Mitchell to Menoher, July 11, 1919, NARA, RG 18, Air Service 1917–1926, "General Correspondence, 1919-1921," box 17.

104 **He shielded his eyes . . . until the wings stalled:** "Flyer Tells," *Evening World* (New York, NY), 5.

104 **The Frenchman later said:** Bob Campbell, "Late Arrivals Tell Thrilling Tales of Experiences in the Air," *Morning Sun* (Binghamton, NY), October 11, 1919, 3.

104 **"Believe me":** "Thrilling Day for Fliers in Cross-Country Contest," *Rochester Herald,* October 9, 1919, 1.

104 **"I would not":** "Thrilling Day for Fliers," *Rochester Herald,* 1.

104 **"nice cozy hotel":** "Thrilling Day for Fliers," *Rochester Herald,* 1.

104 **De Lavergne resumed . . . secured another DH-4:** Campbell, "Late Arrivals," *Morning Sun* (Binghamton, NY), 3.

104 *Junk:* Photograph of Gish's plane at Cheyenne, NARA Still Photos Archive, box 2111, #38-7286.

104 **Mitchell, too . . . extreme stress:** James J. Cooke, *Billy Mitchell* (Boulder, CO: Lynne Rienner, 2002), 99.

105 **"during this period" . . . "his nerves":** Memo from Capt. James P. Kerby, Ward Surgeon, Fort Douglas, Utah, July 9, 1919, Maughan personnel file, NPRC.

105 **thirty days of medical leave:** Handwritten letter from Maughan to Adjutant General of the Army, July 22, 1919, Maughan personnel file, NPRC.

105 **Maughan then appealed:** "Aviators Are Off on Big Race from Coast to Coast," *Evening Star* (Washington, DC), October 8, 1919, 1.

105 **his engine was running hot . . . direct line:** Maj. Carl A. Spaatz, pilot report.

106 **They would fly no farther:** Daily report, Capt. T. S. Voss, Salt Lake control stop commander, October 8, 1919, NARA, RG 18, "Reliability Test Flights," box 4.

106 **After waiting for the snow:** Daily report, Green River control stop, October 9, 1919, NARA, RG 18, "Reliability Test Flights," box 3.

106 **it still needed time:** Telegram from Voss to Menoher, October 9, 1919, NARA, RG 18, "Reliability Test Flights," box 3.

106 **Crissy made one complete circuit:** "Two Plunge to Death in Pond," *Salt Lake Telegram*, October 9, 1919, 13.

107 **highly regarded . . . Junior Military Aviator:** Army press release, "Transcontinental Flight, Oct. 10, 1919," NARA, RG 18, "Records Relating to Aeronautics, 1917–1927," Entry 117, box 27.

107 **Crissy's wife:** "Commandant of Mather Field and Observer Die in Aerial Derby Mishap," *San Francisco Chronicle*, October 9, 1919, 1.

107 **who had been cheering . . . Both men died:** "Two Plunge to Death," *Salt Lake Telegram*, 13.

108 **"Ninety percent":** Maj. Carl A. Spaatz, pilot report.

108 **nearly 25 percent:** David Jack Kenney, "Stall and Spin Accidents: Keep the Wings Flying," AOPA Air Safety Institute, n.d., p. 2, https://www.aopa.org/-/media/files/aopa/home/pilot-resources/safety-and-proficiency/accident-analysis/special-reports/stall_spin.pdf.

108 **"Corpses Mark Trail":** "Corpses Mark Trail of Aerial Derby," *Atlanta Constitution*, October 9, 1919, 1.

CHAPTER TWELVE: "God's Given Children"

109 **Billy Mitchell believed:** William Mitchell, *Skyways* (Philadelphia: J.B. Lippincott, 1930), 71.

109 **"The horse-rider with good hands . . . a horse's mouth bleed":** Capt. T. S. Rippen and Lt. E. G. Manuel, *Report on the Essential Characteristics of Successful and Unsuccessful Aviators*, Royal Air Force, n.d., p. 3, NARA, RG 18, "Records Relating to Aeronautics, 1917–1927," Entry 117, box 26.

109 **German aviators:** H. Graeme Anderson, *The Medical and Surgical Aspects of Aviation* (London: Hodder & Stoughton, 1919), 19, Hathi Trust; https://hdl.handle.net/2027/mdp.39015005989853.

109 **"an increased sense of responsibility":** Rippen and Manuel, *Report on the Essential Characteristics*, 2.

109 **a racist qualifier:** Mitchell, *Skyways*, 71.

109 **"alert, cheerful":** Rippen and Manuel, *Report on the Essential Characteristics*, 3.

110 **"God's given children":** Reminiscences of Carl A. Spaatz, 1959, Douglas Waller Papers, Wake Forest University, ZSR Library Special Collections and Archives, box 4.

110 **"flies like the devil":** "Three Dead, Many Hurt, in Start of 2700 Mile Air Race," *The Sun* (New York, NY), October 9, 1919, 1.

111 **Some of the first such maps . . . "aerial navigation maps":** James R. Akerman, ed., *Cartographies of Travel and Navigation* (Chicago: University of Chicago Press, 2006), 217, 223–24.

112 **Post Office maps:** Akerman, *Cartographies of Travel and Navigation*, 232.

112 **"The issued maps":** Lt. Guy H. Gale, pilot report.

112 **Rand McNally state maps . . . large paperclips:** Lt. Alexander Pearson, Jr., pilot report.

112 **For American aviators . . . enemy guns:** Erik M. Conway, *Blind Flying: Low Visibility Operations in American Aviation 1918–1958* (Baltimore: Johns Hopkins University Press, 2006), 13–14.

112 **notorious incident . . . "would have been with us":** Steven A. Ruffin, "Major Harry Brown and His 'Lost Flight' of the 96th Aero Squadron," *Over the Front* 19, no. 3 (Fall 2004): 196–207.

113 **lakes and rivers:** Belvin W. Maynard, " 'Flying Parson' Tells of Experiences in First Flight Over Continent," *Washington Times*, October 13, 1919, 17.

113 **To guide them in . . . Coast Artillery:** Ray Landis Bowers, "The Transcontinental Reliability Test: American Aviation After World War I" (master's thesis, University of Wisconsin, 1960), 81–82.

113 **As he approached Binghamton . . . flying in circles:** Belvin W. Maynard, "Blazing the Air Trail from Coast to Coast with Tar Heel Aviator in Army Race," *News & Observer* (Raleigh, NC), October 24, 1919, 1.

113 **Lt. John Marquette . . . drop out of the race:** Capt. John P. Marquette, pilot report.

114 **Maynard had no difficulty . . . boiled ham:** Maynard, "Blazing the Air Trail," 1.

114 **He knew, counterintuitively:** Herbert M. Friedman and Ada Kera Friedman, "The Great Transcontinental Air Race," *Aviation History* 21, no. 2 (November 2010): 50.

114 **The crowd was even bigger . . . better view:** "Thrilling Day for Fliers in Cross-Country Contest," *Rochester Herald*, October 9, 1919, 1.

114 **"hated black cross of the Boche":** "Thrilling Day for Fliers," *Rochester Herald*, 1.

114 **one of forty-five Fokkers:** "4 Planes in Omaha All Night," *Omaha Daily Bee*, October 14, 1919, 1.

114 **the best fighter of the war:** Jack Herris and Bob Pearson, *Aircraft of World War I* (London: Amber Books, 2010), 163.

115 **Allied powers required:** "Fokker D V.II," Smithsonian National Air and Space Museum, https://airandspace.si.edu/collection-objects/fokker-dvii/nasm_A19200004000.

115 **Mechanics were unfamiliar with:** Harold Hartney, "Col. Hartney's Trip in the German Fokker," *Air Service News Letter*, November 7, 1919, 2.

115 **He followed a compass line:** Maynard, "Blazing the Air Trail," 1.

115 **Glenn Martin came out:** Maynard, "Blazing the Air Trail," 1.

115 **made a tactical error:** Hartney, "Col. Hartney's Trip," 2.

116 **control officer stopped:** Capt. J. O. Donaldson, pilot report.

116 **"Breakfast in Long Island":** "Flyer Does N.Y.-Chicago in 6 Hrs., 45M.," *Chicago Tribune*, October 9, 1919, 1.

116 **By Maynard's account:** Maynard, "Blazing the Air Trail," 1.

116 **Aero Club of Illinois . . . dormitory:** Chicago control stop final report,
     Capt. Earl S. Hoag, November 3, 1919, NARA, RG 18, "Reliability Test
     Flights," box 2.
117 **"I'm tired":** "Flyer Does N.Y.-Chicago," *Chicago Tribune*, 1.
117 **At the first opportunity . . . delay his getaway:** Maynard, "Blazing
     the Air Trail," 1.
117 **The mattresses . . . hauled out of bed:** Maynard, "Blazing the Air
     Trail," 1.
117 **tossed and turned:** Maynard, "Blazing the Air Trail," 1.

CHAPTER THIRTEEN: "Snow Hurricane"

118 **Scattered across thirty-one states . . . crude daily weather map:**
     Donald R. Whitnah, *A History of the United States Weather Bureau* (Urbana:
     University of Illinois Press, 1961), 12–13.
118 **In 1870, the U.S. Weather Bureau:** Whitnah, *A History*, 19.
118 **initially relied on the Signal Corps . . . Gulf and Atlantic:** Whit-
     nah, *A History*, 22.
118 **daily national weather map:** Whitnah, *A History*, 28.
119 **manned balloons:** Whitnah, *A History*, 39.
119 **kite observation station in Drexel:** Whitnah, *A History*, 169.
119 **500 men . . . theodolite:** George Owen Squier, "Aeronautics in the
     United States at the Signing of the Armistice: An Address Before the Insti-
     tute of Electrical Engineers," November 11, 1918; Hathi Trust, https://hdl
     .handle.net/2027/ucl.$b106232.
119 **"every hour, night and day":** *Reorganization of the Army: Hearings Before the
     Subcommittee of the Committee on Military Affairs*, U.S. Senate, 66th Congress,
     August 7, 1919 (testimony of William Mitchell).
120 **"Good flying weather today":** Whitnah, *A History*, 171.
120 **daily observations at kite stations:** Whitnah, *A History*, 170.
120 **thirty-hour aviation forecasts . . . "accuracy":** "Weather Reports
     Available," *Aircraft Journal*, July 26, 1919, 5; Hathi Trust, http://hdl.handle
     .net/2027/ucl.c2638493.
120 **a Weather Bureau meteorologist:** Telegrams from "Bowie" to Raw-
     lins control stop, Rawlins control stop final report, NARA, RG 18, "Reli-
     ability Test Flights," box 3.
120 **8:00 a.m., 12:00 noon, and 3:00 p.m.:** Message from Menoher to control
     stops, October 7, 1910, NARA, RG 18, "Reliability Test Flights," box 5.
120 **Fort Omaha Balloon School:** Message from Col. C. D. Chandler, Bal-
     loon and Air Division, Air Service headquarters, to commanding officer, Fort
     Omaha Balloon School, NARA, RG 18, "Reliability Test Flights," box 5.
121 **"a trip of this nature":** Maj. Henry Abbey, Jr., pilot report.
121 **"accurate weather reports":** Lt. Col. T. S. Bowen, pilot report.
121 **visiting the local Weather Bureau:** Lt. Robert S. Worthington, pilot
     report.

121 **a worrying picture:** Daily Weather Map, October 9, 1919, National
     Oceanic and Atmospheric Administration Central Library, U.S. Daily
     Weather Maps, https://library.noaa.gov/Collections/Digital-Collections
     /US-Daily-Weather-Maps.

122 **At 10:30 p.m. . . . "dangerous conditions":** Copy of telegram from
     Bowie to Rawlins control stop, Rawlins control stop final report, NARA,
     RG 18, "Reliability Test Flights," box 3.

122 **11:00 a.m. . . . "dangerous conditions":** Copy of telegram from Bowie
     to Rawlins control stop, Rawlins control stop final report.

122 **They had agreed:** Telegram from Voss, Salt Lake City control stop com-
     mander, to Menoher, October 8, 1919, NARA, RG 18, "Reliability Test
     Flights," box 3.

123 **His aviation résumé:** Pioneers of Flight Gallery, Smithsonian National
     Air and Space Museum, https://pioneersofflight.si.edu/content/lt-lowell
     -smith-0.

124 **"Snowing with gradual increase":** Copy of telegram from Maj. Fran-
     cis B. Longley to Green River control officer, October 8, 1919, Rawlins
     control stop final report.

124 **would never get that message:** Rawlins control stop final report.

124 **shutters on the nose:** Maj. Carl A. Spaatz, pilot report.

124 **craned his neck:** Brian Karli (pilot and specialist in vintage airplane res-
     toration), email correspondence with the author, January 19, 2020 (describ-
     ing technique for landing DH-4 and other open-cockpit biplanes).

124 **200 pounds of ice:** Extract from Smith's logbook, Rawlins control stop
     final report.

124 **Much to his irritation:** "Smith Outflies Spatz Coming from New York,"
     Binghamton Press (Binghamton, NY), October 16, 1919, 12.

125 **"A very poor Field":** Extract from Smith's logbook, Rawlins control stop
     final report.

125 **twelve-minute delay:** Maj. Carl A. Spaatz, pilot report.

125 **a nerve-wracking departure:** Maj. Carl A. Spaatz, pilot report.

125 **He could see that it would be folly:** Maj. Carl A. Spaatz, pilot report.

125 **follow the railroad:** Maj. Carl A. Spaatz, pilot report.

125 **about seventy-five miles:** Belvin W. Maynard, "'Undaunted by Mis-
     fortune,' Maynard Pushes on After Losing Half a Day in Race," *News &
     Observer* (Raleigh, NC), October 26, 1919, 1.

125 **"snow hurricane" . . . banking sharply:** Maj. Carl A. Spaatz, pilot
     report.

125 **clear skies . . . a wing skid:** Maj. Carl A. Spaatz, pilot report.

126 **"snow and blow":** "Four Fliers Are Near Goal," *Cleveland Press*, October
     11, 1919, 1.

126 **"really a race":** Letter from Mitchell to Arnold, September 11, 1919,
     William Mitchell papers, Library of Congress, Manuscript Division,
     box 7.

126 **"a sporting event"**: "The Transcontinental Reliability Race," *Air Service News Letter*, October 8, 1919.

126 **"score board"**: Memorandum for Information Group from Lt. Col. W. C. Sherman, acting assistant chief, Air Service Training & Operations Group, September 26, 1919, NARA, RG 18, box 5.

126 **"the human element"**: Lt. Walter E. Richards, pilot report.

127 **about 150 feet**: "U.S. Military Airplane Wrecked Near Saratoga, Pilot Killed," *Saratoga Sun* (Saratoga, WY), October 16, 1919, 1.

127 **slumped motionless . . . small fire**: "U.S. Military Airplane Wrecked," *Saratoga Sun* (Saratoga, WY), 1.

127 **broken aileron**: "A Heroic Incident of Transcontinental Air Race," *St. Louis Post-Dispatch*, November 23, 1919, 87.

127 **Goldsborough was disoriented**: "He's Idol of Wyoming," *The Sun* (Baltimore, MD), November 30, 1919, 13.

128 **Cowboys saddled**: "U.S. Military Airplane Wrecked," *Saratoga Sun* (Saratoga, WY), 1.

128 **trail made in the snow**: "U.S. Military Airplane Wrecked," *Saratoga Sun* (Saratoga, WY), 1.

CHAPTER FOURTEEN: Rain

129 **At 5:00 a.m. . . . . not be safe**: Telegram from Cleveland control stop to Mitchell, October 9, 1919, NARA, RG 18, "Reliability Test Flights," box 2.

129 **"very, very poor"**: Telegram from Cleveland control officer to Mitchell, October 9, 1919, NARA, RG 18, "Reliability Test Flights," box 2.

130 **"before the weather report from Cleveland"**: Lt. William C. F. Brown, pilot report.

130 **a violent storm**: Lt. William C. F. Brown, pilot report.

130 **close to 400 miles an hour:** J. O. Donaldson, address to American Flying Club, n.d., NASM Technical Reference Files, Drawer J1, Folder 1919-890-01.

130 **fray and start to splinter**: Capt. J. O. Donaldson, "District 'Ace' Tells How He Won Air Race of U.S. Army," *Washington Times*, October 23, 1919, 1.

130 **replace his propeller four times**: Lt. H. W. Sheridan, pilot report.

130 **mixed with hail**: "8 More Derby Flyers Arrive Despite Storm," *Cleveland Plain Dealer*, October 10, 1919, 1.

130 **Brown and three other DH-4 pilots . . . Girard, Ohio**: Lt. William C. F. Brown, pilot report.

130 **a meal and cider**: Letter from Lt. Ralph Bagby to his mother, October 12, 1917, provided to the author by Betty Goerke (Bagby's daughter).

130 **chewed-up propeller blades**: "8 More Derby Flyers," *Cleveland Plain Dealer*, 1.

130 **"The nastiest day"**: "8 More Derby Flyers," *Cleveland Plain Dealer*, 1.

130 **Lt. H. G. Norris . . . fetch a new one:** "8 More Derby Flyers," *Cleveland Plain Dealer*, 1.

131 **"beautifully balanced":** Maj. John C. Bartholf, "From Pacific to Atlantic in an SE-5," *U.S. Air Service* magazine, November 1919; Hathi Trust, https://hdl.handle.net/2027/mdp.39015024398896.

131 **manufactured under license:** Manufacturers Aircraft Association, Inc., "Technical Development Airplanes, 1914 to 1919," *Aircraft Year Book 1920* (New York: Doubleday, Page, 1920), 126.

132 *Gloomy Gus . . . yellow letters:* "Eleven Air Racers Pause in Flight at Omaha Friday," *Omaha World-Herald*, October 11, 1919, 1.

132 **flew at just 250 feet:** Donaldson, "District 'Ace'," 1.

132 **The son of an Army general:** "John Owen Donaldson" [biography], South Carolina Encyclopedia, https://www.scencyclopedia.org/sce/entries /donaldson-john-owen/.

132 **sent him to Canada and Texas . . . pursuit tactics:** "Captain John O. Donaldson to Be Discharged," *Air Service News Letter*, July 10, 1919, 10.

132 **about 300 Americans who flew for Britain:** "Americans in the British Flying Services," 1914–1945, Royal Air Force Museum, https://www .rafmuseum.org.uk/research/online-exhibitions/americans-in-the-royal-air -force/americans-in-the-british-flying-services-1914-1945/.

132 **one of the first ten . . . "you can't fly":** Letters from Donaldson to aunt, John O. Donaldson Correspondence, Special Collections and Archives, Furman University.

132 **Planques Aerodrome . . . seven more would follow:** James J. Hudson, "Lieutenant John O. Donaldson, World War I Air Ace and Escape Artist," *Air University Review* XXXVII, no 2 (January–February 1986), 88.

133 **"the man who fought upside down":** Obituary, *New York Herald Tribune*, February 9, 1930, 9.

133 **fitted with metal stirrups:** Frederick Johnsen, "British SE-5 earned its place in the fighter pantheon," *General Aviation News*, January 8, 2020, https://generalaviationnews.com/2020/01/08/british-se-5-earned-its -place-in-the-fighter-pantheon-2/.

133 **"solely by instinct":** "Donaldson Describes His Record-Breaking Flight," *Binghamton Press* (Binghamton, NY), October 23, 1919, 19.

133 **Distinguished Service Cross:** "John Owen Donaldson," South Carolina Encyclopedia.

133 **Alone against three enemy aircraft:** John O. Donaldson, "My Capture and Escape," *Harper's Monthly*, July 1919, 244.

133 **"burnt to death":** Letter from Donaldson to parents, October 31, 1918, John O. Donaldson Correspondence, Special Collections and Archives, Furman University.

133 **On his third night . . . recaptured a few days later:** Donaldson, "My Capture."

134 **another prison near Belgium . . . walk across the occupied coun-try:** Donaldson, "My Capture."

134 **Two of the escapees . . . shower of sparks:** Donaldson, "My Capture."

134 **made a speech at the New York Aeronautical Exposition:** "Another Ace on Cornell's Service Roll," *Ithaca Journal*, March 24, 1919, 5.

134 **"The boat of the air":** John O. Donaldson, "Aviation Is Coming into Own as Sport," *The Sun* (New York, NY), March 16, 1919, 24.

134 **an "aerial steeplechase":** Donaldson, "Aviation Is Coming," 24.

135 **cracked crankcase:** Handwritten draft of telegram written by Donaldson, Central Decimal Files, 1917–38, box 719, folder 373.

135 **The rain had chewed:** Donaldson, "District 'Ace'," 1.

135 **"sweet little bus":** "8 More Derby Flyers," *Cleveland Plain Dealer*, 1.

135 **the "Hoodoo Quartet":** "Five Air Visitors Anchor for Night at West Endicott," *Morning Sun* (Binghamton, NY), October 11, 1919.

135 **pie and sandwiches:** "Aviators Arrive Here Out of Luck Because of Rain," *Binghamton Press* (Binghamton, NY), October 10, 1919, 17.

136 **makeshift nine-gallon fuel tank:** Telegram from Hartney to Mitchell, October 9, 1919, NARA, RG 18, "Reliability Test Flights," box 2.

136 **Other pilots tried . . . thirty-nine minutes:** "Planes Off Again for Aerial Derby," *Buffalo Enquirer*, October 10, 1919, 1.

136 **"No orders to stop":** Col. C. C. Culver, pilot report.

136 **Lt. H. D. Smith . . . a gust blew his plane:** "Transcontinental Plane En Route to Buffalo Is Wrecked Near Lockport," *Buffalo Enquirer*, October 9, 1919, 1.

136 **Lt. Alexander Roberts . . . Canadian steamer:** Lt. Alexander Roberts, pilot report.

136 **"volplaned" . . . Roberts yelled:** Lt. Alexander Roberts, pilot report.

137 **righted itself:** Lt. Alexander Roberts, pilot report.

137 **missing in a snowstorm:** "Air Racers Battle Mountain Blizzard Two Lost Is Fear," *Nevada State Journal*, October 19, 1919, 1.

137 **Bitter Creek, Wyoming:** Air Service press release, October 11, 1919, NARA, RG 18, "Records of the Office of the Chief of the Air Service, 1917–21," "Records Relating to Aeronautics," Entry 117, box 27.

137 **funeral of his old friend:** William Mitchell diary, October 9, 1919, William Mitchell papers, Library of Congress, Manuscript Division, box 4.

137 **consoling Dodd's widow:** Caroline Mitchell diary, October 7, 1919, Douglas Waller Papers, Wake Forest University, ZSR Library Special Collections and Archives, box 15.

138 **"the great necessity":** Ray Landis Bowers, "The Transcontinental Reliability Test: American Aviation After World War I" (master's thesis, University of Wisconsin, 1960), 139.

138 **"Without the stimulus":** Editorial, "As Bad As War," *Buffalo Express*, October 11, 1919, 6.

CHAPTER FIFTEEN: Time and Space

139 **nearly airsick . . . "the roughest weather":** Belvin W. Maynard, "'Bumps' Caused Maynard to Think Billy Sunday Surely Was Reviving the Elements," *News & Observer* (Raleigh, NC), October 25, 1919, 1.

139 **He circled the field . . . "knocking the chimney":** "Leading Planes Reach Rock Island in First Cross-Country Air Derby," *Rock Island Argus*, October 9, 1919, 1.

139 **"I'm a little late":** "Leading Planes Reach Rock Island," *Rock Island Argus*, 1.

139 **temporarily deafened:** "Leading Planes Reach Rock Island," *Rock Island Argus*, 1.

140 **slowed their ground speed . . . "visions":** Maynard, "'Bumps' Caused Maynard to Think," 1.

140 **gold dome . . . "fair women reporters":** Maynard, "'Bumps' Caused Maynard to Think," 1.

140 **dead reckoning:** "East Meets West at North Platte in Airplane Race," *Omaha World-Herald*, October 10, 1919, 1.

140 **About 200 people . . . three point landing:** "East Meets West," *Omaha World-Herald*, 1.

140 **"every newspaper reporter":** Maynard, "'Bumps' Caused Maynard to Think," 1.

140 **"large and commodious" . . . "retired farmer":** Maynard, "'Bumps' Caused Maynard to Think," 1.

141 **"the disk of a gramophone":** Maynard, "'Bumps' Caused Maynard to Think," 1.

141 **"don't need any lunch":** "East Meets West," *Omaha World Herald*, 1.

141 **glass of milk:** Maynard, "'Bumps' Caused Maynard to Think," 1.

141 **"When did you leave New York":** "Transcontinental Landing Field a Popular Place," *The Phonograph* (St. Paul, NE), October 16, 1919, 1.

141 **they could warm:** Maynard, "'Bumps' Caused Maynard to Think," 1.

141 **friendly chat:** Maynard, "'Bumps' Caused Maynard to Think," 1.

142 **faces reddened:** "Five Army Planes Reach North Platte Yesterday," *North Platte Semi-Weekly Tribune*, October 10, 1919, 1.

142 **"That's hardship":** "Maynard May Fly Toward the Sun on Tuesday," *Daily Sentinel* (Rome, NY), October 13, 1919, 1.

142 **send up flares:** "Aviators Pass in Nebraska," *Omaha Daily Bee*, October 10, 1919, 1.

142 **bombers after dark . . . "night pursuit":** William Edward Fischer, Jr., *The Development of Military Night Aviation to 1919* (Maxwell Air Force Base, AL: Air University Press, 1998), 31, 35, 115.

143 **attached to the wingtips:** Roger Connor (aeronautics curator, Smithsonian National Air and Space Museum), email correspondence with the author, January 16, 2020.

143 **automobile headlights:** Eldon Wilson Downs, "Contribution of

U.S. Army Aviation to Uses and Operation of Aircraft" (PhD diss., University of Wisconsin, 1960), 173.

143 **speculation in the press:** "Aviators Pass," *Omaha Daily Bee*, 1.

143 **failing to circle the field:** Memo from Arnold to Training and Operations Group, Air Service, October 20, 1919, NARA, RG 18, "Reliability Test Flights," box 1.

143 **"annihilated time and space":** "Washington Reports on Progress of Flyers," *New York Times*, October 11, 1919, 3.

143 **"remarkable performances":** "Purpose of Race Demonstrated," *New York Tribune*, October 10, 1919, 2.

143 **"did not contemplate penalizing":** "Maynard Held at Cheyenne by Accident," *Rockford Daily Register-Gazette*, October 10, 1919, 1.

143 **"All I want is sleep":** "Clergyman Arrives at Fort D.A. Russell from Chicago," *New York Times*, October 10, 1919, 2.

143 **oyster stew:** Maynard, "'Bumps' Caused Maynard to Think," 3.

143 **draining the radiator:** Maynard, "'Bumps' Caused Maynard to Think," 3.

144 **"put on the wire for us":** Telegram from city editor, *San Francisco Examiner*, to Maynard, October 9, 1919, NARA, RG 18, "Reliability Test Flights," box 5.

144 **"make San Francisco":** Lieut. B. W. Maynard, untitled dispatch from Cheyenne, *San Francisco Examiner*, October 10, 1919, 1.

CHAPTER SIXTEEN: Hungry Hogs and a Telegraph Pole

145 **thirty-one gallons:** "Aviator Charges Unfair Tactics in Aerial Derby," *Binghamton Press* (Binghamton, NY), October 18, 1919, 8.

145 **sputtered to a stop:** "Donaldson Describes His Record-Breaking Flight," *Binghamton Press* (Binghamton, NY), October 23, 1919, 19.

146 **"Fields of rocks":** Maj. Hollis Leroy Muller, *Manual of Military Aviation* (Menasha, WI: George Banta, 1917), 43; Hathi Trust, http://hdl.handle.net/2027/uc1.b3141330.

147 **until paved runways made them necessary:** Roger Connor (aeronautics curator, Smithsonian National Air and Space Museum), email correspondence with the author, November 6, 2021.

147 **Manzelman had arrived over Chicago . . . phoning the *Tribune*'s newsroom:** "Human Anchor Averts Wreck of Race Plane," *Chicago Tribune*, October 10, 1919, 2.

147 **After his water pump failed:** Maj. Henry Abbey, Jr., pilot report.

147 **"bald hill":** Lt. H. W. Sheridan, pilot report.

147 **turned turtle in mudflats:** Lt. G. B. Newman, pilot report.

147 **"slept in a snowdrift":** "Eleven Air Racers Pause in Flight at Omaha Friday," *Omaha World-Herald*, October 11, 1919, 1.

148 **spent the night in a sheep wagon:** "Lieutenant Worthington, SE5.

Started from West," anonymous account, NASM Technical Reference Files, Drawer J1, Folder 1919-890-01.

148 **push it across the desert:** Lt. William C. F. Brown, pilot report.

148 **hogs with a taste:** "Hungry Hogs Ate Rudder of Airplane," *Wyoming State Tribune*, October 13, 1919, 1.

148 **spent the night with it:** Letter from Bagby to his mother, October 12, 1917.

148 **leaning over his gas tank:** "Plane After Plane Drops Out of Sky," *Democrat and Chronicle* (Rochester, NY), October 9, 1919, 28.

148 **flew bare-handed:** W. Yates, oral history, Aviation File, Sweetwater County Historical Museum, Green River, Wyoming.

148 **Below him was Highland Park:** Des Moines control stop final report, Lt. Col. Jacob E. Fickel, NARA, RG 18, "Transcontinental Reliability Test Flights," box 18.

149 **"back yard" . . . "stopped within ten feet":** "Donaldson Describes," Binghamton Press (Binghamton, NY), 19.

149 **drafted three men:** "Donaldson Describes," *Binghamton Press* (Binghamton, NY), 19.

149 **twenty-eight gallons:** Des Moines control stop final report, Lt. Col. Jacob E. Fickel.

149 **"dragonfly on a thistle top":** "Eleven Air Racers Pause," *Omaha World-Herald*, 1.

149 **"don't touch that!" . . . smeared his throat:** "Eleven Air Racers Pause," *Omaha World-Herald*, 1.

150 **new emergency fuel tank:** Harold Hartney, "Col. Hartney's Trip in the German Fokker," *Air Service News Letter*, November 7, 1919, 2.

150 **"dreary, dismal place":** Hartney, "Col. Hartney's Trip," 2.

150 **risk his propeller:** "16 Air Racers Land Here and 16 Leave in Day," *Chicago Tribune*, October 12, 1919, 2.

150 **Red Cross canteen:** "16 Air Racers Land Here," *Chicago Tribune*, 2.

150 **lost air pressure . . . completed the leg:** Hartney, "Col. Hartney's Trip," 2.

150 **a service led by Billy Sunday:** Hartney, "Col. Hartney's Trip," 2.

151 **"I'm going out to overhaul":** Bob Campbell, "Late Arrivals Tell Thrilling Tales of Experiences in the Air," *Morning Sun* (Binghamton, NY), October 11, 1919, 3.

151 **Thomas-Morse Aircraft Corporation factory:** "Crippled Aviator Asks Help Here," *Ithaca Journal*, October 10, 1919, 3.

151 **a six-penny nail:** Lt. Daniel Brailey Gish, pilot report.

151 **Pitts was worried:** "Flyer Killed in Crash at Local Field," *Buffalo Express*, October 11, 1919, 1.

151 **marked with red flags:** "Flyer Killed in Crash," *Buffalo Express*, 1.

151 **nearly out of gas:** "Flyer Killed in Crash," *Buffalo Express*, 1.

151 **slid back:** "First Fatality in Cross-Country Derby Occurs at Curtiss Field, When Plane 24 Crashes to Earth," *Democrat and Chronicle* (Rochester, NY), October 11, 1919, 1.

152 **"the only 'movie stuff'":** Belvin W. Maynard, " 'Bumps' Caused Maynard to Think Billy Sunday Surely Was Reviving the Elements," *News & Observer* (Raleigh, NC), October 25, 1919, 1.

152 **"clinging for dear life":** "Great Coast to Coast Air Race," *San Francisco Chronicle*, October 8, 1919, 2.

152 **Sweeley decided:** Capt. Harry C. Drayton, pilot report.

152 **"pilots wear spurs":** Capt. Harry C. Drayton, pilot report.

152 **"like a stone":** "Would Bar Men from Riding on Tail of Machine," *Buffalo Evening News*, October 11, 1919, 1.

152 **Red Cross ambulance:** "Would Bar Men," *Buffalo Evening News*, 1.

153 **"John L. Hoodoo":** Campbell, "Late Arrivals," 3.

153 **just 200 feet:** "Leaves Hospital to Be in Race," *Air Service News Letter*, November 15, 1919, 1.

153 **in need of repair:** "Leaves Hospital to Be in Race," *Air Service News Letter*, 1.

153 **warmed up the Liberty . . . joined his mechanic:** Belvin W. Maynard, " 'Undaunted by Misfortune,' Maynard Pushes on After Losing Half a Day in Race," *News & Observer* (Raleigh, NC), October 26, 1919, 1.

153 **"You have burst your radiator":** Maynard, " 'Undaunted by Misfortune,' " 1.

153 **Water in the overflow pipe:** Maynard, " 'Undaunted by Misfortune,' " 1.

153 **rose at 5:30 a.m.:** Maynard, " 'Undaunted by Misfortune,' " 1.

154 **telegraphed the control stop . . . solve the problem:** Maynard, " 'Undaunted by Misfortune,' " 1.

154 **only one hole . . . oyster stew:** Maynard, " 'Undaunted by Misfortune,' " 1.

154 **"would stand in the pulpit":** Maynard, " 'Undaunted by Misfortune,' " 1.

155 **"every mile counts":** Maynard, " 'Undaunted by Misfortune,' " 1.

155 **spilled from tiny schoolhouses:** Maynard, " 'Undaunted by Misfortune,' " 1.

155 **empty of human beings . . . "a long walk at least":** Maynard, " 'Undaunted by Misfortune,' " 1.

155 **turning purple:** "Stops Short Interval for More Fuel," *Salt Lake Tribune*, October 11, 1919, 1.

155 **"Lookit 'im come!":** "Parson Is Welcomed in S.L.," *Salt Lake Telegram*, October 11, 1919, 1.

156 **ran out of gas:** "Flying Parson Describes His Great Aerial Adventure," Lieut. Belvin W. Maynard, *San Diego Union*, October 12, 1919, 6.

156 **scrambled from the cockpit . . . smiled and waved:** "Parson Is Welcomed," *Salt Lake Telegram*, 1.

156 **red-rimmed and inflamed:** "Stops Short Interval," *Salt Lake Tribune*, 1.

156 **"The roar of the motor":** "25 Hours' Flying Carries Pastor Across the Continent," *New York Times*, October 12, 1919, 1.

156 **Mechanics at Salt Lake City:** "Stops Short Interval," *Salt Lake Tribune*, 1.
156 **"Parson, the sinners are with you":** "'Flying Parson'" Expects to Eat Luncheon in 'Frisco," *Omaha World-Herald*, October 11, 1919, 1.

CHAPTER SEVENTEEN: Spaatz vs. Kiel
157 **200 and 600 feet . . . he was lost:** Maj. Carl A. Spaatz, pilot report.
157 **former schoolteacher:** "3 Flyers Span Nation," *Chicago Tribune*, October 12, 1919, 1.
157 **waving as he passed:** "Eight Planes Pass Over City," *Omaha Daily Bee*, October 11, 1919, 1.
157 **human counterweight:** "Eight Planes," *Omaha Daily Bee*, 1.
157 **"If I don't beat you into Mineola":** "Eight Planes," *Omaha Daily Bee*, 1.
158 **closed it temporarily:** Rock Island control stop final report, Lt. E. S. Hansberger, November 3, 1919, NARA, RG 18, "Reliability Test Flights," box 4.
158 **got on the phone . . . "over-bearing attitude":** "Three Planes Race," *Rock Island Argus*, 1.
158 **"Do all you men know how to find Grant Park?":** "Three Planes Race from City for East," *Rock Island Argus*, October 10, 1919, 1.
158 **Spaatz was grateful:** Maj. Carl A. Spaatz, pilot report.
158 **"quick succession":** "Three Planes from West Reach Chicago," *Chicago Daily News*, October 10, 1919, 1.
158 **Spaatz dropped off a letter:** "Three Planes from West," *Chicago Daily News*, 1.
158 **"Squally weather":** "Three Planes Race," *Rock Island Argus*, 1.
158 **After leaving the lakeshore . . . finding six men:** Maj. Carl A. Spaatz, pilot report.
159 **desperate for a room and a hot bath:** "Spatz and Kiel Land Almost Side by Side," *New York Times*, October 12, 1919, 3.

CHAPTER EIGHTEEN: Salduro
160 **breakup of a Boeing 707:** Flight Safety Foundation, Aviation Safety Network, crash report, https://aviation-safety.net/database/record .php?id=19660305-1.
160 **lenticular clouds:** "Tips on Mountain Flying," FAA Aviation Safety Program, https://www.faa.gov/regulations_policies/handbooks_manuals /aviation/media/tips_on_mountain_flying.pdf.
160 **"Air currents are much more violent":** C. Lamar Nelson, "'Fly High' Is Safe Rule," *Salt Lake Telegram*, October 9, 1919, 13.
161 **"What's the use of wasting time":** Capt. J. O. Donaldson, "Twice Across the Continent in a Single-Seater," *U.S. Air Service* magazine, November 1919, 25.
161 **just twenty-five feet:** Capt. J. O. Donaldson, "District 'Ace' Tells How He Won Air Race of U.S. Army," *Washington Times*, October 23, 1919, 1.

161 **24 degrees below zero:** "America Beautiful Land from Air, Says Capt. Donaldson," *Greenville News* (Greenville, SC), November 4, 1919, 5.

161 **"jump straight up":** "Donaldson Describes His Record-Breaking Flight," *Binghamton Press* (Binghamton, NY), October 23, 1919, 19.

161 **looked on in horror:** "Donaldson Describes," *Binghamton Press* (Binghamton, NY), 19.

162 **marking of its corners in black:** Belvin W. Maynard, "'Undaunted by Misfortune,' Maynard Pushes on After Losing Half a Day in Race," *News & Observer* (Raleigh, NC), October 26, 1919, 1.

162 **"like drunken sailors":** "Donaldson Describes," *Binghamton Press* (Binghamton, NY), 19.

162 **Temporarily blinded:** Donaldson, "Twice Across the Continent," 25.

CHAPTER NINETEEN: Hello Frisco!

163 **Confusion momentarily:** "Maynard Here, Wins Race," *San Francisco Chronicle*, October 12, 1919, 1.

163 **a few leisurely circles:** Belvin W. Maynard, "'Undaunted by Misfortune,' Maynard Pushes on After Losing Half a Day in Race," *News & Observer* (Raleigh, NC), October 26, 1919, 1.

163 **a hot bath and a restful night:** Maynard, "'Undaunted by Misfortune,'" 1.

163 **bags of salt:** Lieut. Belvin W. Maynard, "Blazing Air Trail Over Snow Capped Peaks of the Sierras Maynard Lands at Presidio," *News & Observer* (Raleigh, NC), October 27, 1919, 1.

164 **only place for miles with any trees . . . "without the usual loss of wife":** Maynard, "Blazing Air Trail," 1.

164 **13,000 feet . . . eye on his temperature gauge:** Maynard, "Blazing Air Trail," 1.

164 **cherry red:** "Aircraft in Forest Service," *Air Service News Letter*, December 26, 1919, 5.

164 **With the city shrouded . . . spotted tall buildings:** Maynard, "Blazing Air Trail," 1.

164 **"the whole city":** "'Flying Parson' Gives History of Transcontinental Derby," *The Sun* (Baltimore, MD), October 19, 1919, 3.

164 **some doubted it was him:** "Maynard Here," *San Francisco Chronicle*, 1.

164 **sideslipping twice:** "Sky Pilot at Presidio," *San Diego Union*, October 12, 1919, 6.

165 **"the machine would skid to the ground":** "Maynard Here," *San Francisco Chronicle*, 1.

165 **three days, six hours:** *Report on the First Transcontinental Reliability and Endurance Test* (Washington, DC: Government Printing Office, 1919), 13; Hathi Trust, http://hdl.handle.net/2027/uiug.30112112405466.

165 **108 miles an hour:** "25 Hours Flying Carries Pastor Across Continent," *New York Times*, October 12, 1919, 1.

166 **Trixie was the first to alight:** "The 'Flying Parson' Arrives," *Mansfield News* (Mansfield, OH), October 12, 1919, 12.

166 **Hap Arnold shouldered:** "Lieut. Maynard Safe at Presidio Field," *New York Times*, October 12, 1919, 3.

166 **"until my cheeks became cramped":** Maynard, "Blazing Air Trail," 1.

166 **"It was a great trip":** "Maynard in San Francisco," *Omaha Sunday Bee*, October 12, 1919, 12.

166 **"almost wide open":** "3 Flyers Span Nation," *Chicago Tribune*, October 12, 1919, 1.

166 **"dusty and bedraggled":** "Maynard Here," *San Francisco Chronicle*, 1.

166 **extra uniform . . . "a safe means of travel":** Belvin W. Maynard, "'Flying Parson' Tells of Experiences in First Flight Over Continent," *Washington Times*, October 13, 1919, 17.

166 **Alaska, Cuba, Panama . . . $15 million:** "Recommend $15,000,000 More for Airplanes," *New York Times*, October 11, 1919, 13.

166 **morning of bird shooting:** William Mitchell diary, October 11, 1919, William Mitchell papers, Library of Congress, Manuscript Division, box 4.

166 **"Convey to Lieutenant Maynard":** Telegram from Mitchell to Arnold, October 11, 1919, NARA, RG 18, "Reliability Test Flights," box 5.

167 **"Congratulations upon your marvelous feat":** Lieut. Belvin W. Maynard, "Maynard Declines Invitation to Dine with King in Order to Get Started on Time," *News & Observer* (Raleigh, NC), October 28, 1919, 1.

167 **at Roosevelt Field:** "Mrs. Maynard Much Relieved," *Boston Globe*, October 10, 1919, 8.

167 **"The children and I":** "Maynard's Wife Asks Him Not to Make Return Flight," *Riverside Daily Press* (Riverside, CA), October 13, 1919, 1.

167 **heartfelt plea:** "Maynard's Wife Asks Him," *Riverside Daily Press* (Riverside, CA), 1.

167 **"I had heard that":** "Maynard Ready to Start Flight Back Eastward," *St. Louis Post-Dispatch*, October 14, 1919, 1.

CHAPTER TWENTY: Roosevelt Field

168 **"the best thing for you both":** "First Racers from Coast Arrive and Depart at West Endicott in Pouring Rain," *Morning Sun* (Binghamton, NY), October 13, 1919, 3.

168 **Rain fell in sheets . . . "They ought not":** "First Racers from Coast," *Morning Sun* (Binghamton, NY), 3.

168 **no sensible person:** "First Racers from Coast," *Morning Sun* (Binghamton, NY), 3.

168 **"We'll start" . . . "We'll get there":** "First Racers from Coast," *Morning Sun* (Binghamton, NY), 3.

168 **returned to their plane:** "First Racers from Coast," *Morning Sun* (Binghamton, NY), 3.

169 **Spaatz followed:** Maj. Carl A. Spaatz, pilot report.

169 **could not locate the field:** "Smith Loses His Lead in Flight East," *Rockford Daily Register-Gazette* (Rockford, IL), October 11, 1919, 1.

169 **map that had blown out:** "First West Ships Here," *Bryan Democrat* (Bryan, OH), October 14, 1919, 1.

169 **ride to the Glenn L. Martin Company plant:** "Spaatz Sets Pace in West to East Flight," *East Liverpool Review* (East Liverpool, OH), October 11, 1919, 1.

169 **oil-stained coveralls . . . "no other explanation":** "Lead Lost in Aerial Race Near Finish," *Democrat and Chronicle* (Rochester, NY), October 12, 1919, 4.

170 **"terrific rate of speed":** "Captain Smith Delayed Near Cleveland by Accident to 'Plane," *Buffalo Evening Times*, October 11, 1919, 1.

170 **circled for several minutes:** "Captain Smith Delayed," *Buffalo Evening Times*, 1.

170 **a beeline for Pitts:** "Kiel and Spatz Leave Rochester," *Buffalo Evening Times*, October 11, 1919, 1.

170 **"visibility was not so bad":** "Kiel and Spatz," *Buffalo Evening Times*, 1.

170 **instructions from Washington:** Ray Landis Bowers, "The Transcontinental Reliability Test: American Aviation After World War I" (master's thesis, University of Wisconsin, 1960), 147.

170 **"Where is Lt. Maynard":** "First Racers from Coast," *Morning Sun* (Binghamton, NY), 1.

170 **"The Flying Parson":** "First Racers from Coast," *Morning Sun* (Binghamton, NY), 1.

170 **"If you give me permission":** "First Racers from Coast," *Morning Sun* (Binghamton, NY), 1.

170 **"It would be foolhardy":** "First Racers from Coast," *Morning Sun* (Binghamton, NY), 1.

170 **"The rain doesn't bother":** "First Racers from Coast," *Morning Sun* (Binghamton, NY), 1.

170 **"That's Lieutenant E. C. Kiel":** "First Racers from Coast," *Morning Sun* (Binghamton, NY), 1.

171 **light a fire:** "First Racers from Coast," *Morning Sun* (Binghamton, NY), 1.

171 **"present weather conditions":** "First Racers from Coast," *Morning Sun* (Binghamton, NY), 1.

171 **"right on your tail":** "First Racers from Coast," *Morning Sun* (Binghamton, NY), 1.

171 **urging the flyers:** "Flying Parson Lands Winner at Frisco; Two East Bound Men Finish Near Tie," *Des Moines Register*, October 11, 1919, 1.

172 **lost "considerable time":** Maj. Carl A. Spaatz, pilot report.

172 **station signboards:** "Doesn't Want to Race Back," *New York Times*, October 12, 1919, 3.

172 **About 300 people:** "Spatz and Kiel Land Almost Side by Side," *New York Times*, October 12, 1919, 3.

172 **flew out to meet:** "Spatz and Kiel Fly in Neck and Neck," *The Sun* (New York, NY), October 12, 1919, 2.

172 **"Here they come!":** "Spatz and Kiel Land," *New York Times*, October 12, 1919, 3.

172 **The Air Service originally:** "Spatz and Kiel Fly," *The Sun* (New York, NY), 2.

172 **soldiers rushed:** "3 Flyers Span Nation," *Chicago Tribune*, October 12, 1919, 1.

173 **gasoline had been dumped:** "Spatz and Kiel Fly," *The Sun* (New York, NY), 2.

173 **"Anyone else here?":** "Spatz Third in Race Because Beacon Was Not Lighted in Time," *New York Tribune*, October 12, 1919, 10.

173 **"Yep, he just landed":** "Spatz Third in Race," *New York Tribune*, 10.

173 **exchanged handshakes:** "Spatz and Kiel Land," *New York Times*, 3.

173 **"I'm awfully dirty":** "Spatz and Kiel Land," *New York Times*, 3.

173 **"I don't care":** "Spatz and Kiel Land," *New York Times*, 3.

173 **the light of two oil lamps:** "Spatz and Kiel Land Neck and Neck at Mineola to Cheers of Waiting Crowds," *Sunday Star* (Washington, DC), October 12, 1919, 23.

173 **"To be perfectly frank":** "Spatz and Kiel Land," *New York Times*, 3.

174 **the Air Service had announced:** "Maynard Wins First Honors in Race West," *Sunday Star* (Washington, DC), October 12, 1919, 1.

174 **thirty-seven from New York:** "Transcontinental Reliability Test," *Aircraft Journal*, October 18, 1919, 4; Hathi Trust, https://hdl.handle.net/2027/nyp.33433090904735.

174 **"pursued by a jinx":** "Belated Flyer in Air Race Is Pursued by Jinx," *Buffalo Morning Express*, October 13, 1919, 4.

174 **"a strenuous event":** Telegram from Glidden to Newton Baker, secretary of war, October 11, 1919, NARA, RG 18, "Reliability Test Flights," box 2.

174 **a grieving Uncle Sam:** Editorial cartoon, *Denver Post*, October 12, 1919 (described in Michael E. Kassel, "Thunder on High: Cheyenne, Denver and Aviation Supremacy on the Rocky Mountain Front Range" [master's thesis, University of Wyoming, 2007]).

175 **the return journey:** "Maynard Wins First Honors," *Evening Star* (Washington, DC), 1.

175 **"No one can make me race back":** "Doesn't Want to Race Back," *New York Times*, 3.

CHAPTER TWENTY-ONE: Donaldson and Hartney

179 **a stop on the transcontinental railroad . . . closed to Native American children:** Dana R. Bennett, *All Roads Lead to Battle Mountain* (Battle Mountain, NV: Lander County Historical Society, 2012), 1–135.

179 **spent $2,000:** Lieutenant B. W. Maynard, "Most Dramatic Incident of

My Flight," *U.S. Air Service* magazine, November 1919, p. 26; Hathi Trust, https://hdl.handle.net/2027/mdp.39015024398896.

179 **Smith had briefly lived:** Bennett, *All Roads*, 135.

180 **"notably Battle Mountain":** Capt. H. C. Drayton, pilot report.

180 **"rip-roaring Western town":** John Donaldson, speech to American Flying Club, New York, reprinted in *Salt Lake Tribune*, October 27, 1919, 18.

180 **cleaning his spark plugs:** Capt. John O. Donaldson, pilot report.

180 **the rest of his journey:** "Donaldson Describes His Record-Breaking Flight," *Binghamton Press* (Binghamton, NY), October 23, 1919, 19.

180 **seaplanes landing tourists:** "Donaldson Describes," *Binghamton Press* (Binghamton, NY), 19.

181 **radiator was patched with tin:** "It Is Great Race Says Man Who Arranged It," *Reno Evening Gazette*, October 17, 1919, 1.

181 **"dangerously" warped:** Harold Hartney, "Col. Hartney's Trip in the German Fokker," *Air Service News Letter*, November 7, 1919, 2.

181 **a DH-4 circling . . . "This was a terrible trip":** Lt. Col. Harold E. Hartney's flight log, NPRC.

181 **"my greatest bugbear":** Hartney, "Col. Hartney's Trip," 2.

181 **"unique experience":** Lt. Col. Harold E. Hartney's flight log, NPRC.

181 **flew into a snowstorm:** Hartney, "Col. Hartney's Trip," 2.

182 **performed poorly . . . about 20 percent less:** Hartney, "Col. Hartney's Trip," 2.

182 **a few hundred feet . . . forty miles an hour:** John Weatherseed (The Vintage Aviation Team), email correspondence with the author, April 21, 2021.

182 **"the most wonderful dinner":** Hartney, "Col. Hartney's Trip," 2.

182 **"a very delightful trip":** Hartney, "Col. Hartney's Trip," 2.

182 **ground-looped:** Hartney, "Col. Hartney's Trip," 2.

183 **"The Germans evidently" . . . five-hour delay:** Hartney, "Col. Hartney's Trip," 2.

183 **"most unpleasant":** Hartney, "Col. Hartney's Trip," 2.

183 **"lightning bug":** "Famous Ace Here in First German Fokker to Arrive in Derby," *San Francisco Chronicle*, October 18, 1919, 1.

183 **"I arrived there happy":** Hartney, "Col. Hartney's Trip," 2.

CHAPTER TWENTY-TWO: "The Man of a Hundred Wounds"

184 **bracing wires . . . gas, oil, and water:** Lt. Daniel Brailey Gish, pilot report.

184 **call for the ambulance . . . "night bombing attack":** "Giant and Pygmy of Air Race Drop in Upon Chicago," *Chicago Tribune*, October 14, 1919, 5.

185 **"tail of his plane":** "Flier Killed in Making Landing," *Buffalo Courier*, October 11, 1919, 1.

185 **"man of a hundred wounds":** "Aviators Arrive Here Out of Luck Because of Rain," *Binghamton Press* (Binghamton, NY), October 10, 1919, 17.

185 **guided by flares:** "4 Planes in Omaha All Night," *Omaha Daily Bee*, October 14, 1919, 1.

185 **below 200 feet:** "Leaves Hospital to Be in Race," *Air Service News Letter*, November 15, 1919, 1.

185 **landed in a field:** "Leaves Hospital," *Air Service News Letter*, 1.

185 **leaky radiator:** Salt Lake City control stop final report, Lt. James G. Hall, NARA, RG 18, "Reliability Test Flights," box 4.

185 **engine oil changed:** Airfield logbook, Reno control stop, p. 3, NARA, RG 18, "Reliability Test Flights," box 3.

185 **second landing attempt:** San Francisco control stop final report, Lt. H. A. Halverson, October 31, 1919, NARA, RG 18, "Reliability Test Flights," box 3.

186 **broke the tail skid:** "Derby Airplane Named 'Junk' Is Just That Now," *San Francisco Chronicle*, October 19, 1919, 4.

186 **Gish's parents:** "Five Planes Land at S.F.; One Wrecked," *San Francisco Examiner*, October 19, 1919, 2.

186 **flat left tire:** Lt. Daniel Brailey Gish, pilot report.

186 **"Derby Airplane Named 'Junk'":** "Derby Airplane," *San Francisco Chronicle*, 4.

CHAPTER TWENTY-THREE: Homeward Bound

187 **snow squalls:** Lieut. Belvin W. Maynard, "Sliding Between Storms Maynard Flies Eastward," *News & Observer* (Raleigh, NC), October 29, 1919, 1.

187 **nose in the wind:** "Maynard Wins Great Aviation Test," *Reno Evening Gazette*, October 18, 1919, 1.

187 **congratulatory telegrams . . . "resting and sleeping":** Lieut. Belvin W. Maynard, "Maynard Declines Invitation to Dine with King Albert in Order to Get Started on Time," *News & Observer* (Raleigh, NC), October 28, 1919, 1.

187 **delivered the bags of salt . . . mailed a stamped letter:** Lieut. Belvin W. Maynard, "Over Snow-capped Peaks," News & Observer (Raleigh, NC), October 27, 1919, 1.

188 **one from King Albert:** Maynard, "Maynard Declines Invitation," 1.

188 **a change in plans:** "95 Hour Limit Set on Stay at Trip's End," *San Francisco Chronicle*, October 13, 1919, 1.

188 **"If the Air Service says":** "95 Hour Limit," *San Francisco Chronicle*, 1.

188 **Tuesday, October 14, at 1:12 p.m.:** "95 Hour Limit," *San Francisco Chronicle*, 1.

188 **soaped and rinsed:** San Francisco control stop final report. NARA, RG 18, "Reliability Test Flights," box 4.

188 **trial "jazz":** "Maynard Will Begin Return Flight at 1:12," *San Francisco Chronicle*, October 14, 1919, 13.

188 **physical exam:** San Francisco control stop final report.

188 **a diet of roast chicken:** "Maynard Plane on Return Trip," *Christian Science Monitor*, October 15, 1919, 2.

188 **dine with his wife and children:** "Flying Parson Says He Has Engagement at New York Friday," *Salt Lake Telegram*, October 15, 1919, 1.

188 **a *third* crossing:** "Maynard Plane," *Christian Science Monitor*, 2.

189 **whimpering and resisting:** "Winner in Race Gets Off in Fine Start," *San Francisco Chronicle*, October 15, 1919, 13.

189 **pointed straight at the Golden Gate:** "Winner in Race," *San Francisco Chronicle*, 13.

189 **cheering wildly . . . three arrowheads:** Maynard, "Maynard Declines Invitation," 1.

189 **Nevada Hotel:** Dana R. Bennett, *All Roads Lead to Battle Mountain* (Battle Mountain, NV: Lander County Historical Society, 2012), 36, 103, 106.

190 **"up before the chickens":** Maynard, "Sliding Between Storms," 1.

190 **ground fog:** Maynard, "Sliding Between Storms," 1.

190 **he was disappointed:** Maynard, "Sliding Between Storms," 1.

190 **shrouded in smoke:** Maynard, "Sliding Between Storms," 1.

190 **"a dinner engagement":** "Lieut. Maynard Hops Off for East," *Deseret Evening News* (Salt Lake City, UT), October 15, 1919, 1.

190 **"did not much care " . . . "shaky all over":** Maynard, "Sliding Between Storms," 1.

191 **lunched on steaks:** Maynard, "Sliding Between Storms," 1.

191 **"a narrow opening of light" . . . 150 feet:** Maynard, "Sliding Between Storms," 1.

191 **where Wales had died:** "Maynard Wins Air Derby, Racing 125 Miles an Hour," *New York Times*, October 19, 1919, 1.

191 **snow was falling . . . "might just be the margin":** "Maynard Hurtles Across State at Terrific Speed," *Cheyenne State Leader*, October 16, 1919, 1.

191 **another bowl of oyster stew:** Maynard, "Sliding Between Storms," 1.

191 **a wingtip nearly brushed:** "Flew to City at 158-Mile an Hour Clip," *Wyoming State Tribune*, October 16, 1919, 1.

191 ***The Woman on the Index*:** U.S.A. Theatre advertisement, *Sidney Telegraph* (Sidney, NE), October 10, 1919, 6.

CHAPTER TWENTY-FOUR: A Telegram from Omaha

192 **back on Capitol Hill:** *War Expenditures: Hearings Before Select Committee on Expenditures in the War Department*, 66th Congress, 1st sess., October 15, 1919 (testimony of William Mitchell).

192 **Mitchell was asked:** *War Expenditures* (testimony of Mitchell).

192 **"you cannot do anything":** *War Expenditures* (testimony of Mitchell).

192 **"knows the game":** *War Expenditures* (testimony of Mitchell).

192 **"He cannot know":** *War Expenditures* (testimony of Mitchell).

193 **5:20 p.m.:** *War Expenditures* (testimony of Mitchell).

193 **went to the movies:** Caroline Mitchell diary, October 15, 1919, Douglas Waller Papers, Wake Forest University, ZSR Library Special Collections and Archives, box 15 (hereafter Waller papers).

193 **snowing along the route:** "Two Air Racers Killed in Storm," *New York Times*, October 16, 1919, 1.

193 **their engine stopped . . . 200 feet:** "Two Killed When Plane Comes Down," *Wyoming State Tribune*, October 16, 1919, 1.

193 *Defender*: "Storm Ties Up Racers Here," *Cleveland Plain Dealer*, October 11, 1919, 2.

193 **arrival of a doctor:** "Lieutenant Kirby and Observer Miller Crash to Death," *Omaha World-Herald*, October 16, 1919, 1.

193 **telephoned Salt Lake City:** "Two Killed," *Wyoming State Tribune*, 1.

193 **nine-year-old daughter:** "Hold Funeral of Washington Flier," *Washington Times*, October 22, 1919, 22.

193 **began the journey to Utah:** "Lieutenant French Kirby Will Be Buried Here," *Washington Herald*, October 17, 1919, 1.

194 **"more in the public mind":** Statement distributed by Spokane News Bureau, NARA, RG 18, "Reliability Test Flights," box 2.

194 **"mere sporting event":** "California Cities Must Have Landing Sites, Convention Delegates Told by Crozier," *Riverside Enterprise* (Riverside, CA), October 22, 1919, 3.

194 **flown Caproni Bombers:** Fiorello H. La Guardia, *The Making of an Insurgent* (Philadelphia: J.B. Lippincott, 1948), 182.

194 **starve the Air Service . . . "incompetent officers":** Ray Landis Bowers, "The Transcontinental Reliability Test: American Aviation After World War I" (master's thesis, University of Wisconsin, 1960), 24.

194 **"most pathetic display":** "Flying 5400 Miles in Fifty Hours," *Literary Digest*, November 1, 1919, 20.

194 **"ninety percent":** "Flying 5400 Miles," *Literary Digest*, 20.

194 **"rank stupidity":** Editorial, *Chicago Tribune*, October 18, 1919, 8.

195 **"rather a high price":** Editorial, *San Francisco Chronicle*, October 22, 1919, 8.

195 **"done little to strengthen":** Editorial, *Buffalo Morning Express*, October 17, 1919, 8.

195 **"Death Rides with the Airmen":** Editorial, *Deseret Evening News* (Salt Lake City, UT), October 20, 1919, 4.

195 **a rare exception:** Editorial, *New York Times*, October 17, 1919, 16.

195 **"entrants were cautioned":** "It Is Great Race Says Man Who Arranged It," *Reno Gazette-Journal*, October 17, 1919, 1.

195 **half a degree:** Telegram from Halverson, control stop commander, to Training and Operations, October 21, 1919, NARA, RG 18, "Reliability Test Flights," box 4.

195 **no higher than 9,500 feet:** "Dangerous Air Trip Halted by Chief of Derby," *San Francisco Chronicle*, October 21, 1919, 3.

196 **proper angle . . . train to New York:** Telegram from Halverson, October 21, 1919, NARA, RG 18, "Reliability Test Flights," box 4.

196 **"his ship in such condition":** Telegram from Halverson, October 21, 1919.

196 **three small holes:** "Aviator Charges Unfair Tactics in Aerial Derby," *Binghamton Press* (Binghamton, NY), October 8, 1919, 8.

196 **The holes had jagged edges:** "Says Vandals Damaged Plane," *New York Tribune*, October 19, 1919, 2.

196 **clearing telephone wires . . . Worthington speculated:** "Aviator Charges," *Binghamton Press* (Binghamton, NY), 8.

196 **Worthington telephoned Mineola:** "Says Vandals," *New York Tribune*, 2.

197 **"bad flying" . . . "as soon as practicable":** Memo from Mitchell to Menoher, October 24, 1919, Waller papers, box 14.

197 **a telegram from Omaha:** Telegram from Lt. Harold R. Wells, Omaha control officer, Air Service headquarters, October 16, 1919, NARA, RG 18, "Reliability Test Flights," box 3.

CHAPTER TWENTY-FIVE: Buffalo

198 **"take his own time" . . . to San Diego:** "Fliers Don't Want to Race on Trip Back," *Buffalo Morning Express*, October 14, 1919, 1.

198 **replaced their DH-4's propeller . . . Splitdorf Mica:** Maj. Carl A. Spaatz, pilot report.

198 **planned to start:** "Kiel and Spatz Declare They Will Not Make Return Flight to Frisco," *Morning Sun* (Binghamton, NY), October 14, 1919, 1.

198 **he learned that Lowell Smith:** "Two Cross-Country Air Racers Killed," *The Sun* (New York, NY), October 16, 1919, 1.

199 **plugged with cornmeal:** Binghamton control stop final report, Capt. C. C. Mosely, November 14, 1919, NARA, RG 18, "Reliability Test Flights," box 1.

199 **file a formal complaint:** "Smith Charges He Was Held Up in His Flight Across Country," *Binghamton Press* (Binghamton, NY), October 13, 1919, 1.

199 **twenty-four hours and thirty minutes:** "Smith Claims Best Record," *The Sun* (Baltimore, MD), October 14, 1919, 1.

199 **he could still win the race:** "9 More Cross Continent in Big Air Race," *New York Tribune*, October 14, 1919, 1.

199 **throttled back to 1,450 rpm:** Maj. Carl A. Spaatz, pilot report.

199 **"We hope to show":** "Smith Outflies Spatz Coming from New York," *Binghamton Press* (Binghamton, NY), October 16, 1919, 12.

200 **"tired and worn" . . . push it too hard:** "Smith Outflies Spatz," *Binghamton Press* (Binghamton, NY), 12.

200 **headed into the city:** "Air Race Leader Loses Plane by Fire in Buffalo," *Buffalo Morning Express*, October 16, 1919, 3.

200 **what they thought was kerosene:** "Smith Explains Hard Luck," *Nevada State Journal*, October 18, 1919, 2.

200 **offered to loan . . . an Oriole:** "Spatz, Air Race Leader, Gives Plane to Smith," *Buffalo Evening News*, October 17, 1919, 1.

200 **Menoher granted permission:** Telegram from Menoher to Buffalo control stop commander, October 16, 1919, Buffalo control stop final report, Lt. A. B. Pitts, November 5, 1919, NARA, RG 18, "Reliability Test Flights," box 2.

200 **rescinding his approval:** Telegram from Menoher to Buffalo control stop commander, October 17, 1919, Buffalo control stop final report, Lt. A. B. Pitts.

200 **a bold request:** "Captain Smith Feted Here as Race Ends," *San Francisco Chronicle*, October 22, 1919, 13.

200 **After fifteen minutes:** "Captain Smith Feted," *San Francisco Chronicle*, 13.

200 **"I wanted to fly bad":** "Smith Explains," *Nevada State Journal*, 2.

201 **"all parties concerned":** Telegram from Pitts, Buffalo control officer, to Menoher, October 17, 1919, NARA, RG 18, "Reliability Test Flights," box 2.

201 **lost two days:** Logbook entry, October 20, 1919, Cheyenne control stop, NARA RG 18, "Reliability Test Flights," box 2.

201 **knocked unconscious:** "Hard Luck Trip Is Finished by Capt. Smith," *Evening Tribune* (San Diego, CA), October 21, 1919, 1.

201 **delayed his departure:** "Maynard Starts on Return Flight," *New York Times*, October 15, 1919, 3.

201 **smashing his landing gear:** Untitled item, *Washington Post*, October 21, 1919, 1.

201 **hopped on a train:** Carl A. Spaatz's personal diary, October 17, 1919, Library of Congress, Papers of Carl Spaatz, "Diaries," box 31.

CHAPTER TWENTY-SIX: The Mechanic

202 **an icy wind . . . hold on any departures:** Lieut. Belvin W. Maynard, "Two Happy Fliers Until Motor Goes Dead in Nebraska," *News & Observer* (Raleigh, NC), October 30, 1919, 1.

202 **searched the eastern horizon:** Maynard, "Two Happy Fliers," 1.

202 **seven pilots . . . because of fog:** North Platte control stop final report, Lt. J. MacEwan VanderVoort, November 10, 1919, NARA, RG 18, "Reliability Test Flights," box 3.

203 **"I believe it is in better condition":** Belvin W. Maynard, "'Flying Parson' Tells of Experiences in First Flight Over Continent," *Washington Times*, October 13, 1919, 17.

203 **expected to make Bryan:** "Lt. Maynard Reaches City," *Evening Telegraph* (North Platte, NE), October 16, 1919, 1.

203 **2,500 feet . . . "two more jubilant spirits":** Maynard, "Two Happy Fliers," 1.

203 **Without so much . . . "Our hearts":** Maynard, "Two Happy Fliers," 1.

204 **telephone wires and a fence:** "Maynard Expects to Fly Again at Daylight," *New York Times*, October 17, 1919, 3.

204 **scrambled from his cockpit . . . could find nothing:** Maynard, "Two Happy Fliers," 1.

204 **"Turn the propellor" . . . without resistance:** Maynard, "Two Happy Fliers," 1.

204 **"We have broken":** Maynard, "Two Happy Fliers," 1.

204 **"I guess" . . . get some rest:** Maynard, "Two Happy Fliers," 1.

204 **a newspaper report:** Maynard, "Two Happy Fliers," 1.

204 **heavy fog . . . damaged beyond repair:** "Fog Halts Flyers; One Wrecks Plane in Farmer's Yard," *Omaha World-Herald*, October 15, 1919, 1.

205 **a couple of days:** "Maynard Is Down but Still in Race," *New York Times*, October 17, 1918, 3.

205 **called the control officer . . . waved down an automobile:** Maynard, "Two Happy Fliers," 1.

205 **an Army detail . . . back to Wahoo:** Maynard, "Two Happy Fliers," 1.

206 **"more useless than a sandbag":** *Report on the First Transcontinental Reliability and Endurance Test* (Washington, DC: Government Printing Office, 1919), 27; Hathi Trust, http://hdl.handle.net/2027/uiug .30112112405466.

206 **filled his oil reservoir:** "Reasons for Holding the Test," n.d., unsigned report, NARA, RG 18, "Reliability Test Flights," box 5.

206 **served with Maynard in France:** "'Sky Pilot' Lands at Mineola, Winning 5,400-mile race," *New York Tribune*, October 19, 1919, 1.

206 **one of the best mechanics:** "'Flying Parson' Gives History of Transcontinental Air Derby," *The Sun* (Baltimore, MD), October 19, 1919, 3.

206 **a mechanic who lived nearby . . . hauled out the old engine:** Maynard, "Two Happy Fliers," 1.

206 **"I am still in the race":** "Maynard Is Down," *New York Times*, 3.

206 **portable Delco lighting system:** Maynard, "Two Happy Fliers," 1.

206 **a *New York Times* reporter:** "Maynard Expects to Fly Again," *New York Times*, 3.

206 **fitting the propeller:** "Flyers West of Rockies," *Los Angeles Times*, October 18, 1919, 6.

207 **"O.K., warm 'er up":** "Flyers West of Rockies," *Los Angeles Times*, 6.

207 **Red-eyed, grimy:** "Maynard Retains Lead," *The Sun* (Baltimore, MD), October 18, 1919, 3.

207 **Kline let it idle . . . joined Trixie:** "Flyer Cuts Over Lake Michigan," *Omaha Daily Bee*, October 18, 1919, 1.

207 **If it were up to him . . . Menoher had turned down:** Telegram from Menoher to Omaha control officer, October 17, 1919, NARA, RG 18, "Reliability Test Flights," box 2.

207 **slept most of the way:** "Maynard Retains Lead," *The Sun* (Baltimore, MD), 3.

207 **a bearing in his engine:** Lt. Alexander Pearson, Jr., pilot report.

207 **"engine from a flivver":** "Takes Second Engine from Wrecked Plane," *Omaha World-Herald*, October 21, 1919, 3.

208 **"royally entertained":** Capt. J. O. Donaldson, "District 'Ace' Tells How He Won Air Race of U.S. Army," *Washington Times*, October 23, 1919, 1.

208 **"driving such a car":** John Donaldson, speech to American Flying Club, New York, reprinted in *Salt Lake Tribune*, October 27, 1919, 18.

208 **got his boots shined:** Itemized bill, NARA, RG 18, "Reliability Test Flights," box 1.

208 **$16:** Itemized bill, NARA, RG 18, "Reliability Test Flights," box 1.

208 **replacing its tachometer:** San Francisco control stop daily report, October 15, 1919, NARA, RG 18, "Reliability Test Flights," box 4.

208 **The linen had separated:** Airfield logbook entry, Mather Field, Sacramento, October 15, 1919, NARA, RG 18, "Reliability Test Flights," box 1.

208 **"nothing startling":** Capt. J. O. Donaldson, "Twice Across the Continent in a Single-Seater," *U.S. Air Service* magazine, November 1919, 25.

208 **"willing to bet $10" . . . shaking their heads:** "Maynard in Ohio; Flies Right Over Lake Michigan," *Omaha World-Herald*, October 18, 1919, 1.

CHAPTER TWENTY-SEVEN: Victory

210 **he'd forgotten to display:** "Maynard in Ohio; Flies Right Over Lake Michigan," *Omaha World-Herald*, October 18, 1919, 1.

210 **set down in a field:** "Preacher Flies Over Iowa with Borrowed Engine," *Daily Gate City and Constitution-Democrat* (Keokuk, IA), October 17, 1919, 1.

210 **grinned broadly . . . with lunch:** "Maynard Lands in Rock Island First," *Rock Island Argus*, October 17, 1919, 1.

211 **"he leads, others follow":** "Plenty of Pleasure in Navigating Air, Says Flying Parson," *Atlanta Constitution*, October 20, 1919, 3.

211 **3,000 people:** "Coast to Coast with One Stop, Maynard Test," *Chicago Tribune*, October 18, 1919, 2.

211 **steep fishtailing descent:** "Flyer Cuts Over Lake Michigan," *Omaha Daily Bee*, October 18, 1919, 1.

211 **"Don't you get awfully tired" . . . licked his nose:** "Flyer Cuts Over," *Omaha Daily Bee*, 1.

211 **"please don't talk of it":** "Coast to Coast," *Chicago Tribune*, 2.

211 **at a right angle to the wind . . . a hundred yards:** "Flyer Cuts Over," *Omaha Daily Bee*, 1.

211 **chatted briefly with Lowell Smith:** "Maynard Wins 5,400 Mile Flight, Made Two Stops Here in Air Derby," *Bryan Democrat* (Bryan, OH), October 21, 1919, 1.

212 **grand family home:** Lieut. Belvin W. Maynard, "Reaching Mineola, Maynard Enjoys Chicken Dinner," *News & Observer* (Raleigh, NC), October 31, 1919, 1.

212 **"Mineola by two o'clock"**: Maynard, "Reaching Mineola," 1.

212 **It took some doing**: Maynard, "Reaching Mineola," 1.

212 **within gliding distance**: Maynard, "Reaching Mineola," 1.

212 **blasted their steam whistles**: "Maynard Receives Warm Greetings as He Arrives Here," *Buffalo Courier*, October 19, 1919, 1.

212 **"Welcome back, ace"**. . . **"not an idea for a picture"**: "Flying Parson Stops Here for Forty Minutes," *Democrat and Chronicle* (Rochester, NY), October 19, 1919, 44.

212 **Boy Scouts and clergymen**: "Maynard Praises West Endicott Aviation Field," *Binghamton Press* (Binghamton, NY), October 20, 1919, 9.

213 **"a heavy blue haze"**. . . **"falling leaf"**: "Maynard Wins Air Derby, Racing 125 Miles an Hour," *New York Times*, October 19, 1919, 1.

213 **in front of the headquarters tent**: "Maynard Ends Flight at Mineola," *Evening World* (New York, NY), October 18, 1919, 1.

213 **flat-brimmed hat**: Photo of Maynard and family in the *Brooklyn Daily Eagle*, October 19, 1919, 4.

213 **big red apple**: "Lt. Maynard Wins Sea to Sea Flight," *Washington Herald*, October 19, 1919, 1.

213 **Trixie . . . barking and wagging her tail**: "Maynard's Story of Flight," *New York Times*, October 19, 1919, 3.

213 **embraced his wife**: "Maynard's Story," *New York Times*, 3.

213 **tears of happiness**: "Maynard's Story," *New York Times*, 3.

213 **"Kiss her again"**: "Maynard's Story," *New York Times*, 3.

213 **Maynard laughingly**: "Maynard's Story," *New York Times*, 3.

213 **scrubbed the grime . . . a little thinner**: "Maynard's Story," *New York Times*, 3.

213 **"Atta boy!"**: " 'Sky Pilot' Lands at Mineola Field Saturday at 1:30," *Sandusky Star-Journal* (Sandusky, OH), October 19, 1919, 1.

213 **rudder was covered**: "Maynard's Story," *New York Times*, 3.

214 **"the best mechanic"** . . . **"natural born flier"**: "Parson Ready for Long One-Stop Go Within Few Days," *Des Moines Register*, October 19, 1919, 1.

214 **"Liberty motor"**. . . **"safe as the Brooklyn Bridge"**: "Maynard Describes Flight Twice Across Continent," *Sunday Star* (Washington, DC), October 19, 1919, 3.

214 **"back to the ministry"**: "Maynard Describes Flight," *Sunday Star* (Washington, DC), 3.

214 **horseback riding**: Caroline Mitchell diary, Oct. 18, 1919, Douglas Waller Papers, Wake Forest University, ZSR Library Special Collections and Archives, box 15.

214 **"The air distance covered . . . military control"**: "Derby Shows U.S. Isolation Gone," *Sunday Star* (Washington, DC), October 19, 1919, 7.

214 **"As an individual performance"**: "Derby Shows," *Sunday Star* (Washington, DC), 7.

214 **"victory cake":** Maynard, "Reaching Mineola," 1.

214 **a long walk:** "'Flying Parson' Tries Land Legs After 50-Hour Voyage of 5,402 Miles," *Washington Times,* October 19, 1919, 1.

214 **"Pilot's luck" . . . "It was uncanny":** "Flying to 'Show,' Capt. Donaldson Here in Air Race," *Chicago Tribune,* October 19, 1919, 2.

215 **worst of the entire trip:** Capt. J. O. Donaldson, "District 'Ace' Tells How He Won Air Race of U.S. Army," *Washington Times,* October 23, 1919, 1.

215 **Maynard was among the few:** "Air Post to Span Continent in 1920," *New York Times,* October 21, 1919, 1.

CHAPTER TWENTY-EIGHT: Flying Blind

216 **vestibular system . . . "graveyard spiral":** "Spatial Disorientation," Federal Aviation Administration brochure, https://www.faa.gov/pilots/safety/pilotsafetybrochures/media/spatiald.pdf.

216 **researchers at the University of Illinois:** "Which Way Is Up?" Aircraft Owners and Pilots Association, https://www.aopa.org/news-and-media/all-news/2002/february/pilot/which-way-is-up.

217 **Sperry and other companies:** Erik M. Conway, *Blind Flying: Low Visibility Operations in American Aviation 1918–1958* (Baltimore: Johns Hopkins University Press, 2006), 15.

217 **Doolittle took off . . . blind flight:** Conway, *Blind Flying,* 23.

217 **a compass . . . a bubble to show the angle:** L. F. E. Coombs, *Control in the Sky: The Evolution and History of the Aircraft Cockpit* (Barnsley, England: Pen and Sword Aviation, 2005), 32.

217 **"entered with caution":** Maj. Hollis Leroy Muller, *Manual of Military Aviation* (Menasha, WI: George Banta, 1917), 183; Hathi Trust, http://hdl.handle.net/2027/ucl.b3141330.

217 **jackknife:** Belvin W. Maynard, "'Undaunted by Misfortune,' Maynard Pushes on After Losing Half a Day in Race," *News & Observer* (Raleigh, NC), October 26, 1919, 1.

218 **close call:** Harold Hartney, "Col. Hartney's Trip in the German Fokker," *Air Service News Letter,* November 7, 1919, 2.

218 **lost his way in heavy fog . . . returned to North Platte:** Telegram from North Platte control officer to Air Service headquarters, October 23, 1919, NARA, RG 18, "Reliability Test Flights," box 3.

218 **mandolin-playing:** Betty Goerke, *A Broken Propeller: Baz Bagby and America's First Transcontinental Air Race* (Washington, DC: New Academia Publishing, 2017), x.

218 **reconnaissance mission in heavy fog:** Goerke, *A Broken Propeller,* 34.

218 **yearned to be a pilot:** Goerke, *A Broken Propeller,* 20.

218 **changed his plans:** Goerke, *A Broken Propeller,* 40.

219 **maps or goggles . . . never argued:** Letter from Bagby to his mother, October 12, 1919, provided to the author by Betty Goerke.

219 **"return trip slowly":** Letter from Bagby to his mother, October 19, 1919, provided to the author by Betty Goerke.

219 **drop a letter:** Goerke, *A Broken Propeller*, 100.

219 **bent an axle:** Letter from Bagby to his father, October 23, 1919, provided to the author by Betty Goerke.

219 **climbed to 2,800 feet:** Copy of Bagby's logbook, October 27 entry, provided to the author by Betty Goerke.

219 **just 100 feet:** "Puts Air Service on Map," *The Republican* (St. Paul, NE), October 30, 1919, 1.

219 **indicator had frozen . . . coated in ice:** Bagby logbook, October 27 entry.

219 **"lost all sense of direction" . . . sixty miles an hour:** Hartney, "Col. Hartney's Trip," 4.

220 **vertical dive . . . "freezing mist":** Hartney, "Col. Hartney's Trip," 4.

220 **a load of ice:** "Air Racers Flying in Coatings of Ice," *Evening World* (New York, NY), October 28, 1919, 3.

220 **agreed to complete . . . "put it all over me":** Letter from Bagby to his mother, October 30, 1919, provided to the author by Betty Goerke.

220 **"We used to fly in France":** Letter from Bagby to his mother, October 30, 1919.

221 **Kiwanis Club lunch:** "Kiwanians Get Few Pointers on Aviation," *Binghamton Press* (Binghamton, NY), October 30, 1919, 5.

221 **mutual agreement:** Letter from Bagby to his mother, October 30, 1919.

CHAPTER TWENTY-NINE: Three Horses

222 **The latest had occurred . . . would have to be shipped:** Logbook entry, October 23, 1919, Rawlins control stop, NARA, RG 18, "Reliability Test Flights," box 5.

222 **35-mile-per-hour crosswind:** Logbook entry, October 23, 1919, Rawlins control stop.

222 **tried to wave him off:** Rawlins control stop final report, 3.

223 **another DH-4 . . . no wish to repeat the experience:** "Dangerous Air Trip Halted by Chief of Derby," *San Francisco Chronicle*, October 21, 1919, 3.

223 **engine started missing:** "Leaves Hospital to Be in Race," *Air Service News Letter*, November 15, 1919, 1.

223 **missed telephone wires:** "High Wind Stops Aviation Race," *Deseret Evening News* (Salt Lake City, UT), October 23, 1919, 2.

223 **found lodging:** Daily report, Green River control stop, October 24, 1919, NARA, RG 18, "Reliability Test Flights," box 3.

223 **landing T . . . leading edges:** Rawlins control stop final report, 3.

224 **stocks kept at the field . . . linen and dope:** Rawlins control stop final report, 3.

224 **"pluck and grim determination":** Editorial, *New York Tribune*, October 24, 1919, 10.

224 **"bad weather":** Bulletin from Capt. Howard T. Douglas, Air Service headquarters, October 25, 1919, NARA, RG 18, "Reliability Test Flights," box 2.

225 **"suffered severely" . . . coated with ice:** "Leaves Hospital," *Air Service News Letter*, 1.

225 **hole in his radiator:** "Leaves Hospital," *Air Service News Letter*, 1.

225 **"possibility of getting thru":** Telegraph from Clune, Cheyenne control stop commander, to Air Service headquarters, October 25, 1919, NARA, RG 18, "Reliability Test Flights," box 2.

225 **thirty-three miles:** "Air Racer Driven Back by Storm Near Sidney," *Omaha World-Herald*, October 26, 1919, 4.

225 **installed a new propeller . . . stagger wires:** Logbook entry, October 27, 1919, Cheyenne control stop, NARA, RG 18, "Reliability Test Flights," box 2.

225 **forced back . . . as far as North Platte:** "Leaves Hospital," *Air Service News Letter*, 1.

225 **wheels needed attention:** "Four Planes Here on Home Stretch," *Des Moines Register*, October 29, 1919, 9.

226 **brief sightseeing flight:** "Air Man Takes Passenger for Ride in Plane," *Rock Island Argus*, October 30, 1919, 11.

226 **thirty miles from Chicago . . . land immediately:** Lt. Daniel Brailey Gish, pilot report.

226 **sank to its wheel hubs . . . three horses:** Lt. Daniel Brailey Gish, pilot report.

226 **the Liberty engine started missing . . . electrical system:** Lt. Daniel Brailey Gish, pilot report.

CHAPTER THIRTY: A Sour Parting

231 **a brief controversy:** Editorial, "Maynard the Real Winner," *Reno Evening Gazette*, October 23, 1919, 4.

231 **"Maynard is the winner":** Editorial, "Maynard the Real Winner," 4.

231 **"skill, pluck":** Editorial, "Maynard's Flight," *New York Times*, October 20, 1919, 14.

232 **a victory lap:** "Lt. Maynard Flies to Raleigh Two Days Ahead of His Scheduled Arrival," *News & Observer* (Raleigh, NC), November 2, 1919, 1.

232 **a waiting crowd:** "Governor Bickett Takes Air Flight," Raleigh *News & Observer* (Raleigh, NC), November 4, 1919, 1.

232 **"the largest assembly" . . . silverware service:** "Silver Service to Lt. B. W. Maynard," *News & Observer* (Raleigh, NC), November 7, 1919, 1.

232 **ballroom at the Hotel Commodore:** "American Flying Club Reunion," *U.S. Air Service* magazine, December 1919, 30; Hathi Trust, https://hdl.handle.net/2027/mdp.39015024398896.

232 **"shocked by the lack of clothes":** "New York's Low-Back Gowns Shock Maynard," *New York Tribune*, December 1, 1919, 8.

232 **"unless they were half intoxicated":** "Drunkenness Worst Foe of Fliers, Says Maynard," *New York Tribune*, December 9, 1919, 24.

233 **"a really riotous evening":** Capt. T. S. Rippen and Lt. E. G. Manuel, *Report on the Essential Characteristics of Successful and Unsuccessful Aviators*, Royal Air Force, n.d., p. 3, NARA, RG 18, "Records Relating to Aeronautics, 1917–1927," Entry 117, box 26.

233 **"an ill-advised 'bracer'":** "The Medical Aspects of the Transcontinental Air Race," report to Menoher from Col. Albert E. Truby, Air Service flight surgeon, February 26, 1920, 6, NARA, RG 18, "General Correspondence, 1919–1921," box 14.

233 **"This is not only not true":** Statement by Mitchell, December 9, 1919, William Mitchell papers, Library of Congress, Manuscript Division, box 7.

233 **a board of inquiry:** "Flying Parson Must Face Quiz: Called to Explain Remarks About Air Fatalities," *Washington Post*, December 11, 1919, 4.

233 **a meeting with Menoher:** "Maynard Explains 'Air Booze' Story to Chief," *New York Tribune*, December 13, 1918, 7.

233 **"juggling" his words:** "Mitchell Denies Accusing His Co-Fliers of Inebriety," *New York Tribune*, December 17, 1919, 11.

233 **the league had Maynard's typewritten statement:** "League Answers Maynard," *New York Times*, December 18, 1919, 13.

234 **"I am an old man of eighty":** "'Flying Parson' Goes Back to Pulpit Soon," *New York Tribune*, December 22, 1919, 5.

234 **hoped to shed his uniform in January:** "'Flying Parson' Goes Back," *New York Tribune*, 5.

234 **ordered to repay $825:** Statement from C. K. Younger, Vice Chairman, American Flying Club, January 13, 1920, NARA, RG 18, "Reliability Test Flights," box 2.

234 **threatened to dock his paycheck:** Memo from Col. William F. Pearson, Air Service director's office, January 7, 1920, NARA, RG 18, "Reliability Test Flights," box 2.

234 **an Army photographer:** "Aerial Tour for Army," *The Sun* (New York, NY), February 5, 1920, 6.

234 **recently given birth:** "Maynard Will Come to Kinston if Public Is Disposed to Want Him," *Daily Free Press* (Kinston, NC), February 21, 1919, 1.

234 **"a trusted war horse":** Maurer Maurer, *Aviation in the U.S. Army 1919–1939* (Washington, DC: Office of Air Force History, 1987), 36.

234 **broke a propeller . . . running out of gas:** Thomas C. Parramore, *First to Fly: North Carolina and the Beginnings of Aviation* (Chapel Hill: University of North Carolina Press, 2002), 267.

234 **a flight with a reporter:** Ben Dixon MacNeill, "Half Century of Tar Heel Wings," *News & Observer* (Raleigh, NC), December 13, 1953, 45.

235 **his prickliness . . . "surly as Lindbergh":** MacNeill, "Half Century," 45.

235 **nine cracked wing ribs . . . as many flying hours:** Maurer, *Aviation*, 36–37.

CHAPTER THIRTY-ONE: The Woodrow Wilson Airway

236 *second* **transcontinental race:** Memo from Mitchell to Menoher, September 22, 1919, William Mitchell papers, Library of Congress, Manuscript Division, box 7 (hereafter Mitchell papers).

236 **$358.99 worth of food:** Letter from Omaha Chamber of Commerce to Col. Joseph Morrow, Air Service Central Department commander, November 19, 1919, NASM Technical Reference Files, "1919 Transcontinental Reliability and Endurance Test Omaha Control Stop Information," Acc. No. 2009-0004, box 1.

236 **"square deal":** Handwritten letter from W. J. Franing to Air Service director, November 22, 1919, NARA, RG 18, Central Decimal Files, 1917–38, box 1220.

236 **Mitchell replied:** Letter from Mitchell to Franing, December 16, 1919, NARA, RG 18, Central Decimal Files, 1917–38, box 1220.

236 **"there is no question":** *Report on the First Transcontinental Reliability and Endurance Test* (Washington, DC: Government Printing Office, 1919), 30; Hathi Trust, http://hdl.handle.net/2027/uiug.30112112405466.

237 **"certain speed indicators":** *Report on the First Transcontinental Reliability and Endurance Test*, 31.

237 *"sine qua non":* *Report on the First Transcontinental Reliability and Endurance Test*, 29.

237 **The first wireless signal:** "Development of the Radio Telephone," *Aircraft Journal*, January 25, 1919, 7; Hathi Trust, http://hdl.handle.net/2027/ucl.c2638493.

237 **radio telegraphs:** "WW1 & WW2 Communications," Royal Signals Museum, Blandford Camp, Dorset, United Kingdom, https://www.royalsignalsmuseum.co.uk/ww1-ww2-communications/.

237 **used by the French over Verdun:** Carl Bobrow (former Verville fellow, Smithsonian National Air and Space Museum), email correspondence with the author, December 31, 2021.

237 **hundreds of the wireless devices:** Carl J. Bobrow, "The U.S. Military and the Paradigm Shift to Wireless Communications in World War I," *Over the Front* 30, no. 2 (2015): 184.

237 **a practical version:** A. H. Morse, *Radio Beam and Broadcast; Its Story and Patents* (New York: D. Van Nostrand, 1925), 48.

237 **"radio compass" . . . electrical interference:** Eric J. Silberg and David J. Haas, "Developing the Navy's NC Flying Boats: Transforming Aeronautical Engineering for the First Transatlantic Flight," Naval Surface Warfare Center, Carderock Division, paper presented at the

AIAA Centennial of Naval Aviation Forum, September 21–22, 2011, Virginia Beach, Virginia, https://www.navsea.navy.mil/Portals/103 /Documents/NSWC_Carderock/Developing%20the%20NC%20 Flying%20Boats.pdf.

237 **life span of a Liberty engine . . . luminous instrument dials:** *Report on the First Transcontinental Reliability and Endurance Test*, 30, 31.

238 **spurred the Air Service:** Capt. Ray L. Bowers, "Aviation on Trial— Success and Catastrophe," *Airpower Historian* VIII, no. 2 (April 1961): 97.

238 **Fifty-four planes:** *Report on the First Transcontinental Reliability and Endurance Test*, 18.

238 **estimated at $500,000:** Memo from Col. William F. Pearson to Menoher, October 23, 1919, NARA, RG 18 "Reliability Test Flights," box 14.

238 **$10,000 benefit:** "Lt. Maynard Wins Sea to Sea Flight," *Washington Herald*, October 19, 1919, 1.

238 **"less danger in aeroplaning":** Harold Hartney, "Col. Hartney's Trip in the German Fokker," *Air Service News Letter*, November 7, 1919, 2.

238 **a tortured comparison:** Glenn L. Martin, "Airplanes Safer than Automobiles," *Air Service News Letter*, October 31, 1919, 1.

238 **two drivers and a mechanic:** "1919 Indy 500 Comes Roaring Back Following War Break," Indystar.com, https://www.indystar.com/story /sports/motor/2016/02/26/1919-indy-500-comes-roaring-back-following -war-break/81014690/.

238 **one fatality for every 180 hours:** William M. Leary, *Aerial Pioneers* (Washington, DC: Smithsonian Institution Press, 1985), 108.

238 **one fatal accident per 100,000 hours:** "2018 Data Show Increase in U.S. Aviation Fatalities," Flight Safety Foundation, https://flightsafety .org/2018-data-show-increase-in-u-s-aviation-fatalities/.

238 **"homicidal insanity":** "Not Progress but Homicide," *The Sun* (New York, NY), October 23, 1919, 10.

239 **"Woodrow Wilson Airway" . . . Aero Club of America:** "The Woodrow Wilson Airway," *The Aero Blue Book and Directory of Aeronautic Organizations* (New York: The Century Co., 1919), 8.

239 **a jeweler in Ogallala . . . "small bumps":** Letter from Robert A. Goodall to Capt. A. J. Clayton, office of Air Service director, October 13, 1919, Central Decimal Files, 1917–38, box 1225.

239 **"Your field":** Letter from Lt. Col. H. M. Hickam to mayor of St. Paul, November 15, 1919, Central Decimal Files, 1917–38, box 1225.

239 **"municipal aviation station":** "New York State News," *Wyoming County Times* (Warsaw, NY), December 18, 1919, 3.

239 **"As this race has progressed":** "Air Post to Span Continent in 1920," *New York Times*, October 21, 1919, 21.

240 **more than triple . . . $1,375,000:** Leary, *Aerial Pioneers*, 113–14.

240 **half a dozen . . . Elko:** "Airmail: A Brief History," U.S. Postal Service, https://about.usps.com/who-we-are/postal-history/airmail.pdf.

241 **nearby suburb of Maywood:** Helen Knight, "Chicago Airmail History: McGirr and Waterman Airports," *ESSAI* 13 (2015): article 22, https://dc.cod.edu/essai/vol13/iss1/22/.

241 **Meeting with local officials in Cheyenne:** Leary, Aerial Pioneers, 116.

241 **Elected officials in Salt Lake City . . . Six years later:** *H.R. 4326 and H.R. 4642: Hearings Before a Subcommittee of the Post Office and Post Roads,* U.S. House, 69th Congress, 1st sess., May 3, 1926, pp. 2–5 (testimony of Rep. Elmer O. Leatherwood).

241 **focused on communications . . . coast to coast:** Leary, *Aerial Pioneers,* 120–21.

242 **a new, purpose-built mail plane:** Leary, *Aerial Pioneers,* 116–17.

242 **"a dreadful abortion of a plane":** Leary, *Aerial Pioneers,* 116–17.

242 **a structural member snap . . . walked away:** Leary, *Aerial Pioneers,* 121.

242 **a sleek low-wing monoplane . . . the purchase of eight:** Leary, *Aerial Pioneers,* 118–19.

243 **nine forced landings . . . waved down a car:** Leary, *Aerial Pioneers,* 121–23.

243 **Max Miller . . . tossing mailbags:** Leary, *Aerial Pioneers,* 123–24.

243 **dove into the ground . . . recently gotten married:** Leary, *Aerial Pioneers,* 123–24.

243 **morning of September 8 . . . strapped it to a wing:** Leary, *Aerial Pioneers,* 125.

244 **relays . . . eighty-three hours:** Leary, *Aerial Pioneers,* 125.

244 **Plane No. 151 . . . "We must hurry":** "First Official N.Y. Air Mail Reaches S.F.," *San Francisco Examiner,* September 12, 1920, 1.

244 ***The Restless Sex:*** "'Restless Sex' Films Reach S.F. Via Air," *San Francisco Examiner,* September 12, 1920, 2.

244 **an "epoch-making event":** "The Transcontinental Aerial Mail," *Aerial Age Weekly,* September 12, 1920, 1.

244 **"Then off with hats":** "Transcontinental Aerial Mail," *Aerial Age Weekly,* 1.

245 **"the first airway":** William Mitchell, speech manuscript, Mitchell papers, box 27.

245 **"the establishment of the airmail system":** William Mitchell, "The Army Flies the Mail," manuscript, Mitchell papers, box 27.

245 **"might sanctify to some degree":** William Leary, "The Great Transcontinental Air Race of 1919," handwritten manuscript, William M. Leary papers, University of Texas at Dallas, box 103.

246 **"airplane journeying":** Editorial, "The Racing Planes," *Rockford Morning Star* (Rockford, IL), October 23, 1919, 2.

246 **unable to meet demand:** Binghamton control stop final report, NARA, RG 18, "Reliability Test Flights," box 1.

246 **dove into a clover field:** Leary, *Aerial Pioneers,* 126.

247 **just thirty-three hours:** Leary, *Aerial Pioneers*, 143.

247 **night operations:** Leary, *Aerial Pioneers*, 178–80.

247 **a law that allowed the Post Office . . . last flight:** Leary, *Aerial Pioneers*, 223, 236.

247 **Colonial Air Transport . . . TWA:** F. Robert van der Linden, *Airlines & Air Mail* (Lexington: University Press of Kentucky, 2002), 23, 61, 112, 150, 180, 284.

EPILOGUE

249 **blue squadron leader's pennant . . . reporters:** Douglas Waller, *A Question of Loyalty: Gen. Billy Mitchell and the Court Martial That Gripped the Nation* (New York: HarperCollins, 2004), 141.

249 **blimps and planes:** Thomas Wildenberg, *Billy Mitchell's War With the Navy* (Annapolis, MD: Naval Institute Press, 2013), 75.

249 **"we can destroy or sink" . . . "I would be perfectly willing":** Wildenberg, *Billy Mitchell's War*, 53, 58.

249 **storms forced:** Wildenberg, *Billy Mitchell's War*, 76–77.

249 **eleven Army bombers . . . over in minutes:** Wildenberg, *Billy Mitchell's War*, 79–80.

250 **carried from his cockpit . . . fueling talk:** Waller, *Question of Loyalty*, 154, 156.

250 **Menoher had petitioned:** James J. Cooke, *Billy Mitchell* (Boulder, CO: Lynne Rienner, 2002), 127.

250 **only 754:** Roger F. Bilstein, *Flight in America* (Baltimore: Johns Hopkins University Press, 2001), 42.

250 **drinking heavily . . . Elizabeth Trumbull Miller:** Waller, *Question of Loyalty*, 159–67.

251 **a clear breach:** Wildenberg, *Billy Mitchell's War*, 118–19.

251 **"more brass than a monkey":** Reminiscences of Gen. Leslie P. Arnold (ret.), 1960, p. 22, oral history collection, Rare Book & Manuscript Library, Columbia University.

251 **aviation command in San Antonio:** Wildenberg, *Billy Mitchell's War*, 127.

251 **Mitchell summoned reporters . . . "almost treasonable administration":** Waller, *Question of Loyalty*, 11–20.

252 **a forum on air power:** Waller, *Question of Loyalty*, 168–82, 233.

252 **guilty of insubordination:** Waller, *Question of Loyalty*, 324.

252 **heart disease:** Waller, *Question of Loyalty*, 350.

252 **"personal souvenirs":** Letter to American Flying Club from Col. O. Westover, office of Air Service director, February 4, 1920, NARA, RG 18, "Reliability Test Flights," box 2.

252 **shotgun:** Advertisement for Abercrombie & Fitch Co., *U.S. Air Service* magazine, November 1919, 1.

252 **Mackay Trophy:** Description and names of winners can be found at

"Mackay Trophy," National Aeronautic Association, https://naa.aero
/awards/awards-and-trophies/mackay-trophy/.

253 **"spirit of pioneer endeavor":** Letter to Gish from Westover, office of
Air Service director, December 29, 1919, Gish personnel file, NPRC.

253 **purchase a ranch . . . shortage of funds:** Ruth Spaatz reminiscences,
United States Air Force Oral History Program, Washington, DC, 1981
(Montgomery, AL: Alfred F. Simpson Historical Research Center, Max-
well Air Force Base), 23–24.

253 **world endurance record:** "Gen. Carl Andrew Spaatz," Defense
Department biography, https://media.defense.gov/2016/Mar/11/2001
479297/-1/-1/0/AFD-160311-586-021.PDF.

253 **"the moral choice":** David R. Mets, Master of Airpower (Novato, CA:
Presidio Press, 1988), 303.

254 **offers from industry . . . *Newsweek*:** Ruth Spaatz reminiscences,
United States Air Force Oral History, 36.

254 **second-place finish:** "Army Pilot Wins Pulitzer Air Race," *New York
Times*, November 26, 1920, 1.

254 **"my whole enthusiasm" . . . crashed near Omaha:** Harold E. Hartney, *Up and at 'Em* (London: Cassell and Company, 1940), 299–300.

254 **Sikorsky . . . passenger airline:** "Harold Hartney Dies; Air Hero of
World War I" [obituary], *New York Herald Tribune*, October 6, 1945, 10B.

254 **the strong endorsement of Billy Mitchell:** Letter from Mitchell to
Senator Royal S. Copeland, June 24, 1935, NASM Technical Reference
Files, American Institute of Aeronautics and Astronautics, box 35.

254 **adviser to the Civil Aeronautics Administration:** "Hartney Dies,"
New York Herald Tribune.

254 **heart ailment:** "Hartney Dies," *New York Herald Tribune*.

254 **eldest son:** "Harold Hartney, Noted Flier, Dies" [obituary], *New York
Times*, October 6, 1945, 11.

255 **shot down over North Vietnam:** "Col. James Cuthbert Hartney," personnel profile, Defense POW/MIA Accounting Agency, https://dpaa-mil
.sites.crmforce.mil/dpaaProfile?id=a0Jt000000sxxJXEAY.

255 **sold Hendrick automobiles:** Advertisement, *Washington Times*, April 17,
1920, 6.

255 **gas-filtering device . . . Thompson submachine guns:** Application
to Officers' Reserve Corps, January 10, 1022, Gish file, NPRC.

255 **company in Massachusetts:** Letter from Gish to adjutant general, War
Department, August 25, 1941, Gish file, NPRC.

255 **house with a swimming pool:** Letter from Gish to Air Force Retired
Activities Branch, November 11, 1958, Gish file, NPRC.

255 **complaining about taxes:** Letter to the editor, *Ft. Lauderdale News*, July
22, 1958, 4.

255 **flogging as a punishment:** Letter to the editor, *Ft. Lauderdale News*, February 3, 1958, 4.

255 **grandiose and paranoid:** Letter from Gish to Directorate of Administrative Services, Air Force, December 29, 1960, Gish file, NPRC.

255 **no longer be answered:** Letter from Col. Ellis B. Craig, chief, military personnel records division, to Gish, May 25, 1919, Gish file, NPRC.

255 **died of heart disease:** Casualty assistance form, June 3, 1963, Gish file, NPRC.

255 **the Texas oilfields:** "Capt. John O. Donaldson to Be Discharged," *Air Service News Letter*, July 10, 1920, 10.

255 **flight school at Newark:** "John O. Donaldson, Noted Ace, Dies as His Plane Crashes," *Greenville News* (Greenville, SC), September 8, 1930, 1.

255 **September 7, 1930 . . . died a short while later:** "John O. Donaldson, Noted Ace," *Greenville News* (Greenville, SC), 1.

256 **some of the bombing tests . . . under his own name:** Betty Goerke, *A Broken Propeller: Baz Bagby and America's First Transcontinental Air Race* (Washington, DC: New Academia Publishing, 2017), 126–27.

256 **North Africa and Italy:** Goerke, *A Broken Propeller*, 126–27.

256 **without bothering to ask permission . . . "AWOL more than 48 hours":** Walter Cronkite, "Goes AWOL so He Can Be an Invader," *Shreveport Times* (Shreveport, LA), June 10, 1944, 1.

256 **reprimanded and awarded a medal:** Goerke, *A Broken Propeller*, 137.

256 **reunion of World War I aviators:** "Ralph Bagby, War Hero, Dies in Car Crash," *Chicago Tribune*, June 24, 1961, 16.

256 **"bee out of his thoughts":** "Maynard Still Has Ambitions as Clergyman," *Rochester Times-Union*, October 21, 1919.

257 **"The Motor Troubles of Society":** "Flying Parson Is Heard in New Bern," *New Bern Sun Journal* (New Bern, NC), June 14, 1920.

257 **aerial-photography business:** Thomas C. Parramore, *First to Fly: North Carolina and the Beginnings of Aviation* (Chapel Hill: University of North Carolina Press, 2002), 268.

257 **Queens Village Airdrome . . . got it flying:** Russell F. Holderman, *Between Kittyhawk and the Moon*, ed. Nancy Holderman Durante (Charleston, SC: BookSurge, 2009), 122, 124.

257 **alarmed . . . mismatched wires:** Holderman, *Between Kittyhawk and the Moon*, 124.

257 **flying circus . . . wooden bench:** Holderman, *Between Kittyhawk and the Moon*, 125.

257 **climbed to 2,000 feet . . . spiraled into a field:** " 'Flying Parson' Dies, 3 Other Air Men Killed During Fair," *New York Times*, September 8, 1922, 1.

257 **broken under the weight:** Holderman, *Between Kittyhawk and the Moon*, 125.

258 **still breathing:** " 'Flying Parson' Dies," *New York Times*, 1.

258 **four oak trees:** "More than Three Thousand Attend Funeral of Lieutenant Maynard at Former Sampson County Home," *Wilmington Morning Star* (Wilmington, NC), September 11, 1922, 1.

INDEX

Page numbers in *italics* refer to map and illustrations.